MARRIAGE
and the FAMILY

an integrated approach for Catholics

ALPHONSE H. CLEMENS, Ph.D.

Director, Marriage Counseling Center
The Catholic University of America
Washington, D. C.

PRENTICE-HALL, INC.

Englewood Cliffs, N. J.   *1957*

Nihil obstat
Edwin Foley, C.SS.R.
Censor deputatus
Imprimatur
✠ Patrick A. O'Boyle
Archbishop of Washington
January 11, 1956

PRINTED IN THE UNITED STATES OF AMERICA
55846

To

OUR LADY,

MY WIFE,

and

MY MOTHER

Acknowledgments

ALL AUTHORS must be tempted, at times, to accept exclusive acclaim for their work. However, it is evident that without Divine assistance, the cultural heritage of the past, and the contributions of contemporaries, this book would not have been possible.

A debt of gratitude is due to the Blessed Trinity for having disclosed the Divine Plan for Marriage, and to Our Lady Immaculate, patroness of the Catholic University of America under whose auspices the contents of this book were largely developed.

My wife has cooperated in every phase of the work. In most respects it is as much her work as mine. The sacrifices of my father and mother have also helped to make this book possible.

The constructive suggestions of the readers appointed by the publisher proved invaluable. Portions of the work were read by:

The Most Reverend Charles Helmsing, D.D. and Most Reverend Leo Byrne, D.D., Auxiliary Bishops of the Archdiocese of St. Louis; Rev. Dr. Paul H. Furfey, Head, Department of Sociology, Catholic University of America; Rev. Dr. Henry Sattler, Roxbury, Massachusetts, author and lecturer; Rev. Dr. Thomas Reese, Wilmington, Delaware; Dr. and Mrs. Clarence Enzler, writers and book reviewers; Dr. Kerby Neill, Professor of English, Catholic University of America; Mr. and Mrs. V. J. Clemens.

Technical suggestions, references and revisions came from:

The Very Rev. Dr. Francis J. Connell, Dean, School of Sacred Theology; Rev. Dr. Bernard Mulvaney and Rev. Dr. Thomas Hart, Department of Sociology; and Mr. Eugene Wilging and his staff, Libraries, all of the Catholic University of America; Dr. Albert Motzel, Senior Instructor in Surgery, School of Medicine, St. Louis University; and Dr. John Cavanagh, psychiatrist, Washington, D.C.

"Unless God build the house, they labor in vain who build." Our sincere gratitude to all whose prayers compensated for the inadequacies of the authors, especially to the Mother Superiors and Sisters in the Carmels of St. Louis, Missouri, and Little Rock, Arkansas.

Preface

CHESTERTON closed one of his books by indicating that all he needed to write another was a challenge. A series of challenges inspired this book. There was, in the first place, the challenge of translating the Divine Plan for Marriage into a design for twentieth-century marital living, of integrating it with the findings of modern science. A second challenge was the insistence of Pius XI that "since everything must be referred to the law and mind of God, in order to bring about the universal and permanent restoration of marriage, it is indeed of the utmost importance that the Faithful should be well instructed concerning matrimony; and that . . . *by the written word, not cursorily but often and fully* . . . so that these truths will strike the intellect and will be deeply engraved on their hearts" [italics ours]. There have also been challenges from many colleagues and students who have generously urged the publication of lectures on this subject. None, however, has offered a more persistent incentive than my immediate academic superior, advisor and friend, Dr. Paul Hanley Furfey. Still another challenge has come from the needs of married couples themselves, discovered by intimate contact with people in various parts of the nation and by repeated surveys made at the Catholic University of America.

This book was written to help solve the problems of couples preparing for marriage, of couples successfully married, of couples with marital difficulties, of students in our schools and colleges, and of marriage educators and counselors. These needs can best be met by emphasizing the positive design for marriage rather than by citing individual problems that might arise. For this reason, a constructive approach is used; the problematical is introduced only incidentally. This book is intended to serve realistically the practical, functional needs of married life. To this end, its contents must deal with all major influences on life itself—theology, philosophy, sociology, psychology, physiology, education, recreation, economics and law.

Success in marriage must be based upon the Divine Plan, which can be understood adequately and completely only by consulting all available sources. From religion and revelation come our goals, the broad and indispensable outlines of the design for successful marriage. From true science we fill in many details of this design. For this reason, this book tries to reflect the best in scientific discovery, and a number of empirical studies made at the Catholic University of America and not before published have been introduced. (Although this type of finding is freely used in this book, the reader should be warned of the extremely limited value of such data, as is explained further in the Appendix. Actually, empirical science has not yet afforded conclusive data on the nature of a single relationship in marriage!) The laws of both Church and State furnish additional guides to marital living by applying general principles to specific situations. In addition, this book tries to emphasize common sense, and calls upon the past experiences of the race, which Monsignor Fulton Sheen has called "the memory of civilization."

This book is *religious* in the sense that it is based on the Divine Plan; it is *scientific* in that this Plan encompasses the natural and social sciences as well as the sacred sciences; it is integral in that it attempts to integrate the supernatural with the natural, the sacred with the secular, the philosophic with the scientific. The deeply serious reader is urged to read the final chapter, which deals in great detail with the full nature of the Divine Plan, before delving into the contents of the book proper.

This book intends to be both idealistic and realistic. It explains the Divine Ideal for Marriage as well as the practical design for living this ideal amid the difficult realities of our present culture and civilization. Chesterton once observed, "Ideals are the most practical thing in the world." Such ideals for marriage are practical only when they are applied to the specific, detailed and concrete situations of daily marital and family living. Whether this book has succeeded in so doing remains to be judged by the indulgence of its readers.

It is to this end that I humbly invoke the blessings of the Triune God-Head—the Divine Exemplar of "life together."

ALPHONSE H. CLEMENS

Contents

1

Preparing for Marriage

BEFORE you finish reading this chapter over two hundred marriages will have been contracted. During the same time more than fifty marriages will have ended in divorce, separation, annulment, or desertion. This high rate of marital breakdown is becoming more and more a matter of national concern. Millions of individuals are seeking the means of avoiding such a tragedy in their lives. Churches, schools, homes, and scientific agencies are hastening to find the answer to this problem. Certainly never before in our national experience have so many labored so long and with such resources at their command to discern the reasons for marital failure and to find the plan for marital success.

At this time both religion and science agree that the chief reason for failing marriages is the absence of proper and adequate preparation. For the past several generations we have been approaching marriage with the attitude that anyone, regardless of capacity, training, or preparation, can make a success of it. We seem to have been acting on the assumption that individuals have an *innate* ability and do not need any *acquired* knowledge or training for marriage. This, in part, is probably the result of the notion that, unlike other professions, the responsibilities of marriage are quite simple and require little more than ordinary common sense for their successful discharge.

1

MARRIAGE IS A PROFESSION

Apparently there is a serious lack of perspective about this whole matter. Marriage is the oldest natural profession, having started with the human race itself.[1] On the natural level, it is the *noblest* profession; no other has the dignity and privilege of producing and shaping the noblest handiwork of creation—human beings. Artists may produce lasting works on canvas, stone or wood; physicians may treat ailing bodies; lawyers may assist in effecting justice in present human relationships; but parents alone assist in the creation of human beings *who will live for eternity*.

Important as are the other professions, none (except the priesthood or the religious life) can equal marriage. No other natural profession—in fact, not all others combined—have the effect for good or evil upon the race, the nation, the Church, and the world. Nor does any other natural profession require the versatility and the broad scope of qualities and knowledge that marriage demands. To attain success in marriage, both as a partner and a parent, implies competency in the art of human relations, knowledge of physical health and care, and an understanding of adult and juvenile human nature, human education, the techniques of homemaking, the earning of a living, the art and science of holiness, and many other accomplishments. This is just one reason why the chores of family living and homemaking, far from being dull, should be stimulating and challenging.

Another fact often escaping our attention is the constant striving for progress and improvement which has brought about the raising of standards in other professions. A century ago, for instance, the young man aspiring to become a physician simply acted as an assistant to some practitioner before engaging in the practice of medicine on his own. Today society thinks the responsibilities of this profession too weighty to permit it to be pursued by any without many years of study, research, and internship. Yet when it comes to preparation for marriage, we still act today as the medical profession did a century ago. It is left to the reader to determine the reason for our failure to recog-

---

[1] A profession is here understood as a life work requiring extensive knowledge, information and skill dedicated to the service of others in a direct manner.

nize the desirability of improving and perfecting the profession of marriage with an equal vigor and preparation.

Associated with this failure is another; we have neglected to provide facilities for study, research, and expertness in marriage. Every profession except marriage has had its scholars and experts. The Church has had its theologians; the state has had its political scientists; the world of business and finance has had its economists; the sick in body and mind have had doctors of medicine and psychiatry. However, the most important of the natural professions—marriage—has not until quite recently trained experts or specialists to study it, to counsel it, to improve it!

This widespread neglect of preparation for marriage induced Pius XI to write:

We wish to call your attention in a special manner to the present-day lamentable decline in family education. The offices and professions of a transitory and earthly life, which are certainly of far less importance, are prepared for by long and careful study; whereas for the fundamental duty and obligation of educating their children, many parents have little or no preparation, immersed as they are in temporal cares.[2]

This position was confirmed by Pius XII when he noted:

. . . that whereas no one would dream of suddenly becoming a mechanic or an engineer, a doctor or a lawyer, without an apprenticeship or preparation, yet every day there are numbers of young men and women who marry without having given an instant's thought to preparing themselves for the arduous work of educating their children which awaits them.[3]

WHY PREPARE FOR MARRIAGE

Despite these warnings given by wise counsel, many still persist in refusing to acknowledge the need for better preparation of youth for marriage. Many prefer to believe that in the pioneer days youth was not given such education, yet there was less divorce than today. Such a view fails to grasp the fact that the

---

[2] Pius XI, *Christian Education of Youth* (New York: The America Press, 1936), p. 24; also *Acta Apostolicae Sedis*, Vol. XXI (December 1929), pp. 723–762.

[3] Pius XII, "Davanti a Questa," *Acta Apostolicae Sedis*, Vol. XXXIII (1941), p. 451.

pioneer home was, in the main, vastly different from the modern home in its training of children, and that the need always remains to raise the standards of marriage just as those of other professions.   Perhaps the chief fact neglected by this position is that married life and its duties of rearing children have become more and more complicated as the general environment of the family has grown in complexity.   Pioneer parents were not confronted with the neurotic pressures of our age.   They had no need for concern about the effect of radio and television on children; they were not faced with the problem of censoring comics, books, periodicals, and movies.   In their simple economy, there was little need of the complicated arts of budgeting, buying, insuring, and financing.   Attractive wages were not present to allure mothers from the home to the office or factory, and women did not question their role as mothers.   Automobiles and commercialized amusements did not threaten the pattern of home recreation.   Wild theories of romantic love, freedom of sex, divorce, birth control, and the like were not so prevalent, pulling youth and adults into insane concepts of the meaning of marriage.

The tragic fact cannot be ignored that today our culture and civilization are to a large extent a conspiracy against marriage. The home is basically at fault, especially the city home.   Not only is distorted child training giving us increasing amounts of delinquency, but the art of homemaking and the appetite for domesticity are not being imparted to our youth, and sex education has been almost totally ignored or fraught with damaging Puritanism.

Yet all the while this failure to educate aright for marriage has been in evidence, the secular media of education and propaganda have been feverishly active.   Irreligious professors, authors, dramatists, producers, and editors have been influencing youth through classroom, lecture platform, radio, press, and television with their secularistic notions of marriage.   They did not and do not hesitate to insist that marriage is not God-made but man-made, that it can be changed to suit our whims, that divorce is a blessing and children are a curse.

The further fact remains that a weighty moral responsibility exists to prepare youth for marriage.   One of our noted theologians reminds us of this responsibility when he writes:

Hence, all agencies that have the opportunity of exerting any influence on the youth of our nation should deem it *one of their chief duties* to direct the minds and hearts of young men and women in such wise that we can expect from them a practical acceptance of the ideals of Christian marriage. The three agencies on which this *obligation principally devolves* are *the home, the schools and the church* [italics ours].[4]

Our youth share the responsibility of preparing themselves for their own marriages in addition to or in lieu of the efforts of others.

CONTENT OF MARRIAGE PREPARATION

The proper preparation for marriage actually starts in infancy; it is then that the initial seeds are planted which will in childhood and adolescence mature into habits of personality. "For it cannot be denied that the basis of a happy wedlock and the ruin of an unhappy one is prepared and set in the souls of boys and girls during the period of childhood and adolescence." [5] This early training is usually referred to as *remote* preparation for marriage; it is more important by far than that *proximate* preparation that starts with the dating or courting period.

Proper preparation for marriage depends upon two factors— what we are and what we know. Empirical studies [6] confirm the position of the Holy Father that marital success depends *chiefly* upon traits of character and personality—upon habits of will, mind, emotions, and body. In addition, proper attitudes of mind and heart, and adequate information about things marital are likewise essential to success. Both *formation* and *information* are necessary. Yet while such information is wide in scope —embracing a knowledge of the religious, social, educational, psychological, physiological, economic, and legal aspects of marriage—it remains quite secondary in importance to character and personality. The technical knowledge of budgeting is important; more important, however, are habits of industry, thrift, and detachment. A certain amount of information about physi-

---

[4] F. J. Connell, "The Obligation of the Home, School, and Church to Educate for Family Living," *Marriage and Family Relationships*, ed. A. H. Clemens (Washington, D. C.: The Catholic University of America Press, 1950), p. 6.

[5] Pius XI, *op. cit.*, p. 58.

[6] See Chapters 7 and 19 for such studies.

cal sex is imperative; yet more imperative are such correct attitudes and traits as consideration and unselfishness. A knowledge of child training is indispensable; more important still is a genuine love and understanding of children.

The conditions desirable for marriage further indicate the need for preparation. The responsibilities of rearing a family are onerous in many ways. If physical health and an abundance of nervous vitality are not absolute requisites, they are, at least, highly desirable assets. On the other hand, a certain economic basis is imperative; despite romantic illusions, two cannot live as cheaply as one. Yet more important than both of these, is the development of a truly mature personality—an adult mental, moral, and emotional stature that is ready to assume the weighty responsibilities of marriage rather than veer from them.

TYPES OF PREPARATION

While the content of preparation for marriage should demand attention, the types and methods of premarital education also need consideration. This need is being accentuated by the haste with which, in all too many instances, persons lacking in depth and scope of knowledge about marriage are devising lecture programs and literature. Even a cursory review of these attempts evidences a superficiality and lack of perspective which must be inadequate and in some instances is actually harmful.

Some of the current mistakes being made might be labeled as "pragmatic," "theoretical," or "incomplete." There is, first, the attempt to be utterly and excessively practical which ends in being merely pragmatic. The desire to be realistic and specific to such an extent that the *exact* and *precise* answer to each couple's problem is attempted often leads to the failure to meet the needs of any couple. This penchant for a pragmatic impracticability tends to minimize or ignore *principles* and *theory*. Even if and when this type of education succeeds in meeting the *present* problem of a couple, it rarely affords the tools (principles) with which to solve their *future* problems.[7] Furthermore, only too often this attempt to be "down-to-earth" results in being "earthy" and not sufficiently "up-to-heaven." At best, it be-

---

[7] For detailed example see "Family Budgeting" in Chapter 17.

comes a secular lecture series sprinkled with a bit of Holy Water, instead of a genuine integration of the supernatural and the natural. This type of program assumes its own practicability and the *theoretical* uselessness of all other types.

There is, secondly, the "unrealistic" approach to premarital and marital preparation, which delights in generalities, unapplied and unexemplified principles, platitudes, and "old bromides." This usually emanates from individuals lacking a realistic grasp of present-day marital life, though sometimes well-read in marriage literature.

Thirdly, we find the type of approach evidencing a competency in one or several aspects of marital living but lacking that full scope of knowledge and insight which can alone insure a proper perspective and a well-rounded program. This may be the "supernaturalist" who thinks success in marriage can be attained exclusively through religion and prayer. It may, on the other hand, be the "naturalist" who hopes to solve all problems by science without the aid of religion. It might, again, be that person who treats topics such as sex, money, in-laws, from a practical or theoretical viewpoint but not from both points of view; under their religious or mundane aspects but not under both aspects; or in a material or spiritual manner but not in an integrated manner. It may also be the type of person bent more upon enlisting a huge audience than imparting a sound education. Such a person is likely to be very solicitous about providing what couples *want,* while neglecting to give them what they *need.* This type of approach affords only that *partial view* so characteristic of our highly specialized civilization and so offensive to the integrity of the Catholic viewpoint.

HOW TO PREPARE FOR MARRIAGE

Most of us are either poorly or partially prepared for marriage, but few of us are *adequately* prepared. A widespread observation and intimate contact with married couples throughout the nation, impels the conviction that few enjoy the security in their marriages which adequate preparation would have insured. Couples who after many years of marital living attend their first marital education program, seem unanimous in voicing their regrets that this type of preparation had to arrive so late in their careers. They realize that many difficulties and problems would then have been avoided.

For those experiencing retarded growth in marriage, it is necessary that an inventory be taken *now*. They need to examine their character and personality traits; they must determine their religious and moral stature; they should appraise their economic competency and their knowledge of all aspects of marital living. *For self-knowledge is the inescapable first step to re-education.* If childhood and adolescence have not matured character and personality, the need exists to engage in a program of self-reform *now*. Though such personality and character conversion is a time-consuming process, it generally can be done by force of character and the grace of God. Without it, marriage easily can become a mirage. Should such unfavorable traits be deep-seated and not subject to personal efforts of re-education, the advice of a psychiatrist is indicated.

The importance of physical health, freedom from contagious disease, and ability to reproduce is significant to make premarital examination highly desirable. The growing recognition of neuroses and psychoses, in like manner, indicate the wisdom of a premarital personality inventory also. Those experienced in marriage counseling realize that many mismated marriages would be obviated were such premarital care exercised. The readiness for physical examination coupled with the reluctance to be psychologically tested indicates either a lack of realization that marriage is more a soul-mating than a physical experience or that personality disorders cause more trouble in marriage than physical defects. Economic incompetency often can be removed by vocational guidance which will help to discover a career more suitable to one's talents. It can be removed further by increased industry, greater thrift and economy in handling funds, and more training or education.

Today, those seriously bent on preparing carefully for marriage have a wide variety of resources at their disposal. They have ever had and still have the wise counsel of parents and pastors which only the foolhardy would ignore. In addition, they have now a growing number of books, magazines, and pamphlets available. There are more courses in schools and colleges and more adult lecture programs than ever before. There is also the expert guidance of professionally trained marriage counselors now at the disposal of many.

PREPARATION IN THE DIVINE PLAN

When God, in His Infinite Wisdom, conceived the Divine Plan of marriage, He could have decided to prepare men and women by innate abilities. However, He decided otherwise; He would not have us born with all traits and knowledge required for success in marriage. Rather would His Plan embrace the need for children to *acquire* these through early family education, social environment, the grace of God, the assistance of church and school. In fact, He would impose this as an obligation upon all agencies responsible for the education of youth; and He would impose it upon the youth themselves. Like other professions, marriage was to attain success only by long, arduous, and careful preparation *before* marriage and an equally arduous cultivation *after* marriage. This remains the continuing responsibility and challenge of parents, educators, clergy, youth, and married couples. This is that Prudence embodied in the Divine Plan by which we are mandated to employ all available means, natural and supernatural, for the successful attainment of marital goals and purposes.

2

Three Marriage Patterns

In our culture we like to make a distinction between the practical man and the idealist. We further prefer to believe that philosophy has no relation to practical living. Actually, in both these points of view our culture is very unrealistic and impractical. The bald fact remains that the most practical of persons *must* and *does* have an ideal and a philosophy from which that ideal springs. The apparent difficulty here is that many do not know what their ideal or their philosophy is, simply because they have never *consciously* formulated either of the two. On the contrary, they have borrowed them *without thinking* from others.

This is true in the area of marriage and the family also. All entering marriage do so with ideals and a philosophy of marriage, though they may not be aware of it. This ideal may follow consistently one set of principles—one philosophy—though it usually is an ideal comprising several and often conflicting philosophies. The husband, for instance, whose marriage ideal includes dominating his wife and indulging his children, does not have a consistent philosophy but a mixed and contradictory one. Few things seem more important, therefore, in our current approach to marriage than the clarification of our principles and ideals. Only by so doing can we hope to avoid a contradictory pattern in marriage. Even more, only then can we hope to enter marriage or conduct our family life in accordance with the *one correct ideal*.

THE LARGER VIEW NEEDED

Few things are more clear than that our marriage and family patterns are being changed. The current scene presents little uniformity in marriage. We hasten to attach labels such as "conservative," "independent," "progressive," "emancipated," "democratic," "companionate," to various married couples and families. All of this merely confirms the fact that marriage and family life are in a state of flux and change. But more than this, we are revolutionizing our patterns of marriage and family living. Serious students of sociology are working feverishly to devise a new pattern, while the rank and file either consciously or unconsciously are joining this endeavor. Each youth approaching marriage is faced with the need to determine his or her ideal for marriage. Every newly married couple is faced with the decision of which one of several possible patterns they will follow in their marital life. Most, it would seem, formulate this all-important choice on the basis of preference; whim; prejudices; the example of others; the trend of the times; and opinions garnered from novels, magazines, newspapers, radio and television skits, and columns to the love-lorn. Even few of our serious students have come to an understanding of just what is happening to our marital and familial living, because few have traced this problem through to its basic factors.

To determine the divinely right and socially advantageous pattern of marriage in the midst of the current babel of tongues is not an easy task. To resolve this problem nothing less than the broader perspective arrived at through history, sociology, philosophy, and theology is indicated. Those who have gained this larger view are faced with the fact that, from a certain aspect, in all of human experience there have been only three types of marriages and family patterns. Amongst the sociologists who have addressed themselves to this problem, perhaps five stand out for their studious attempt to discern marriage patterns from all of history (Table 1). LePlay first was impressed by the changed aspects of family life after the Industrial Revolution. His study is based on firsthand observation and participation. Sorokin made an exhaustive statistical study (the only such study available) of all known cultures and civilizations. Burgess and Locke reviewed some of the highlights of historic experience, and Zimmerman gave us one of the best documented histories of marriage and the family available.

THREE FAMILY TYPES

Only three patterns are found by these five scholars. While the names and the characteristics of each pattern vary somewhat from scholar to scholar (Table 1), there remains a large measure of agreement. In the first type they find a strong kinship family, where the clan exercises a dominance over the family that at times is excessive and a serious infringement of conjugal, family, and personal rights; force and fear frequently are the only bonds welding the family together. The second type accords a larger measure of self-government to the conjugal family; kinfolk are respected, loved, and assisted, and while their advice is sought and usually heeded no significant interference on their part is tolerated; the chief bonds of this family type are those of genuine love, mutual respect, and mutual interests. The third type consists of not only the divorce of the conjugal family from the kinship group, but a large measure of independence on the part of each member of the family; group solidarity and loyalty no longer take precedence over personal preferences; equalitarianism is extant, divorce and separation are widespread.

A second area of agreement between the five sociological scholars is that family types are cyclical, one following the other in orderly procession throughout history. All have detected on the historical horizon a gradual lessening of authoritative control from the state or clan, to the conjugal family unit, to the individuals themselves within the family. Sorokin, Burgess and Locke, and Zimmerman are further united in their observations that our present chaotic marriage and family pattern is characterized by a transition from the conjugal family type to the equalitarian type of family life. This change represents to Burgess and Locke a note of progress; to Sorokin and Zimmerman it represents the final stage of family decay and deterioration.

TABLE 1. TYPES OF MARRIAGE AND FAMILY

Sociologist	Marriage and Family Types		
LEPLAY *	*Patriarchal* Stability, supervision, kin dominance and assistance, low material and high spiritual standard of living, strong traditions	*Souche* Conjugality, mobility, preserved traditions, prosperity, combination of traits of other types	*Independent* Instability, change desired, discarded traditions, self-sufficiency, government aid, fluctuating prosperity and depression
SOROKIN †	*Compulsive* Bond of force, not love; exploitation; degradation; cruelty; deprivation of rights; tyranny	*Familistic* Mutual love, devotion, sacrifice, solidarity, permanence, community living and sharing	*Contractual* Bond is a contract, cold, self-seeking, utilitarian, divorce, birth control, child neglect, loss of most functions to outside agencies
BURGESS AND LOCKE ‡	*Large Patriarchal* Absolute control over wife and children; power of life and death sometimes; power to marry off, divorce or sell his children	*Small Patriarchal* Conjugal family, dominance of husband	*Equalitarian* Weak parental authority, arrangement of own matches by children, spouse selection by romance or companionship, equal status of husband and wife, maximum freedom
ZIMMERMAN §	*Trustee* Kinship structure, sacred property held as trust for entire clan, family law supreme, maximum power by clan rather than Church or state	*Domestic* Strong conjugal family, little in-law interference, self-rule, strong internal bonds	*Atomistic* Minimum state regulation, rejection of Church regulation, divorce, birth control, adultery, fewer children, companionate marriage, rejection of traditions, independence of youth, juvenile delinquency, sexual perversions

* LePlay, *Les ouvriers européens*, 2nd ed. rev. (Paris, 1879).
† P. Sorokin, *The Crisis of Our Age* (New York: E. P. Dutton & Co., Inc., 1942), chap. v.
‡ E. W. Burgess and H. J. Locke, *The Family from Institution to Companionship* (New York: American Book Company, 1945), chap. i.
§ Carle C. Zimmerman, *Family and Civilization* (New York: Harper & Brothers, 1947), chap. vi.

13

FACTORS IN FAMILY CHANGE

In the plethora of sociological writings on marriage and the family, numerous causes are alleged for the currently observable change. Most of them, however, fail to make any distinction between basic and superficial causes, or even between causes and mere symptoms of marriage and family transition. The resultant confusion makes it extremely difficult to arrive at any clear body of agreement in the matter. In an attempt to determine the dominant thinking of writers of college texts on sociology, a personal survey was made of sixteen prominent authors. The over-all trend of their combined opinions indicated the following factors in family change as most important.

Decline of religious influence

Marriage was once generally thought to be a sacred, sacramental affair subject to regulation by the Church. God was deemed its author, the family was conceived of as a little church, marriage was a symbol of the union of Christ and His Church. Today marriage is progressively being more secularized; Church laws are ignored; the state has taken over its jurisdiction; marriage is thought a man-made affair or a social convention; and moral teachings against divorce, birth control, and abortion are not only avoided but even ridiculed.

Idealized changes and cultural lag

As a result of religious decline, attitudes toward marriage and the family are changing. Once considered spiritual-supernatural, marriage is now more and more deemed purely material and natural. Instead of being ratified in heaven, marriages are often merely recorded on legal forms in the offices of Justices of the Peace. Children were once thought the primary goal of marriage; now it is thought to be chiefly personal happiness. Wives, once rightfully submissive to husbands, now claim an equal status and authority. Children, once deemed properly subject to parental authority, now are thought of as equal partners in the family council.

At the same time the family is straining to catch up with the current trends of so-called "scientific progress." In an attempt to adapt itself to industrial, urban, scientific culture, the family is going through a veritable revolution.

Industrialization

The emergence of factory and office work has taken the father out of the home and, in many cases, wives and children also. Husbands, wives, and children no longer find family solidarity increased by working together through the day. In addition, industrialization has brought impoverishment to many, and inadequate housing in slum areas. It has brought the commercialized attractions that lure the members of the family apart even in their leisure hours.

Urbanization

The growth of city life has placed the family in an artificial environment made for industry and business rather than for domestic living. The quiet relaxation of the rural home is giving way to the noisy tensions of city life. The spaciousness of the rural environment is giving way to cramped living quarters, lack of privacy, and paucity of play space for children. The home, once the center of work, recreation, and religion, now finds itself in competition with factory and office, the theatre, and other outside amusements.

Growth of science

The rapid progress made in the natural sciences has led many to believe that similar changes must be made in marriage and the family. Pseudo-science is leading families to believe in the threat of overpopulation, the use of contraceptives, and the desirability of sterilization and abortion. Furthermore, science with its laborsaving devices has changed the nature of homemaking in many respects; it has freed the housewife from many chores and (in smaller families) has afforded a degree of leisure never before experienced.

Transfer of function

Not only have home chores been reduced by "gadgets," they have to an even greater extent been eliminated by the simple procedure of transferring them to outside agencies. The home, once a school, is now replaced by the public or private institution of learning. The home, once a center of recreation, is forsaken by children occupied in playgrounds, boys and girls clubs, scouting groups, community centers, and day nurseries. The home, once a laundry and a tailoring shop, is now supplanted by the "laundromat" and the "ready-to-wear" store. Even religious training of children is being transferred to the teachers and ministers of religion.

While quite a number of other factors are listed by these sixteen sociologists, these six are most frequently mentioned. It seems significant that eleven of the sixteen recognized the change in religious influence as one of the most important reasons for the variations in our current marriage and family pattern. In so doing, they are probing beneath the more superficial and symptomatic factors to causes, and to causes that are seemingly basic.

CAUSES IN FAMILY CHANGE

Human beings generally shape the outlines of their overt conduct by their inner beliefs and attitudes. That segment of human conduct which can be observed, therefore, bespeaks a more basic cause. *External* actions are usually nothing more than the outward expression of an *inner* philosophy of life.

The real purpose (or purposes) of family sociology is to examine this process as outlined. . . . It seeks the *causes* of family-civilization change, if there are such. . . . The science of family sociology cannot be mere statistics or *surface causes*. . . . Acts are social facts only when the *meaning-values* are attached to them. . . . Men do not want descriptions of society or unusable, even though interesting, statistical relations without *causal-functional connections*. . . . Changes in the family are changes in *basic meanings* given to the fundamental relations which compose the family. . . . Unless we consider the *real meaning* given these relations, we can speak of no fundamental social change in the family [italics ours].[1]

In this pursuit of a meaningful cause of family change, we are ultimately thrown back to the varying definitions given of man himself. Marriage is made of men and women; philosophers like to call them its *material cause*. Were we to build or change

---

[1] Carle C. Zimmerman, *Family and Civilization* (New York: Harper & Brothers, 1947), pp. 664–671.

a house, we would first want to know the nature and purposes of the people for whom it is to be built or altered. Were it to be for a large family, we would doubtless build or remodel it so as to include a nursery, many bedrooms, a large dining room, and perhaps a recreation room. Were it for a childless couple, we could dispense with nurseries and extra bedrooms, substitute a breakfast nook or small dining alcove and perhaps eliminate the recreation room.

In identical fashion, before we set about the formidable task of remodeling our marriage and family patterns, we would be well advised first to determine for whom we are to change them. The reason we have so many erratic suggestions for marital-familial reform, is that too many reformers (unlike architects) are rushing pell-mell ahead with their plans before answering the all-important question: "For whom are we altering marriage?" And if the answer is "for man," then a second question: "But what is man?"

THE THREE ANSWERS

Ultimately we need to have recourse to philosophy and theology for the answer to this question. Historically there have been three—and only three—answers given about man's nature. Just as sociologists have found only three basic types of marriage and family patterns, so philosophers and theologians in their speculations have arrived at only three general theories about man. In fact these three theological opinions can be logically associated with the three sociological-historical family patterns, and the transition from one type of marital-familial pattern to the other would seem to have as its ultimate cause a shift in the appraisal of the meaning of man himself.

The history of theology clearly indicates that man has been thought to have been either corrupted (depraved), wounded (imperfect), or unwounded (perfect).

Sociologists have found three family patterns in the historic experience of mankind. Theologians and philosophers similarly, have laid down three sets of principles for family behavior. However, it should be noted that rarely does any one pattern prevail to the exclusion of the other two. Rather there is usually found in a given culture, a mixture of the three. For instance, in our American culture today we find the liberalism of divorce side by side with the regimentation of sterilization by the state.

On the other hand, it seems true that at any given time a certain culture will be *dominantly* one of these three. A definite tendency to override the other two will usually be present. In our contemporary American family, for instance, the observable *over-all trend* is toward increased equalitarianism and freedom from restraints. This is true despite the fact that perhaps no other culture is so mixed, so heterogeneous, and so full of inner conflict and contradiction.

That the direction of the changes in marriage and the family are not basically due to factors such as industrialization and urbanization is self-evident; amidst the industrial-urban milieu we can and do find families of all types. In fact, in some quarters, despite the above adverse factors, we find in recent years families reverting to the more conservative types in considerable numbers.

Corrupted nature and marital totalitarianism

One of the three opinions on the nature of man is found in the theological theories of Calvin. Adhering to a belief in the fall of man in the Garden of Eden, he envisioned man's nature so irreparably damaged that it became utterly depraved. In similar fashion Hobbes devised the theory that man was intrinsically evil, a lawless creature given only to an unreasoning quest of selfish personal interests.[2] Upon the heels of this concept, which denies the dignity of man's personality, quickly followed the "blue law" state and the autocratic family. If man's nature is so utterly degraded, he must not be given any liberties; rather must he be controlled in every action by the dictates of an overbearing family pattern. Courtship under this system is tightly chaperoned; mates are selected by parents; affectionate display is minimized; sex is considered evil and sex expression an indication of degradation; sex education is taboo; wives are subjected to husbands even in unreasonable matters; the conjugal family does not enjoy self-government; children are regimented, not respected. In short, the dignity and rights of the conjugal family, of wives and of children, are seriously curtailed, and a form of marital and

---

[2] *Elementa Philosophica de Cive.*

TABLE 2

NATURE OF MAN AND FAMILY TYPES

NATURE OF MAN	Corrupted (depraved)	Wounded (deprived)	Unwounded (perfect)
BASIC ATTITUDES	Regimentation	Regulation	Liberalism
COURTSHIP	Strict chaperonage	Supervision	No supervision, much freedom
DISPLAY OF AFFECTION	Prohibition or minimization	Moderate kissing and embracing	Passionate necking, petting
MATE SELECTION	Choice of parents, "scientific breeding" by state	Choice of youth with advice of parents	Choice of youth, advice of parents not sought or rejected
PURPOSES OF MARRIAGE	Children only, happiness not considered	Children primary, happiness secondary	Personal happiness dominant, children secondary or not wanted
PROPERTY	Ownership by kinship group, not conjugal family	First claim to property to family needs	Individual ownership and use by husbands and wives for own purposes first
SEX	Necessary evil	Goodness, nobility, sacredness, virtue	Tool of pleasure to be used without restrictions
SEXUAL EXPRESSION	For child rearing; sterilization and denial of sex rights	For both children and personal happiness	Chiefly for personal gratification and pleasure
EXTRAMARITAL FRIENDSHIPS	Frowned upon with opposite sex	Allowed with caution and reserve	Much freedom permitted with opposite sex; kissing, etc.
FUNCTIONS OF HUSBAND AND WIFE	Strict division of labor	Participation in all functions jointly	Husband mere "breadwinner," wife working or at leisure
ROLE OF HUSBAND AND WIFE	Dictatorial role of husband	Husband, senior partner; wife, junior	Equalitarian
PLACE OF CHILDREN	Being seen but not heard	Respect for dignity as human beings	Rather complete equality; vote in family decisions
CHILD REARING	All children possible; no regard for prudence	Number dictated by prudence and morals	Contraceptives, childlessness, abortion

19

TABLE 2 (*Continued*)

NATURE OF MAN	Corrupted (depraved)	Wounded (deprived)	Unwounded (perfect)
CHILD TRAINING	Strictness; harsh discipline	Moderate supervision and discipline	Progressivism, little or no discipline or supervision
STABILITY	No separation for any reason	Separation for compelling and approved reasons only	Divorce and separation for any slight pretext
IN-LAWS	Domination, interference, dictation	Acceptance of in-laws, aid and advice but not domination, mutual love and assistance between couples and relatives	Rejection of both domination and good advice of in-laws, extreme independence of couples

familial totalitarianism holds sway. A modern version of this pattern was found in 1917 in Soviet Russia when Communism taught that men were corrupted by Capitalism (not by original sin). The Soviet family was completely under the control, not of the kin, but of the tyrannical State. In its contradictory position, it permitted a system of marriage akin to "free love" predicated upon the perfection of man. Since 1932 Communistic Russia has reversed this position for one of "regulation" of marriage. This form of absolutism, still extant today in some cultures, is interestingly portrayed in recent missionary annals:

The same situation prevails in Black Africa today where the tightly organized family structure comprises several generations of the same ancestry, living under the authority of a single head, grandfather or, perhaps, great-grandfather. . . . He decides on the marriages of the girls in the family, and whether this or that child shall be sent to school. He can give one sex to the mission and refuse another one permission to attend catechism classes; his orders, approved by all the members of the family, are ordinarily carried out without question.

Nearly always the heads of families arrange the marriages, one asking a girl, born or to be born, of the other group, in order to strengthen the bonds of friendship already existing among them.

Often the designated little girl is sent, at the age of four or five, to her future in-laws where her education takes place. When she reaches the age of puberty, they decide who her husband will be. In other tribes, the fiance goes often to the home of his fiancee to help with the farming, repairing of huts, etc., and the young girl will pass the seasonal festivals with the family of her future husband. . . .

In still other tribes, the young man and the young girl are ignorant till the day of the wedding as to whom their partner is going to be. . . .

The marriage does not give the young couple legal autonomy, it does not emancipate them from clan trusteeship; the husband remains subject to the authority of his family chief. . . .

The wife's position on the other hand becomes ambivalent; she is bound to respect and obey her husband and his parents, and is henceforth at the disposition of her husband's family (in several tribes, she is passed to one of his brothers in case of impotence, or prolonged absence). But at the same time she must submit to the orders of the head of her own family, since she still remains a part of the family who retain the right to see how she is treated; on this basis they often assume the additional right to repeatedly demand numerous gifts, even going so far as to take the wife back if the husband does not give in to demands he feels exaggerated.[3]

Unwounded nature and marital license

The extreme opposite opinion of man's nature had as perhaps its most prominent spokesman, Jean Jacques Rousseau of French Revolutionary fame. Unlike Calvin, Rousseau denied the Biblical account of man's fall in Eden, labeling it a "myth." Rather did he contend that man still enjoys the natural perfection and goodness he possessed before the fall. This natural goodness remains intact as long as the individual follows the promptings of lower nature and is not restricted by rules and regulations imposed from without. Rousseau called for the complete freedom of man and for his return to nature (to instincts, urges but not to reason). Upon this concept is based the free and easy, the *laissez-faire*, the unrestricted premarital and postmarital pattern of today.[4]

Youth can be trusted to the promptings of good Mother Nature and allowed to date without any supervision at twelve or even eleven years of age. Sex instruction replete with sensational and tempting physical detail can be given without injury to the youngest child. Passionate necking and petting can be, at least, winked at; they are, after all, natural. Men and women are free to ape current styles of progressive undress—Rousseau pictured the near-naked American Indian as the highest type of manhood. Mates are selected without the advice of or consultation with parents. Once married, couples do not foster deep and abiding ties with relatives. Parents are free to follow lower nature's promptings to limit childbirth through contraceptive use. If happiness is not found in marriage, divorce affords a facile and proper escape. Children are liberated from disciplinary measures and allowed to grow up in accord with the unfolding of their lower natures. In brief, no rules of religion, morality, or higher

---

[3] Soeur Marie-Andre du Sacre Coeur, "Woman's Indignity in Africa," *World Mission*, Vol. IV, No. 3 (Fall 1953), pp. 277–278.

[4] Louis Veuillot, *The Liberal Illusion*, trans. George Barry O'Toole (Washington, D. C.: National Catholic Welfare Conference, 1939), pp. 11–17; also Cardinal Louis Billot, *Liberalism: A Criticism of Its Basic Principles and Divers Forms*, trans. George Barry O'Toole (Beatty, Pa.: St. Vincent Seminary, 1922), pp. 40–42.

nature's law are to restrict the freedom of man or the egocentrism of the individual. A partial picture of this type of marriage and family was given us by one of America's pioneer family sociologists:

This does not mean, however, that the children hold the same subordinate position which was once theirs. They, in fact, tend to dominate the scene, their wishes determining the policy of the family. Thus the trend seems to be toward the filiocentric family in which the child plays the dominant role. He is, of course, controlled by the parents on occasion, to be indulged the next moment. . . . He has never heard the dictum that "children should be seen and not heard," and parental commands serve the function of suggesting what not to do.

The result is that parents are more and more experimenting with child rearing along lines quite alien to their grandparents. The child is not to be disciplined or coerced, but is to be given the privilege of choosing for himself. Application of "psychology" takes the place of the older controls. Persuasion and suggestion supplant the more direct methods dependent upon physical force. . . .

The husband is no longer the head of the household in many families, in spite of the fact that he still provides the family name, as well as the Christian name which his wife uses upon more formal occasions. Within the family circle, however, he is no longer the autocrat whose word is law. In fact, he is lucky if his children look upon him other than as a meddlesome outsider, or as an ally to be catered to when support is needed in breaking down his wife's opposition to some program of the children.

The wife, on the other hand, finds herself quite the equal of her husband in the family circle, if not the superior. She rules the destiny of the family group with a sympathetic, but nonetheless determined hand. . . . So far as the children are concerned, her commands are even more to be taken into account than those of the father.[5]

Wounded nature and marital regulation

The pure Christian tradition has always held that when man fell in the Garden of Eden he was *deprived* of some of the perfections previously enjoyed. Despite his imperfection, however, he

---

[5] E. Mowrer, *The Family: Its Organization and Disorganization* (Chicago: The University of Chicago Press, 1932), pp. 274–275. Copyright 1932 by the University of Chicago.

did not become *depraved*. Attracted to what is good, he also is prone to that which is evil. He is a composite of saint and sinner. "If angelism does not become a man, neither does bestiality. We are not angels, but then neither are we merely animals." [6] Because we are not angelic we cannot be allowed complete freedom from rules and regulations. Because we are inclined to evil, laws are necessary for our guidance and protection. But since we are merely imperfect and not utterly depraved, it is not regimentation stifling all liberty but regulation safeguarding true freedom that is indicated. The Catholic position on man and marriage always has been that both are benefited, prospered, and protected by the wise limitations of religion, morality, natural law, and proper civil legislation.

In accord with the true nature of man, the best interests of youth are served when they are supervised in their dating relationships, especially in the initial stages. Parents not only supervise the selection of dates but mixed parties as well. They also control the books, comics, movies, radio-television programs, and similar media used by their children, conscious of the tendency to evil lurking always in fallen human nature. Sex education is given at the time and in the quantity needed. Children are not prematurely and needlessly tempted by mere physical facts but have their wills disciplined to handle those facts safely. Affectionate display (when reflective of true love) is encouraged, with appropriate limitation and moderation. Sex is considered a good and sacred thing, proper sexual expression in marriage an act of high virtue. The selection of mates belongs ultimately to our youth, but the advice and counsel of parents is always present. Marriage is not for the depraved but for the strong; it implies unity and permanency despite difficulties and disappointments. Divorce is outlawed, but separation is thought proper for special and compelling reasons. The inclination of imperfect nature to limit offspring without a justifiable reason or by unnatural methods is curbed. The selfishness of depraved men and women who would make personal convenience and happiness the chief purpose of marriage gives way to the altruism of child rearing

---

[6] W. Farrell and M. J. Healy, *My Way of Life: The Summa Simplified for Everyone* (Brooklyn: Confraternity of the Precious Blood, 1952), p. 5.

and training. Children are given the incentives, rewards and sanctions which imperfect natures need for their improvement. Child "permissiveness" gives way to discipline; harsh over-strictness is dissipated by gentle firmness. In short, the rules of religion, morality, and natural law are considered the best safeguard of true liberty and the only protection against the imperfect tendencies of wounded human nature. A glimpse of this type of marriage and family pattern is given us by a pioneer Catholic sociologist in his original text on marriage:

Under the Christian law, then, there were to be no more bills of divorce. Both simultaneous and successive polygamy were excluded . . . the marriage promise was considered to partake of the nature of a vow. It was a sacred promise made to God. . . . By means of this ideal of a vow the Church sought to combine at once the fixity that goes with finality and the self-respect that goes with freedom. As Chesterton has well pointed out, *it is the only system that history has given us that combines stability with any degree of liberty* [italics ours]. . . . This safeguarded human conduct from temporary whim and from the caprice of fickle human nature. Marriage was looked upon as a matter of deepest loyalty, an affair of honor and of chivalry that, in turn, begot a pronounced sense of responsibility and a willingness to meet the difficulties and trials of married life. . . . In marriage the child holds first place. . . . There is the mutual love and assistance of the spouses. . . . The teaching of the Church on sex morality . . . led to a view of marriage that made the perpetration of the race, under conditions most favorable for its development, a noble task, one whose accomplishment is deserving of very serious sacrifice. It was a view that saw the glory of marriage to consist in fertility, in children. It was a view that gave man and woman a task that transcends them, a task that consists in fashioning an environment under which children may be born and may grow up under the best conditions attainable, an environment in which they may be prepared to carry forward a treasure of honorable traditions given them by their parents. It was a view, in a word, that was dominated by the family's transcendent importance and dignity.[7]

THE MARRIAGE PATTERN OF THE DIVINE PLAN

Marriage and the family were made for man, not man for marriage and the family. When God designed marriage and the

---

[7] E. Schmiedeler, *An Introductory Study of the Family* (New York: Appleton-Century-Crofts, Inc., 1947), pp. 40–43.

family, He did so in full accord with the nature of man, both before and after the Fall. To insure success, marriage was accomplished by regulations of Divine Wisdom intended to protect imperfect human beings from the vagaries of their own deprived natures.

Since man's nature was an imperfect one, His Wisdom provided rules to guide marriages away from the reefs and shoals of its imperfect members. The many fallacies current today resulting from the liberalistic attitudes in our culture, fail to realize the need for such wise control through natural laws.

Every man or woman, even before marriage, has the choice of conforming his or her premarital and marital conduct to the pattern forged by the Divine Inventor of marriage, or to the patterns devised by the infantile romanticism of Rousseau or by the gloomy speculations of Calvin. The first alone insures success. The latter two spell out for us the marital wreckage and family failure littering the pages of history and cluttering the divorce courts of today. They effect the recurring tendencies toward marital and familial totalitarianism, indicated by the emerging insistence on practices such as legal sterilization, compulsory physical examinations coupled with denial of license to marry, and the supposedly scientific mating of couples by governments through eugenic selection. The pendulum of history tends to swing back and forth from one unholy extreme to the other. Nothing but religion can arrest its swing and poise it in the mid-position termed by some the "happy medium."

3

Nature and Purposes of Marriage

N OT ONLY the nature of man but also the nature of marriage need to be understood if marriage is to be approached intelligently. Doubtless one of the chief reasons why mistaken notions about preparation for marriage and the conduct of it are so widespread today, is the simple failure to have learned its *full* scope and nature. That many couples have, at best, only a partial insight into this problem is a matter of common observation to those engaged in marriage and family education.

NATURE OF MARRIAGE

The complete nature of marriage indicates that it is in every instance a natural contract and a social institution; in most instances a God-given vocation and a legal contract; and in many instances a sacrament.

Unfortunately in few other respects does the inadequate preparation for marriage of our Catholic couples show greater weakness than in this. One study of 182 Catholic husbands and wives who had completed a premarital series of lectures indicated that only 114 knew marriage was a sacrament, only 37 that it was a legal contract and only 31 that it was a natural contract.[1] Another study of 167 Catholic husbands and wives revealed that only 13 (7.8 per cent) saw the full scope of marriage, while 154 (92.2 per cent) did not.[2] Similar findings resulted from a personal study of 75 couples, only seven of which knew marriage was a natural contract.[3] In a careful survey of 186 seniors in one of our most prominent Catholic universities, taken just before they took a senior marriage course, 184 (99 per cent) realized the sacramental nature of marriage; only 85 (45 per cent) that it is a natural contract; and only 104 (55 per cent) that it is a legal contract.[4] It seems apparent that the dominant blind spot of these couples relates to marriage being a *natural contract;* yet that is the very *essence* of marriage. One may speculate as to how a couple can have any real understanding of marriage (or of annulments) if they fail to grasp its essential nature.

This error is widespread not only among married couples but also among those who profess expertness in marital affairs and set themselves up as professional advisors. In a personal survey of marriage counselors in the nation, half of the oldest agencies admitted the absence of any consciously formulated philosophy of marriage; almost a third of the "functioning" services refused to answer this question, indicating either inability or confusion; and four-fifths of the remaining replies indicated no recognized philosophy of marriage. Apparently, a large number of couples are being counseled by individuals who have no clear-cut, well-defined concept of the nature of marriage.

---

[1] P. M. James, "The Expressed Results of a Certain Premarital Lecture Course" (Master's thesis, Catholic University of America, 1953), p. 56.

[2] R. Feiten, "An Investigation of the Knowledge and Attitudes of Catholic Married People on Moral Relations in Marriage and the Family" (Master's thesis, Catholic University of America, 1948).

[3] A. H. Clemens, "An Opinion Poll of Cana Conference Couples in Washington, D. C." (Unpublished monograph, Catholic University of America, 1952).

[4] Norman Galloway, "An Investigation of the Knowledge and Attitudes of the Seniors of the Arts and Science School of a Catholic University Relative to Marriage" (Master's thesis, Catholic University of America, 1950).

Marriage a natural contract

The essential factor in marriage—the thing which determines whether a marriage really exists—is the presence of a contract.[5] As all others, the marriage contract consists of an agreement—a consent between a man and a woman to take each other as husband and wife. This implies that they are entering an agreement to effect certain purposes or goals in a certain way. The question confusing most marriage students today is whether these goals and means are entirely subject to the personal choice of the individuals, whether they are to be determined by society or whether they are indicated by nature and God.

Perhaps a dominant majority of family sociologists reject the position that marriage—its contract, goals, structure—is determined by nature. With this rejection comes a large measure of freedom to experiment with, to change, to revolutionize marriage. With many, however, this is merely a matter of semantics; actually most admit "natural laws" regarding marriage despite the refusal to accept that terminology. The new science of "human relations"—widely heralded and being introduced into more universities almost daily—deals with the rules requisite to maintain peace and to attain the goals of industry, organizations, and family living. The marriage sociologist, counselor or specialist is unknown who fails to realize that cooperation is indispensable to successful relations. Who would be so puerile as to attribute these *imperatives* to any source other than *nature;* all recognize that these rules for human relations are *in the nature of things, viz.,* they are laws of nature. This is especially true of marriage since marriage is nature's invention, having its structure determined and its goals posited by nature. These are the *absolutes* of marriage—the natural imperatives—unchanging and unchangeable.

Let it be repeated as an immutable and inviolable fundamental doctrine that matrimony was not instituted or restored by man but by God; not by man were the laws made to strengthen and confirm and

---

[5] St. Thomas Aquinas, *In IV, Sentences,* 30, 2, 2; also *The Summa Theologica of St. Thomas Aquinas,* tr. by the Fathers of the English Dominican Province (New York: Benziger Bros., 1948), Vol. III, Q. 29, art. 2.

elevate it but by God, the Author of nature . . . and hence these laws cannot be subject to any human decrees or to any contrary pact even of the spouses themselves.[6]

Those who reject this position as confirmed in the above passage of Pius XI, and follow those false prophets who admit they have no clearly defined philosophy, soon learn that nature is an inexorable taskmaster. The millions milling through divorce courts and counseling agencies evidence the fact that certain *absolute* "rules of the game" have been fixed by nature and cannot be violated with impunity.

Is marriage man-made?

Yet despite this patent fact, most of our family specialists—sociologists, counselors, and writers—insist that marriage is an artificial device or a mere convention of society. The opinion dominates our marital literature that there are no absolute and fixed natural laws; rather has marriage emerged as the result of an evolutionary process. This theory was resurrected by Bachofen [7] in 1861 from the discredited writings of ancient philosophers; quickly gaining adherents, it blossomed into practical experimentation in Soviet Russia in 1917. The followers of this school of thought, including the authors of most textbooks on the family today, assert without proof that the human race originally had no marriage system; instead there was complete "free love." Gradually socio-economic changes indicated the desirability of marriage and society fashioned various marriage patterns to meet its subjective desires. One scholar has said:

The main postulates of the evolutionary school may be termed erroneous, *not in agreement with empirical fact* and not sufficiently thought through by the devotees of the family evolutionary school themselves [italics ours].[8]

Today we are assured by an internationally famous anthropologist that no true scientist subscribes any longer to the opinion

---

6 Pius XI, "On Christian Marriage," *Catholic Mind,* Vol. XXIX, No. 2 (January 22, 1931), p. 22; also *Acta Apostolicae Sedis,* Vol. XXII (December 31, 1930), pp. 539–592.

7 Bachofen, *Das Mutterrecht,* (Stuttgart, 1861).

8 Carle C. Zimmerman, *Family and Civilization* (New York: Harper & Brothers, 1947), pp. 62–63.

that free love originally prevailed. Rather does the evidence indicate that "marriage among primitive peoples was probably monogamous. . . . The essential thing in human marriage is not a sexual relationship; rather is this a development of relatively recent times." [9]

The great sociological experiment

Heedless of the unscientific nature of the evolutionary theory and unmindful of the inexorable laws of nature protecting marriage, Soviet Russia in 1917 embarked on the greatest empirical test of free love ever attempted in all human experience. With a laboratory of 165 million human guinea pigs that extended from the Dnieper River to the Ural Mountains—a laboratory of over eight million miles—the experiment was conducted based on the theory of Friedrich Engels: "A positive cessation of fondness or its replacement by a new passionate love makes a separation a blessing for both parties and for society." [10] Compared to this empirical study in free love and divorce, the Kinsey study is an extremely diminutive endeavor. Yet most have heard of Kinsey; few have heard of the great Russian experiment in family folly.

After 17 years of trial and error, in the huge city of Moscow alone 57,000 children were born but 154,000 abortions were performed.[11] Eighteen years of free love brought 38 per cent more divorces than marriages and over seven million homeless children, roaming the roads in the country and the streets in the cities. Soviet Russia today admits marriage has a natural basis; it has made abortion illegal and divorce almost impossible to obtain, insisting that women are by nature intended to become mothers. It has given irrefutable and conclusive empirical proof that marriage is based on certain inviolable, absolute natural laws and that nature punishes in no unmistakable fashion the society that dares to thwart her designs.

---

9 H. Guenther, *Frommen und Urgeschichte der Ehe* (Goettingen, Germany: Nusterschmidt Wissenshaftlicher Verlag, 1951), p. 296.

10 F. Engels, *Der Ursprung der Familie, der Privateigenthums und des Staats,* (Hollingen-Zurich, 1884), tr. by E. Untermann (Chicago, 1902).

11 F. J. Sheen, *Communism and the Conscience of the West* (New York: Bobbs-Merrill Co., Inc., 1948), Chap. vii.

Marriage a social institution

In the design of nature marriage is also a social institution. Its social aspect is indicated by the fact that its chief purposes are not individual but social. Not only the generative act in marriage but also the rearing and education of the children are social functions. After reviewing all the extant literature on the early history of marriage, an eminent anthropologist assures us it is only in recent history that sex for personal gratification has loomed so large; in all cultures reviewed he found the *social* roles dominant—rearing, protecting, and educating children. He further indicates that any society not dedicated to the social purposes of the family is doomed to extinction.[12] It is precisely this social task imposed by nature that makes marriage an institution —a social relationship tending toward permanency. Without stability and perpetuity, children could not be trained properly, the rights of children to both parents would be violated, and the need for companionship in old age would remain unsatisfied.[13]

As in all social institutions a series of relationships arise between the various members. There are many such in marriage —religious, moral, sociological, psychological, physical, economic, legal, recreational, educational. It is the knowledge and mastery of these relationships which constitutes the art of a successful and happy marriage.

Marriage a legal contract

Since few marriages are contracted outside the rightful jurisdiction of some government, marriage is usually a legal contract. No government is so unaware of the impact of marriage and the family on social welfare or ruin as to leave the conduct of its affairs completely in the hands of individuals. The role of the civil law is twofold: on the one hand, it should confirm the natural laws and not violate them (as too often it does today); on the other hand, it should recognize that certain cultural differences exist in various places and at various times. Accordingly, permanency of marriage should be reflected in civil law, but laws of inheritance may well be changed, within certain limits, in

---

12 Guenther, *op. cit.*
13 St. Thomas Aquinas, *Summa Contra Gentiles,* c. 124, c. 122; also *Supplement to Summa Theologica,* Q. 65, art. 1.

accord with the fluctuating needs and customs of a given culture.
The Church also has established legislation for marriage. The
marriage of baptized persons is always a sacrament, and the
Church is the rightful custodian of the sacraments. Accordingly, she has both the right and the duty to enact such laws as
will protect marriage, the Church, human society, and human
souls from the pitfalls in marriage. The Church has watched
marriage and family living for almost two thousand years, and
should at this late date know its dangers and necessary conditions.
If people resort to obtaining advice from marriage counselors
with perhaps twenty years' experience, they should stand more
ready to be guided by the Church with her twenty centuries of
experience. Furthermore, these laws are meant for the welfare
of the couples and their children and are based upon revelation
and theology as well as experience. It is only the unwise who
will reject or circumvent them.

Marriage a sacrament

Whenever baptized persons contract a marriage, they always
and at the same time receive a sacrament. This implies that
marriage is for them supernatural as well as natural. The entire
married life of the couple is elevated to this supernatural level;
grace is imparted not only on the day of the wedding but whenever needed throughout the married life, and the bonds of unity
and of permanency are deepened. Even in its sacramental aspects marriage is *social;* for the primary graces of the sacrament
flow not to the individual purposes, but to the *social purposes* of
this institution. It is, further, a *lay* sacrament in that none but
lay people receive it, and none but a lay person can administer it.

The high dedication and the many difficulties of married life
call for the extra help of a special sacrament. At the same time
the fact that Christ so elevated marriage to the supernatural, is
evidence enough of the great dignity and nobility of the married
state. It further implies that we gain all the graces possible out
of this sacrament by a more religious preparation for it and a
more prayerful attitude toward it after marriage.

Marriage a vocation

Relatively few seem to realize adequately that marriage is one
of four *major* vocations—the other three being the priesthood,

the religious life, and single life in the world. Pius XII did not hesitate to speak to newlyweds of the family "which they are *called upon* to found [italics ours]." [14]   Others have pointed out that it "is a calling, a high vocation" [15] and that "it is at the disposal of certain people who received a special vocation to it." [16]

In its *social* aspect this vocation of marriage implies a life of consecration of all one's powers—supernatural and natural, of soul and of body—to the extension of the Church, the Mystical Body of Christ on earth.   In its *personal* aspect, it has implications of being a "religious vocation," for it is a call to the higher realms of spirituality.   Christian marriage is "a source of great holiness, a most effective means of advancing in spiritual perfection to the sublime heights of heroic sanctity." [17]   Few couples as they walk down the aisle on their wedding day seem conscious of this call to a higher life.   No priest, brother, or nun on the day of his ordination or taking of vows would fail to sense this fact; but many, if not most, couples do.   And marriage is a state conducive to holiness, *not in spite of, but precisely because of the circumstances of married life.*   Were this known more widely, doubtless many would advance in holiness more quickly and would appreciate their vocation more fully.

Since marriage is one of the four major vocations, any career or occupation must, at best, remain a mere *avocation.*   Perhaps no clearer indication of the loss of a sense of marital vocation is discernible than the intense preoccupation of fathers (and sometimes mothers) with their careers to the neglect of marital and familial duties.   This sense also seems lost by those husbands who abdicate their roles to their wives and by those mothers who foist more and more of their responsibilities to their children upon outside agencies.

---

[14] Pius XII, "I Fini del Matrimonio," *Atti e Discorsi de Pio XII,* III (Rome: Instituto Missionares Pia Societa San Paolo, 1941), p. 243.

[15] D. von Hildebrand, *Marriage* (New York: Longmans, Green & Co., Inc., 1947), p. 44.

[16] Dom J. Scheuber, *Nazareth* (Westminster, Md.: Newman Press, 1948), pp. 7–8.

[17] F. J. Connell, "Marriage as a State of Religious Perfection," *Marriage Education and Counseling,* ed. A. H. Clemens (Washington, D. C.: The Catholic University of America Press, 1951), p. 32.

PURPOSES OF MARRIAGE

To properly prepare for marriage, to understand and live it successfully requires a clear and correct notion not only of the nature of man and of marriage, but also of the *purposes* of marriage. A current weakness in marriage literature is the discussion of functions, roles, and success in marriage without first having determined its goals.

Goals and success

Since success implies attaining goals, our norms for success will depend upon the determination of such goals. Many writers are snarled in confusion by positing certain purposes in marriage and then defining success without the attainment of those purposes. Few, if any, refuse to include "procreation" as a proper goal,[18] but many, if not most, exclude children from their notion of marital success. Further, *every* empirical study available on success in marriage [19] is based on the assumption that there is only one main purpose—happiness. Yet these same scholars in their other publications usually list additional purposes. Apparently, too many "learned" marriage counselors and family sociologists fail to see the common sense nexus between purposes and success in marriage. They would admit that a watch that does not keep time is not productive, but they do not see that a marriage that does not achieve its purposes is a failure also.

Goals of marriage

The purposes marriage is intended to serve are not simple; on the contrary they are quite complex. They are at once natural and artificial, social and individual, objective and subjective, generic and specific. In the Divine Plan for marriage certain unmistakable goals are imbedded in the very nature and structure of marriage itself. They are *natural* since marriage is a natural contract implying certain purposes, *artificial* in that some reasons for marriage are made by those entering it (prestige, wealth, and the like), *social* in that some goals serve society, *individual* since

---

18 See "Functions in Marriage" at the end of this chapter.
19 See Chapter 9 for further discussion.

personal advantages are also served, *objective* because certain goals are placed in marriage by its Author and are not subject to human change, *subjective* since rightful personal desires may be present, *generic* because marriage has at least one goal in common with other societies, *specific* since the family has its own unique purposes also. "From God comes the very institution of marriage, *the ends for which it was instituted,* the laws that govern it, and the blessings that flow from it [italics ours]."[20] The first and most important is a *dual* and a *social* one—the procreation and education of the human race. The second is that long list of individual benefits accruing to married people which result in the development of their personalities.

The failure to include either of these two sets of goals is a grave omission. Marriage is primarily a *social* institution designed to perpetuate the human race; only secondarily, is it intended for personal gain. The inverting of their order so that personal advantages take precedence over the welfare of the race is a serious distortion of the Divine Plan; the emphasizing of either to the diminution or neglect of the other is a tragic error. Yet all three of these mistakes are rife today, even at times in Catholic circles. In a study of 120 Catholic husbands and wives who had taken a premarital lecture course, only 92 considered children a primary goal;[21] in another study, out of 399 Catholic husbands and wives 285 thought "partnership" between them the main element, while only 114 considered "parenthood" the chief factor in success;[22] a third study of 185 seniors in a Catholic university indicated that 164 considered "procreation of children" primary while 21 considered "companionship" primary.[23] In a personal study of 202 Catholic college seniors, 172 thought children the primary purpose while 29 thought mutual companionship and love primary.

In any given culture the ends or goals of marriage are colored by that culture itself. Some past civilizations, such as ancient

---

[20] Pius XI, *op. cit.,* p. 24.

[21] P. M. James, *op. cit.,* p. 55.

[22] H. Dunn, "A Study of Some Catholic Marital Attitudes, Practices and Problems with Special Reference to the Implication for Premarital Instructions," (Doctoral dissertation, Catholic University of America, 1956), p. 11.

[23] Galloway, *op. cit.,* p. 126.

Sparta or Italy under Mussolini, have emphasized the *social* purposes of marriage to the neglect of the personal advantages; this is typical of *Socialism*. Others have maintained a happy balance between the two goals, neither exaggerating the importance of children nor of personal happiness, yet maintaining the prior importance of child rearing. This is to be expected in a culture adhering closely to *nature* or to the *Christian* tradition. Still others, as our own current American pattern, exalt the *individual* purposes and minimize or ignore the social goals. This bespeaks the *individualism* so rampant today.

Personal happiness

Personal happiness is a righful goal of marriage as of all human living. However, it is a "generic" goal, since it is common to all other societies. That is, it is not a "specific" goal of marriage since happiness is not the unique goal of marriage alone. If the "generic" goal of happiness is to be attained, obviously it must be through the accomplishment of "specific" goals. In other words, happiness, rightly understood, is a by-product or an end result of having achieved parenthood, companionship, and other unique marriage goals. This is quite different from the current widespread secular concept that happiness is *the* unique goal and end of marriage. This secular concept believes that happiness can be attained directly by marriage regardless of whether such a marriage achieves its rightful goals of parenthood and complementary living or not. In other words, the current trend is to regard happiness as the *exclusive* and *primary* goal, failing to recognize parenthood as the primary specific goal without which maximum happiness in the married state is not likely to be achieved.

This tendency to stress the personal advantages of marriage has gained such strength that it has distorted the sense of values of many of our learned scholars. One prominent family sociologist states in his preface that half of his book will be given to the question of happiness in marriage.[24] All of the empirical studies of success in marriage have taken happiness as their chief norm. The theory dominating the thinking of American marriage and

---

[24] M. Nimkoff, *Marriage and the Family* (New York: Houghton Mifflin Company, 1947), p. x.

family experts accepts the position that the drift from an "institution" with high social purposes to a "companionship" emphasizing personal advantage, is a mark of true progress. In fact, freedom from social duties (child rearing) permits more time to cultivate love [25]—as though love would grow in a vacuum! Yet before this thinking had become prominent, an American sociologist was perplexed by the growth of divorce accompanying the growth of this theory, when he wrote:

Yet it is not inconsistent to say that this aim at love increases divorce. The theory being that the contracting parties are to be made happy; then, if they are not, it seems to follow that the relation is a failure and should cease: the brighter the ideal the darker the contrast. Where interest and custom rule marriage those who enter into it may not expect congeniality, or, if they do, they feel that it is secondary and do not dream of divorce because it is not achieved.[26]

This theorizing has finally trickled down to the masses where it is now commonly held. We date, court, select spouses, and enter marriage largely because "we are in love." We expect to get out of marriage a presumed "happiness" rather than the gratification of achievement, the sense of worthwhile contribution. "Now, it is not wrong for people to enter marriage with such *personal subjective* motives, as long as they do not reject the purposes and qualities of marriage as established by the Creator . . . [italics ours].[27] However, even though morally justifiable, this approach to marriage is extremely hazardous. It is likely to color the entire set of expectations and goals, and to eventuate in frustrating the objective purposes should they clash or interfere with subjective aims.

Viewed from this standpoint, the contemporary Western family leaves much to be desired. It has increasingly failed in its main task; has increasingly generated the forces of egoism and demoralization. The principal reason for this is to be found in the growing transformation of the family from a familistic union of husband and wife into an

---

[25] E. W. Burgess and H. J. Locke, *The Family, from Institution to Companionship* (New York: American Book Company, 1945), pp. 26 ff.

[26] Charles Horton Cooley, *Social Organization* (New York: Charles Scribner's Sons, 1929), p. 366.

[27] F. J. Connell, "The Ends of Marriage," *The Catholic Family Monthly,* Vol. XL (August 1945), p. 7.

implicitly egoistic contractual association of a male and a female in the interest of pleasure and utility.[28]

Personal advantage is obviously a secondary goal. But many have failed to realize that these advantages and this sought-for happiness is a *by-product* arising from the full attainment of the social goals of marriage.

Catholics and personal goals

Even some Catholic scholars have fallen prey to the individualism of our culture. With the avowed purpose of correcting the earlier neglect of the personal purposes they have swung to the opposite extreme and exalted them to an equal place with the social purposes or have denied that there are really two distinct sets of goals.[29] Some Catholics taught that both children and personal gain were of equal importance; others held that both were the same purpose and did not represent two distinct goals. This position gained increasing numbers of adherents until the Holy See decided the situation should be clarified.

This new mode of thinking and speaking is destined to promote error and uncertainty, the Decree read: seeking to avert such happenings, the Eminent and Reverend Fathers of this Sacred Congregation, pledged to safeguard matters of faith and morals, in plenary session on twenty-ninth day of March 1944 proposed to themselves this question: "Can the opinion of certain writers be admitted who either deny that the procreation and education of offspring is the primary end of marriage, or teach that secondary ends are not essentially subordinated, but equally principal and independent"? They decreed in response: "No." [30]

Social goals of marriage

That marriage, like all other professions, should have primarily social goals should be obvious to any thinking person. Society expects the physician to conform his life to his oath of Hippocrates in which he promises to place the welfare of his patient

---

[28] P. Sorokin, *The Reconstruction of Humanity* (Boston: The Beacon Press, 1948), p. 144.

[29] H. Doms, *The Meaning of Marriage* (New York: Sheed & Ward, Inc., 1939).

[30] Decree of the Holy Office, April 1, 1944, *Acta Apostolicae Sedis*, Vol. XXXVI (1944), p. 103.

above personal advantage; society expects the lawyer to pursue justice for others before fees for himself; it expects the soldier to expose even his life for the common good. In none of these does it tolerate the frustration of social purposes for the sake of individual convenience or gain. On the contrary those placing self before service are disqualified or removed from their posts by society. Only in the world's most important natural profession —marriage—does contemporary society place personal advantage above social welfare by encouraging birth control, divorce and similar antisocial practices. In a study of ten different family cultures from primitives to civilized peoples the social goal of procreation was found in all of them as primary but personal gain as a goal was not.[31] This would seem to confirm the naturalness and the primacy of the social function.

Sacred Scripture, tradition, Canon Law, philosophy and truly scientific sociology agree upon the importance of child rearing as a family goal. The motivation of Tobias by the Holy Spirit caused him to pray: "And now, Lord, Thou knowest, that not for fleshly lust do I take my sister to wife, but *only* for the love of posterity, in which Thy name may be blessed for ever and ever."[32] Despite the fact that this high ideal is not for all, the law of the Church places childbearing first: "The primary end of marriage is the procreation and education of children; the secondary end, mutual support and the relief of concupiscence."[33] This traditional position is confirmed by Pius XI in the words: "Thus amongst the blessings of marriage, the child holds the first place."[34] The Catholic ideal has ever emphasized the social and religious significance of marital goals.

The humblest of laboring men should regard his home life as an apostolate out of which Church and nation may draw the priests, missionaries and apostles they need. For the basic ideal of family life is to 'multiply the number of the elect'. . . . Family life inspired by this high ideal affords a proper basis for the decent education and moral training of the young. It gives a truly supernatural foundation to

[31] S. A. Queen and J. B. Adams, *The Family in Various Cultures* (Philadelphia: J. B. Lippincott Company, 1952).

[32] Tobias 8:9.

[33] Canon 1013, 1–2.

[34] Pius XI, *op. cit.*, p. 24.

their courtships and their friendships, which alone is able to withstand the teaching and morals of modern paganism.[35]

The fact remains that while both the primary (social) and the secondary (personal) goals of marriage are distinct, they are not independent of each other. It is not difficult to agree with the position maintained by a distinguished Catholic family scholar:

It would appear better, if one speaks of two ends, to call them complementary and to lay stress upon their complementary character . . . it is impossible to speak of conjugal love without going on to reproduction, or of reproduction without going back to married love.[36]

Development of personality

Another source of confusion to some is the apparent contradiction between primacy of child rearing and the statement of Pius XI in his Encyclical:

This mutual inward perfecting of husband and wife, this determined effort to perfect each other, can in a very real sense, as the Roman Catechism teaches, be said to be *the chief reason and purpose of matrimony* [italics ours] provided matrimony be looked at . . . more widely as the blending of life as a whole and the mutual exchange and sharing thereof.[37]

This position should prove a wholesome antidote to the thinking of those who believe that the insistence upon the priority of child rearing makes of marriage merely a "breeding" institution and the wife and mother a mere "brooder" of children. On the contrary:

It is repugnant to the Catholic way of thinking to look upon marriage as nothing else but a union for the production of children. Marriage serves this purpose and derives from this basic end its essential constitution, but it is also capable of realizing personal values of a high order. The kind of union demanded by marriage calls for mutual love, without which it would be farcical and revolting. But when based on love, it contributes in an eminent degree to the welfare of

---

[35] Canon Cardijin, *The Spirit of the Y. C. W.* (Toronto, Canada: The Catholic Truth Society, 1940), pp. 13–14.

[36] Jacques Leclercq, *Marriage and the Family,* tr. by T. R. Hanley (New York: Frederick Pustet Co., Inc., 1941), p. 15.

[37] Pius XI, *op. cit.*

the contracting parties, enhances their personal life, enriches them emotionally, and contributes in every respect to their happiness.[38]

The seeming contradiction between the primary end consisting on the one hand of child rearing and on the other of perfecting the personality, is easily removed in the light of traditional Catholic philosophy.   Marriage and the family, as all societies, have both *specific* and *generic* goals.[39]   One purpose of the family is the development of personalities; this goal is also that of *all other societies*—the Church, state, economic society, educational society, and so forth.   This is why the development of personality is called a "generic" purpose.   However, each society also has goals peculiar to it—specific purposes—which no other society can attain.   The procreative and child rearing purposes of marriage are peculiar to the family; no other society can achieve these goals.   This distinction was clearly in the mind of Pius XI when he wrote his message.   It should be noted that the Pope qualified his statement that personality perfection can be considered the chief purpose with the words *"provided matrimony be looked at" from a certain (the* generic*) point of view.*

FUNCTIONS IN MARRIAGE

Whatever the goals of marriage, they can be realized only through the discharge of certain functions.   It is not recognized generally enough that between goals and functions there is an inescapable relationship.   This failure leads many to discuss changing functions or the loss of function in the modern family without noting whether such change or loss is related to success or failure in marriage.   Some even contend that the decline of the child rearing function results in a much higher degree of marital success.[40]   This position is reflected in most of the most widely used textbooks in sociology a few years ago.   It is phrased in these words, by one of them:

---

[38] R. Geis, *Principles of Catholic Sex Morality,* tr. by C. Bruehl (New York: Joseph F. Wagner, Inc., 1930), p. 40.

[39] St. Thomas Aquinas, *Summa Theologica,* Vol. II, Pt. 2, Q. 141, Art. 5; *De Regimine Principisum,* I, c. 14; also H. Pesch, *Lehrbuch der Nationalokonomie, Vol. I* (Freiburg in Breisgau: Herder, 1914), pp. 467–469.

[40] Burgess and Locke, *op. cit.,* p. 715.

However, the loss of traditional functions by the family brought compensatory forces into play, resulting in the marked accentuation of the residual affectional functions. Here, then, is the principal explanation as to why the modern family has become the great agency concerned with the problem of human happiness.[41]

Functions are changing

The change of functions of the family is noted by all marriage and family specialists; and only a few fail to agree that this change also represents a loss of family functions to outside agencies. The decline of family size, home production, home recreation and family prayer, on the one hand, and the increased use of extra-domestic agencies—bakeries, laundries, schools, nurseries, playgrounds, theatres, dance halls, night clubs and so forth—on the other, stand as mute but eloquent testimony of both the change and the loss of functions in the family circle.[42] This is indicated in the opinions of the authors of nineteen sociology textbooks, who agree that in varying degrees the economic, religious, educational, welfare, protective and recreational functions have been lost.[43] However, quite a number of functions are being retained, at least in part, especially reproduction, maintenance, socialization, companionship, inheritance, sex satisfaction, economic support, education, recreation, religion and the provision of a home. A few authors think no economic functions remain in the family; others recognize no function at all except companionship.[44] One of the textbooks states that children could be reproduced either inside or outside marriage, and that the children might well be socialized by agencies other than the family; in fact, this might result in increasing the life-chance of the child.[45] This Socialist doctrine is apparently being taught students in some of our colleges and universities.

---

[41] Nimkoff, *op. cit.,* Preface p. x.

[42] For additional facts see Chapters 14, 16, and 17, Education, Recreation, and Economics.

[43] J. A. Curtin, "Analysis of Family Theory as Found in Some Standard Textbooks Commonly Used in the Basic Sources in Sociology in Colleges and Universities" (Master's thesis, Catholic University of America, 1951), p. 21.

[44] *Ibid.*

[45] J. W. Bennett and M. M. Termin, *Social Life: Structure and Function* (New York: Alfred A. Knopf, Inc., 1948), p. 551.

Loss of function

Few have indicated more alarm over this loss of function than one economist turned sociologist.[46] In his listing of eleven different functions he emphasizes how much most have waned. He thinks the *need for survival* is being frustrated by the decline of home production and the low standard of living. The *security* function is weakened by neglect, rejection, breakdown of the kinship family, inadequate protection in case of the death of the breadwinner, and the encroachment of outside agencies including the state. The *endowment* function no longer provides dowries to subsidize early marriages; as a result economic hardship forces wives to work, causes quarrels and induces birth control. He sees the *disciplinary* function disappearing in the growing indulgence of children by parents and the disappearance of physical punishment. The *vocational* function is declining with a loss of the vision of the home as a center of work, production, and education. The *recreational* function suffers when homes are intended to be show places, home parties are not tolerated, most amusements are sought in commercialized forms or little yard space is available for children at play. The lack of privacy and the atmosphere of noise from radio and television inside and from bustle of traffic outside militate against that relaxation which the *recuperative* function should afford. One of the most tragic losses stems from the difficulty of discharging the *character building* function by the home when so many children are handed over to nursery schools and institutions, when so little religion and prayer remain in the family circle and when children are shaped by adverse influences in the neighborhood. Nor does he think the *eugenic* function very strong in families which fail to impart sex education, prepare youth for marriage or assist them in getting an economic start in marriage. The loss of love, the *erotic* function, is attested by preferring the office job to mothering children, by child rejection and neglect and juvenile delinquency. In similar fashion, the *harmonic* function's decline is indicated by the divorce rates, by separations and desertions, and

---

[46] Ralph Borsodi, *Education and Living* (New York: The Devin-Adair Co., 1948), chap. x, part II, sec. 2.

by the growing quest for marriage counseling. In the words of Pius XII this type of debilitated home is "a transient, cold, deserted, changeable, obscure habitation, without the serenity and warm light of a family living together . . . it is not a true home." [47]

Results of loss of function

There are those who view the decrease in function with little or no alarm. They harbor the optimistic belief that marriage is working its way to a more perfect pattern of companionship. They see the loss of function as a temporary disturbance due to the transition of the family from a rural to an urban pattern and from an institution with social goals to a companionate arrangement for personal advantage. Others do not fear that the loss and transfer of some functions will affect the internal solidarity of the family. There are also those who remain aware of the natural goals of marriage and the family, and of the fact that these goals can best be served *only* by preserving certain functions intact within the family itself. To them the loss of certain functions spells partial or total frustration of nature's plan for marriage.

"Social history and cultural anthropology prove that one cannot disturb the functional balance of the family without disturbing simultaneously that of society, because the family is and remains not only the cradle but also the prototype and nursery of society." [48] This seems true because in the first instance the family is not a mechanistic but an *organic* unit; it has the principle of vital activity *within* not outside of it. In practical terms this implies that the family (like all living organisms) thrives and prospers by *functioning,* but it atrophies and deteriorates through lack of functions. Again it is largely through the joint discharge of these functions that bonds of unity, attachment and love are deepened. "The family that prays together, stays together"; but so does the family that works together and plays together. Bonds are forged only in a true functionalism, never

---

[47] Pius XII, *Atti e Discorsi di Pio XII,* V (Rome: Instituto Missionares Pia Societa San Paolo, 1943), p. 26.

[48] F. Mueller, *American Institute of Socio-Political Thought,* Vol. II, No. 4 (January 1946).

in a vacuum left by the loss of function. Love by its very nature cannot feed upon itself without exhausting itself. It needs to be nourished by other functions in marriage and the family. Furthermore, the loss of function to the family means its transfer to some outside agency. Few in number are those functions which can be better discharged by such external establishments; usually such a transfer means a less effective performance of a function. There is no substitute for the family as a teacher of religion or an educator of character; just as there is no bakery or grocery substitute for a homemade piece of bread. Not only does the individual suffer by a lesser function but society at large becomes afflicted with irreligion, delinquency and other social ills.

At the conclusion of a scholarly study conducted by the noted family experts comprising the President's Research Committee on Social Trends we find a striking reference to the effect of loss of function in the family:

Finally a major problem of the family is its instability. Divorce is still increasing. Although the rate of this increase in the past decade has slowed up, a study of the long time trends gives no confidence in a prediction that the rate of divorce itself will decrease in the near future, though it must do so in the long run. *Increased divorce is due to the weakening of the functions which served to hold the family together,* and no doubt of public opinion, which would appear to be correlated with the exercise of these functions. *If, say six of these eight functions or bonds are weakened, then more divorce is to be expected, unless there is a corresponding strengthening of the other two* [italics ours].[49]

THE NATURE, PURPOSES, AND FUNCTIONS OF MARRIAGE IN THE DIVINE PLAN

In the Divine invention of marriage God formed its essential nature, which is unchanging and unchangeable. In many nonessential aspects He left it free to the changes and modifications of existing cultures. Marriage, accordingly, is subject to certain inalienable laws of nature which posit its basic structure and purposes. It has been granted the privilege and dignity and the

---

[49] Report of the President's Research Committee on Social Trends, *Recent Social Trends in the United States* (New York: McGraw-Hill Book Company, Inc., 1933), p. 708.

resources of a special sacrament. With the aid of these sacramental graces marriage will ensure growth in holiness, will extend the Mystical Body of Christ on earth. Its effects are intended to transcend limits of time and space, and to penetrate into and populate the very courts of heaven itself.

Accordingly, the chief purpose of marriage has been placed by its Divine Author in the generation and education of children. It is also intended to serve the personal need for self-development and the desire for happiness. The norm for success in marriage according to the Divine Plan implies the attainment of both purposes. Far from being mutually exclusive, both purposes assist and serve each other.

But to attain these goals and so enjoy success, certain functions in marriage and the family are imperative. The loss of function today is debilitating and is contributing to divorce and marital breakdown. The transfer of these functions to outside agencies generally diminishes the vigor and vitality of the family, weakens bonds of attachment, substitutes an inferior function, and abets the growth toward socialism.

4

The Quality of Love

Few things are more necessary for human well-being than love. It is almost as important as the food we eat or the air we breathe. Physical health, emotional and mental poise, and spiritual progress must have love as a component element of their diet. It is required alike in infancy, childhood, adolescence, adulthood, and old age. The infant deprived of it suffers from an arrested development; the child without it becomes a twisted personality; the adolescent often turns out delinquent; the adult becomes haggard, embittered, and prematurely old; the aged live out their lives frustrated by disappointment, disillusionment, and loneliness. It is true, even though trite, that "love makes the world go round."

Love's most natural habitat is marital and family living. Marriage is the fulfillment of man's instinctive yearning for the embrace of marital love. The family is the society which finds its deepest bond and its greatest contribution in and through love. Doubtless this is a major reason why marriage and family life enjoy such unique advantages, benefits, and blessings.[1] This is also a reason why an undying love which breaches all obstacles and permits no diminution is the perpetual and weighty responsibility of husband, wife, and children to one another.

---

[1] For further development of this point see Chapters 11 and 12.

INFATUATION

One of the chief reasons that so few understand this continuing duty of love, is precisely that few understand the true nature of love. They confuse true love with passion, infatuation, sentiment, or romance—none of which is constant or permanent. This type of infantilism, referred to as being "head over heels in love," is as different from true love as a counterfeit coin is from a genuine one. Perhaps its most tragic aspect is that it is a form of self-deception leading to a marriage which proves to be nothing more than a mirage. For infatuation is based only on some attraction, not on the more stable elements of respect, reason, and will.

The combined opinions of experts [2] indicate that infatuation is changeable and unpredictable, love is constant and enduring; the former is physical or emotional alone, love is also rational and volitional; infatuation has a sudden onset, love grows gradually; the former is fascinated by appearance and mannerisms, the latter is based on admiration for human qualities of mind and character; infatuation is absorbed by the present moment, love looks to the future; the former is totally blind to defects, the latter is conscious of them; infatuation idealizes the other person as being "perfect," love realizes the presence of both virtues and limitations; infatuation is based upon an attraction to some one quality only, love embraces the total personality makeup. In the words of Pius XI infatuation is based on "the passing lust of the moment" and "in pleasing words only"; while love enjoys that "deep attachment of the heart, which is expressed in action, since love is proved by deeds." [3]

THE ROMANTIC CONCEPT

Another mistaken notion widely accepted, even by supposedly intelligent persons, is the romantic concept of love. In this concept the attraction between two people is based largely, if not entirely, upon emotion, sentiment, and romance. Its extremely

---

[2] Robert Tyson, "Current Mental Hygiene Practice," *Journal of Clinical Psychology,* Vol. VII, No. 1 (1951), p. 55.

[3] Pius XI, "On Christian Marriage," *Catholic Mind,* Vol. XXIX, No. 2 (January 22, 1931), p. 28.

widespread acceptance in our nation betrays the deep-seated emotionalism and immaturity of our national temperament in matters marital. Even many experts who decry the romantic complex seem unable to escape its foibles when they attempt to define love. Words such as "sentiment," "feeling," "emotion," appear almost constantly in our marriage literature; definitions such as "love is the positive emotion experienced by one person . . . in an interpersonal relationship . . ." [4] are not uncommon. Specialists and experts in marriage are almost unanimous in thinking the romantic complex extremely dominant in our culture today. In a study of 8,000 high school students selected out of a nationwide sample, the question was asked whether any two people were meant for each other in the sense of being "the one and only" or "a soul-mate." In replying 31 per cent answered "yes," 35 per cent "no" and 29 per cent "don't know." [5] Apparently, almost a third were deceived by the romantic concept; over a fourth were so confused about the matter that they would not reply decisively; and only a little more than a third were definitely not victims of the romantic complex. Marlene Dietrich gave expression to the romanticism of our age when she advised: "If your brain, instead of your heart, pilots your emotions, there must be regrets. You *cannot* trust your brain. You *can* trust your heart" [italics ours].[6]

The romanticist firmly believes that love is a profoundly mysterious thing, which arrives suddenly, without any bidding, and whose snares are inescapable. In the language of infantilism the lover awakens one morning in the middle of a sub-zero winter to find robins singing on his window sill. His otherwise sound heart skips its normal beat at the thought of the beloved, his blood pressure rises, his appetite disappears, there is a marked stare in his eyes and his ability to concentrate has gone. For he is in ecstasy with the person who is the only one in the world and without whom life is simply not worth living. The whole matter

4 R. F. Winch, *The Modern Family* (New York: Henry Holt & Co., Inc., 1951), p. 333.

5 A. J. Drucher, H. T. Christenson, and H. H. Remmers, "Some Background Factors in Socio-Sexual Modernism," *Marriage and Family Living*, Vol. XIV, No. 4 (November 1952), Table 1, p. 336.

6 Marlene Dietrich, "How to be Loved," *Ladies' Home Journal* (January 1954), p. 37.

was, is, and will remain out of his or her control; and there can be no escape except through marriage! It is a sad commentary upon our culture that such infantile emotionalism and incipient neuroticism can be mistaken for love. It is equally perplexing that our culture fails to protect our youth from romantic love but heaps coals of condemnation upon them when they suffer from its effects. Yet the causes are not difficult to discern. "With the shift of functions away from the family, romantic love has taken over marriage. . . . Whether the wife is a good cook is a secondary consideration. It is not necessary that she be a good seamstress any more than she needs to know how to spin and weave. Hence there are more hasty marriages."[7] In addition, practically all our mass media of propaganda—movies, pulp magazines, radio, television, novels, periodicals, theatres, newspapers—are ceaselessly portraying the romantic complex as proper and true. Unfortunately, youth and adults alike can scarcely avoid being caught in the trap of this fallacy. There is no proportionate counterpropaganda to offset the persistent outpourings of romantic love.

COUNTERFEITS OF LOVE

One of the reasons for the rising divorce rate is surely the self-deception which leads many to believe they are in love when actually they are not. A list has been made of some of the psychological cravings which such persons find satisfied by another and which induce them to conclude unsuspectingly that they are in love.[8]

1. Romance, glamour and adventure
2. Parasitic dependence by individuals too weak to stand alone
3. Sexual fascination
4. Seeking self-assurance, money, prestige, or power
5. Inability to be one's self, leading to an attempt to live through another person
6. Compulsive desire to feel needed
7. Wanting to be mothered
8. Avoiding spinsterhood

---

[7] W. F. Ogburn, "The Changing Family," *The Family,* Vol. XIX (1938).
[8] F. Alexander Magoun, *Love and Marriage* (New York: Harper & Brothers, 1948), Chap. i.

9. Obtaining a "meal ticket"
10. Acceptance for what one wants to be but actually is not
11. Being "in love with love"

NATURE OF TRUE LOVE

Few things are more necessary than an understanding of the nature of true love to avoid the snares our present culture lays for us on the road to success in marriage.

There is no more difficult or thankless task than that of treating . . . love in a scientific manner.   There is a reason for this: we are so accustomed to eloquence and the flight of fancy when the word *love* is mentioned that we tend to regard the disciplined mental process of the scientist as pedantic or ridiculous. . . .   We concede the truth of the statement that all the world loves a lover.   But the scientific attitude is difficult to preserve when we are treating this subject.   The poet has sung his best about love, and the cynic has said his worst, but the scientist has said very little that is worth remembering.[9]

While science has given us practically no help in understanding love, theology and philosophy have for centuries analyzed the nature of love with great accuracy and precision.   None has given us a more *complete* and *practical* understanding than St. Thomas Aquinas.

Human love, according to the Angelic Doctor, is the inclination of one human being toward another, craving a union which leads to mutual self-improvement and ultimately to a greater union with God.   There are four elements here: a mutuality of desire, the union of two in one, mutual growth toward perfection of personalities, and increased affinity to and union with Divine Love.

All erotic love presupposes incompleteness, deficiency, yearning for completion, and an attraction for enrichment, for all love is a flight for immortality.   There is a suggestion of Divine Love in every form of erotic love, as the lake reflects the moon.[10]

This craving for union has been further pointed out by Bossuet:

[9] W. Waller and R. Hill, *The Family—A Dynamic Interpretation,* p. 107. Copyright 1951 by The Dryden Press, Inc., New York.   Reprinted by special permission.
[10] F. J. Sheen, *Three to Get Married* (New York: Appleton-Century-Crofts, Inc., 1951), p. 50.

In the raptures of human love, what mother, what lover knows not the impulse to consume, nay, to absorb, after any fashion whatsoever to be incorporated with the beloved? . . . As though by devouring the loved one it were possible to possess his soul and body, to feed thereon, to be one with him, to live in him. This is that fury of tenderness which can never be satiated by any human passion.[11]

Anatomy of love

Since love implies the inclination and union of two persons, it can be best understood by a brief analysis of human personality. The latter consists of an intellect, a will, a set of emotions and a body. Accordingly human love must mean the desire for union between two intellects, two wills, two hearts, two bodies; anything less than this is something less than the totality of love. Emotional rapport and affectionate display may be the romantic language of love, but they are not love itself. Intellectual admiration may be a noble thing; but it, too, falls short of being love. *For human love, contrary to current practice, is not best symbolized by the heart (seat of the emotions) pierced by a dart; rather should it be symbolized (as is the love of the Christ) by a heart surmounted by a Cross—the symbol of the* will *to sacrifice.* "Love is primarily in the will, not in the emotions or the glands." [12]

Love is not just "two in one flesh." It is more; it is "two in one personality." Its full expression is not found in "two *hearts* that beat as one" but in "two *wills* that want as one, two *intellects* that think as one, two sets of *emotions* that respond as one, and two *bodies* that react as one." For to be full and complete, the love of two human beings must be that of the total human personality and not merely a part of it. In a study of 61 Catholic husbands and 59 Catholic wives it was found that the majority understood true love; 62.5 per cent indicated that love was chiefly spiritual; 29.2 per cent that it was chiefly emotional; and 3.3 per cent chiefly physical.[13]

---

[11] Bossuet, quoted by Abbe Constant Fouard, *The Christ the Son of God* (New York: Longmans, Green & Company, Inc., 1923), p. 205.

[12] Sheen, *op. cit.,* p. 1.

[13] P. M. James, "The Expressed Effects of a Certain Premarital Lecture Course" (Master's thesis, Catholic University of America, 1953), p. 52.

The meaning of love

Pius XI pointedly reminded us of the totality of love and the priority of the *will* in love when he wrote: "By matrimony therefore the *souls* of the contracting parties are joined and knit together *more directly and more intimately* than are their bodies, and that not by any passing affection of sense or spirit, but by a deliberate and firm *act of the will*" [italics ours].[14]   In general we can agree that "Those who love are one in will, willing and not willing all that their Beloved wills or wills not; and they come to adopt the same thoughts, the same opinions, the same convictions, the same desires, and the same affections as the loved one." [15]   He is here merely restating what the Angelic Doctor taught five centuries ago, that while love implies union of all facets of the human personality, it is essentially an act of the will. "And this is love's definition: to will good to another and to have it done." [16]   Intellectual respect, emotional attachment and physical appeal must, accordingly, *remain accidental or non-essential* aspects of human love.   This, of course, does not imply that these accidental qualities of love are not desirable; rather does it indicate that, though desirable, they are yet not essential to an act of human love.   While at first sight this may seem difficult to accept, we actually do realize it in practical living.   The mother fatigued in body and emotionally apathetic, who yet rises at three in the morning *by sheer force of will* to nurse a sick child, is considered devoted and loving.   In fact, we will credit her with greater love, the more "her spirit was willing though her body (and emotions) were weak."   This is another way of asserting that true love can be greatest when the elements of emotional and physical attraction are least; for then a greater act of the will must be employed.   "Whereas, in the love of friendship, the lover is in the beloved inasmuch as he reckons what is good or evil to his friend, as being so to himself; and his friend's will as his own,

---

14 Pius XI, *op. cit.,* p. 23.

15 J. B. St. Jure, *Knowledge of Jesus Christ,* II, II, 4 (New York: P. O'Shea, 1868–70).

16 W. Farrell and M. J. Healy, *My Way of Life: The Summa Simplified* (Brooklyn: Confraternity of the Precious Blood, 1952), p. 37.

so that it seems as though he felt the good or suffered the evil in the person of his friend." [17]

Actually the various levels of the human personality are so intimately associated with one another that any action on any level will find its resonance on all others. We never love on one level alone. Knowledge of another's good qualities must bring with it a certain attachment of the will. An emotional and sentimental inclination toward another, will invariably induce an expression of physical love. How else can we explain the significance of a hand shake, a pat on the back, the holding of hands, embracing, kissing and other physical love acts generally accorded relatives, friends and even mere acquaintances? For the same reason it is inevitable that any *normal* person deeply in love by intellect and will, with a member of the opposite sex, will, in time, experience an inclination toward the expression of love in some form of physical embrace.[18]

In a study of 226 engaged men and women it was found that 28.4 per cent of the men and 26.3 per cent of the women felt strong physical attraction before the end of the first month; and 33.1 per cent of the men and 37.1 per cent of women felt no strong physical attraction until after six months of steady dating.[19] On the other hand, physical and emotional love can redound to the deepening of the higher love of intellect and will. This is one of the reasons for sex expression and for the encouragement of romantic love after marriage. Even before marriage it is a good omen for future marital success when the two are drawn together by emotional and physical as well as spiritual attractions; though clearly such must be kept orderly and controlled.

Four-dimensional love

Perhaps the reason love is so seldom seen to be a four-level process, is that its emotional and physical components are so evident that they obscure the spiritual elements. Some have

---

[17] St. Thomas Aquinas, *The Summa Theologica of St. Thomas Aquinas,* tr. by the Fathers of the English Dominican Province (New York: Benziger Bros., 1948), Vol. III, Pt. I, Q. 28, art. 2.

[18] See Chapter 12 for further discussion.

[19] E. W. Burgess and P. Wallin, *Engagement and Marriage* (Chicago: J. B. Lippincott Company, 1953), p. 161.

compared love to an iceberg—one-fourth visible and three-fourths invisible.[20] It is this unitive process of intellect, will, emotions and body that is commonly termed "compatibility." A study was made of 1,000 engaged couples, 666 of whom were followed into their early years of marriage. This study was concluded with the observation:

> The love relation of husband and wife appears from our interview data to be closely related to the compatibility of the couple. Irritations arising from clashes of temperament and conflicts caused by cultural differences and certain situations may develop into tensions that weaken and sometimes disrupt the marital relation. Incompatibility, if not resolved or controlled, may take the form of a vicious cycle progressively alienating the husband and the wife, and leading finally to the disruption of the marriage.[21]

Many are confused as to exactly what compatibility on each personality level implies. In practice, the affinity of two intellects means similar intellectual interests, viewpoints, attitudes, principles and philosophy of life on at least the truly important issues. It is evident that mixed marriages—cultural, social, religious or otherwise—militate against a deep union on this level. The affinity of two wills implies character traits which are similar, mutually desired ambitions and goals, expectations and determinations which are alike. Clearly a couple with divided loyalties and purposes in life's important matters have little similarity on the level of unity of will. Emotional affinity means the obvious affectionate disposition toward each other; it further implies the less evident similarity in preferences, interests and tastes. A couple enjoying similar leisure time pursuits such as music, cards or literature are emotionally compatible. Physical affinity quite clearly implies a mutual sex attraction. It is true that the possibilities of love increase with greater similarities on all four levels of the personalities of lover and beloved. Conversely, the probability of nourishing love becomes increasingly difficult as there are more and greater dissimilarities between the two. For this reason, adjustment is relatively easy between well-matched

---

[20] E. A. Dowling, *Cana Conference Outline on Emotional Intercourse* (St. Louis: Queen's Work, 1943).

[21] Burgess and Wallin, *op. cit.*, p. 467.

couples and extremely difficult for those mismatched.   Under no circumstances ought we lose sight of the fact that it is natural to love in others the same good intellectual, volitional, emotional or physical qualities which we ourselves possess.   God's love for us is due, at least in part, to the image of His likeness stamped upon our natures.   A noted theologian has written: "I hold . . . that God first loves Himself.   Following this, *God loves Himself in other beings . . .*" [22]   Parental love is partly explained in the affinity and similarity between parent and child.   Marital love, likewise, is founded upon jointly shared qualities of mind, heart, will and body.

Types of love

After the love of God, man's next inclination is to love himself. Properly understood, this is also his next duty.   For true self-love means the quest for perfection of one's personality on both the natural and supernatural levels.   It is to be expected that marital love would also include this element of self-seeking.   It is entirely proper that people marry for subjective reasons such as convenience, love, or security, provided they do not eliminate the objective purposes of marriage.   However, a too narrow concept of self-centered love can easily lead to the defeat of one's own personality development.   The person marrying just for personal convenience will end in suffering inconvenience.   True love of self must reach out and embrace love of others.   For it is only through sacrificing for others that our own personality can be *fully* developed.

Man was created both an individual and a social personality. To prosper he must develop both aspects.   Individual self-love can never alone lead to the full maturity of his *social* personality. He must love others by sacrificing self if he would expand himself; for ". . . he that shall lose his life for My sake shall find it." [23]

There are three stages of love . . . The first love is *digestive* love, the second is *democratic* love, and the third is *sacrificial* love.   *Digestive* love centers in the person whom one loves.   It assimilates per-

---

[22] Blessed John Duns Scotus, *Reportata Parisientia*, Vol. XXIII, No. 5, p. 303.
[23] St. Matthew 16:25.

sons . . . using them as means to either its own pleasure or utility.
. . . Above digestive love is *democratic* love, in which there is a reciprocal devotion founded on natural honor, justice, common likes,
and a sense of decency. . . . Over and above this is what might be
called sacral or *sacrificial* love, in which the lover sacrifices himself for
the beloved, and desires even to immolate self that the other might be
glorified.[24]

*True love does not reach its fullest stature until it carries its cross
to Calvary. Only there can it truly say "It is consummated."*
This was apparently well understood by the 476 Catholic spouses
married ten years or longer who when questioned as to the meaning of love, *placed in the order of importance* their answers as
follows: [25]

1. Understanding
2. Self-giving
3. Unselfishness
4. Mutuality
5. Unity
6. Physical union
7. Cooperation
8. Deeper if less emotional
9. Children
10. De-emphasize sex

The three most important qualities of love mentioned in this study
were unmistakably sacrificial aspects. For the test of love is
sacrifice. This outgoing of love toward the welfare of the beloved has been called a "love of friendship." It is ready at all
times (as is a true friend) to overlook faults and weaknesses, to
share every least possession and to work for the advantage of
the beloved.

THE PROGRESS OF LOVE

In "As You Like It," Shakespeare penned this phrase: "Men
are April when they woo, December when they wed." Realistically there is an unfortunate element of truth in the observation.
In the Divine Plan for love, however, love should grow and not
lessen with marriage and the passing of time. For love to wane
after marriage is clearly unnatural.

---

[24] F. J. Sheen, *The World's First Love* (New York: McGraw-Hill Book Company, Inc., 1952), pp. 167–168.

[25] Hugh Dunn, S.J., *A Study of Some Catholic Marital Attitudes, Practices
and Problems with Special Reference to the Implication for Premarital Instructions* (Washington, D. C.: The Catholic University of America Press, 1956),
Table 24, p. 80.

The progress of love from its incipient to its most advanced stages is earmarked by nature.   Firstly, it scarcely needs to be observed that one cannot love what one does not know.   Knowledge is the first requisite of growing love.   Shakespeare noted that "love looks not with the eyes but with the mind."   Because love presupposes knowledge, there really are no bad marriages unless there were first "bad dates," for dating is the pathway to knowledge of the other party in marriage.   Secondly, the will (theologians and philosophers assure us) is made for *good;* it cannot help but reach outward to embrace anyone whom the mind presents to it as being good.   This attachment of the will is automatic and is the very *essence* of love.   This is to say that any quality which we think good in another, *automatically* evokes an act of the will which is at once an act of love.   Thirdly, once the intellect and will have arrived at the knowledge and embrace of another, the emotions *normally* respond by sentimental, affectionate or romantic impulses.   Fourthly, in any *normal* person the love in the intellect, will and emotions flows over, as it were, into the physical, completing the attraction to the other sex.

This is the orderly progress of love as nature has intended it. To disturb or invert this process in any way is to court danger. Becoming physically or romantically infatuated first blinds the mind and perverts the will.   It is apt to lead to selecting a partner with whom we are not truly in love.   Following the orderly processes of natural love demands two things: firstly, that precautions be taken to avoid infatuation and romantic love *before* adequate knowledge of the other person has evoked the love of the will; secondly, that ample time be allotted for nature's process to work its way through the intricacies of the complex personality.

True love usually is of slow growth.   It feeds upon knowledge, and knowledge of another must generally be gathered piecemeal and over a considerable period of time.   We do not usually "fall into" love; we can only "grow into" true, genuine love.   Clearly, love at first sight is an impossibility unless it is through "intuitive knowledge"; this is so rare and undependable that one would be extremely foolish to be guided by it.   This *time* imperative of growing into love is also the clue to the problem of the length of courtship and engagement.   Combined, they should be long enough for a genuine love adequate for marriage to mature, but no longer.

Growing into love

To grow into love and to deepen love, either before or after marriage, requires cultivation. The great mistake of our times is to forget that *love cannot be taken for granted.* It grows on proximity to the other person—either physical or psychological; on the discovery of similarities; on the sharing of possessions and experiences which induce a greater like-mindedness; on preoccupation with and attention to another. It grows with acts of generosity toward another. Every date, even though it be just a good time, is an exposure to the possibility of growing in love. Love is fostered by reflecting on and thinking seriously of another, by keeping mementos—pictures, letters, gifts—and by paying attentions to the other—remembering anniversaries, giving gifts —small attentions and large sacrifices. This is indicated in some measure by a study of 119 husbands and wives. The chief way of showing love for their spouses was listed as "making sacrifices for them" by 84; the second was "giving compliments" by 22; the third was "remembering anniversaries and the like" by 10.[26]

Before the onset of love itself and certainly before the deepening of love, members of the two sexes may first be attracted emotionally or physically in a sense. Perhaps the generally accepted position is true that women are first attracted emotionally while men are first attracted by physical beauty or charm. It is commonly enough heard on feminine lips that a certain man is "homely but cute"; while equally common is the male statement "she is beautiful but dumb." Emotion plays a rightful part in attracting the female to a proximity (dating) which can lead to knowledge and to love. Physical beauty and charm appeal to men and invite the same proximity with the same possibilities of eventual love. Both are allurements to proximity; neither should be confused with love itself. The growth of real love comes only through knowledge, which cannot issue to any significant extent from romanticism or physical charm.

The capacity to grow into love differs widely between various persons. For love is a habit which is largely *learned* by the early experiences of childhood. Some people are incapable of gen-

---

26 James, *op. cit.*, p. 58.

uinely growing into love without a major change of personality and habit pattern. As an adult the child who is neglected or starved for affection either will be ignorant of how to cultivate love or will have developed an excessive craving for it. In neither instance is that person a likely partner for a well-ordered love life. An attempt was made to discover the extent to which love is an acquired habit, by questioning 200 college girls.[27] On the basis of the data obtained, it was concluded that:

1. Love is a learned reaction determined by:
   a. Love in early family life
   b. The start or delay of early contact with opposite sex
   c. The number of friendly contacts with men
2. Adult love relations are conditioned by early love pattern in the family
3. Children not loved by their fathers may not permit their love to grow for mates later in life.

Still another way in which love grows is from a partial to a total love. The first attractions of beauty, charm, refinement, manners, and the like can mean little more than a love of those particular superficial qualities. As knowledge of the more essential traits of the other person grows, love transfers itself from the surface traits to more profound aspects of the personality. From an incomplete attachment it grows to a love of the entire person— mind, will, emotions and body. It is this perpetual revelation of the hidden facets of the personality of one's marriage partner, which permits an unending growth in love throughout the many years of married life. This is given some confirmation by a study of a group of Catholic husbands and wives; their almost unanimous experience was that their love had grown from a decidedly emotional type to a more complete love of the entire person.[28]

Growing out of love

While all agree that people "fall" or "grow" into love, few seem to realize that one can also "grow out of love." Doubtless

---

27 Albert Ellis, "Some Significant Correlates of Love and Family Attitudes and Behavior," *Journal of Social Psychology*, Vol. XXX, pp. 3–16.
28 Dunn, *op. cit.*, Table 26, p. 84.

this, too, is a result of the romantic fallacy that once the mystery of love enmeshes us in its web, there is no escape!   Yet a careful consideration of the nature of love makes it clear that one *can* grow out of love by simply reversing the process of the growth into love.   If only those who by force of circumstances *must* or *should* remove their deep attachment to another could come to understand this, much unnecessary heartache and misery could be avoided.   If love prospers by proximity, sharing, attention and preoccupation it can be starved by remoteness, refusal to share, inattention and neglect.   Those who would grow out of love should observe the following:

1. Break off all contact (proximity) in person, by phone, by mail
2. Remove all reminders of the other party—photos, gifts and the like—which will keep the attention focused on him or her
3. Cease to think or speak of the separated beloved
4. Fill the vacuum created by him or her with other dates; care must here be taken lest one be "caught on the rebound" and marry unwisely
5. Pray that the natural process of forgetting be hastened, that another will soon fill the vacuum left, and that courage mark this trying period of transition.

Some are deterred from "making the break" which they realize should be made, because they are afraid of the emotional consequences.   The various studies now at our disposal would suggest that in most cases no serious results follow disappointment in love.   In one study [29] the 141 male students reported 314 love affairs, 230 of which had been broken at the time.   The 258 women reported 582 love affairs, 414 of which had been broken.   These breakups of love affairs in a majority of instances (61.4 per cent of the men and 56.3 per cent of the women) did not result in any serious disturbances.   Hostility was felt by 91.9 per cent of the men and 13.2 per cent of the women.   Ambivalent reactions were experienced by 13.8 per cent of the men and 15.6 per cent of the women.   Only 14.9 per cent of the men and women found their attraction increased.

---

[29] C. Kirkpatrick and T. Caplow, "Emotional Trends in the Courtship of College Students as Expressed by Graphs with Some Observations on Methodological Implications," *American Sociological Review*, Vol. XX (October 1945), pp. 619–626.

In another study [30] 320 formerly engaged students (249 men and 71 women) indicated the length of time taken to return to a normal emotional state after the break. Within two weeks 22 per cent, within five months 69 per cent, and within a year 71 per cent had done so. In Chicago 2,000 men and women (mostly college students) who had experienced broken engagements were studied.[31] The authors summarized part of their findings in this way:

To the "jilted" person the broken engagement occasions an emotional crisis something like direct proportion to its unexpectedness. . . . Time, the comforting counsel of friends, the routine of life, new interests and especially the formation of another attachment, gradually heal the injuries caused by the emotional wounding. Later, the person tends to minimize the degree of stress and strain experienced and to express satisfaction that the break occurred.

LESSONS OF LOVE

The close scrutiny of the nature of love and its natural growth to maturity can give the clue to many otherwise perplexing problems. You must only accept the inescapable conclusions that become apparent; some of which are here enumerated:

1. *The test of love is sacrifice.* If love is essentially an act of the *will* reaching out to the welfare of another, it must imply willingness to deny oneself for the other. There can be, then, no real test of being in love or being loved, unless it be the test of *sacrifice*. Judging love by the amount of flattery, affection or romance may indicate emotional arousal; it does not necessarily point to that act of the will which alone can be called love. Many a thoughtless wife could save herself the needless agony of thinking her husband not in love with her because his ardor has cooled, were she to recognize the really great sacrifices he is daily making for her—sacrifices beyond the call of duty. His lack of ardor may be due to nothing more than worry, fatigue or preoccupation with his career. While his lessened ardor is a mistake on his part, it is not necessarily an indication of lessened

---

30 J. T. Landis and M. G. Landis, *Building a Successful Marriage* (Englewood Cliffs, N. J.: Prentice-Hall, Inc., 1948), pp. 177–178.
31 Burgess and Wallin, *op. cit.,* pp. 298–299.

love. It is tragically true that once a couple is emotionally "head over heels" in love even the test of sacrifice no longer proves of value. This test must be made *before* such emotional involvement or it is entirely untrustworthy. Who has not witnessed the exaggerated sacrifices which romantically involved lovers will make while in the throes of their emotional imbalance? In the words of the old cliché, they will "climb the highest mountains," to be with the object of their romance.

As basically an act of the will, love has as its *only* norm the measure of willingness to deny oneself for the advantage of the beloved. In the Nuptial Mass we read: "When the sacrifice is complete, love is perfect." Love knows nothing short of surrender of oneself to and for the person beloved. Flattery and romantic appeal may be the language of one bent upon exploiting another; only genuine renunciation of self for the beloved is the language of love.

2. *Love is based on respect.* Since true love has its origin in knowledge, it must rest upon a knowledge of genuinely desirable traits in the person loved.

3. *Love must be total.* To love another with one's will is *essentially* human love but not *completely* human; we are personalities with emotions and bodies also. The frigid wife and the unaffectionate husband might well heed this lesson of love by giving to their spouse that part of their personality that now they are withholding.

4. *There can be no love at first sight.* Love requires knowledge and knowledge requires time. Even couples married many years find continuous revelations of hidden traits of their partners. That many are tricked into believing this romantic illusion is suggested by the replies of 740 college students; [32] 476 (64.3 per cent) thought love did not occur at first sight; 167 (22.5 per cent) didn't know; 97 (13.1 per cent) thought it did. In other words, more than a third were not sure but that they might fall in love at first sight.

5. *Love is also emotional and physical.* To react against romanticism by making love exclusively an act of the will is a mistake. Romantic and sexual love are the normal result of

---

[32] R. A. Skidmore and A. S. Cannon, *Building Your Marriage* (New York: Harper & Brothers, 1951), p. 60.

intellectual and volitional love; furthermore they serve the important purpose of increasing and deepening the latter. Every *normal* person desires and every person has a right to the totality of love in marriage.

Taking love for granted and divesting it of its affectionate aspects is all too common a mistake after marriage today. Human nature is such that it expects more than an act of the will; it has a right in marriage to the warmth and romance of affectionate display. It is most ironic that before marriage, when emotional love has great dangers, we cultivate it ardently. However, after marriage when it should be given maximum development, we tend to lessen it or reject it entirely.

6. *The absence of affectionate or physical love is a symptom.* It points to the fact that either the two do not genuinely love each other, or that, though love does exist, an emotional or physiological block is present, preventing higher love from spilling over into the affections and body. To correct this abnormal condition the aid of a physician or psychiatrist may be required.

7. *Love is not blind, but bound.* This is Chesterton's observation. The knowledge that true love implies keeps it from being blind. Yet despite the clear awareness of defects and shortcomings in another, love is cemented by the firmness of the will and by emotional and physical attachment. Love exists, not because of the absence of defects, but in spite of them. This was agreed to by most of the 120 Catholic married persons who were asked whether their love for their partners blinded them to his (or her) faults; 105 replied "No," 12 replied "Yes" and 5, "Don't Know." [33]

8. *Love implies permanency.* The unnatural aspect of divorce can be seen in the innate expectation of constancy in the human heart. In all advanced cultures love knows no language other than "always," "forever," "eternal." This is a universal concept of the nature and meaning of love. The growth of love toward a likeness bordering on identification has led St. Paul to assert: "He that loveth his wife, loveth himself" [34]—and self-love is always permanent.

9. *Love is not single.* Contrary to the romantic fallacy, more

---

[33] James, *op. cit.*, p. 43.
[34] Ephesians 5:28.

than one person can be the object of true love, since more than one person can be the object of *knowledge*. Though it may shatter the human ego, the bald fact remains that any married person could have been equally well matched with another. To the "jilted" lover this should remain a source of consolation and encouragement. When St. Thomas More, who married a second time after his first wife's death, was asked by Erasmus which of the two he would have preferred, he replied: "If it were not against the laws of God and man, I should have wanted to marry both at the same time."

10. *Love teaches a lesson about matching.* The similarities which love implies call for the selection of partners who are as alike as possible on each of the four levels. Further, the wise selection by "the eyes of the mind" is seriously endangered by permitting emotional and physical love to expand significantly and early. A basic rule in psychiatry—"Never make an important decision when the emotions or passions are high"—is applicable here. Emotion blinds reason. For this reason, those "head over heels in love" rarely heed the advice of common sense.

11. *Love indicates the proper pattern for dating and courtship.* From the above it should be clear that the current dating and courting pattern with its tendency to freedom in "love-making," defeats its own real purpose. Extensive kissing, embracing, necking and petting, stimulate the emotions and passions (and so becloud the mind) *before* the all-important decision of a life-mate (and of a lifetime) has been made. Restrained affection alone makes sense here.

12. *Love indicates selection of dates.* Since dating leads to knowledge and knowledge leads to love, every date is an exposure to the possibility of growing into love. Clearly to date one who at first thought is not a desirable mate, is to court the possibility of eventual love and marriage. Countless are the Catholic youth who have been caught in this snare. "I wouldn't marry him, if he were the only man left; but he *is* a good date," only too often ends in eventual marriage. For this reason, it has been observed, there would be no mixed marriages if there were no mixed dates.

13. *Love is dynamic, not static.* It either grows deeper or weaker; love never stands still. If this be the case, love can never be taken for granted. It must be attended, nursed, culti-

vated or it will tend to wither and recede. The nagging wife or unaffectionate husband has completely forgotten this lesson of love.

14. *Love is humble.* It does not bedeck itself with the mantle of pride. All our literature on love speaks of self-abasement and surrender to the beloved. The words of love, "sweet nothings," are replete with phrases of praise for the beloved and abasement of the self. The union of love demands an abasement. This is the reason for the God-man assuming human nature. Without the humility of the Eucharist, human beings could never enjoy the profound merger of the Divine with the human in Holy Communion.

15. *Love means peace and unity.* Neither peace nor unity are virtues in themselves; they are rather, the fruit of love. Most marital discord stems from the absence of mature love, on the part of at least one partner. For according to St. Paul, love is patient, kind, does not envy, does not boast, is not proud, does not provoke another, does not seek its own comfort at the expense of the other, is not irritated, thinks no evil of its partner, *excuses all things,* hopes all things, *endures all* things, and *never* falls away.

In no way can the importance of love be better recognized than in its widespread effects. Not only are the individuals benefited but also the marriage, the children, society at large, and religion in particular. To the individuals comes that ecstatic enjoyment which is a foretaste of the joys of the Beatific Vision. With the growth of love comes that increasing similarity which culminates in the profound merger of "two in one." With it comes the completion of one's personality and a flight toward perfection.

Marriage, likewise, shares in its fruits; the mutual understanding of two persons not yet completely alike, can be effected only through love. St. Bernard had pointed out long ago that if we are to understand another, we can do so in no other way than through the eyes of love.[35] For love enables us to refrain from fixing our attention exclusively upon another's defects which is the basis of misunderstanding. Love sees nothing less than the totality; it sees virtues and noble traits as well as weaknesses.

---

[35] St. Bernard, *De Gradibus Humilitatis,* No. 14.

The love between partners in marriage is not meant only for their mutual joy and advantage. Rather does this proper love-relationship between parents create the best possible environment for the growth of the children's personalities. Children best learn how to love from the example of their parents. It is only through a genuine parental love for them that wholesome personalities can be formed, for love is as necessary for the soul of a child as food is for its body.[36]

Just as higher love spills over into emotional and physical love, so love within the family circle spills over into society at large. "Love is always an outward-turning; and as the love of man and woman is made by, as well as expressed in, the making of a family, so the love of the family is made by and expressed in the making of the world."[37] It is in the home that we learn or fail to learn the habit of love. If society at large today reflects "man's inhumanity to man," it is simply because the home has failed to develop charity in the hearts and wills of its children. After spending large sums of money, much time and energy in an intensive study, a group of social scientists has come to the conclusion that the basis of all the world's ills is simply a lack of love, and that this lack is traceable to the failure of the home.[38]

True love also has a religious significance. The highest and noblest type of love—that by which the lover admires most the Christlikeness of the beloved—comes from religion. The improvement of personality which love fosters is not complete until and unless it has led both lover and beloved closer to spiritual and moral perfection. If love is truly operative this must be the result, for right human love must bring us to the love of God. "He that loveth not knoweth not God: for God is charity. . . . He that loveth not his brother whom he seeth, how can he love God whom he seeth not? . . . If we love one another, God abideth in us: and His charity is perfected in us."[39] Love of

---

[36] For further discussion see Chapter 15.

[37] G. Vann, *The Heart of Man* (New York: Longmans, Green & Company, Inc., 1946), p. 116.

[38] P. Sorokin, *Altruistic Love, A Study of American Good Neighbors and Catholic Christian Saints; The Ways and Power of Love;* and *Forms and Techniques of Altruistic and Spiritual Growth* (Boston: The Beacon Press, 1954).

[39] I John 4:8, 20, 12.

another leads to love of God also because human love never fully satisfies. Complete union between two human beings remains unattainable; yet the human heart craves the "perfect union" which can be found only in the love of God. This inadequacy of human love was voiced by St. Augustine, one of the world's great lovers: "Our hearts were made for Thee, O God; and they are not at rest until they rest in Thee."

LOVE IN CONFLICT

Lovers' quarrels are common enough to indicate that human love does not always run smoothly. The imperfections of humans make it possible for love and conflict to exist side by side; in fact, on occasion conflict does arise precisely because of the loving solicitude of one partner for the other. To be sure such love is not perfect on the part of both, for perfect love would cause or tolerate no conflict. Disagreements between those truly in love never, however, degenerate into bitterness or antagonism; nor do they ever lead to separation, for true love brooks no obstacles.

Someone has said that hate is simply love turned inside out. The element of truth in this is that human beings do not pay the attention which hate implies to an object totally unloved. The object fully disliked is that which we ignore and to which we are completely indifferent. The "jilted" woman knows this; she would rather have her former lover call on her and insult her than be completely ignored by him. In this context, it is extremely useful to observe that at times we tend to turn most against that person we love best. This is quite characteristic of those in the throes of a nervous breakdown, of children in their adolescence, and of women experiencing their climacteric or menopause. The apparent antagonism and hatred at such times is, rightly understood, a convincing proof of genuine love.

On the other hand, hatred differs from love. Hatred is possible only when we preoccupy ourselves with the defects of another to the exclusion of his virtues. Love encompasses all aspects of another's personality, both good and evil. For this reason a lesson which all married persons should learn is that we cannot hate what we fully know. If one is torn asunder by antagonistic feelings toward his mate, he might well consider

70 • THE QUALITY OF LOVE

these measures: firstly, rivet his attention on the good qualities of the partner; secondly, try to forget the bad qualities; thirdly, grow in knowledge of one's mate.

LOVE IS THE DIVINE PLAN

In the Master-Plan of the universe the attraction of things to each other is an element of order. Molecules attract each other, as do opposite magnetic poles; there is an attraction between the various stars and planets and an attraction that draws objects earthward. In all animate creation there is an attraction between the male and female that insures the continuance of the various species of plants, flowers, vegetables and animals.

Human beings, too, would be ordered by this universal law of attraction or love. However, in the designs of Infinite Wisdom, human beings (unlike plants and animals) were to share in love Divine. The infinite love which God had for us, He wanted us in our finite way to have for each other. This is true in a special sense for married couples. For they alone were to exhaust the possibilities of human love on all levels. From this "mutual crucifixion" of sacrificial love, husband and wife were to become more like each other and more like God. In the raptures of love's ecstasy they were to enjoy a foretaste of love in the Beatific Vision. Love exhausting itself in mutuality would give birth to God's children. That same love would afford the affectionate warmth so necessary for the growth and formation of the children's personalities. Parents and children in the embrace of their common loves, were to go forth into society at large radiating to others the love given them in their families. Through their common loves they would grow together in moral and spiritual stature, until their earthly love was to be swallowed up in the infinite ocean of God's eternal Love.

5

Roles in Marriage

SHAKESPEARE wrote that all the world is a stage upon which men and women are acting the drama of life. Much the same thing might be said of marriage, for the successful attainment of marital goals requires that each person play a particular role in marriage. If it be true that goals in marriage cannot be achieved without retaining and performing certain functions, it is equally true that these functions cannot be performed unless each family member plays a certain role. An inescapable relationship exists between goals, functions and roles—a relationship which many do not detect today as they toy with the changing of marital roles. The determination of these roles depends upon not only the nature and purposes of marriage but also the nature and purposes of men and women and the requirements of a given socio-cultural milieu. Since the nature and purposes of marriage and of men and women are both objectively fixed by the Author of man and marriage, some marital roles are unchanging and unchangeable. The cultures of various societies differ and their impact on marriage indicates variations and changes in some marital roles. Such culturally influenced roles may indicate progress or retrogression, but they cannot violate nature's goals for marriage and yet spell out success in married and family living.

71

IMPORTANCE OF ROLES

Only when men play their proper roles as husbands and fathers and when women adhere to their natural roles as wives and mothers can marriage be successful. Certain roles are also needed between parents and children, between the members of a family and between blood relatives. There are the economic roles of father, mother and children; and there are educational, religious, recreational and sex roles. The actual execution of these roles in marriage is indispensable for the attainment of proper goals but the concepts of the roles they must play with which the couple enters into marriage are also basic factors in adjustment. If children can be reared properly only when both parents play their full roles as educators, it is also true that two lives can be welded into one only when the couple have similar role concepts or expectancies. Every successful marriage indicates similarity of expectations; every broken marriage attests to a disparity in the couple's concept of their roles and a disillusionment regarding their original expectations. Doubtless this is one of the most basic reasons for marital breakdown. The husband who thinks of himself as nothing more than a breadwinner has failed not only as a man but also as a marital partner. The wife who thinks of herself as a deliberately sterile working wife has failed both as a woman and as a mother. When husbands generally expect wives to play conventional roles as homemakers while wives in increasing numbers prefer to be office or factory workers, continued family failures can be anticipated. In such circumstances, according to one marriage expert:

There is nearly always a maneuvering for personal status, for changes in the personality or behavior of the other member of the union. Much of the tension immediately developing into incompatibility in married life comes from this mutual maneuvering. It nearly always has a double strategy, each attempting to establish his preconceived role in the comradeship while at the same time leading the other to adopt the role already assumed by husband or wife to be good for the other. The fact that this maneuvering may be largely unconscious, or may be interpreted by both in terms of unselfishness, in no degree lessens its significance or removes the possibility of tension.[1]

---

[1] E. Groves, *The American Family* (Chicago: J. B. Lippincott Company, 1934), p. 166.

ROLES TODAY

In our culture this disparity in role concept is so widespread that we cannot speak with conviction of the American wife's role or the American husband's role.   Instead of a clear and fixed pattern, we find in our current culture only confusion and chaos. No longer can boy and girl marry secure in the knowledge that each brings to the marriage the accepted role concept of the existing culture—for there is no such stable concept of the wife or husband role which is accepted throughout our social structure.

Evidence of this division and confusion abounds.   In a study of 936 men and women 63.4 per cent of the men and 47.3 per cent of the women thought woman's role after marriage was that of a homemaker, while 36.6 per cent of the men and 52.6 per cent of the women held just the opposite role concept for married women.[2]   In another instance, two contradictory roles were found dominant in our social environment.   From 73 autobiographies and 80 interviews of college students a "feminine role" concept (a different role for women than men) was found; and also a "modern role" concept (an identical role of behavior and conduct for men and women of the same age).   It is interesting that 26 per cent indicated *resentment against their families for failing to impart to them a clear-cut concept of roles.*[3]   One family sociologist tries to resolve this confusion in part by pointing out that there are four different role concepts of husbands and wives prevalent in our society today.   The first role portrays the husband as dominant, the wife as submissive, feminine and dependent.   The second role concept for women stresses the importance of motherhood and homemaking.   The third envisions a shifting role, from one with limited leisure while children are young to one with greater leisure and other activities as children mature.   The fourth role concept indicates that as a duty women should play a very active part in political and economic life.[4]

Unfortunately Catholic families are not spared the impact of

---

[2] E. W. Burgess and P. Wallin, *Engagement and Marriage* (Chicago: J. B. Lippincott Company, 1953), Table 63, p. 407.

[3] Mira Kamorovsky, "Cultural Configurations and Sex Roles," *American Journal of Sociology,* Vol. LII (November 1946), pp. 184–189.

[4] Ruth S. Cavan, *The American Family* (New York: Thomas Y. Crowell Company, 1953), pp. 441–442.

this confusion upon their thinking and acceptance of roles in marriage. Some studies suggest that this influence is greater than most recognize. A nationwide study of 4100 Catholic people asked whose role it was to decide whether to purchase a new radio or television set or to save the money. If the mother alone opposed the purchase 77.9 per cent thought it should not be bought; if the mother also was working 67.4 per cent thought she should have as much to say about it as the father; and if the children were working 31 per cent thought they should have an equal voice with the parents.[5] This seems to suggest a probable shrinking of the father's role and an emergence of the mother's and children's roles in economic decisions within the family. It further lends some confirmation to the theory that the growing economic independence of women and children is a significant factor in the change of roles today. Perhaps the current confusion is better illustrated by a joint interview-questionnaire study of 120 Catholic husbands and wives. Asked who was the chief authority in the home, 36 thought it was the husband, 1 the wife and 83 indicated husband and wife had equal authority. Yet when queried about the moral obligation of wives to obey the reasonable decisions of the husbands, 78 out of 120 thought it to be a grave responsibility, 12 a light one, and 20 no obligation at all; 10 failed to reply.[6] Apparently the thinking of these couples was quite confused.

CHANGING ROLES

Sociologists have been quick to note the social factors inducing roles to change and bringing about the present chaotic condition in role concepts. (Doubtless the Industrial Revolution, emancipation of women, urbanization, the feminist movement, preoccupation of men with careers instead of domestic duties, employment of women and children outside the home and similar factors have left their imprint upon family roles.) However, the rejection of the Christian and the natural position on the nature and goals

---

[5] T. Harte, J. Nuesse and B. Mulvaney, "Catholic Opinion Survey II," *American Catholic Sociological Review*, Vol. XVI, No. 1 (March 1955), p. 39.

[6] P. M. James, "The Expressed Results of a Certain Premarital Lecture Course" (Master's thesis, Catholic University of America, 1953), Q. 37, p. 49 and Q. 39, p. 52.

of marriage and the family and the loss of the vision of the distinctive natures and roles of men and women seem much more basic. Catholics immersed in the secularized culture of our times are confronted with a genuinely difficult problem. Many will first need to recapture the full Catholic vision of the unchangeable roles of men, women and children in the Divine Plan for Marriage. Yet the Catholic minority will best be able to retain proper roles only if it recognizes the need for some measure of adjustment to the changed social structure of today. This task, perilous but imperative, implies neither compromise nor that abject surrender (too often witnessed) to our secular culture. It does indicate the precise limit of adaptation, so that the divinely natural roles remain intact while current social needs are accommodated so long as they do not militate against the basic Christian tradition. (As a result, for instance, of the greater freedom and education of women, husbands would do well to modify their right to make decisions by a greater consultation with their wives than was formerly the custom.) (As a result of the increased difficulties of child rearing in our urban milieu, husbands might well help more than formerly in the chores related to child care.)

In addition, "when a current social practice must be rejected, the minority must take positive steps to meet the need which the rejected practice was designed to fill." [7] The heavy burden carried by Catholic couples in a social system geared to small families calls for certain practical measures of justice and charity— both personal and social. "Girls must be prepared not only for marriage but motherhood. Young men must be taught the virtue of prudent saving and responsibility. Heavily burdened households must be aided by relatives, or, in their absence, by parish members. Programs for slum clearance, adequate housing, health insurance should be initiated and supported." [8] To these might be added a revival of something akin to the discarded dowry system and an inheritance in advance of the death of parents.

---

[7] J. Thomas, "Catholic Family in a Complex Society," *Social Order,* Vol. IV, No. 10 (December 1954), p. 453.

[8] *Ibid.,* p. 457.

EQUAL BUT DIFFERENT

(The determination of roles in marriage depends upon the determination of the respective natures of the men and women who make up marriage.) This controversial subject is discussed by everybody, yet few have troubled themselves to obtain the relevant facts. Like the nature of true love, the nature of men and women has had little light shed upon it by the physical or social sciences.[9] Here again we need to consult theology and philosophy, ordinary observation and common sense to garner the facts. Actually much of the current controversy about men and women is clouded by misleading and inaccurate suppositions. Many like to interpret differences between men and women as implying inequalities;(they seem unable to understand that they may be different and yet equal.)(Or they will confuse inequality of status with personal inferiority, again failing to realize that men and women might have varying positions and yet retain the essential equality of personality.) Apparently women are more liable to this error than men. In our economy of women workers many men find themselves inferior in status to a feminine supervisor, dean or officer; few of these individuals, however, seem to complain of a sense of personal inferiority as a result.

The Christian tradition has ever held that men and women are equal in essential respects while unequal in accidental respects. Pius XII has restated this position repeatedly. On one occasion he said:

In their personal dignity as children of God a man and a woman are *absolutely equal,* even as they are in relation to the last end of human life, which is everlasting union with God in the happiness of heaven. But a man and woman cannot maintain and perfect this equal dignity of theirs except by respecting and activating the *characteristic qualities which nature has given each of them, physical and spiritual qualities* which cannot be eradicated, and which cannot be reversed without nature itself always establishing a new balance [italics ours].[10]

Not only does Pius XII speak of essential equality and accidental differences, but he also emphasizes that the retention of

---

[9] For empirical studies on this topic see Chapter 9.

[10] Pius XII, "Questa Grande," *Acta Apostolicae Sedis,* Vol. XXXVII (1945), p. 285.

accidental differences safeguards the basic equality common to both sexes. This stands in direct opposition to the feminist position which contends that equality is best preserved by eliminating differences.

(As equal human beings husbands and wives, therefore, have the same basic needs, drives and desires. Both need to find in marriage and through their marriage partners the perfection of their personalities, the delights of children; both need and desire mutual companionship, love and affection, understanding, respect, sexual surrender, acceptance and security. These and other goals and benefits of marriage relate to both husbands and wives since they are essentially *human* needs and desires.) "We are not real men and women unless we are both lovers and makers, and unless our making is the expression of our love." [11]

Role of man

Ever since God assigned to Adam the role of "dressing the garden," man's over-all vocation has been to share in the creative, protective and governing functions of Providence. Man's role may be both lover and maker; but his role as lover expresses itself pre-eminently through the latter, as all history testifies. The progress of civilization and culture is an array of man's conquest over the forces of lower nature. Man's efforts have tunneled through mountains, drained swamps, spanned rivers with bridges, erected skyscrapers and revealed the secrets of atomic power. Even in fields thought distinctively feminine man often remains the maker. Feminine fashions are created by male artists; the world's most noted chefs are men!

Doubtless man achieves his greatest work in his role as the active principle of generation. In it he not only begets the masterpiece of creation but comes closest to a creatorship with God. "The father according to the flesh has in a particular way a share in that principle which in a manner universal is found in God." [12] However, his part in protecting the children he has generated is

---

[11] G. Vann, *The Heart of Man* (New York: Longmans, Green & Co., Inc., 1946), p. 104.

[12] St. Thomas Aquinas, *The Summa Theologica of St. Thomas Aquinas*, tr. by the Fathers of the English Dominican Province (New York: Benziger Bros., 1948), Vol. II, Pt. 2, Q. 52, art. 7.

being minimized by some sociologists today. (With the disappearance of the frontier and its physical dangers and with the increasingly protective resources of outside agencies, some think this role is almost extinct. Yet in our economy maintaining economic security for the family remains a difficult task. Children no longer threatened by the vicissitudes of nature, now are preyed upon by the evils of civilization. Secular and unethical influences in movies, literature, comics, radio, companions and other environmental forces, seem only to have shifted the protective functions of fatherhood.)

Beyond this protective role lies that developmental one that can be discharged only when the father retains his role of leadership. The impact of the industrial and urban culture has removed the father from the home for long periods of time. His leadership role tends to be reduced proportionately. Many seem to have abdicated their moral roles as leaders in things religious and educational, retaining perhaps nothing more than the responsibility for economic provision. The absence of the working father, made imperative by our economy, clearly indicates the need to delegate increased responsibilities to the mother. Yet there remains a vast difference between *delegation* of leadership role and *abdication* of it. Despite cultural forces to the contrary, the role of the father must remain intact as the leader and supervisor of all family endeavors, including the role of religious leadership. Pius XII has reminded husbands to "sanctify your wives by your example of virtue; give them the proud experience of imitating your good and spiritual life, your industrious habits and your courage under hardships and the sufferings that are never lacking in human life." [13] St. Thomas had earlier reminded us that "the father is the principle of generation, of education and discipline and of everything that bears upon the perfecting of human life." [14] This is obviously quite different from the matriarchal tendencies of our current culture that would relinquish religious and educational leadership to the wives and mothers, to churches and schools.

A factor which doubtless diminishes his leadership is the dual

---

[13] Pius XII, "Gran fonte," *Atti e Discorsi di Pio XII,* Vol. IV (Rome: Instituto Missionares Pia Societa San Paolo, 1943), p. 97.

[14] Aquinas, *op. cit.,* Vol. II, Pt. 2, Q. C 11, art. 1.

role of man—familial and social. Lord Byron warned us that "love is of man's life *a part;* tis woman's whole existence." Husbands and fathers must apportion their time between the home and the outside arena of business and political affairs. This was strikingly symbolized in the wedding ring of St. Louis, King, which bore the inscription: "God, France, Marguerite." The intense competition in the business-professional world today, coupled with the ambitions for wealth and position, easily blind husbands and fathers to the fact that their primary vocation and major duty is to their families. Marriage counselors daily witness marriages tottering because of the preoccupation of men with careers to the neglect of wives and children. Added to this is frequently found an immersion in countless extra-familial social activities in the evenings and over week ends. Such men have forgotten that their families have first claim to their leisure time. This is so true, moralists point out, that spending many evenings a week away from home even in the best of charitable work is stealing time belonging to the family and is a matter of sheer and simple injustice.[15]

The deterioration of the man's role in the family is mirrored in our culture in the declining respect for husbands and fathers. This has been noted by a distinguished psychiatrist who asserts that since men are too busy working to be effective fathers, children are left to become semi-orphans, and society comes to stigmatize fathers as something akin to nitwits.[16] A Catholic sociologist has given this picture in some detail by instances of our view of the paternal roles in our current culture.

Take "Make Room for Daddy," for instance. It's a rather amusing show, but who is always wrong, befuddled and confused? Father, of course. Then there is the William Bendix show, "The Life of Riley," equally amusing and equally hard on fathers. Add to these, comic strips like "Bringing Up Father," an old standby, or "Blondie," and what do you have? Father is weak, well-meaning, but somewhat stupid, even by a ten-year-old's standard; invariably he gets himself into trouble from which only the wisdom of his wife and young chil-

---

15 M. E. Boylan, *This Tremendous Lover* (Westminster, Md.: Newman Book Shop, 1948), p. 287.
16 O. S. English and C. J. Foster, *Fathers Are Parents Too* (New York: G. P. Putnam's Sons, 1954), p. viii.

dren eventually saves him. If instead of watching TV shows or reading comic strips to learn father's role, a son observes his own father, he is likely to find that his father is rarely available for observation. Even if he is physically present he is likely to be concealed by a newspaper or magazine.[17]

The mass media of propaganda seem to be adept at belittling fathers.

A study of more than 100 recent American films revealed that not one of them represented a father as the hero. Father was usually portrayed as a weak, colorless fellow who ultimately faded into the background of the plot.[18]

Two scholars, B. O. Rubenstein and M. Levitt, studying the effects of paternal neglect and maternal domination upon disturbed children, investigated this problem. They found that fathers are reacting in one of several ways: "1. withdrawing from any situation of stress and letting mother handle it; 2. staying away from home as much as possible or becoming hypochondriacs to avoid responsibility; 3. doing what they think is expected of them by their wives and society." [19] The observed results were sons who were weak, anxious, overaggressive and antagonistic.

Perhaps it was results such as these that impelled a noted psychiatrist to write:

Plainly this nation needs father in the arm-chair at the head of the table again, carving the roast, disciplining the children, keeping the peace, settling disputes, loving his wife for sewing his pants for his own use, serving as an example for his sons to emulate and daughters to seek in husbands of their own. For it is from and through father that the entire family should receive a steadfastness of purpose, an enthusiasm of interest, a sense of justice and fair play, an awareness of the world's problems, and an inspiration to be useful, friendly and to participate in making the world a better place to live in. Father is essential. Home requires him. Children must have him to round out their development. He can be firm without being despotic, decisive and still not dictatorial, gentle and yet not weak.[20]

---

[17] J. Kane, "What's Happened to Daddy?" *Jubilee,* Vol. II, No. 3 (July 1954), p. 24.

[18] R. P. Goldman, "What's Wrong With American Fathers?" *Parade,* (October 17, 1954), p. 10.

[19] *Ibid.,* p. 11.

[20] O. S. English and C. J. Foster, *op. cit.,* Foreword, p. xi.

Despite these tendencies to minimize paternal roles, a significant number of husbands still seem to retain a dominant position. One study of husband-wife relationships assures us that "the majority of wives must still achieve their aims in subtle and indirect ways which evidence the dominance of their husbands." [21] In a study of 167 Catholic husbands and wives 89.6 per cent of the husbands and 94.5 per cent of the wives believed that the husband's reasonable decisions should be followed; [22] in a personal study of male seniors in a Catholic college 98 out of 102 thought the husband should be the chief authority in the home.

Role of women

The role of women in marriage and the family is perhaps even more distorted by society than that of men. Secularism and feminism have taken such a toll that throughout their lives many women apparently never capture the vision of their truly Providential role. Yet science sheds no conclusive light on this problem. It is chiefly from religion, philosophy, common sense and observation that the role of woman can be known and appreciated.

Christian tradition is entirely clear and constant in its portrayal of woman's role. It has been pointedly expressed in the words of Pius XII:

Every women is made to be a mother in the physical sense of the word or indeed, in the more spiritual and exalted but no less real sense . . . to this end the Creator ordained the whole characteristic constitution of woman, her organic make-up, but even more her spirit, and above all her delicate sensitiveness [italics ours].[23]

In contrast to man, the maker and initiator, woman is intended to *mother,* to nurse, to preserve and to develop what man has originated. This motherhood role, Pius XII assures us, is given to *all women* without exception; whereas, shaping means to serve appropriate ends, the Divine Plan has given woman a set of innate

---

21 E. Burgess and L. Cottrell, *Predicting Success or Failure in Marriage* (Englewood Cliffs, N. J.: Prentice-Hall, Inc., 1939), p. 342.

22 R. Feiten, "An Investigation of the Knowledge and Attitudes of Catholic Married People on Moral Relations in Marriage and the Family" (Master's thesis, Catholic University of America, 1948), pp. 36–37.

23 Pius XII, "Questa Grande," *Acta Apostolicae Sedis,* Vol. XXXVII (1945), pp. 285–287.

characteristics intended to make her capable of her role as mother. This seems the dominant agreement of writers (both ancient and modern) concerned with the nature and role of women (Table 3).

TABLE 3

THE PSYCHOLOGICAL TRAITS AND CHARACTERISTICS OF WOMEN:
THERE ARE THREE TENDENCIES *

To Be Reserved	To Conserve	To Serve
More shrinking, more difficult to arouse to action (Aristotle)	More retentive memory (Aristotle)	More compassionate (Aristotle)
Reflective intelligence (Marholm)	Nourishing passion (Marholm)	Solicitude (Marholm)
More affectable (Ellis)	Inward creative power (Key)	Tactfulness (Ellis)
Passive self-dependence (Mayreder)	Conservative or centripetal tendency (Mayreder)	Alterocentrism (Lombroso)
Personality and Charm (Lombroso)	Centripetal character (Farnham)	Intuitiveness (Lombroso)
Receptivity (Menninger)	Tenderness (Comte)	Adaptability (Menninger)
Passivity (Deutsch)	Guardian of hereditary qualities (Ward)	Intuition (Scheinfeld)
Self-realization, deeply internal (Farnham)	Faculty of reproduction (Wieth-Knudsen)	More Sensitive (Ross)
Purity (Comte)	Ideal of thrift (Chesterton)	Particularism (Wieth-Knudsen)
Passive-defensive (Ward)	More passionate (Leclercq)	Pliability (Chesterton)
Coyness (Westermarck)	Conserver (Vann)	Power of observation (Leclercq)
Ideal of dignity (Chesterton)	Motherhood (Pius XII)	Orientation toward man (Maritain)
Receptive (Vann)		Perspicacity and finer touch (Pius XII)
Delicate sensitiveness (Pius XII)		

* Louis Ryan, "The Characteristics and Social Role of Women," *American Catholic Sociological Review*, Vol. IX, No. 4 (December 1948), pp. 230–253.

The tendency To BE RESERVED involves a certain feminine biological and psychological passivity or receptivity spoken of by the ancients and moderns alike; the more shrinking, more difficult to arouse nature indicated by Aristotle; the ideal of dignity, or isolation and of purity; reflective intelligence; deeply internal self-realization; the delicate sensitiveness spoken of by Pius XII.

The tendency To Conserve is exemplified by the basic motherly, protective qualities noted by almost all writers and especially the present Pontiff; an organic tendency to stability and conservatism; more retentive memory; warm, nourishing passion; the centripetal tendency; the ideal of thrift; patience, self-sacrifice, and domestic prudence, so characteristic of the Valiant Woman.

The tendency To Serve proceeds from the fundamental alterocentrism of woman, aided by some intuitive superiority; compassion and solicitude; a particularism involving adaptability and pliability; perspicacity and a finer touch in dealing with personal problems; the fundamental orientation toward man, and hence toward love.

Physical motherhood expresses itself not only through childbirth but likewise through occupations such as nursing, child care and social work; spiritual motherhood evidences itself not only in the educative efforts of mothers of families but also in the religious vocations of nuns and work such as teaching. For in the Divine Plan women have been reserved the task of "childbirth, the work of nursing and the first education of the children," as well as "those thousand particular but demanding little tasks, those imponderable daily attentions and cares, that are the elements of the *internal* atmosphere of the family [italics ours]." [24]

Today, however, woman's role is no longer exclusively confined to the home. The spiritual poverty of our age, the conspiracy against the family in our culture has extended her role to the forum of social and political life. Pius XII apparently thought this new role so significant that he gave it the attention of a special message.

The fate of the family, the fate of human relations are at stake. They are in your hands. *Every* woman has then, mark it well, the obligation, *the strict obligation in conscience,* not to absent herself but to go into action in a manner and way suitable to the condition of each so as to hold back those currents which threaten the home, so as to oppose those doctrines which undermine its foundations, so as to prepare, organize and achieve its restoration [italics ours].[25]

---

[24] *Ibid.*

[25] Pius XII, *Woman's Duties in Social and Political Life* (New York: The Paulist Press, 1945), Sec. 36, p. 14; also *Acta Apostolicae Sedis,* Vol. XXXVII (December 28, 1945), pp. 284–295.

The emergence of women into the social and political arena does not signal a departure from her basic home-family orientation. On the contrary, as Pius XII took pains to point out, woman was to enter these areas precisely for the purpose of protecting and restoring the normal home and family. While this new role devolves upon the wives and mothers to the extent to which their other family cares permit, it is chiefly the role of "those on whom unavoidable circumstances bestowed a *mysterious vocation,* whom events have destined to a solitude which was not in their thoughts and desires, and which seemed to condemn them to a selfishly futile and aimless life [italics ours]." [26] Even here woman is expressing her motherhood vocation and defending its integrity and continuance, by engaging in that type of employment which will most benefit the family and the home.

The extent to which the Christian vision of woman as mother has been lost or blotted out seems evident in the preferences and activities of women in our culture. The girl student in high school and college preparing more intensely for a position in the business world than for her future role as homemaker; the guidance of such young women into clerical occupations, although they cannot mother a typewriter, an adding machine or a set of business files (but can mother the boss); the clearly discernible preference of millions of wives for the office rather than the home; the rejection of motherhood visible in the small family system and the foisting of motherhood cares onto agencies outside the home—all attest to the loss of this vision of woman's central role of motherhood. Marriage counselors stand witness almost daily to the discontent and friction arising from this rejection of her true role. The single woman who has failed to orient her single endeavors toward some type of motherhood career is easily detected as the cynical, frustrated and prematurely aged woman, whom, in our lack of charity, we label "old maid." Apparently some graduates of our more sophisticated secular women's colleges have caught the vision of their destined roles in motherhood and are taking positions as *maids* in homes of culture and refinement rather than positions in stores and offices.

---

[26] *Ibid.,* Sec. 41, p. 15.

Relative roles of men and women

The confusion in our culture over the distinct roles of men and women in marriage, is accompanied by a distortion of the roles which each is to play toward the other. The available factual studies do not dissipate this confusion by revealing a definite pattern of husband-wife relationships, but merely add more confusion. /The father's role in many instances is quickly shrinking to nothing more than that of the family breadwinner interested in little other than his career; many husbands and fathers are also taking a greater measure of responsibility in domestic chores and child care than formerly./ The six billion dollars spent in 1954 for do-it-yourself tools seem to indicate a large interest by fathers in homemaking arts. In a study of 982 men and women, 71.6 per cent of the men and 48.1 per cent of the women expected the husband to help with housekeeping chores.[27] Though many wives are taking an increased interest in extra-domestic activities and in working outside the home more magazines and books on homemaking are being read and more lectures on mothercraft are being attended than ever before.

Apparently no consistent pattern in the American family can be drawn of the roles of husbands and wives. The same confusion seems present in exclusively Catholic circles. In a study of 90 Catholic wives and 77 Catholic husbands 92.2 per cent thought wives were subordinate to husbands, but only 38.4 per cent agreed that the husband was the head of the house.[28] In another study of 120 Catholic married people, only 30 per cent thought the husband the chief authority in the home.[29] In a third study consisting of 186 Catholic college seniors, only 52 per cent thought the husband should be the family head.[30]

In another respect a new husband-wife pattern seems rapidly emerging. The dominance of the father seems to be giving way to equalitarian roles between husband and wife and to a falsely

---

[27] Burgess and Wallin, *op. cit.,* Table 64, p. 408.
[28] Feiten, *op. cit.,* p. 35.
[29] James, *op. cit.,* p. 49.
[30] Galloway, N., "An Investigation of the Knowledge and Attitudes of the Seniors of the Arts and Science School of a Catholic University Relative to Marriage" (Master's thesis: Catholic University of America, 1950), p. 17.

labeled "democratic" type in which children have an equal vote in making decisions through a "family council" arrangement. These are facts to be reckoned with, especially since children reared in such families are likely to continue the pattern into their own marriages.

In a study of 2,596 families married at least five years and located in most states of the Union, 61 per cent of the husband-dominated marriages, 47 per cent of the wife-dominated and 87 per cent of the "50–50" marriages were considered happy by close friends or relatives.[31]   A study of this nature might tempt one to conclude that the family not only *can* have two heads but *ought* to have two heads.   However, it should be noted that many one-partner dominated families were also deemed happy.   A more valid interpretation would seem to be that people will be happy if their *anticipated* roles are realized regardless of whether such roles be husband or wife-dominated.   However, one must hold suspect any allegation of a workable marriage arrangement with two heads who are such in practice as well as in theory. To assume that any two heads will in every instance and decision be in full agreement is fantastically unrealistic.   Before the present trend toward equalitarian family control reached any marked stature an American sociologist detected its meaning.

The old traditional subordination on the part of the wife had its uses . . . and however distasteful to modern ideas of freedom, was a factor in holding the family together.   For, after all, no social organization can be expected to subsist without some regular system of government.   We say that the modern family is a democracy; and this sounds very well; but anarchy is sometimes a more correct description. . . . *So long as members are one in mind and feeling* there is an unconscious harmony which has nothing to do with authority; *but with even slight divergence comes the need of definite control* [italics ours].[32]

The impact of our culture upon the traditional Catholic position as to the role of the husband as head of the family is evident in various studies made of Catholic people.   In one such study

---

[31] P. Popenoe, "Can the Family Have Two Heads?" *Sociology and Social Research,* Vol. XVIII (September-October 1933), pp. 12–17.

[32] C. H. Cooley, *Social Organization* (New York: Charles Scribner's Sons, 1929), pp. 368–369.

of 186 college seniors, 47 per cent thought equalitarian roles of husband and wife desirable;[33] in another study of 167 Catholic married couples, 59.8 per cent thought the same;[34] in a third study of 120 married people 67 per cent held the equalitarian notions of family headship.[35]

Ever since St. Paul wrote: "But I would have you know that the head of every man is Christ: and the head of the woman is the man,"[36] the Christian tradition has held fast to the position that the role of the husband is one of decision-making, and that of the wife is one of acceptance of such decisions in all *reasonable* matters. The exercise of leadership is a duty on the part of the husband and its acceptance is an obligation on the part of the wife. Contrary to feminist notions, it does not imply either inferiority of the wife or absolute rulership of the husband. No Catholic will deny the personal superiority of Our Lady as compared to St. Joseph; yet the greatest of all women was subordinate to her less graced husband! Too many have forgotten, however, that the Magnificat of our Lady is the Magna Charta of Christian womanhood—"because He hath regarded the *humility* of His handmaid" (St. Luke 1:48). Wives are in some instances actually superior in mentality or character to their husbands; their role in marriage arises not from personal qualities but rather from status. Accordingly, such wives even though superior in person remain obligated to a subordinate position. This is not unlike everyday experience in the extra-domestic world in which many persons of superior ability and attainments must subordinate themselves through status to an inferior personality. Civil rulers enjoy a superior status and our obligation to respect it remains, even though we may realize that they are not always the most able or brilliant persons in the nation. However, by virtue of training (if not innate ability) most men enjoy a facility in making decisions, a bodily vigor, an orientation to contacts outside the home which impels them into positions of leadership.

It is not by accident that St. Paul followed his admonition to wives to obey their husbands with a warning to husbands that

---

33 Galloway, *op. cit.,* p. 72.
34 Feiten, *op. cit.,* p. 35.
35 James, *op. cit.,* p. 49.
36 I Corinthians 11:3.

they *love* their wives. The Christian tradition has tempered the right of the husband's headship of the family with both charity and rationality. Charity, including kindness, patience, humbleness, will indicate a consultation with one's wife on decisions affecting her intimately; rationality implies respect for the opinions and judgments of one's mate and above all, restraint from unreasonable demands to which the husband does not have a right nor the wife a duty of submission.

If "to the husband falls the greater responsibility—in assuring the sustenance and subsistence care—the welfare of the persons and the house, in the decisions that engage him and his children for the future," [37] such cares and privileges often need the wisdom which comes only through the mutual interchange of ideas. In a culture such as ours in which women are more highly educated and share in the knowledge of extra-familial affairs more profoundly and in which many (if not most) girls are reared in an equalitarian atmosphere—ordinary prudence would seem to indicate the need of a delicate and tactful exercise of the power of family headship by the husband. An autocratic exercise of such powers under the cultural conditioning of today, will probably lead not to family harmony but to anarchy and rebellion—a fact evident in the case records of many broken marriages.

The rights of leadership are not, however, without corresponding responsibilities. "Since honor and decorum in the woman is the husband's public pride and esteem, the man out of consideration for her must make every effort to excel and distinguish himself among his equals in his own profession." [38] To his leadership of the family he should add excellence and success in his creative role outside the family. The danger of our civilization seems to be that many men will so emphasize this external role as to minimize or forget their internal domestic duties. The fiercely competitive struggle can all too easily preoccupy a man so as to leave little time and energy for his home, wife and children. This leads not only to a disproportionate execution of his over-all role but also to injustice. Mindful of this Pius XII advised husbands and fathers that "The perfection of the family

---

[37] Pius XII, "So la Vita," *Acta Apostolicae Sedis,* Vols. XII, IV (1942), p. 38.
[38] Pius XII, "Non Merovig Liateri," *Acta Apostolicae Sedis,* Vol. XLI (1942), p. 89.

bonds consists not only in fulfilling the actions pertaining to your profession, your trade or your particular work inside or outside the home; *in the house itself which is the particular* sphere of your wife, you also have an active part to fulfill [italics ours]." [39]   For instead of an autocratic aloofness, the husband's role consists in sharing the work of the wife in the home. Charity compels him to assist her when she is overburdened with household chores and with the physical care of the children.   It will not permit him to stand by while she struggles with the pressures and cares of the family.   Not infrequently such women will try to find an escape through a job outside the home or through birth control practices.

Many of the relative roles of husband and wife have a high degree of mutuality.   By emphasizing differing roles, we may easily lose sight of those which are similar.   If men marry because, "It is not good for man to be alone," they cannot afford to forget to be companions to their partners—as wives frequently complain they do today.   On the other hand, women marrying "to be loved" must remember that husbands crave tenderness and affection almost as much as they—that they forget this is another frequent complaint in failing marriages.   Both crave, furthermore, that sympathy, understanding and compassion which find their origins in the deep intimacy of life together.   Both have the capacities and responsibilities of child rearing and education; both have the economic roles of industrious application to work and wise handling of family finances; and both share the responsibility for the moral and religious growth of each other and of the children.

Women working outside the home

A role which nature had not intended but which our culture has fashioned for women is that of working outside the home. This role is becoming more significant since the trend is toward more rather than fewer women working in extra-domestic employment.   Those thinking that necessity is the greatest motive for women in gainful employment would have been disillusioned

---

[39] Pius XII, "Gran Fonte," *Acta Apostolicae Sedis,* Vols. XII, IV (1942), p. 45.

had they attended the "Conference on the Effective Use of Womanpower" held in Washington, D. C., in March 1955. In this meeting, sponsored by the Women's Bureau of the Department of Labor, it was widely agreed to be most desirable that more and more women leave the home for the office, store and factory.[40] In 1953 over 19 million women were in the labor force; this represented about 33 per cent of all women of working age. Of these 10.7 million, or more than half, were married women. While the number of married women increased by 30 per cent since 1940, the number of married women in the labor force increased by more than 100 per cent.[41] One-fourth of all the women living with their husbands were working, 10 per cent more than in 1940 even though the number of children requiring their care increased about 20 per cent.[42] In 1952, two million of the working mothers had children under 6 years of age and 5.3 million had children under 18 years of age.[43] In the first year of marriage 40 per cent of married women were working wives; in the second year 30 per cent. About 15 per cent of the mothers of pre-school age children worked and nearly one-third of the mothers of school-age children were in the labor force.[44]

Not only is the increasing trend toward women in the labor force significant, but so is the shift from one type of employment to another. *Since 1940 there has been a striking shift from employment in private households to clerical positions and work machine operators.*

The largest increases are in four clerical or sales occupations . . . Together they added over 75 per cent more women than they had in 1940, and now employ a third of all women at work . . . Over the past decade women have moved away from household employment

---

[40] Women's Bureau, U. S. Dept. of Labor, *The Effective Use of Womanpower,* No. 257 (Washington, D. C.: United States Government Printing Office, 1955).

[41] Women's Bureau, *What About Women Workers: A Few Facts,* Leaflet 18 (Washington, D. C.: United States Government Printing Office, 1954).

[42] P. C. Glick, "The Life Cycle of the Family," *Marriage and Family Living,* Vol. XVII, No. 1 (February 1955), p. 8.

[43] Women's Bureau, *op. cit.*

[44] Glick, *op. cit.*

and the distinctly laboring jobs to those as operatives, clerical workers, and into service, sales, professional, and management occupations.[45]

Most of these are the farthest removed from any implications of motherhood. The loss of the vision of women's true role is reflected in the preference of many for certain types of work. Comfort or income (unless necessity compels) does not warrant forsaking her womanly role for a masculine one. It may be more convenient or lucrative to assume a man's role, but at the same time, less natural.

Few seem to realize that this trek of women from the home is not only un-Christian but also often uneconomic. One survey pointed out: For over 15 years a homemaker who is the wife of a well-known economist has kept a scientific record showing what it cost to produce things for her family in her kitchen, which has all modern equipment. She has proved to her satisfaction that the average woman who prepares meals, cans, preserves, bakes and launders at home, for her own family, produces substantially the equal value of the man's economic contribution in industry.[46]

Another view of the economic value of the homemaker would be the cost of replacing *all* her services by a salaried maid. If one were also to add the cost of those services which a homemaker can offer but which maids usually refuse to do (sewing, mending, repairing household items and the like), the full worth of a homemaker becomes clear.

In 1952 the average wage of male workers in manufacturing industries was $67.97 a week or $3,534.44 a year.[47] In the same year half of the working women earned less than $1,398 a year; three-eighths earned between $1,398 and $3,000; and only one-eighth earned over $3,000.[48] *Probably only about one-eighth of all women workers earned as much in the office or factory as they might have in the home.* This consideration becomes even more striking when we realize that the extra ex-

[45] Women's Bureau, U. S. Dept. of Labor, *Changes in Women's Occupations 1940–1950,* No. 253 (Washington, D. C.: United States Government Printing Office, 1954), p. 16.

[46] H. E. Pidgeon, *Women in the Economy of the U. S. A.* (Washington, D. C.: United States Government Printing Office, 1937), p. 32.

[47] *Monthly Labor Review,* Vol. LXXVIII, No. 1, Table C-4 (January 1955), p. 143.

[48] Women's Bureau leaflet, *op. cit.*

penses entailed by women in outside employment often seriously reduce their net earnings. Pius XII pointed out that "this supplement to the earnings [of her husband] which she gets by working outside of the home is easily eaten up by other expenses or even waste which is ruinous to family economics." [49] In many cases if working wives were to compare their salary minus the costs of clothing, outside meals, transportation, baby-sitters, maids and the like with their value as producers in the home, they would find to their amazement that they are actually losing money and reducing the family standard of living by holding a position. A nationally famous financial advisory service has given us a sample estimate of the outlay for 1951 entailed by a working wife (See Table 4).

TABLE 4

AVERAGE WEEKLY DEDUCTIONS OF WORKING WIVES (1951) *

Weekly salary		$58.00
Weekly payroll taxes	$12.00	
Weekly part-time maid and carfare	16.00	
Weekly lunches	2.50	
Weekly additional clothes	4.00	
Total deductions	$34.50	34.50
		$24.50

* *Changing Times—The Kiplinger Magazine* (September 1951), pp. 29–30.

TABLE 5

AVERAGE ANNUAL DEDUCTIONS OF WORKING WIVES (1955) *

Annual salary		$2,860.00
Additional income tax	$569.05	
Social Security	43.16	
Transportation	100.00	
Food and drinks	380.00	
Extra clothes and cleaning	300.00	
Extra medical bills	40.00	
Baby-sitter	1,040.00	
Total deductions	$2,472.91	2,472.91
		$387.09

* Henry Cooke, "A Husband's Report: Why We Can't Afford to Have My Wife Work," *Work*, Vol. X, No. 9 (March 1953), p. 3.

[49] Pius XII, "Questa Grande," *Acta Apostolicae Sedis*, Vol. XXXVII (1945), p. 290.

The experts concluded: "But if it is money she [the wife] wants, better take the time to do a bit of arithmetic before she swaps her dishpan for a typewriter." [50]   The organ of the Catholic Labor Alliance gave a more recent calculation which indicated similar large deductions (See Table 5).

Combined studies on working women indicate "that most frequently half or well over half of the women at work in all types of occupations consider themselves in some degree responsible for dependents." [51]   This is especially true of the divorced and widowed; it indicates one of the evils of divorce and also the failure of our society to provide adequate widow's pensions. Sometimes it is necessary for married women to work; this indicates the need for a system of family allowances to permit mothers to remain at home with their children.   The United Nations Organization has taken cognizance of this problem and has stated its position clearly:

We must work towards a general economic organization, an economic policy and a family policy which would not oblige women to carry out the two-fold work of wage-earning outside the home and family and household tasks in the home.   Some kind of allowance, to be paid by enterprises and States, should be considered and put into effect, so that the mother may remain at home . . . for the benefit of her children and family.[52]

In a study of 652 instances of gainfully employed wives scattered in 9 geographical sections of the nation, 18 states and 36 cities, 438 claimed economic necessity and 179 the need to support dependents.[53]   However, one may suspect any *genuine* need for so many working since 527 of the 652 drove at least one car while 62 of these 527 owned 2 cars and 4 had 3 cars.   Only 167 stated they needed cars for their work.   Car ownership in this group of working wives was proportionately higher than for the nation as a whole.   Actually 50 per cent of these women ad-

---

[50] *Changing Times—The Kiplinger Magazine* (September 1951), p. 30.

[51] H. E. Pidgeon, *Women Workers and Their Dependents*, Women's Bureau, Bulletin No. 237 (Washington, D. C.: United States Government Printing Office, 1952), p. 3.

[52] U. N. Economic and Social Council, *District General* E/CN. 9/ngo/3 (January 20, 1953), p. 35.

[53] C. T. La Follette, *A Study of the Problems of 652 Gainfully Employed Women Homemakers*, Contribution to Education No. 619 (New York: Bureau of Publications, Teachers College, Columbia University, 1934), Table 7, p. 29.

mitted that if they did not work their standard of living *would be well above the minimum comfort level.*[54]   This suggests that the luxury standard is often being attained only through working wives.   A review of various studies made by the government showed that many wives work to be able to purchase more expensive automobiles, television sets and homes.[55]   Such women are unwittingly in accord with the Soviet policy as indicated in the rhyme:

> Formerly women only knew how
>   to cook soup and porridge,
> Now they go to the foundry—
>   At the foundry it is nicer.[56]

The highest percentage of employed married women is found among women in the first years of marriage.   Infrequently lecturers and writers urge this practice as wise and economic. Again the full economic value of the wife as a producer in the home seems not to be realized.   The city-bred wife especially would be much better guided to use the first year of marriage to develop skills in homecraft; this would repay her throughout her life as a homemaker, while her income from employment will cease after children arrive.   Of the 652 gainfully employed wives in the study earlier mentioned [57] 305 felt they needed more education in meal preparation; over a third stated the need for more information on nutrition, diets, marketing, child care, home management and home economics; and almost a third wanted further knowledge of clothing, child development and care of the sick.

When 279 women who were *above average* as household managers were studied, only 16 per cent of them possessed skill in household tasks.   Unfortunately, these women were of the lower economic group where such skills could increase their standard of living significantly.[58]

---

[54] *Ibid.,* chap. vii, pp. 123–126.

[55] E. S. Herbert, "When the Homemaker Goes to Work," *Journal of Home Economics,* 44 (April 1952), pp. 257–259.

[56] Maria Shaburova, *Zhenshchina Bol'shaia Sila* (Moscow: Partizdat, 1935), p. 32.

[57] La Follette, *op. cit.*

[58] D. Dickins, *Effects of Good Household Management on Family Living,* Bulletin 380 (State College, Mississippi: Mississippi State College Agricultural Experiment Station, May 1943), p. 6.

This emphasizes the tragic fact that when our culture hastens unmarried women into employment it not only fails to prepare them for marriage but actually deters their more complete education for family life.   In encouraging women to find employment in industry before marriage we forget that "Women again are not suited to certain trades; *for a woman is by nature fitted for homework,* and it is that which is best adapted at once to preserve her modesty, and to promote the good bringing up of children and the well-being of the family [italics ours]." [59]   Industrial or commercial employment means working in the man's world—frequently one of crudity, to say the least.   The feminist boast to have women clean up the man's world has ended in women becoming almost as immune to man's immodesties and deviations as he.   Pius XI recognized this when he stated: "The mind shudders if we consider the frightful perils to which . . . the virtue of girls and women is exposed in modern factories." [60] The close proximity of men and women at work has clearly lessened man's respect for womankind; it has also given us the phenomenon—born of spending longer hours with one's secretary than one's wife—secretaries labeled "office wives" by Hollywood.

The young girl may delight in dressing daily for public display in an office, but the habit will ill-adjust her for her future role in a house dress as a homemaker.   Her deeply social nature will thrill to its further cultivation by working with adults daily in office or factory or store until she needs to learn anew the adjustment to the solitude of the home after marriage.   "There is an isolation about life in the urban home for which some preparation should be given [in] the girl's earliest years.   Ordinarily her education is one for activity.   The trouble begins when she is thrown back on the limitations of the home.   Then it becomes evident that she has not developed the resources and the capacities which such a role demands." [61]   The frequent

---

[59] Leo XIII, "Rerum Novarum," *Social Wellsprings,* Vol. I, ed. J. Husslein (Milwaukee: The Bruce Publishing Company, 1943), p. 192; also *Acta Sanctae Sedis,* Vol. XXIII, pp. 641–670.

[60] Pius XI, "Restoring the Christian Social Order," *Social Wellsprings,* Vol. II, ed. J. Husslein (Milwaukee: The Bruce Publishing Company, 1943), p. 227; also *Acta Apostolicae Sedis,* XXIII (June 1, 1931), pp. 177–228.

[61] John J. O'Sullivan, *The Moral Obligation of Parents to Educate Their Children for Marriage* (Washington, D. C.: The Catholic University of America Press, 1955), p. 31.

words of praise employed to stimulate her morale as a hired worker may not be duplicated by a husband all too often thoughtless and usually not present during her day of homemaking triumphs. The economic independence learned through years of employment cannot be discarded lightly for the rather complete economic dependence of marriage without a major adjustment. This is doubtless why Pius XI encouraged the Woman's Social and Civil Union of France which was dedicated to inducing women to return to domestic types of employment.[62] There is little wonder that so many housewives speak with such nostalgia of their premarital jobs and consider it a boon when the former boss requests them to help him through an emergency situation for a short time. Conversely, it is not surprising that many women find their homemaking jobs—varying from cooking to cleaning, to sewing, to child care, to interior decorating, to laundering—utterly "monotonous, routine, slavish"; while the prospect of sitting at the same Comptometer or typewriter day after day appears challenging and stimulating.

Once the woman has learned the pleasure of working in company with others, keeping house in isolation becomes boring. A social worker connected with a large department store, who is familiar with the home life of the sales girls who marry and leave the store to begin housekeeping, testifies that in a very little while a great proportion of these young women return to the store, stating that they want their old jobs back, not because they are unhappy in their marriage or contemplate leaving their husbands, but because they find working alone in the house so dull that they are driven to tears.[63]

By force of family circumstance many girls and women are compelled in our unfamilial economy to earn a living. Others against their preference must remain unmarried and pursue the "mysterious vocation" (Pius XII) of the single woman in the world. Such women should first try to obtain a type of employment in accord with their feminine, motherly natures. One of the closest students of the Church's attitude on this question, interprets the mind of Pius XII as follows:

---

[62] Pius XI, "Anno Sellantaduesimo," *L' Osservatore Romano,* Vol. CXXXVIII (1932), p. 1.

[63] E. Groves, *The American Family* (Chicago: J. B. Lippincott Company, 1934), p. 157.

From the teaching of the Pope that motherhood is the sphere of all women, . . . the conclusion naturally follows that he would favor the choice by unmarried women of life tasks that concern themselves with child care. Such would be nursing, teaching, family case work, specialization in children's diseases by women doctors, play directing, youth guidance, recreational leadership, educational administration, and welfare work.[64]

The effect of women in gainful employment after marriage is even more clearly discernible. A report of the United Nations states:

It is common knowledge that the practice of married women working away from their homes, combining the work of wage-earners with that of running the house and bringing up their children, has its effect on the birth-rate, on the mother's health, on the physical and mental health of the children and on the family institution as a whole. *Scientific studies have been made to these effects* [italics ours].[65]

That our civilization is tending to grant priority to woman as a worker rather than woman as a mother can be seen in prevailing fertility rates. In 1949 there were 658 children under 5 for every thousand non-working wives and only 216 children for every thousand working wives.[66] Low fertility was also noted at the World Population Conference in Rome in 1954 where population experts pointed out that "Current fertility of women in the labor force is still not more than one-third as high as that of other women." [67] In a study of 652 employed married women, 433 (66 per cent) had no children of their own; 113 had 1 child each; the average number of children was about one-half a child each; only 39 of the 359 married less than 10 years had any children; *out of 433 without children only 275 wished they had them.*[68] Associated with women working is a high

---

64 W. B. Faherty, *The Destiny of Modern Woman* (Westminster, Md.: The Newman Press, 1950), pp. 74–75.

65 United Nations Social and Economic Council Report, *op. cit.,* p. 2; also Expert Committee on Mental Health, report of second session, World Health Organization.

66 United States Census Bureau, *Population Report,* P-20, No. 27, p. 8.

67 H. Shyrock, C. Seigel and C. Beale, "Future Trend of Fertility in the U. S.," (*United States Census Bureau Report* E/Conf./13/242) Meeting No. 6, Rome (September 1954).

68 La Follette, *op. cit.,* pp. 53–57.

incidence of abortion—a fact which our wartime experience brought out into the open with striking emphasis.

The doctor in one of the largest woman-employing concerns in the nation estimated that one quarter of the pregnancies among his workers end in abortion. In a southern munitions factory forty-five of two thousand women were brought to the company hospital in less than a year with "incomplete abortions." The physician in charge believes that eight times as many such operations were not discovered during that time. . . .

In another midwest town I sought out one of the law-breaking midwives. . . . "There's an abortion boom," she said. "I had forty-five patients on Saturday. The girls like Saturday because that gives them the weekend to rest. They come here straight from the factory, in slacks and overalls." Her rates had climbed from fifty to sixty-five dollars and finally seventy-five dollars, she said. . . .

In Buffalo a girl aircraft worker told me, "There are only three subjects we discuss in the women's rest room—my operation; how to keep from getting pregnant if you aren't; how to get rid of the baby if you are." [69]

The effects of neglect of children by employed mothers are likewise, at this time, clear and unmistakable. Our national experience with defense plants clearly identified the enormous growth of juvenile delinquency with the absence of the mother from the home. The White House Conference on Child Health and Protection reported on this fact. "The mothers of fully 50 per cent of the delinquent girls were employed outside the home; the mothers of 43 per cent of the delinquent boys also were employed." [70] In a study of 109 working mothers and 159 non-working mothers the following effects were noted upon the children in the order of their importance.[71]

Out on streets after school
Don't obey those with whom they are left
Poor school work resulting from lack of home attention

---

[69] Gretta Palmer, "Your Baby or Your Job," *Woman's Home Companion* (New York: The Crowell-Collier Publishing Company, October 1943). Reprinted by permission of The Crowell-Collier Publishing Company and Brandt & Brandt.

[70] *Controlling Juvenile Delinquency,* Publication 30. (Washington, D. C.: United States Government Printing Office, 1943).

[71] La Follette, *op. cit.,* Table 28, p. 68.

Development of poor food habits
Development of traits such as selfishness, rudeness, etc.
Apparent lack of love for parents
Nuisance to others in the neighborhood.

Nor does the strain of carrying a double load of work outside and inside the home enhance the relationship between husbands and wives. Out of 652 couples questioned about this matter 183 husbands felt disappointed, inadequate, inferior and frustrated; 357 husbands felt that their wives neglected them; 144 wives admitted they failed to mend the husbands' clothes; 118 wives admitted they did not serve well-prepared meals; and 119 wives stated that they were too tired to live up to their husbands' social inclinations.[72] In addition many refused sex rights to their husbands either because of fatigue or the fear of pregnancy.[73]

Despite the increasing numbers of employed wives, there still remains an apparently large segment of the nation opposed to this trend. In one group of 936 men and women studied, only 15.7 per cent of the men and 22.5 per cent of the women thought that wives should work if it isn't necessary.[74] When 104 Catholic married men, whose wives are working, were asked about the effects, 32 stated it interfered with their happiness and 25 thought it made the wives less cooperative.[75] In another study of 381 Catholic marriages, it was disclosed that when the wife worked there was less home life, husbands felt inadequate as providers and lost part of their self-esteem; wives, on the other hand, showed fatigue, neglect of home duties, emotional strain, independence, and neglect of children; whereas the children suffered from lack of care, supervision and affection, and showed a lack of esteem for their parents.[76] When students in 11 colleges were asked what they thought of a young woman's combining home and a career, most of them indicated they wanted a homemaker and not a working wife.[77]

---

[72] *Ibid.*, pp. 150–151.
[73] *Ibid.*, p. 145.
[74] Burgess and Wallin, *op. cit.*, Table 63, p. 407.
[75] *James, op. cit.*, p. 76.
[76] Dunn, *op. cit.*, Table 103, p. 266; Table 105, p. 270; Table 107, p. 274.
[77] M. Little, "Are College Men Boys?" *Mademoiselle* (September 1954), pp. 150–151.

Doubtless these individuals would agree with Pius XII's observation that often the woman in outside employment tends to become "bewildered by the highly distracting world in which she lives; dazzled by the glitter of false luxury, she develops a thirst for "shady" pleasures that distract but do not satisfy or recreate— pleasures in those night-clubs or dance halls . . . which corrupt." [78] Perhaps they further agree with him when he notes that as a result of wives being employed there is a loss of affection and of home ties; bonds are severed and proximity shattered; young girls are no longer prepared for homemaking; the wife and mother is often exhausted while she loses her dignity and influence in the home.[79] Or perhaps they will agree with Cardinal Manning who early in our industrial era tagged the trek of women to outside employment *a lack of a decisive Christian conscience.*

Serious as are the results of this practice, there are many married women who must by force of necessity risk the hazards of such employment until our economy and government take the rightful and dutiful measures to make it unnecessary. Such women, impelled against their wishes by necessity, may find useful the experiences of some 652 gainfully employed wives: these wives concluded as *absolutely necessary* for the double role of job-holder and homemaker, (in the order most frequently mentioned):

1. Good health of the woman worker
2. A husband who appreciates her helping to support the family
3. A husband who is willing to help with household chores
4. An employer who is sympathetic
5. Sufficient pay to enable the hiring of household help
6. A husband who sympathizes with her need to help
7. A family all of whose members are willing and able to do many things for themselves.[80]

ROLES IN THE DIVINE PLAN

When God made men and women, He made them *equal in all essential respects* and gave them identical roles as human beings,

---

[78] Pius XII, "Questa Grande," *Acta Apostolicae Sedis,* Vol. **XXXVII** (1945), p. 290.
[79] *Ibid.,* p. 289.
[80] La Follette, *op. cit.,* Table 14, p. 45.

to work out their salvation here and to enjoy the Beatific Vision for all eternity. However, when God made marriage and assigned certain purposes to it, He gave men and women different roles and gave them the peculiar traits required to fulfill those roles. Accordingly, in the Divine Plan they were to be *accidentally different*. Both were to be *lovers* but man was to express his love role through *creativity* which would reach its highest form in the generation of other human beings. Woman was to live out her love role in *motherhood*. Man's creativity was to be both inside and outside the home; woman's motherhood was to be sometimes outside the familial context as a nun or as an unmarried woman, but usually inside the domestic circle as a married person. Mothers were to leave the home and enter into social and political life only when the home itself was at stake and only in order to rescue it. She was not intended, as a rule to work outside the home in gainful employment. Experience and science both indicate that complete success and happiness in marriage are most likely to be attained only when both men and women retain their respective roles.

6

When the Sexes Meet

Not the least of the marvels of human nature is the development of a human being from an infant to a mature adult. The egocentric infant, whose every cry is a demand for attention, finds his latent and innate social nature turn outward to others by gradual stages of growth and proper education until he enjoys the stature of adult selflessness. The young child early associates with members of both sexes without any consciousness of sexual differences. Frequently enough *he* will spend as much time playing with feminine toys as *she* will engaging in masculine games. By the age of twelve, however, boys and girls tend to drift apart, preferring the company of their own sex. In fact, during this "gang age" either is embarrassed if found associating extensively with the opposite sex; his "gang" will label him a "sissy" while her peers will call her a "tom-boy." Doubtless this grouping according to sexes is an instinctive thing, intended to bring to a fuller development the distinctive characteristics of boys and girls. This process should result in developing masculine men and feminine women.

Both boys and girls, however, have yet to learn the distinctive and differing traits of the opposite sex and how to adjust to them before they are fully socialized. At about 14 years of age an aroused sex consciousness not only deepens the awareness of the opposite sex but also develops a curiosity about and desire to associate with its members. Boys and girls will now associate together without fear of ridicule, and even with evident signs of recognition and acceptance. In its earliest phase, however, boys are not ready to pair-off with individual girls and vice verse; rather do we find both preferring to associate in mixed groups.

DATING

In the latter phase there is a tendency, for boy and girl to pair-off as individual couples. This is the dating process so pronounced in our culture. One close study of this age-pattern revealed that:

Between the beginning of the fourteenth and the end of the sixteenth years the associational pattern changes from almost exclusive inter-action with members of their own sex to a mixed associational pattern similar to that found in adult life . . . such as dances and parties . . . almost exclusively mixed.[1]

If today we witness dating at increasingly earlier ages, it is doubtless due to the premature exposure of children to the love-making scenes in movies, comics, television and radio; in some instances it is due to parents—ambitious but illiterate—who fail to realize that a premature shortening of the "gang age" will mean more feminine boys and more masculine girls. Any chaperone of an *early* teen-age mixed party realizes how very *unready* the boys and girls are (especially the former) for this intersex experience.

The importance of dating

While there is complete agreement on the pairing-off process there is rather complete confusion among specialists on the purpose of dating. An opinion which for some time has been widely accepted, known as the "dalliance theory," indicates that dating is a thrill seeking and prestige seeking adventure with no reference whatever to either courtship or marriage and with no educational value for either.[2] Recent studies, however, reveal more

---

[1] A. B. Hollongshead, *Elmtown's Youth* (New York: John Wiley & Sons, Inc., 1949), p. 225.

[2] W. Waller, *The Family a Dynamic Interpretation* (New York: The Dryden Press, Inc., 1938), p. 235.

serious purposes in dating. In one of these studies 1,595 high school juniors and seniors and 384 youths in the first 3 years of college were given questionnaires in which they were asked which were the three most important reasons for dating; 25.9 per cent stated "affection," and 14.9 per cent said "selection of mate." [3] When another group of 300 young men and women were asked similar questions, fourth in the list was "as a means of finding a life-mate." [4] Studies made at Michigan University, Penn State College, Hope College and other places seem to have rendered untenable the theory that dating has no serious purposes.[5] Rather does it seem that many important results accrue from dating such as a broader experience, greater poise and balance, learning and adjusting to the traits of the opposite sex and a large number of contacts for mate selection.

Pairing-off boys and girls during the dating period is not a universal custom. Its prominence in our culture, however, may have a very special importance. In a small family system such as ours, youth does not enjoy the educational advantages which come to those born into a family of several brothers and sisters each. Dating affords these contacts denied the only child or the child who is one of a twosome. Again, our culture is one of many often conflicting sub-cultures; it is one in which the equalitarian ideal leads to a considerable amount of intermingling between boys and girls of varying social, economic, educational and religious backgrounds. This poses an added difficulty in spouse selection that has hazards even in a society with a homogeneous culture pattern. Dating with its wide and enriching contacts permits the finding of those relatively few out of many who might prove proper life-partners. In the mixture of varying cultures which is ours, the likelihood of finding a more suitable life-partner would seem to be increased as a result of the wide contacts which our dating pattern generally encourages. Dating may well be likened to window shopping, and like window shop-

---

[3] S. H. Lowrie, "Dating Theories and Student Responses," *American Sociological Review*, Vol. XVI, No. 3 (June 1951), pp. 334–340.

[4] J. F. Cuber, "Changing Courtship and Marriage Customs," *Annals of the American Academy of Political and Social Sciences*, 229 (1943), p. 32.

[5] R. A. Blood, "A Retest of Waller's Rating Complex," *Marriage and Family Living*, Vol. XVII, No. 1 (February 1955), pp. 41–47.

ping, it should enable youth to arrive at a better, more discriminating choice than would be likely without a search of such scope and magnitude.

Success in dating

Popularity in dating is not a condition for success in marriage; nor are popular boys and girls usually the best spouses. Perhaps this is true since not a few try to achieve popularity at the expense of their integrity of character, good morals and other basically sturdy qualities. However, that one need not sacrifice such desirable qualities seems evident in the many studies now available on desirable traits in boys and girls. Studies [6] indicate that, in general, both sexes place a premium upon genuinely good characteristics such as dependability, maturity, cleanliness in thought and action and being considerate. In one study both sexes definitely preferred masculine men and feminine women. It seems even more striking that, while appearance in the sense of neatness and good grooming, are given high ratings in each study and by both sexes, good looks do not even appear among the most desired factors. It should also prove gratifying to all decent youth to note that necking and petting are not listed by any of these studies among their ten highest rated factors. The study of 12,500 high school students from all parts of the nation indicated the same fact. Some undesirable traits in males were listed as vulgarity, withholding of compliments, disrespect, demanding of too much necking and petting, being overtalkative and loud, using dishonest flattery. Some undesirable traits in girls were being over-dependent, too serious, flighty, flirtatious, childish and silly, complaining, cold, money-minded, sensitive and stuck-up.[7]

However, the possession of desirable traits alone will not ensure dates; in addition, boys and girls need to "put themselves into circulation" by frequenting those places where they are most likely to meet desirable persons of the opposite sex. In a nation-

---

[6] H. T. Christensen, "Dating Behavior as Evaluated by High School Students," *American Journal of Sociology*, Vol. LVII, No. 6 (May 1952), p. 580; and *Marriage Analysis* (New York: The Ronald Press Company, 1950), pp. 255–260; also Blood, *op. cit.*, pp. 41–48.

[7] H. T. Christensen, "Dating Behavior as Evaluated by High School Students," p. 582.

wide study of 9,081 married couples [8] the places which served this purpose best were school and homes of friends. It was found that pickup dates rarely result in good marriages. Other studies tend to confirm the fact that the most usual places of meeting future partners in marriage are the school and family friendship circles. Contrary to general belief, life-partners are not as often found in places of gainful employment; in fact, this study indicates that almost as many meet their dates in the church milieu. For those not in school or away from home and family, it seems advisable that they survey the resources of their community and become active in those types of groups—religious, recreational, social—in which the members are the kinds of persons likely to prove good dates and life-partners.

Dangers in dating

The pleasure associated with dating is likely to blind young people to its hidden dangers. One of these dangers, a growing practice, is that of prematurely early dating. The pattern of 602 boys and girls in a dating survey indicated that five per cent of the boys and seven per cent of the girls dated before the age of 12; about 13 per cent of them dated at the age of 12.[9] The same study indicated that about three-fourths (73 per cent) of the city girls started to date before the age of 15.[10] Another study (597 men and 626 women) disclosed that 15.4 per cent of the men and 16.4 per cent of the women dated before the age of 14.[11] Apparently not only the youth but their parents fail to see the dangers inherent in early dating—dangers both moral and social. Also the failure of parents to supervise early teen-age mixed parties becomes increasingly observable. Were more parents to supervise such affairs, they might observe many indications of the lack of readiness of our youth for dating at these early ages and also the temptations to which they are being exposed. Some Catholic parents also fail to see the dangers and

---

[8] Paul Popenoe, *Modern Marriage* (New York: The Macmillan Company, 1947), p. 43.

[9] W. M. Smith, "Rating and Dating: A Restudy," *Marriage and Family Living*, Vol. XIV, No. 4 (November 1952), Table 1, p. 313.

[10] *Ibid.*, p. 313.

[11] E. W. Burgess and P. Wallin, *Engagement and Marriage* (Chicago: J. B. Lippincott Company, 1953), Table 3, p. 119.

effects of frequent dating. According to one investigation 25 per cent of the mothers of Catholic junior high school students and 41.5 per cent of the seniors' mothers approved of their dating three to four times a week.[12]

Another danger largely peculiar to our culture is the failure to be properly selective in choosing dates. The association with persons who are in no way potentially good life-partners is widespread and easily observable. The equalitarian aspect of our culture throws together boys and girls of varying and often conflicting backgrounds. Dating between such mixed personalities is often recognized but minimized. She who says, "Even if he were the only man left in the world, I wouldn't marry him; but he *is* a good date," all too frequently ends in marriage with the person whom she originally knew to be a poor partner. The failure to realize that growing to love others comes from proximity to them and that love comes unbidden—subtly and quietly weaving its spell—leads to the extremely widespread mismating seen daily in offices of marriage counselors. It seems that we need to learn anew that mixed marriages—cultural, social, religious—will not diminish until mixed dating has ceased.

A somewhat similar danger is that of exploitation. Recent studies indicate that although using a date merely or chiefly as a vehicle of "thrill seeking" or gaining a dishonorable personal advantage is not the dominant pattern, it is yet a significant hazard. Girls especially need to recognize that all too many boys and men are ready to resort to those techniques most appealing to women—flattery, affection, romance—to attain ignoble purposes.

Religious and moral hazards

Perhaps the greatest religious hazard facing Catholic boys and girls is that of dating non-Catholics. Here again it bears repetition—if we had no mixed religious dates, we would have no mixed religious marriages.[13] When Catholic youth in various sections of the nation were asked whether they approve of dating

---

[12] Sr. Mary Bridget, "A Study of the Attitudes of Some High School Juniors and Seniors Toward Courtship and the Selection of a Marriage Partner" (Master's thesis, Catholic University of America, 1955), p. 58.

[13] For a discussion of mixed religious marriages, see "Partners in Mixed Religions," Chapter 7.

non-Catholics over three-fourths indicated they did so approve.[14] One might expect Catholic college students to show a deeper insight into this problem. Yet out of 201 asked, only 28 per cent of the boys and only 12 per cent of the girls stated they had never dated a non-Catholic.[15] Among 186 seniors in another Catholic college, 90 per cent could see no reason why dating a non-Catholic could be deemed imprudent.[16] Apparently a larger and more effective emphasis upon this problem is needed in our premarital education.

Doubtless the greatest moral hazard of dating is loss of chastity. Although sinful types of necking and petting are apparently quite common, available studies show it is a minority that either thinks or acts out the misconception that they are necessary. Our culture's confusion about this matter is clear from the failure to protect our youth against this hazard and the condemnation of them if their license leads to mismating, a broken marriage or illegitimacy. This has been noted by an anthropologist who studied adolescents in many societies and cultures.

As a culture we have given up chaperonage. We permit and even encourage situations in which young people can indulge in any sort of sex behaviour that they elect. At the same time we have not relaxed one whit our disapproval of the girl who becomes pregnant, nor simplified the problems of the unmarried mother who must face what to do about her child. . . . We bring up girls to be free and easy and unafraid, without the protections given by shyness and fear to girls of many other societies. We bring our boys up to be just as free and easy, used to girls, demanding towards girls. We actually place our young people in a virtually intolerable situation, giving them the entire setting for behaviour for which we then punish them whenever it occurs.[17]

---

[14] J. H. Fichter and P. W. Facey, "Some Attitudes of Catholic High School Students," *American Catholic Sociological Review*, Vol. XIV, No. 2 (June 1953), p. 105.

[15] M. L. Dwyer, "Some Attitudes Toward Dating and Marriage of 201 Catholic College Students," *American Catholic Sociological Review*, Vol. XIV, No. 3 (October 1953), p. 169.

[16] N. Galloway, "An Investigation of the Knowledge and Attitudes of the Seniors of the Arts and Science School of a Catholic University Relative to Marriage" (Master's thesis, Catholic University of America, 1950), p. 119.

[17] Margaret Mead, *Male and Female* (New York: William Morrow & Company, Inc., 1949), p. 290.

Apparently most of the youth studies so far agree that extensive love-making is undesirable. They seem mindful that kissing and embracing are of three types: the brief, simple type expressive of non-sexual love usually accorded one's parents; the type intended to find its consummation in the physical union of the marital act; and the type expressive of nothing more than animal passion. Since dating is properly conceived as neither the same as marriage nor a situation intended for mere animal indulgence, only a reserved and moderate display of affection can be condoned or vindicated. Furthermore, it is probable that both physical and emotional tensions, with their attendant ill-health, ensue from excessive cultivation of affections—tensions intended by nature to find their proper relaxation in the fulness of marital love. When 159 women were asked about this phase of necking, about 25 per cent admitted it induced nervousness.[18] In the same study the absence of necking was found to relate to good adjustment after marriage; the same finding was noted in a study of the sex life of 2,200 women.[19]

Things to consider

Adolescents are tempted to rebel against the wisdom of experience and observation. Yet boys and girls would be wise to realize that dating has serious meanings and definite hazards. Like other human relations it is successful only when it follows certain rules. Some of these which young daters might well consider are:

1. Dating can be fun without resorting to license and cheap conduct.
2. Avoiding the isolation of secluded spots will do much to minimize the dangers of dating.
3. Group dating is sometimes wise; "there is safety in numbers" but only if the couples are all highly principled.
4. Girls must realize that boys are very much more susceptible to sexual temptation than they are. They should recognize the utter lack of fair play and decency in exciting boy friends by

---

18 W. R. Reevy, "Marital Prediction Scores of College Women Related to Behavior and Attitudes" (Doctoral dissertation, University of Pennsylvania Library, 1954), p. 247.

19 K. B. Davis, *Factors in the Sex Life of 2,200 Women* (New York: Harper & Brothers, 1929).

improper dress or actions and then expecting respect from them.

5. Boys and girls should remember that respect is something which is merited and commanded, and not given gratis.

6. Demands for extravagant entertainment cause the loss of many boy friends; an extravagant boy or girl should not be taken seriously as a possible life-partner.

7. Drinking and dating don't mix well. Liquor has a double-edged effect—it excites the emotions and passions at the same time that it weakens the will.

8. Boys should recognize the hypocrisy and utter ignobility of encouraging girls to be "good sports" and then condemning them behind their backs.

9. Girls would be wise to make the male feel protective and important.

10. Girls should learn to "play hard to get"—but not too hard.

11. Attracting the opposite sex by personality and character traits is much more certain and permanent than by physical charm.

12. Men generally dislike anything beyond a faint suggestion of cosmetics.

13. Being a delightful blend of modernity with old-fashioned virtues and traits, is a safe pathway to success.

14. The domestic type of boy or girl will be more widely acceptable as a date than the sophisticated type.

15. There is a tendency because of late dating hours and pre-occupation with the pleasures of dating, to lessen religious living. However, the great dangers of this period demand more grace, not less. Accordingly, attendance at Mass and Communion is more necessary than previously.

Assisting youth

The perplexities and hazards of the dating age require the assistance of others. Families that encourage the use of the home for youthful social gatherings can do much to reduce teen-age tensions. This is true, however, only if parents discharge their clear moral responsibility to supervise such affairs. Unfortunately today there seems to be a mounting parental neglect in supervision of their children's leisure-time habits—movies, companions, parties, television and radio programs and the like.

The parish church can also perform an invaluable service here. Teen-age social, athletic, recreational and religious functions have proved their worth. Not only will the restoration of the parochial center to its former social role help to keep youth from immoral and unsupervised forms of commercial recreation, it will also enable Catholic boys and girls to meet one another and so render less likely the continued growth of mixed marriages. For similar reasons, schools and colleges should also bring their facilities to bear upon the social problems of our dating youth.

COURTSHIP

While dating serves its function as a "window shopping" period, individuals usually find their interests in the opposite sex narrowing more and more. In time they develop a preference for frequent dates with one person to the exclusion of others and begin to cultivate a more deeply affectionate relationship. This is the concept used here to distinguish between the dating and the courtship periods. This concept is not always accepted in literature on marriage. Some think of courtship as all inter-sex relationships prior to marriage; some think it devoid of serious intent; others envision it as an intensive prelude to marriage; still others think it a social custom devoted to nothing more than pleasure; and still others think it a more or less exclusive relationship with the serious possibility of marriage envisioned.[20]

Empirical studies show that in the minds of many courting has much more serious purposes than dating. When 674 Purdue University students were asked the desired qualifications of a *date* and of a *spouse,* important differences appeared. For dating the men placed pleasant disposition first, good grooming and manners second, sociability third; their most desired trait in a spouse, however, was stability and dependability, their second choice was family-mindedness, the third was considerateness. The women appreciated in a date firstly sociability, secondly pleasant disposition, and thirdly good grooming and manners; for a spouse, however, the women selected as the first qualities stability, dependability and family-mindedness; for the second, considerateness; and for the third trait, emotional maturity.[21] The

---

[20] Opinions of this type vary among Bowman, Burgess and Locke, Cavan, Kane, Merril, Mihanovich and Schnepp and Thomas, and others.

[21] H. T. Christensen, *Marriage Analysis* (New York: The Ronald Press Co., 1950), Figure 5, p. 259.

greater importance attached to traits such as dependability and family-mindedness seems to indicate a deeper seriousness in courtship than in dating. A study of 119 Catholic married persons seems to confirm this deeply serious nature of courting; 76 thought their experience indicated that the best time to learn to adjust was during the courtship; only 12 thought dating was the best period for this purpose.[22]

Courtship serves many purposes. It is the period when two people find each other sufficiently attractive to be considered possible life-partners. It should, through close association, disclose whether those traits are present which would make each a good husband or wife, and whether the personalities of the two are such as to blend and adjust with a minimum of effort. It is a period of personality exploration and a testing of the degree of compatibility between the two. As such courtship assumes the role of a proximate preparation for marriage. The all-important decision of selecting a life-partner confronts the couple while each with a special vigor exerts efforts to improve and perfect himself in those qualifications which make for a successful life-partner and a successful marriage. This is the deeply serious purpose of the close association of courtship—a purpose often drowned out by the romantic glamour and pleasure seeking of the period.

Some courting problems

The problems of courtship are in many respects the same as those of dating, but they are magnified and intensified. There is the same danger of exploitation, of serious persons being led on by frivolous thrill seekers only to find themselves disillusioned and brokenhearted. The moral dangers are greatly enhanced by the deeper attraction between the two, the frequency of meeting and the greater seclusion of the courtship pattern. The exploration of each other's personality traits and the rightful but reserved cultivation of affections vindicate and call for some degree of isolation. However, the idyllic and romantically isolated situations usually depicted in movies—full moon, rippling stream, weeping willows—will prove for most a hazard of great propor-

---

[22] P. M. James, "The Expressed Results of a Certain Premarital Lecture Course" (Master's thesis, Catholic University of America, 1953), p. 87.

tions. Even though a greater affection and isolation can be justified in the courtship than the dating period, at all times both parties should keep the danger of willful consent to sexual arousal remote. This calls for many measures of caution and discretion. "Steady company keeping," as here understood, implies frequent preferential (if not exclusive) and affectionate relationships between a boy and a girl. In some instances, however, the dangers of keeping company are present even if dating is not very frequent; the degree of emotional involvement seems an important factor here. We cannot forget that "steady company keeping in itself is an occasion of sin; however, the hope of marriage *in the near future* will justify it, as long as proper safeguards are observed." [23]

The dangers of loss of chastity in courtship are not easy to exaggerate in a culture which allows an excessive amount of liberty to youth. Both morality and most empirical studies agree that successful marriages are best built upon an unsullied courtship. The studies of many marriage specialists support the position that marriages are most successful when there have been no premarital physical intimacies. These findings have been reinforced by a study of thousands of Catholic marriage failures in which it was disclosed that 50 per cent of the brides who were expectant mothers at the time of their marriages, found their marriages broken within 5 years.[24] Most modern scientific studies merely confirm the traditional position of the Church, no better expressed than in the words of Pius XI:

There is danger that those who before marriage sought in all things what is theirs . . . will be in the married state what they were before, that they will reap that which they have sown; indeed, within the home there will be sadness, lamentation, mutual contempt, strifes, estrangements, weariness of common life, and, worst of all such parties will find themselves left alone with their own unconquered passions.[25]

Another danger that assumes greater proportions daily is keeping steady company with divorced persons. Since marriage

---

[23] F. J. Connell, "Juvenile Courtship," *American Ecclesiastical Review*, Vol. CXXXII, No. 3 (April 1954), p. 184.

[24] J. Thomas, "Marital Failure and Duration," *Social Order*, Vol. III, No. 2 (January 1953), pp. 24–29.

[25] Pius XI, "Casti Connubi," *Acta Apostolicae Sedis*, Vol. XXII, (December 31, 1930).

is not a possibility, courting a divorced person can have no moral justification whatever.   A more widespread practice among Catholics is that of courting non-Catholics.   Apparently many Catholics are unaware not only of the Church's full attitude toward mixed religious marriages but also of the moral aspects of such marriages.   Because there are unusually serious hazards, on both the natural and supernatural levels,[26] mixed religious marriages require equally serious and justifiable reasons.   Since it is a grave sin to enter such a marriage "without a grave and just reason . . . it follows that a Catholic who begins to keep company with a non-Catholic with a view to marriage, having no reasonable probability that there is—or, at least, at the time of the marriage, will be—a grave and just reason for the mixed marriage, also sins grievously." [27]

Dangers in courting

Studies now available differ widely on the problem of length of courtship; this is probably due to the inadequacies of the studies themselves.[28]   However, most agree that a courtship of less than six months is very unpromising.   In a study of Catholic marriages which ended in the Chancery Court, "approximately 17 per cent were acquainted for less than six months and about 45 per cent for less than one year before marriage. . . .   It would seem that nearly half the couples do not meet the minimum prerequisites for length of acquaintance before marriage." [29] The serious tasks of exploring each other's personalities and ascertaining facility for adjustment has generally been thought impossible of accomplishment in less than six months.   In a nationwide poll of women 85 per cent thought a girl should not marry unless she has gone with her prospective partner from six months to two years.[30]   On the other hand, extended courtships are both meaningless and hazardous.   Any two people can probably become sufficiently acquainted in a year.   Courtship continuing beyond the point where this purpose is being served, becomes

---

[26] See "Partners in Mixed Religions" in Chapter 7.

[27] F. P. Connell, "Some Obscure Points of Premarital Morality," (Unpublished workshop lecture, Catholic University of America, June 16, 1952), p. 8.

[28] See Appendix A.

[29] J. Thomas, "Some Group Characteristics and Marriage Problems," (Unpublished workshop paper, Catholic University of America, June 13–24, 1952).

[30] *Woman's Home Companion* (May 1955), p. 11.

fruitless. At the same time, it is inevitable that the longer the two court each other, the greater becomes the physical attraction and the danger of immorality. In a study of 576 engaged couples, it was noted that while not quite 40 per cent of those engaged eight months or less had indulged in physical intimacy, close to half (48.4 per cent) of those engaged 28 or more months had done so. In fact, the same study indicated the presence of strong physical attraction for almost two-thirds in less than six months' time.[31]

A further danger, especially present in urban courtships, is that of mutual observation and association only within the social, recreational and leisure time areas of life. The usual evening or week end date may disclose personality traits associated with a relaxed personality, for most people are quite agreeable in their leisure moments. However, the same person who is a "prince charming" in a drawing room may prove intolerable when at work. Since marriage implies a merger in *all* areas of life—religion, work, affection, recreation—every effort should be made to discover a prospective life-partner's characteristics in each of those areas. If this cannot be done by direct personal participation, it should be learned in other ways.

Many courtships fail to achieve all their purposes because they are taken too frivolously. The fact of being in love and of looking forward to marriage should be a source of joyful anticipation. However, a courtship devoid of serious preparation for marriage will probably find its joy turned into disappointment in time. If the custom of preparing a trousseau is no longer in vogue, the more important preparation of one's self is still wise. Both men and women would be well advised to extend their education for marriage in all respects—religious, moral, psychological, physical, educational, recreational and economic. While men strive to solidify their economic positions and attain a greater security, women (especially in our urban culture) could well apply themselves to the arts of homemaking and child care.

Juvenile courtship

One of the most striking characteristics of our current dating and courtship pattern is the growing prominence of early teen-age

---

[31] Burgess and Wallin, *op. cit.*, Table 31, p. 335 and Chart 17, p. 161.

"steady dating." In one study of 165 students, 11 had gone steady in the first year of high school, 24 in the second year, 50 in the third and 80 in the fourth year.[32] In another study of 24,609 students in 105 Catholic high schools 5,047 (21 per cent) stated that they were going steady. This was defined by 93 per cent of 149 Catholic high school students (female) as meaning going with "only one boy." Among this group 17.9 per cent of the juniors and 37 per cent of the seniors were going steady.[33]

The reasons for these juvenile courtships are frequently not serious ones. Among the 149 Catholic high school female students studied, less than half gave marriage as a reason.[34] When 120 public high school students in grades 9 to 12 were interviewed, the reasons alleged were to obtain security, enjoy status, to broaden acquaintances, and to be invited to social functions.[35] No really serious purpose relating to marriage is indicated. Among the 24,609 Catholic high school students surveyed as to the reasons most often advanced for going steady, only 16 per cent alleged "love with a view to marriage," and less than half were in love.

TABLE 6

REASON ADVANCED BY 24,609 CATHOLIC HIGH SCHOOL
STUDENTS FOR STEADY DATING *

Reasons	Number
Assurance of dates	7,593
Love	5,539
Love with view to marriage	4,636
Others are doing it	3,425
Assurance of a moral date	3,423
Money, automobiles, social connections, etc.	2,594
Fear of criticism	1,167

* Table devised from data in survey by Father Conroy, *When They Start Going Steady* (St. Paul: Catechetical Guild Educational Society, 1954), pp. 60–61.

---

[32] R. D. Herman, "The 'Going Steady' Complex: A Re-Examination," *Marriage and Family Living,* Vol. XVII, No. 1, (February 1955), Table 1, p. 37.
[33] Sr. Mary Bridget, *op. cit.,* p. 59.
[34] *Ibid.*
[35] J. R. Crist, "High School Dating as a Behavior System," *Marriage and Family Living,* Vol. XV, No. 1 (February 1953), p. 26.

An important factor in this situation is the parental attitude toward these youths.   Only 17 per cent of the parents actually approved of their dating steady, and 29 per cent were indifferent to it.   In other words almost half of the parents raised no objection to their children's steady dating.[36]

Results of premature courtship

Apparently a large number of parents and youth do not realize the psychological and moral implications of early steady dating. In a study of 517 college students it was found that those starting to date steadily in grade or junior high school were emotionally maladjusted.[37]   There are, of course, the obvious moral dangers arising from an early sex stimulation which cannot culminate in rightful expression for years to come.   Perhaps the fact that in the past 15 years illegitimate births among teen-age girls has doubled,[38] is an inevitable result.   Another expected result would be an increase in early marriages.   Many high schools are known to have 1 married student to every 20 single students.

A significant aspect of early courtships is the fact that for *most* it is probably immoral.   Steady company keeping (as earlier defined) is *usually* an occasion of sin which may not be entered unless justified by preparation for immediate marriage.[39]   Surely many of the reasons stated by students are in no way a justification for exposure to sinful occasions.   On the other hand, most students, at least in junior high school, *could not* have marriage in view as a possibility in the reasonably near future.   As a matter of fact, the studies cited indicate that most *do not* have that serious purpose in mind at all.

Age of courtship and marriage

The age of marriage in the United States has been steadily decreasing for many years.   In 1890 the median age for men

---

[36] Father Conroy, *When They Start Going Steady* (St. Paul: Catechetical Guild Educational Society, 1954), p. 61.

[37] M. Nimkoff and A. L. Wood, "Courtship and Personality," *American Journal of Sociology*, Vol. LIII (January 1948), pp. 263–269.

[38] Statement made by Dr. Goodrich Schauffer to Congress of Obstetricians and Gynecologists; *Newsweek* (December 27, 1954), p. 49.

[39] F. J. Connell, "Juvenile Courtship," *American Ecclesiastical Review*, Vol. CXXXII, No. 3 (April 1954), p. 184.

was 26.1 years; in 1951 it was 23.6 years. The median age for women in 1890 was 22 years; in 1951, 20.4 years.[40] "About half of the men today who ever marry do so before the age of 23 years, and half of the women, before the age of 20 years. . . .[41] Doubtless if the current trend toward earlier dating and courting persists, we may soon expect a marked decline from the 1951 age of marriage. This is forcing us as a nation to a serious con-, sideration of the entire problem of teen-age marriages.

Neither Church nor state has taken a position against such marriages. Canon law permits boys to marry at the age of 16 and girls at the age of 14 years. The laws of the 48 states and the District of Columbia permit boys to marry at 16–18 and girls at 12–16 years of age. Many distinct advantages accrue from late teen-age marriages when both are adequately prepared. Many believe that the flexibility of personality at such ages makes adjustment relatively easy; the adjustment to and care of infants is less burdensome; juvenile delinquency would be reduced; dangers of childbirth would be lessened; the tensions (both physical and emotional) of deferred sex life would be removed; prostitution and venereal disease would diminish; the general religious and moral tone of families would be heightened; and distinct physical benefits would result. Commenting upon the last alleged benefit, the most noted authority on the growing incidence of tumorous conditions of the generative organs states: "It is my belief that *late marriage* and infrequent childbearing are the reasons for endomitriosis. . . . It is the feeling of this writer, and this has often been repeated, that our children should marry young and they should have families when young [italics ours]."[42] Furthermore, after reviewing the available statistics on infant mortality, another expert concludes: "On the whole, the chances for survival of an infant are greatest where the mother is in her early twenties in her pregnancy; in this combina-

---

[40] *Current Population Reports,* Series P-20 No. 38. (Washington, D. C.: United States Department of Commerce, Bureau of the Census, April 29, 1952).
[41] *Ibid.,* Series P-20, No. 62 (October 31, 1955).
[42] J. V. Meigs, "The Medical Treatment of Endometriosis and the Significance of Endometriosis Surgery," *Journal of Obstetrics and Gynecology,* Vol. 89 (September 1949), p. 320.

tion, the rates of stillbirth, prematurity and infant mortality are at their low points." [43]

Whatever the advantages of late teen-age marriages, it is clear from repeated studies that the incidence of breakdown of such early marriages is much greater than that of marriages contracted in the twenties. In a study of 526 marriages a poor happiness rating was found among marriages in which the husband was under 22 and the wife under 19 at marriage; [44] in another study of 500 marriages, being under 22 for men or under 20 for women spelled unhappiness; [45] in a third study of 409 couples, in which all were under 20, unhappiness was indicated. [46] A study of thousands of broken Catholic marriages revealed that one-third of the husbands were 22 or less when married and nearly 40 per cent of the wives were 20 or under. [47]

Continued investigation is starting to dissociate breakdown in marriage with early age and attach it to other factors which are, however, associated with early marriages. One such investigation disclosed a high degree of in-law interference in early marriages; [48] while another indicated factors such as parental domination and forced marriages present in many early marriages. [49] Whether it be age itself or factors associated with teen-age marriages, the fact remains that in our culture early marriages are fraught with great hazards. For this reason, "Though marriage is valid when these years (16 for boys and 14 for girls) are completed, the pastors of souls should dissuade young people from marriage at an earlier age than is commonly the custom in the respective countries." [50]

---

[43] L. I. Dublin, A. J. Latka and M. Spiegelman, *Length of Life* (New York: The Ronald Press Company, 1949), pp. 139–140.

[44] Burgess and Cottrell, *Predicting Success or Failure in Marriage* (New York: Prentice-Hall, Inc., 1939), p. 117.

[45] L. M. Terman, *et al.*, *Psychological Factors in Marital Happiness* (New York: McGraw-Hill Book Company, Inc., 1938), p. 181.

[46] J. T. Landis and M. G. Landis, *The Marriage Handbook* (Englewood Cliffs, N. J.: Prentice-Hall, Inc., 1948), p. 111.

[47] Thomas, *op. cit.*, p. 8.

[48] Landis and Landis, *op. cit.*, p. 295.

[49] T. P. Monahan, "Does Age at Marriage Matter in Divorce?" *Social Forces*, Vol. XXXII, No. 1 (October 1953), pp. 81–87.

[50] S. Woywood, "Canon 1067," *The New Canon Law* (New York: Joseph F. Wagner, Inc., 1918), p. 216.

The reasons for the high incidence of breakdown are probably obvious. The romantic attitudes of our youth, the lack of maturity and responsibility even at the late teen-age level, the difficulties of attaining economic security at such an early age are, doubtless, important factors operative in breakdown. Generalizations are treacherous, however, since there are some few youths who *are* ready for marriage, even though many are not. Those who have the physical, moral, social, economic and psychological capacities for the responsibilities of marriage should probably not be dissuaded but rather encouraged. Many of the advantages of early marriage could be enjoyed if parents today were as ready to subsidize their sons and daughters as they were yesterday. The discarded dowry system had its merits and might well be revived in more modernistic fashion. In any event, we should face the probability of earlier marriages for some time to come, and employ those steps which will help to render such marriages more stable and successful.

THE DIVINE PLAN AND INTERSEXUAL ASSOCIATION

In the Divine Plan each sex is remotely prepared for marriage roles by the "gang age" process of making boys masculine and girls feminine. A more immediate preparation for marriage is induced by the promptings of nature for intersex contacts and association, culminating in the singling out of just one member of the opposite sex during courtship. Boy and girl need to "go steady" to explore each other's personalities, determine the facility for adjustment and finally decide upon a life-partner. The progressively earlier ages for courtship today are fraught with many dangers. Our culture neither matures youth early nor permits it the opportunity for economic security. It is not part of the Divine Plan that boys and girls should engage in juvenile courtship without the probability of marriage in the reasonably near future. On the other hand, parents and society at large should devise means of assisting those of our youth who *are* ready for marriage at a relatively early age.

7

Selecting a Partner

THE SELECTION of a partner in marriage is one of the most important decisions of a lifetime. It affects not only success in this world, but has a profound effect on happiness or misery in the world to come. Referring to this the late Holy Father wrote:

To the proximate preparation for a good married life belongs very specially the care in choosing a partner; on that depends a great deal whether the forthcoming marriage will be happy or not, since one may be to the other either a good help in leading a Christian life, or on the other hand, a great danger and hindrance. And, so that they will not deplore the rest of their lives the sorrows arising from an indiscreet marriage, those about to enter wedlock should carefully deliberate in choosing the person with whom henceforward they must live continually.[1]

Other decisions can usually be revoked; this one cannot. We can change our careers, our occupations, our homes, our friends —but we cannot change our life-mates; they are partners until death. Even if separation takes place, the intimacy of marital life has left traces on one's personality which are not easily erased.

---

[1] Pius XI, *On Christian Marriage* (New York: The America Press, 1931), pp. 59–60; also *Acta Apostolicae Sedis*, Vol. XXII (December 31, 1930), pp. 539–592.

This proximity of living with one so intimately and for so long a time, usually makes that person the most influential one in our lives. We cannot avoid this influence since to a great extent it is an unconscious process. Were this mutual interchange not to occur, marriage would fail as a vehicle for the growing together of two unlike personalities.

It is widely accepted by marriage counselors that the marriages of those whose attitudes are not shared or which, perhaps, are even opposed to each other, are giving us the numerous marital shipwrecks of today. The burden of marital adjustment is a great one even when both parties are well-matched. Any degree of mismatching simply adds to the already large measure of adjustment required in every marriage. It is true, of course, that one can wrest a significant measure of success from a union with a life-partner who is not the ideal one; such a marriage *need not* end in utter tragedy and defeat. However, if we are to be realistic, many couples seem not to have either the common sense or the willingness to overcome the obstacles and to carry the burden which such mismatching demands. For this reason it seems true that most broken marriages have their seeds of failure planted before the marriage has ever taken place.

FAILURE IN SELECTION

Some evidence of a rather widespread mismatching is given in the various surveys available. In a nationwide poll asking married people whether they would again select the same spouse, only 52 per cent of the men and 47 per cent of the women stated they were certain they would again select the same partner.[2] It is significant that only about half of both husbands and wives were fully *certain* that they were properly mated. The director of this survey commented upon the fact that those who replied "might" and "don't know," comprised just about one out of four—the same proportion as the sometime divorce rate to the marriage rate. In a more limited study of 1,444 couples married 18 years or more, 42 per cent stated they disagreed frequently with their mates and 50 per cent asserted that they were unhappy with their

---

[2] *Public Opinion Quarterly,* Vol. XIII (Princeton, N. J.: Princeton University Press, 1949–50), p. 355.

partners.[3]   When 120 men and women were studied to find out the extent to which their partners in marriage were satisfying major personality needs, slightly more than a third indicated that their mates afforded half the satisfaction they had originally hoped marriage would bring.[4]   Apparently there is much we need to learn about making this important decision of spouse selection.

DESIRABLE CHARACTERISTICS FOR MARRIAGE PARTNERS

Despite the apparently widespread mismatching, some of the studies available indicate a thoughtful, mature and serious view of this problem.   Doubtless the romantic concept of love plays a role in distorting this calmer selection by blinding youth to the true nature of their chosen partners.   Some of the studies among Catholic college and high school students, in any event, indicate a fairly mature judgment in the selection of traits.

A good perspective on the purposes of marriage seems revealed in some studies of Catholic college and high school students; "willingness to rear a family" was the first trait desired in three studies and second in the one remaining study.[5]   "High moral standards" as a first, second and third choice is also revealing. However, it seems clear that these groups did not realize well enough the dangers of mixed religious marriages; the combined percentage for the four groups who thought the "same religion" essential in a life-partner was only a little more than 69 per cent. On the other hand, a genuinely wholesome sense of values is indicated by the large number who did not think "wealth" and "physical attractiveness" essential.

A similar study made among 674 secular university students

---

[3] R. B. Reed, *Social and Psychological Factors Affecting Fertility* (New York: Milbank Memorial Fund, 1947), VII, Tables 2 and 3, p. 390.

[4] Anselm Strauss, *A Study of Three Psychological Factors Affecting the Choice of a Mate* (Chicago: University of Chicago Libraries, Doctoral dissertation, 1945), p. 166.

[5] Studies by the author, of 186 seniors and of 202 male seniors in a Catholic University; also Sr. Mary Bridget, "A Study of the Attitudes of Some High School Juniors and Seniors toward Courtship and the Selection of a Marriage Partner" (Master's thesis, Catholic University of America, 1955), p. 69; also Norman Galloway, "An Investigation of the Knowledge and Attitudes of the Seniors of the Arts and Science School of a Catholic University Relative to Marriage" (Master's thesis, Catholic University of America, 1950), p. 128.

indicated like seriousness.   In the order of their importance the following characteristics were desired: stability and dependability, family-mindedness, considerateness, emotional maturity, good grooming and manners, and being affectionate.[6]   While both Catholic and non-Catholic students indicate a serious approach to this problem, it is clear that Catholic students lay greater emphasis on religious and moral qualities in a life-partner.   The "same religion" was among the first four most desired traits by Catholics, whereas the non-Catholic students placed "religious nature" twentieth on their list.   It remains unfortunate, however, that these and similar studies are largely confined to student populations and do not afford a knowledge of desired traits by the population as a whole.   Furthermore, they indicate what students think are desirable traits but not what traits and types they *actually select*.

How we select partners

Few areas have been more explored by research workers than the current pattern of partner selection.   Among the various findings one of the most scientifically established is that people tend to marry persons who live close to them (about 20 city blocks) geographically.   Nationally available statistics show that one-eighth of the men marry older women; one-fortieth marry women older by five years or more; one-tenth marry women of the same age; and three-fifths marry those less than five years younger.[7]   There is little change in the divorce rate where women are older by not more than five years and men are older by not more than ten years.   The interpreter of these data tells us that: "Where there are *great* gaps between married partners, there is a tendency to extremes in adjustment—either very good or very poor." [8]

It also seems evident from available studies that there is a tendency for people of approximately the same class, social status, religion and education to marry.   Women are likely to

---

[6] H. T. Christensen, *Marriage Analysis,* (New York: The Ronald Press Company, 1950), Fig. 4, p. 256.
[7] L. I. Dublin, *The Facts of Life* (New York: The Macmillan Company, 1951), pp. 44–45.
[8] *Ibid.,* p. 70.

marry slightly above themselves in education and men to marry slightly below, but in general, the higher the educational level of one partner, the higher that of the other. There is also a discernible tendency for women of lower economic classes to marry upward.

In a study comprising 233 items dealing with interests, attitudes, and likes, it was found that 140 of these showed a high degree of correlation.[9] In the 792 couples studied those marriages were happiest where such personality traits were similar. Other studies have indicated the likelihood of more men to select women who resemble their mothers than of women to select husbands resembling their fathers.

The picture one might obtain from these data is that, in general, considerable insight is shown by persons in selecting partners who are similar. However, these studies are not conclusive and their findings must be interpreted in the light of other data and other sources of information.

SELECTING A LIFE PARTNER

Despite the tremendous importance of the task of selecting a partner for marriage, many seem extremely ill-prepared for it. It is debatable whether most people bring to bear upon this most important decision as much thought or common sense as they do upon the purchase of a new suit, dress or coat. This seems true despite the fact that at this stage of human experience and knowledge, there is a vast store of information and wisdom available. Today we can learn the art of spouse-selection from understanding the nature of true love, the nature and purposes of marriage, the conditions for marriage, the nature of men and women, the role of expectations, background factors, psychological factors for happiness and the reasons for breakdown in marriage.

Love and selecting a partner

At the core of marriage is love and at the core of love is the craving for union between two human intellects, wills, hearts and bodies. Among other things, then, marriage is a merger of two

---

[9] L. Terman, *et al.*, *Psychological Factors in Marital Happiness* (New York: McGraw-Hill Book Company, Inc., 1938).

human personalities. This merger, however, cannot be a metaphysical or physical one; it can only be a similarity bordering on identity. We cannot speak of two minds, two wills, two hearts, two bodies that *are one;* we can only speak of two minds, wills, hearts, bodies that *act as one.*

Clearly this shows the need for similarity in each of these respects. Adjustment to each other will be easier or more difficult, depending upon the degree of likeness or difference. For similarity of intellects each partner must embrace the same principles, attitudes, ideas, viewpoints and sense of values, at least on all really important matters; it implies a similar degree of intelligence, cultural development or at least an equal ambition for such; it particularly indicates unity of conviction on matters religious and moral.

A union of wills can be interpreted as meaning similar ambitions, determinations, goals in life. The partner whose chief drive is to amass wealth will have little in common with a partner whose all-consuming aim is more education. On the other hand, two partners with the same sense of values will effect a union of wills in that very similarity.

Since we are creatures who act on the basis of emotions more often than of intelligence, the union of hearts is also important. Many of our deepest interests, leisure time pursuits and hobbies are chiefly emotional preferences. For this reason the enthusiast for high fidelity recordings of symphonic music may find little emotional rapport with the partner who prefers popular music. Affection, too, has a large emotional content so that those are best matched who are capable of equal affection and who know how to express it.

The merger of marriage finds its consummation in the embrace of physical union. Those devoid of such attraction for each other will enter a marriage that is hazardous. But physical matching implies more than a mutual attraction; a similar intensity of sex drives and proper attitudes and actions alone can effect that completely satisfying union which is the end product of the love of two total personalities. Despite the necessary reservations of the premarital relationship, the sex potential of individuals is often discernible; we speak quite widely of people who are "highly sexed," "sexually apathetic" and so forth.

Though much research on this phase of marriage should be done, available data tend to confirm the position that likes should marry. When 476 Catholic husbands and wives were asked how important similar tastes and interests were in marriage, over 87 per cent replied either "important" or "very important." [10] In another instance, a battery of tests given to 80 married couples revealed that persons tend to marry those who are similar. [11]

Marriage and selecting a partner

Perhaps there is no aspect of life from which common sense has departed more generally than selecting a marriage partner. In other areas of life, as a rule, basic good judgment prevails; people generally will select a person with the qualities which will serve the purposes intended. However, the same professional or business man who will with the utmost care select a secretary with the exact qualifications needed, will often choose as a life-partner a wife seriously inadequate for the task of wifehood and motherhood.

It seems that being in love is so dominant that all other factors are ignored. But what sensible woman would engage a maid whom she liked very much but who could neither cook, nor keep house, nor launder! Were we to select partners in marriage with an eye on their ability to serve marital goals, we would have fewer unhappy and unsuccessful marriages.

With procreation of children a primary goal of marriage, an evidently desirable trait is the willingness to raise a family and a genuine fondness for children. In this day of family limitation, this assumes special importance. The education of children being an equally basic goal, spouses should be evaluated in the light of this purpose also. A good educator is a person of sincere religious living, whose example is wholesome, who understands human nature, who can relate effectively to others and stimulate them, and who maintains a painstaking interest in the

---

10 Hugh Dunn, S.J., *A Study of Some Catholic Marital Attitudes, Practices and Problems with Special Reference to the Implication for Premarital Instructions* (Washington, D. C.: The Catholic University of America Press, 1956), Table 36, p. 104.

11 M. Schooley, "Personality Resemblances Among Married Couples," *Journal of Abnormal and Social Psychology*, Vol. XXXI, No. 340 (1936).

education of his charges. Marital dissension arising either from differences of opinion about the education of children or an apathy toward it by one partner, appear frequently in marriage counseling practice. Apparently, the educative qualities of partners are often overlooked in spouse selection. One is led to suspect that some of our available studies on factors in marriage failure are seriously defective since they fail to disclose the frequency of this factor. Associated with the educative aspect is the goal of personality development. Since few persons are influenced by any other person more than by their life-partner, it would seem an important consideration to select the type of partner who will stimulate the development of their religious and moral characters, instill good personality traits and promote educational and cultural attainment.

Among other personal goals of marriage are companionship and mutual assistance. The man who cannot resist the lure of television long enough to dispel his wife's lonesomeness with attention is not a likely companion; nor is he who prefers nights out alone to the exclusion of almost any night out together. The inflexible woman whose major leisure time pursuit is complaining and nagging, will fail equally to play the companionship role which marriage demands. Some of the richest personal rewards of life together are the encouragement, the understanding, the morale building and the sharing in mutual work interests; to serve these purposes definite qualities of mind and heart are needed.

The conditions necessary for marital success should not be ignored. The demands of modern marriage necessitate good physical and emotional health. Economic stability and adequacy of income will act as a potent, though partial, antidote to the prevalent temptation to unnatural family limitation. Maturity alone will bring to marriage the requisite sense of responsibility, self-confidence and rightful adult independence from in-law interferences; emotional maturity will eliminate the blind anger, raging jealousies and adolescent sensitiveness which ruin marital harmony. Only a character based on solid principles and strength of will together with the possession of a set of correct attitudes toward marriage and family living, can give that assurance which all want in their partners for life.

Men, women and marriage

Men and women are called by the philosophers the "efficient cause" of marriage since it is they who are the parties to it. Nature seems, at first sight, to have tricked men and women in that, according to Chesterton, they are naturally incompatible. However, the apparent incompatibility arising from their differing natures, if it is understood and accommodated, is really the basis of a deeper life together. They can act as complements to each other, supplying each other's deficiencies, moderating each other's weaknesses and developing each other's points of strength.

The void in each personality make-up creates an attraction to the person who can fill that need. The quick-tempered individual is not likely to find the same inclination to another "hothead" that he will to an amiable, meek person. It is through such matching that the quick temper may, in time, find itself moderated, while the overly meek person may learn to experience a righteous anger. In this sense, opposites attract. If men tend to be stern and incline to justice while women are more tender and prone to mercy, these differences make for compatibility precisely because they fill a void in each personality. "It is this incompleteness which prompts a being to part, as it were, with its autonomy and seek its perfection by becoming a whole . . . it is man's incompleteness which is the fundamental of his membership in society" [12]—including the domestic society of the family.

Scientific inquiry is tending to confirm this position held by St. Thomas. A study of 423 engaged or recently married people disclosed that a person's major personality needs may influence his choice of life-partner. Some of the needs reflected were attention, prestige, affection, approval or acceptance.[13] Another student of this problem concluded that "In mate-selection each individual seeks within his or her field of eligibles that person who

---

[12] J. F. Cox, *A Thomistic Analysis of the Social Order* (Washington, D. C.: Catholic University of America Press, 1943), p. 45, interpreting *The Summa Theologica,* Vol. I Pt. 2, Q. 11, art. 2 ad. 2.
[13] A. Strauss, "Personality Needs and Marital Choice," *Social Forces,* Vol. XXV (1947), p. 332.

gives the greatest promise of providing him or her with maximum need gratification." [14]

Expectations and partner selection

Each partner should also have similar expectations of marriage. These expectations lie at the basis of marital success or failure. They are largely conditioned by early education and environment. The religion, ethnic group, social class, economic group, and general culture in which one has been reared all contribute to these expectations. For this reason, good matching requires that "like marry like" in these respects.

In a mixed culture such as ours the likelihood is great that partners with different backgrounds and varying expectations will meet and marry. There may be differing or often conflicting notions of the nature and purposes of marriage, the role each partner is to play, the desirability of children, the education and training of children, the handling of family finances, the role of in-laws and many similar factors. Marriage counselors daily witness marriages broken because of different expectations—persons who expected maturity in their partners and found them still tied to their mother's apron strings; the wives who anticipated usurping the husband's headship, and found their partners insisting upon their right to manage the family; the men who preferred expensive automobiles to a comfortable home and found wives who wanted a sizable and attractive home rather than a pretentious car; the partners who anticipated a warm welcome of their own blood relatives and discovered that their spouses resented the in-laws or refused to associate with them; the wives who expected love and affection but found after marriage that they were being taken for granted; the husbands who hoped for understanding and found only nagging and criticism; the partners who wanted a number of children and found their spouses insisting upon family limitation; the wives who expected their partners to share their religious living with them and came to realize that their husbands think religion is "mostly for the wife and kids." Countless similar hopes are daily dashed against the rocks of

---

[14] R. F. Winch, *The Modern Family* (New York: Henry Holt & Company, Inc., 1952), p. 406.

reality, leading to disillusionment and frustration and eventually to the divorce court.

Background factors

At this stage of inquiry there are quite a number of studies which have tried to determine the factors in childhood, adolescence and adult premarital life which promise a successful marriage.[15] Some of these factors would indicate that the best bet in a marriage partner would be one from a small town or the country, raised in a large family, who was a practitioner of some religious creed, whose childhood was a happy one with warm and affectionate relationships with his family. Such a prospect would be raised with firm discipline, would not engage in petting, would have adequate sex education, and would marry with the approval of his parents.[16]

Psychological traits and mate selection

Similar studies have indicated the dangers of certain traits in a life-mate which seem to be related to happiness or unhappiness in marriage. In one of these studies the following traits were found:

Being touchy or grouchy
Losing temper easily
Fighting to get one's own way
Being critical of others
Being careless of other's feelings
Chafing under discipline
Rebelling against orders
Showing dislikes
Being easily affected by praise or blame
Lacking self-confidence
Dominating the opposite sex
Having little interest in old people, children, charity, uplift activities
Being unconventional in attitudes on religion, drinking and sex conduct

---

[15] C. Kirkpatrick, *What Science Says About Happiness in Marriage* (Minneapolis: Burgess Publishing Company, 1947).

[16] Factors taken from studies of Bernard, Burgess and Cottrell, Burgess and Wallin, Davis, Hamilton, Hart, Kirkpatrick, Popenoe, Schroeder, and Terman.

Being often in a state of excitement
Having alternate moods with no apparent cause.[17]

The same investigator has discovered some of the characteristics of happy husbands.

Happily married men show evidence of an even and stable emotional tone.   Their most characteristic reaction to others is that of cooperation. . . .   In money matters they are saving and cautious.   Conservative attitudes are strongly characteristic of them.   They usually have a favorable attitude toward religion.[18]

Some traits usually associated with happy wives were also disclosed.

Happily married women, as a group, are characterized by kindly attitudes towards others and by the expectation of kindly attitudes in return.   They do not easily take offense and are not unduly concerned about the impressions they make upon others. . . .   They are cooperative, do not object to subordinate roles and are not annoyed by advice from others.   Missionary and ministering attitudes are frequently evidenced in their responses.   They enjoy activities that bring educational or pleasurable opportunities to others and like to do things for the dependent and underprivileged. . . .   In religion, morals and politics they tend to be conservative and conventional. Their expressed attitudes imply a quiet self-assurance and a decidedly optimistic outlook upon life.[19]

Breakdown factors and spouse selection

A final approach to the selection of a partner in marriage is that of selecting a person who is devoid of traits characteristic of those who fail in marriage.   The various investigations of breakdown factors will help decide whom *not to marry*.   Some of these traits are: little preparation for marriage, immaturity, irresponsibility, selfishness, incorrect attitudes toward sex, undue attachment to in-laws, strong tendency to drink, inability to handle money wisely, tendency to nag, lack of affection, being a spoiled child, suspicious and jealous attitudes, being a perfectionist, irreligious or lax in religion.[20]

---

[17] Terman, *op. cit.*, chap. v.
[18] *Ibid.*, p. 155.
[19] *Ibid.*, p. 146.
[20] For further factors in breakdown see Chapter 18.

Helps in selecting a partner

Doubtless many who are selecting a life-partner are concerned about the snares laid by our culture. Some considerations gleaned from experience, science and religion are available to help them to a secure choice of a mate.

1. Those dates who clearly lack any one *important* trait of a good partner, should be avoided or at least never permitted to develop into a steady date. Actually most people do exclude others from their dating experience but not always for reasons that are related to their being good partners. It is, of course, unrealistic to expect to find a partner with no defects of any kind. On the other hand, if these defects are of such a nature as to make the goals of marriage unattainable or extremely difficult of attainment, success in marriage is not probable.

2. Those selected for courting should be chosen in the light of the serious purposes of marriage and not merely on the basis of love or some superficial qualities such as appearance or charm.

3. Every effort should be made to learn the reactions of a prospective spouse in *every* area of life—work, religion, affection, recreation.

4. Proper precautions should be employed to keep romantic and affectional development within moderation. Once two unsuited people fall in love, *blind, irrational* mismatching is almost inescapable.

5. Getting acquainted with relatives is perhaps even more important today than formerly. In-law problems are on the increase. Actually one marries not only an individual but his relatives also.

6. Marriage is not a reform school. Men and women do not usually change their basic personality or habits in marriage. On the contrary, such habits can lead marriage toward success or failure.

7. Deceit in courtship is extremely dangerous. It can lead to much disillusionment and mutual criticism later. In the "pursuit" of courtship deceit is often employed.

8. Despite the wisdom of consulting those more experienced (such as one's parents), the independence of our era is moving youth away from this practice. In one study we are told that

"Approximately half (51.3 per cent) of the 975 ﹐
fifths (42.3 per cent) of the 988 women from wh﹐
mation was obtained reported they did not consu﹐
the wisdom of their choice." The same study fo﹐
rental judgments were correct in a high percentage ﹐

9. A good guarantee of correct spouse-selectic﹐
confessor with whom the problem of courtship and﹐
tion can be discussed. The insight of such a cor﹐
him in an unusually good position to give sane advi﹐
solid judgments.

10. Frequent assistance at Mass, reception of th﹐
and prayer are *most important* however. None﹐
better advisor and guide than the Holy Spirit—﹐
knowledge, wisdom, understanding and counsel.

PARTNERS IN MIXED RELIGIONS

A spouse-selection problem requiring special atte﹐
of matching with mixed religions. In 1950 26.4 ﹐
Catholic marriages were mixed ones.[22] When three ﹐ u﹐ ﹐e﹐
valid Catholic marriages in the nation involve mixeu religions,
there is reason for concern.[23] This concern becomes heightened
when we have every reason to believe that the proportion will
increase in the future. The breakdown of ethnic barriers, the
more frequent contacts between peoples of varying religions, the
fact that children of mixed marriages tend to enter mixed marriages themselves, the increasingly tolerant attitudes toward
differing religions and the individualism in the choice of a partner
are factors contributing to a greater number of mixed religious
marriages.[24]

Church's attitude

This increase in mixed marriages is alarming in view of the
Church's rigid attitude against them. Canon law (Canon 1060)

[21] E. W. Burgess and P. Wallin, *Engagement and Marriage* (Chicago: J. B. Lippincott Company, 1953), p. 178, p. 562.

[22] B. G. Mulvaney, "Catholic Population Revealed in Catholic Baptisms," *American Ecclesiastical Review*, Vol. CXXXIII, No. 3, (September 1955), Table 5, p. 192.

[23] J. Thomas, "Are They Marrying Their Own," *Catholic World*, Vol. CLXXIV (November 1951), p. 125.

[24] *Ibid.*, p. 128.

emphatically states that the Church *most severely forbids* them. Doubtless the fact that dispensations are sometimes granted induces many Catholics to assume that the Church has a lenient attitude. This is not correct. On the contrary, *even after she grants a dispensation the Church withholds her approval.* This is evident from her refusal to permit the marriage to occur at Mass and her refusal to impart the nuptial blessing upon the couple.

Her deep concern and anxiety can be seen in the promises made by the non-Catholic partner. These promises include non-interference with the practice of the faith by the Catholic party, adhering to the permanency of marriage, the baptism and rearing of all children in the Catholic faith, the rejection of unnatural birth control practices. The Catholic party must promise among other things, to baptize and rear all children in the Catholic faith; to labor for the conversion of the spouse by example, prayer, and the use of the sacraments; to refrain from unnatural family limitation. A recent complication in this respect is the growing rejection by various non-Catholic denominations of the sacredness and binding power of these promises.

Many mistakenly believe that these promises are the only requirement for a dispensation. But the Church also requires assurance that these promises will be kept and that there be a just reason for a dispensation such as to avoid grave scandal.

Certainly, the mere fact that the two love each other would not constitute an adequate reason for a mixed marriage. It is indeed questionable whether many of the Catholics who enter a mixed marriage have a sufficient reason to justify this course of action. It follows logically from these principles that a Catholic who enters a mixed marriage without a grave and just reason commits a serious sin.[25]

Effects on married couples

The Church *severely forbids* mixed marriages because of her experience with and observation of them for almost twenty centuries. She has seen their dire consequences and has continued to oppose them even when most others thought her motives based upon a sense of snobbish superiority. In recent years, however, one after another of the Protestant denominations have, as a result of similar observation, come to agree with the Church.

---

25 F. J. Connell, "Some Obscure Points on Premarital Mortality," *op. cit.*

Science also has interested itself in this question and has come to confirm the Catholic position.

One of the Church's traditional reasons for opposition is the knowledge that the faith of the Catholic is often weakened or lost entirely. A study of 29,581 mixed marriages tended to confirm this position; 25 per cent never attended Church, while another 20 per cent attended only occasionally.[26] The Bishop's Committee found that about 30 per cent of the Catholics in mixed marriages lose their faith.[27] In a study made by questionnaires sent to all pastors of the United Lutheran Church in America it was reported that out of a total of 2,048 marriages between Lutherans and Catholics, 597 of the Catholics joined the Lutheran Church. It was also disclosed that in about 15 per cent of all Lutheran mixed marriages the spouses either left all religion or the status of their religious living was unknown.[28] Another study indicated that out of 480 Catholic mixed marriages, 10½ per cent missed Mass regularly while seven per cent missed their Easter duties.[29]

Another danger to the couples is the threat to marital stability. It is well established that mixed religious marriages are broken at a higher rate than marriages between members of the same faith.

This conclusion finds ample justification in three studies carried out in widely separated areas of the country. Landis in Michigan (4,108 families), Bell in Maryland (13,528 families) and Weeks in Washington (5,548 families), obtained the following information. In all three studies, approximately 5 per cent of the Catholic and Jewish marriages, 15 per cent of mixed Catholic-Protestant, 8 per cent of the Protestant marriages, and 18 per cent of the marriages in which there was no religious faith, had ended in divorce or separation. . . . Unfortunately, much of the value of these studies is lost because we are not told whether the marriages involving Catholics were valid or

---

[26] J. L. Thomas, "Mixed Marriages—So What?," *Social Order*, Vol. II, No. 4 (April 1952), p. 155–160.

[27] *A Factual Study of Mixed Marriages* (Washington, D. C.: National Catholic Welfare Conference, 1943), p. 14.

[28] Board of the Social Missions of the United Lutheran Church in America, *A Study of Mixed Marriages in the United Lutheran Church in America,* (New York: United Lutheran Publication House), p. 5.

[29] L. I. Dublin, "New Light on Mixed Marriages," *Ecclesiastical Review* (April 1930), pp. 413–414.

not. . . . We have made a detailed analysis of 1,284 *valid* broken mixed marriages. . . . Religious quarrels accounted for only 10.4 per cent of the broken marriages.[30]

In a Lutheran study of 2,674 mixed marriages the following was found:

TABLE 7

MARITAL ADJUSTMENT OF LUTHERANS AND NON-PROTESTANT
MIXED MARRIAGES

Status	Total	Percentage
HAPPY	1414	52.8
MEDIUM	782	29.2
UNHAPPY	288	10.7
BREAK-UP	190	7.4

* Board of the Social Missions of the United Lutheran Church in America, *A Study of Mixed Marriages in the United Lutheran Church in America* (New York: United Lutheran Publication House), p. 5.

Studies in other nations show similar dangers from mixed religions in marriage. In Zurich, Switzerland, the divorce rate was 900 out of every 100,000 marriages, but the mixed marriage divorce rate was 1,425 out of 100,000.[31] In Hamburg, Germany, the divorce rate for 1,000 Protestant marriages was 7.8 per cent; for Catholic marriages it was 7.2 per cent, but for mixed marriages it was 12.1 per cent.[32]

Apparently the irreconcilable issue of contraceptives is a growing factor in breakdown of interfaith marriages. In 78 broken mixed marriages whenever sex was alleged as a breakdown factor, neither sex perversion nor rejection were responsible; in every instance the use of contraceptives was the disruptive factor.[33]

The effects of mixed religions upon marital harmony have

---

30 J. Thomas, "The Pattern of Marriage Among Catholics," *Marriage Education and Counseling*, ed. A. H. Clemens (Washington, D. C.: Catholic University of America Press, 1951), p. 54.

31 P. Popenoe, *Family Life*, Vol. X, No. 8 (August 1950), p. 6.

32 *Schmolers Jahrbuch, Für Gesetzgebung Verwaltung und Volkfwirtschaft im Deutschen Reich*, Vol. 53, p. 33.

33 G. Brinkman, "Some Factors Involved in the Breakdown of Catholic Marriages in Several Eastern Dioceses" (Master's thesis, Catholic University of America, July 1953), p. 57.

been noted in a study of the children of 295 marriages made by a non-Catholic marriage expert. These children indicated that in 18.2 per cent of the cases religious differences had interfered with the marriage "somewhat" and in 5.4 per cent "greatly." [34]

Not the least distressing effect is the intense spiritual loneliness which every sincere Catholic party experiences. Days, such as the First Communion of a child, which should be occasions of maximum spiritual joy are usually marred by the clear knowledge that the day is spiritually meaningless or is interpreted as a form of idolatry by the non-Catholic spouse. It is on such occasions that the sincere Catholic realizes with great acuteness that he or she is treading the road of Catholic spirituality alone.

Effects upon the children

Evidence shows that the primary purpose of marriage, having children, is defeated by mixed religions. A study of 1,805 families showed that "the number of small-sized families is greater among parents one of which is a Catholic." [35] Among 6,551 native white couples in Indianapolis, it was found that childlessness was lowest among Catholic couples (14.8 per cent, and highest among Protestant-Catholic marriages (25.6 per cent).[36] Among 1,284 broken valid mixed marriages, 40 per cent were found childless.[37]

One of the most tragic effects is upon the religious training of children. In the study just cited of Catholic mixed marriages, 97 per cent of the children never went to Catholic schools, 40 per cent were either unbaptized or baptized as Protestants, and in 30 per cent the non-Catholic had broken the pledge in regard to the religious education of the children. A survey from a non-Catholic source indicated similar effects—18.4 per cent of the children were not baptized and 45.6 per cent were brought up

---

[34] J. T. Landis, "Marriages of Mixed and Non-Mixed Religious Faiths," *American Sociological Review* (June 1949), pp. 401–407.

[35] Sr. Leo Marie, "Is the Catholic Birth Rate Declining?" *American Catholic Sociological Review,* Vol. V, No. 3 (October 1944), p. 182.

[36] C. V. Kiser and P. K. Whelpton, "Social and Psychological Factors Affecting Fertility," *Milbank Memorial Fund Quarterly,* Vol. XXII, No. 1, p. 93.

[37] J. Thomas, "Mixed Marriages—So What?", pp. 155–160.

as Protestants.[38]   In Holland it was disclosed that half of the children in mixed marriages were brought up with no religion, one-fifth as Protestants and one-third as Catholics.[39]

Mixed marriages and the future

In spite of the clear agreement between religion and scientific studies on the disastrous effects of mixed religions in marriage, they are continuing to increase.   If we are to entertain any hope for a reversal of this trend, it will be imperative to restore to Catholic youth the deep spiritual meaning of marriage.   Its high vocation in the Mystical Body of Christ and its service as a pathway to holiness, it would seem, need to be appreciated anew. The unrealistic notion that mixed dating is practicable should also be changed.   The home, the school and the parish could play a major role, not only by fostering correct attitudes toward dangers of mixed marriage, but also by providing increased opportunities for social mingling among our Catholic youth.

PARTNER SELECTION AND THE DIVINE PLAN

One of the most striking phenomena in the plan of all creation is the marvelous adaptation of proper means to established goals. If birds were intended to fly, an all-wise Providence gave them wings; if fish were to swim, they have been given fins.   This same adaptation of means to ends is part of the Divine Plan for marriage.   If marriage has certain clearly defined purposes and goals, spouses must be chosen who can serve as fit partners in attaining those goals.   Only those with the required traits of body, heart, mind, personality, character and religion are to be selected for the high and serious purposes of marriage.   Matching people with differing religions clearly destroys the high purposes which belong to marriage.   Non-Catholic fathers or mothers (even if sincerely religious in their own beliefs) can only be expected to serve inadequately as educators of their partners and children in a religion in which they themselves have not been trained and educated.

---

[38] M. H. Leiffer, "Mixed Marriages and the Children," *Christian Century,* (January 26, 1949), pp. 106–108.

[39] *Lumen Vitae* (July-September 1949).

8

Engagement and Honeymoon

SINCE AN engagement is a serious promise to marry, it presupposes that both parties are ready for marriage. It is a time intended for the immediate preparation for marriage. The engagement period is the time when any problems should be settled. Attempting to resolve mutual problems acts as a trial adjustment experience and may help judge the extent to which the two are suited. Frequent bickering or an inability to come to mutually agreeable solutions would not make a marriage very promising.

The significance of the engagement period seems evident in available studies. Most successful marriages have been preceded by an engagement period, whereas elopements prove extremely hazardous. Successful marriages clearly follow on the heels of successful engagements.

There are both informal and formal engagements. The first is the usual type in our culture; it is a simple understanding and promise between the two parties that they will become married. Usually it is associated with the giving of a diamond ring to the girl, though in recent years fraternity pins or other substitutes have been used by students.

A more formal and more binding type of engagement is being reactivated within Catholic circles in recent years. The law of the Church (Canon 1017) provides for a *solemn engagement* for those who wish to avail themselves of it. The promise is made in writing in the presence of witnesses and signed by both partners usually before the pastor. This type of engagement obliges one in conscience to marry the person named and on the date promised. It cannot be broken unless serious reasons are present and it gives the right to claim damages for failure to execute the promise. Even informal engagements permit claims for damages when broken in some states. A growing Catholic custom is to enter into a solemn engagement with liturgical rites or at a special Mass.[1]

THINGS TO DISCUSS AND SETTLE

Many successful marriages are preceded by successful engagements because an engagement properly used will result in settling many differences and problems before the marriage. Every problem solved before marriage is an adjustment rendered unnecessary after marriage. For this reason there should be completely frank and honest discussions between partners before marriage on all problems and especially on those which may be particularly difficult or upon which there is not an immediate and complete understanding between the two. When 476 Catholic husbands and wives, married ten years or longer, were asked the problems which should be agreed upon during engagement, they gave the following answers (listed in the order of frequency mentioned):

Primary purpose of marriage
Finances
Religious practice
Outside interests
In-laws
Goals in family living
Cooperation
Standard of living

Wife working
Place of residence
Rights and duties of partners
Adjustments
Sanctity of marriage
Child rearing
Religious training of children [2]

---

[1] *Promised in Christ* (Loveland, Ohio: Grailville, 1955).

[2] Hugh Dunn, S.J., *A Study of Some Catholic Marital Attitudes, Practices and Problems with Special Reference to the Implication for Premarital Instructions* (Washington, D. C.: The Catholic University of America Press, 1956), Table 12, p. 30.

SOME PROBLEMS IN ENGAGEMENT

One of the chief concerns of engaged couples should be the length of the engagement. Various studies indicate that problems of chastity increase as engagements are prolonged. The 476 Catholic husbands and wives previously mentioned listed the difficulty of remaining chaste *most frequently* among engagement problems.[3] In another study of 576 engaged couples it was found that "intercourse is somewhat more characteristic of the engagements of longer duration . . . the chances are about fifty-fifty that it will occur in engagements which run more than 15 months. . . ."[4] It seems that today many think that with engagement certain liberties, previously sinful, become proper. This is not true, however; being engaged in no way changes the morality of sex for the partners. On the other hand, it is evident that two people sufficiently in love to promise marriage will experience an extremely strong physical attraction which remains a constant danger to them. For this reason, engagements longer than necessary are not wise.

The high rate of broken engagements should also induce caution. From 30 to 50 per cent of engagements are broken, according to some studies. This can only mean that the selection of partners is not being done with sufficient care; or, that many become engaged much too frivolously only to realize it before marriage. Youth would be particularly well advised to be wary of a partner who, without any compelling reason, defers the date of marriage and needlessly prolongs the engagement.

Perhaps one of the chief worries confronting engaged people is the question of revealing secrets about themselves to prospective life-mates. It is well to recognize that one's partner has no right to know all the facts of one's private life; but some of the facts which intimately have or will have a bearing on marriage must be revealed. On the other hand, telling lies about oneself is neither moral nor wise. Those beset with anxieties about such secrets may find the following useful:

---

[3] *Ibid.* Table 51, p. 143.
[4] E. W. Burgess and P. Wallin, *Engagement and Marriage* (Chicago: J. B. Lippincott Company, 1953), p. 335.

1. "A person suffering from a disease that would render cohabitation and sexual relations dangerous to the health of the consort, has a strict obligation in justice to inform the one whom he is planning to marry of this condition.

2. "One who knows that he is sterile, is bound to reveal this fact to the prospective spouse." [5]

3. There is no moral obligation to reveal the fact that one is illegitimate; but it may be best to reveal it if it is likely to become known after marriage and cause serious friction.

4. Sexual transgressions, even fornication or adultery, need not and usually should not be told one's partner.

5. A pregnancy due to relations with another man would bind the girl to disclose her condition to her prospective partner.

6. One need not reveal that he has been adopted. But again, it may be wise to do so if it may become known later and cause serious friction.[6]

7. Public disgrace or "serious moral defects of an external nature (for example, drunkenness, addiction to drugs and so forth)" and "large outstanding debts which he cannot pay" impose a strict obligation to be revealed.

8. "There is no obligation to reveal secret defects which do not make the marriage intolerable or harmful, even though they do render it less desirable." [7]

PREPARING FOR MARRIAGE

The engagement period should be employed for completing one's preparation for marriage. Because of the importance of physical factors, a medical examination of both parties is most desirable. This is demanded by the laws of many states and its value is increasingly recognized by couples themselves. Neither legally exacted nor generally recognized is the desirability of a psychological examination. Yet it is becoming clear that more marriages are intolerably burdened or completely broken by emotional than by physical disease. When half of the nation's hospital beds are occupied by mentally ill patients, urging such psychological attention seems appropriate.

---

[5] J. F. Connell, "Some Obscure Points on Premarital Morality" (Unpublished workshop lecture, Catholic University of America, June 13–24, 1952).

[6] *Ibid.*

[7] E. F. Healy, *Marriage Guidance* (Chicago: Loyola University Press, 1948), pp. 61–62.

Engagement is the time for "putting the finishing touches" to one's education for marriage. Both men and women should conserve their financial resources for the heavy demands ahead and set up a system of handling finances after marriage. Sex education should receive its completion in great detail just prior to marriage. Both men and women might perfect their skills in those home arts and crafts which later they will be expected to employ. Most important, however, is a more extensive knowledge and appreciation of the religious and moral implications of the married state. According to studies made, this type of knowledge is not widespread and yet it is easily available. Because premarital instructions given by the priest are sometimes limited in number is no indication that they are fully adequate preparation for marriage. When 200 Catholic husbands and wives were asked whether the average Catholic couple is well equipped for marriage at the time of the wedding, only 15 answered "Yes"; 157 said "No" and 28 "didn't know." [8]

It is imperative that engaged couples develop that high sense of dedication and vocation enjoyed by priests, brothers and nuns prior to their ordination or the taking of vows. Were couples to sense the spirituality of the married state, they would doubtless approach it with greater devotion, prayer and the use of the sacraments.

WEDDING PLANS

Although it is not expected that Catholic couples will depart entirely from the customs of our times (many of which are commendable), it is well to recognize that wedding plans today are largely the result of the materialism and the secularism of the age. Interviews of some 900 couples married in 1949–1950 in New Haven, Connecticut disclosed that the average cost of the engagement ring was $435, that of the wedding $948 and of the wedding trip $320 for those being married the first time.[9] Since this study was based on a sample including low income

[8] John Knott, "The Cana Conference Movement" (Master's thesis, Catholic University of America, August 1947), p. 63.

[9] A. B. Hollingshead, "Marital Status and Wedding Behavior," *Marriage and Family Living,* Vol. XIV, No. 4 (November 1952), pp. 308–311.

couples, the figures seem extravagantly high. Yet it seems evident that romantic blindness and "keeping up with the Joneses" induce many couples to plan weddings meant to impress friends and acquaintances. Often they spend sums of money entirely disproportionate to either income or social status. This shows an attitude largely unmindful of the huge economic responsibilities awaiting the couple after marriage. Many of the same couples will later resort to family limitation on the plea of inadequate means.

Associated with this wedding extravaganza is the intense preoccupation months in advance, especially by the bride and her mother, with the numerous details involved in such an event. An appropriate attention to the worldly aspects of a wedding does not conflict with Catholic tradition so long as it is in keeping with one's income and position. But the exhaustive preparations that allow only a minimum of time or thought to the spiritual aspects of the great sacramental day are a product of our secularism.

Traditional Catholic customs have, in recent years, enjoyed a revival and are tending to reduce this exclusively secular approach to marriage. Wedding announcements are appearing with religious symbolisms and wording. Cards inviting attendants to participate at the table of the Lord are being sent along with breakfast invitations. Those who realize that their wedding day will have them both receiving and administering a great sacrament, are content with nothing less than a Solemn High Mass. Consciousness of the deep spirituality of the wedding day is leading others to defer night-before celebrations to the night after the wedding. Others possessed of both religious insight and natural wisdom make a retreat immediately prior to the wedding. This affords the spiritual approach proper to one of the great sacramental days of a lifetime and also insures that rest and relaxation for the wedding day that is deemed important even by nonreligious persons.

The Council of Trent has reminded us that a "Wedding is a holy thing; and it should be dealt with holily." Leo XIII wrote:

This religious character of marriage, its sublime signification of grace and the union between Christ with the Church, evidently requires that those about to marry should show a holy reverence toward it, and zealously endeavor to make their marriage approach as nearly as possible the archetype of Christ and the Church.[10]

There are always necessary details in planning the wedding, such as obtaining a license and, in some localities, undergoing the legally required physical examinations. Arrangements should be made with the girl's pastor at least a month in advance, as certain documents such as the baptismal certificates must be obtained. Though many do not, every couple should receive a series of instructions that can be arranged by contacting the priest early enough.

THE HONEYMOON

As well as the romantic concept of love, our culture has given us the conviction that a honeymoon is necessary for marital success. These two concepts are probably associated. The honeymoon pattern common to most American marriages is by no means a universal phenomenon. It is, of course, an extremely enjoyable experience and a useful one, though in no sense of the word a necessary one. It facilitates the making of early adjustments in an atmosphere of relaxation and joy; and it is a memory long to be treasured by those truly in love.

However, the honeymoon's usefulness in adjustment is limited. The adjustments made to a relaxed partner in the glamorous environment of Niagara Falls will prove quite different from those to be made to a fatigued working husband or wife in a small home. If the experience of the honeymoon is "out of this world," it is also somewhat unrealistic.

Those really unable to afford this type of marital vacation need not feel that their marriage will be impaired as a result. Here, as with the wedding itself, there is a tendency to spend foolishly money which could be much more usefully employed for the obligations of marriage. To those able to afford it, the customary honeymoon is a supreme delight but it remains a luxury.

One of the most important aspects of the honeymoon is the

-----

[10] Leo XIII, "Christian Marriage," *Social Wellsprings* (Milwaukee: The Bruce Publishing Company, 1943), Vol. I; also *Acta Sanctae Sedis*, Vol. XI, pp. 372–379.

initial adjustment pattern which emerges. The intensity of emotional and romantic love may lead to expectations certain to be shattered later by the harsh realities of everyday life. The wife who anticipates that her married life will have the same romantic intensity of the honeymoon, is still quite adolescent. The husband who expects the complete attention from his wife on the honeymoon to continue after she has several children to attend is equally immature. Both have failed to see that the honeymoon environment is unrealistic contrasted to the workaday world in which their marriage must eventually weave its adjustment pattern. And neither has recognized that while love grows in depth, it also changes its mode of expression. Romance is rightfully a *permanent* part of every marriage but its nature, frequency and expression must and will change with the passage of time, increasing age and the burdens of married life.

PREPARATION IN THE DIVINE PLAN

Marriage was not devised to permit success without careful preparation and planning. An important part of this preparation is that immediately before marriage. Plans should include preparation in both a worldly and in a deeply spiritual manner. Like a vocation to the religious life, the marriage vocation should also be approached by an increased intensity of religious living. The wedding, being a sacrament, should be treated as such and accorded the full splendor of its liturgical meaning. The honeymoon, though not a part of the Divine Plan for Marriage, can serve useful purposes but it is at the same time fraught with certain very real dangers.

9

Success in Marriage

Every couple setting off on their honeymoon should staunchly hope for the success of their marriage. To this end they should be ready to make certain adjustments. However, not every couple starting married life has a correct notion of what success really means. As studies show, many couples use as their criteria for judging success personal happiness, love and companionship, agreement and compatibility, sexual satisfaction, and the absence of separation or divorce.[1] There is no suggestion here of anything other than adjustment of the partners to each other. For instance, they might conceivably enjoy the above adjustments and yet fail seriously in their religious living or as parents. In fact, the most recent tendency is not to speak of adjustment in marriage but merely of *interpersonal competence*. Obviously, the important adjustment implied in this terminology is that between husbands and wives. A better concept of success was shown in a study of 476 Catholic husbands and wives who in addition to the above named criteria included children, Christian family life, the salvation of one's soul and the training of the children as components of success in marriage.[2]

---

[1] E. Burgess and P. Wallin, *Engagement and Marriage* (Chicago: J. B. Lippincott Company, 1953), p. 484.

[2] Hugh Dunn, S.J., *A Study of Some Catholic Marital Attitudes, Practices and Problems with Special Reference to the Implication for Premarital Instructions* (Washington, D. C.: The Catholic University of America Press, 1956), Table 30, p. 90.

MEANING OF SUCCESS

Adjustment implies changes in attitudes and actions to achieve certain goals. Success, in turn, implies the attainment of the rightful purposes of marriage. These are goals beyond the subjective ones of couples themselves; they relate chiefly to children —their rearing and education. To achieve the success of this primary goal, *vertical* adjustments need to be made by both partners to the Divine Plan for Marriage. Other goals, such as companionship and mutual aid, call for *horizontal* adjustments of husband and wife toward each other. Both adjustments, just as both the primary and secondary purposes of marriage, are not mutually exclusive but rather mutually dependent.

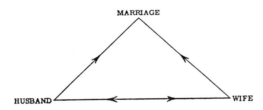

In particular the horizontal adjustments of husband and wife toward each other are intended to promote the welfare of the children and the personality development of all members of the family. Happiness, the chief goal indicated in most studies on marital adjustment, is actually not a goal to be achieved by and in itself; rather is it a by-product resulting from the attainment of all other marital purposes. This seems so little understood that the claim to happiness by couples themselves must often be held suspect. The wife who has frustrated her deepest maternal instincts to live in ease and luxury, often labels herself "happy," but the substitution of artificial for deeply ingrained natural wants cannot spell genuine happiness.

EARLY ADJUSTMENT

One of the most important things at the start of marriage is a correct idea of success. Upon this idea will depend the type of adjustment pattern that will emerge. The first year of marriage is the time for laying firmly the foundations for future success. It represents a gradual transition from the highly romantic to the more practical; from the idealistic to the realistic. The romanticism and idealism of this period serve their purposes in "oiling the machinery of adjustment" and rendering the initial adjustments easier. It is also a time both of happy discoveries and of disillusionment with the demands of marriage and the traits of one's partner. Unexpected difficulties are offset by unanticipated joys; the revelation that one's chosen life-partner has "feet of clay" is often outweighed by the appearance of sterling qualities not previously recognized.

When 476 Catholic husbands and wives were asked the chief problems facing couples in their first year of marriage they listed them as follows (in the order of their frequency):

Sexual adjustment	Finances
General adjustment	Residence with in-laws
Understanding one's spouse	Restraint in the marriage act
Relations with in-laws	Wife working.[3]

To be forewarned about these areas of interpersonal competence is, it is hoped, to be forearmed. If the first year of marriage has been successfully employed, the couple will emerge from it solidly oriented toward the true goals of marriage, with an adjustment pattern firmly fixed, a more realistic love and understanding of each other and a technique established for the resolving of any future problems, tensions or misunderstandings.

Vertical adjustments

For true success it is imperative that the partners both adjust to marriage itself as conceived in the Divine Plan. It is folly to speak of success in mariage when, for instance, a couple mutually agree to the use of contraceptives or to cease the practice of their religion. They may consider themselves successful and happy because they have adjusted to each other. Actually they are dismal failures since the chief purposes of marriage are frustrated even though by mutual agreement. They may have adjusted horizontally but they have not adjusted vertically, which is far more important.

The dedication of marriage requires devotion of all the couple's

---

[3] Dunn, *op. cit.*, Table 53, p. 147.

resources to the goals of marriage. This means that their time, energy, money and the like are no longer to be used exclusively or even primarily for their own comfort. On the contrary, the vertical adjustments of marriage call for the use of these resources primarily for the rearing of a family. Were this kept in perspective it would influence the sums of money spent for the wedding, honeymoon and the setting up of a home and its furnishings. Instead of a showplace intended to impress others, couples would make their new home a nursery and a place for children.

There must also be an early adjustment from the life pattern of a single person to the pattern of group life. For instance, the man or woman who prior to marriage spent considerable time daily in prayer or spiritual reading, may need to reduce such practices or modify them in favor of other things which now are strict duties. This demands endless sacrifice. Nights out alone or with friends now must give way to evenings with one's spouse. Some types of recreation will have to be dropped, changed or modified and new types adopted. Religious practices, also, may need modification or change to accord with group life. Family claims to income will take priority over personal conveniences or preferences. In moderate and low income families this may mean really large sacrifices. The wife will have to adjust to a financially dependant role. Relatives, friends and acquaintances of one's partner must be treated with consideration, and hospitality even though some may prove obnoxious. The rightful demands of sex may call for sacrifices, inconveniences and readjustments of various sorts. These and other vertical adjustments must be made if the high purposes and vocation of marriage are to be successfully attained. To make these adjustments requires a strong sense of dedication, religious motivation, the assistance of grace, willingness to sacrifice and maturity of character.

Horizontal adjustments

Couples are not likely to adjust to marriage very well unless they also have learned to adjust to each other. A part of success in marriage is successful partnership, which calls for an adjustment to any peculiarities and eccentricities of the unique individual one has married. Here reference is not being made to really important traits but rather to those many small characteristics and preferences which one family specialist has well labeled "tremendous trifles." The habits that partners bring to marriage are usually deep-seated and frequently go back all the way to childhood. They are not easily changed and usually must be adjusted to. Odd food preferences, queer notions on home arrangements, uncapped toothpaste, disorderly closets, constant tardiness, tendencies to be quiet and untalkative, sarcasm, minor absences of simple charity in speech and action—these and similar peculiarities must be accommodated in some fashion if successful partnership is to be achieved.

Psychological adjustment

Perhaps the more important horizontal adjustment, however, is that which must be made to living with a member of the opposite sex. It is clear, of course, that men and women have many psychological needs in common. When 476 husbands and wives were questioned on what they expect of each other *both* sexes listed most frequently the identical needs—love, understanding, affection and companionship.[4] This challenges the widespread opinion that the sexes differ in these desires. In addition, both desire appreciation, status and security. In a survey of several hundred college students the six things most desired by both sexes were companionship, love, homelife, children, security and sexual expression.[5] But unless both partners by attitude, word and action communicate these various desires to their spouses, this kind of horizontal adjustment may not be effected.

Equally important, however, is a knowledge and acceptance of the differing psychological traits of the two sexes. It is difficult to see how an ardent feminist, who denies such psychological differences, can either adjust in marriage himself or counsel others to adjustment. It is precisely because of these differences, as was earlier seen, that men and women act out their roles as complements to each other. In marriage, above all, the warning of Dr. Alexius Carrell is meaningful: "What God made distinct, let no man confuse." This seems to reflect the statement of Pius XII: "These characteristic qualities which divide the two

---

4 *Ibid.*, Table 38, p. 108.
5 Clifford Adams, "Making Marriage Work," *Ladies' Home Journal,* Vol. LXXII, No. 2 (February 1955), p. 30.

sexes *are so obvious to all* [italics ours] that only willful blindness or a no less disastrous utopian doctrinaire attitude could overlook or practically ignore their significance in social relations." [6]

Science and sex differences

Modern scientific inquiry is tending to confirm the presence of psychological differences between the sexes.[7] In one study we find that boys from their earliest years show more aggressiveness and are more easily angered than girls; boys excel in social activity but girls in social interests; the play interests of children differ largely between the sexes, as do later their preferences for subjects in school and still later, their occupational interests. The male is definitely more aggressive and dominant, the female more suggestible, nervous, emotional and sociable.[8] Another study tells us that "From a great number of paper and pencil tests on personality, it has been found that women show greater emotionality and neuroticism than men. This has been confirmed by clinical interviews." [9] Women, it seems, have more social, aesthetic and religious interest than men, while men have more economic, political and theoretical interest.[10] Two noted psychologists, Winifred Johnson and Lewis Terman, in a report on their review of 40 of the best research studies, wrote: "Women are consistently more intimately and intensely personal than men. They are strongly interested in persons and spend more time and thought on people and personalities than men do. . . . Excellent studies of young children show that girls very early are more interested in relationships with others, while boys are more interested in material things." [11]

In cases counseled at the Marriage Center of the Catholic

---

6 Pius XII, "Allocution to Italian Women," *Acta Apostolicae Sedis,* Vol. XLI (September 6, 1949), pp. 415–421.

7 C. Zimmerman and L. Cervantes, *Marriage and the Family* (Chicago: Henry Regnery Co., 1956), pp. 137–671.

8 L. M. Terman, *et al.,* "Psychological Sex Differences," *Manual of Child Psychology,* ed. L. Carmichael (New York: John Wiley & Sons, Inc., 1946), chap. xix, pp. 954–1001.

9 P. D'Arcy, *Factual Differences Between the Sexes in the Field of Religion* (Master's thesis, Catholic University of America, 1947), p. 4.

10 G. W. Alport and P. E. Vernon, *A Study of Values* (Boston: Houghton Mifflin Company, 1931).

11 Quoted by J. T. Landis and M. G. Landis, in "What You Should Know About Women," *Collier's* (November 24, 1951), pp. 18–19.

University of America it is noted that the undesirable traits of men and women differ greatly. Traits found in women and rarely in men are nagging, carrying a grudge, living in the past, equating love with affection, overstating cases, minimizing husband's income, self-pity and sensitivity. Some traits found in men but rarely in women were being more career- than family-minded, having little interest in social life, uncommunicativeness, having little interest in home or children, unaffectionate. Psychologists and also anthropologists have noted that there is even a difference between the sexes in the meanings attached to the same words. This has been observed not only in our culture but in a number of others, and is traced not to language differences but to the emotional variations between men and women.[12]

A summary of sex differences as found in scientific studies follows:

1. The general intelligence of both sexes is the same.
2. Slight differences exist in the performance of certain intellectual tasks, of certain skills.
3. Fairly large differences evidence themselves in tasks of an intellectual or physical nature and those of a social nature.
4. Great differences appear in complex activities which are a combination of intelligence, and physical strength or social ability.[13]

For centuries philosophy has insisted that men and women are different and has pointed out some of these variations. In the words of Bishop Fulton J. Sheen:

Man . . . has initiative, power and origin. Woman has intuition, response, acceptance, submission and cooperation. Man lives more in the external world. . . ; it is his mission to rule over it and subject it. Woman lives more in the internal world. . . . Man is more interested in the outer world; woman in the inner world. Man talks about things; woman more about persons. Man fashions the products of the earth; woman fashions life. . . . Man makes sacrifices

---

[12] T. Reik, "Men and Women Speak Different Languages," *Psychoanalysis,* Vol. II (Spring–Summer), pp. 3–15.

[13] C. C. Miles, "Sex in Social Psychology," *Handbook of Social Psychology,* ed. C. A. Murchison (Worcester, Mass.: Clark University Press, 1935), chap. xvi, p. 748; also S. H. Britt, *Social Psychology of Modern Life* (New York: Farrar & Rinehart Inc., 1941), p. 257.

for things which are in the future and which are abstract; woman
. . . is more inclined to make sacrifices for persons and for that which
is immediate. Because more objective, man is inclined to give
reasons for what he loves and what he does; woman, being more
subjective . . . is more inclined to love just for love's sake. Man's
reasons for loving are because of the qualities and attributes of the
beloved. Man builds, invents, conquers; woman tends, devotes,
interiorizes. The man gives; the woman is a gift.[14]

EXPERIENCE, OBERVATION, COMMON SENSE

In the absence of comprehensive scientific knowledge, experience and ordinary observation must be resorted to. That most
uncommon thing known as common sense can also be of assistance here. An interesting observation was made in a national
poll in which 70 per cent of those questioned thought that women
were more talkative than men, with 62 per cent of the women
agreeing; 54 per cent thought women more thrifty, with 52 per
cent of the men agreeing; and 48 per cent thought men more
levelheaded with 40 per cent of the women agreeing.[15]

Other differing traits of men and women in our culture, widely
accepted as such, are the following:

MEN	WOMEN
Men prefer generalities	Women prefer details
Men are more objective	Women are more subjective
Men tend to be stern	Women tend to be tender
Men tend to be forceful	Women tend to be tactful
Men prefer essentials	Women prefer accidentals
Men are more passionate	Women are more romantic
Men are more materialistic	Women are more spiritual
Men are more self-contained	Women are more social
Men are more egoistic	Women are more altruistic
Men tend to dominate	Women are more submissive
Men are more steady	Women tend to moodiness
Men are content with the prosaic	Women prefer the poetic
Men are more conceited	Women are more jealous
Men are more pugnacious	Women are more tenacious

---

14 From *Three to Get Married* by Fulton J. Sheen. Copyright, 1951, Fulton
J. Sheen. Reprinted by permission of the publishers Appleton-Century-Crofts,
Inc., pp. 151–152.
15 *Public Opinion Quarterly*, Vol. XIV, (1950–1951), pp. 373–374.

MEN	WOMEN
Men have more technical skill	Women have more social skill
Men are more secretive	Women are more talkative
Men prefer abstract thought	Women like concrete ideas
Men are more impersonal	Women are more personal
Men are more acquisitive	Women are more seductive
Men are more progressive	Women are more conservative
Men think love more practical	Women think love more romantic.

Doubtless some of these differences are subject to controversy. Despite the difficulties involved, it is important that partners come to know each other's traits. Without such knowledge adjustment is extremely difficult, if not impossible. The husband whose wife attaches importance to small things, will adjust more easily if he understands that this is typical of women at large. The wife who deplores her husband's waning affection although many real sacrifices are being made for her should understand that men do not think affection as important an element in love as do women. It is also important that each sex control those traits which are damaging to marital harmony.

STATUS AND INTERPERSONAL COMPETENCE

One of nature's basic needs is that of status. Everybody wants recognition of his worth, a sense of being wanted and needed and an awareness that he is making a worthwhile contribution. But these are social desires in that they require an element of appreciation by others. Self-esteem is not enough; we expect our contribution to be recognized by others. Without recognition, or worse still, in the face of constant fault-finding, it is almost impossible to preserve a rightful sense of worth—unless we sublimate our lives totally by religion.

This sense of status, of self-esteem in marriage is associated with recognition from our partners of the successful achievement of our respective roles. Men will derive a satisfactory status from being accorded proper respect as heads of their families and as successes in their work. The nagging feminist or working wife seldom gives her husband the esteem he desires, and such a woman may wonder why her husband finds home so unappealing and his secretary so alluring. A study of 61 Catholic husbands found them complaining that the things they obtained least from their wives were compliments, appreciation, confidence and encouragement.[16] The wise wife offers her husband that respect, admiration, deference, and encouragement, without which his morale and status will suffer.

Similarly, women rightfully expect to find their self-esteem preserved and increased by a recognition of their successful roles as mothers, wives and as women. The husband who is inattentive, uncommunicative, unaffectionate, or unappreciative can expect to have a wife whose self-esteem has given way to feelings of rejection. The husband who never consults his wife or never tolerates her opinions, can scarcely expect her to feel "queen of the home." Again, the husband who insists that his wife reject motherhood will find her a frustrated woman, devoid of that peculiar sense of self-esteem which only maternity can bring. In the study mentioned above the statements of 59 Catholic wives disclosed that the things they received least from their husbands were sympathy, compliments and understanding. The wise husband accords his wife her full status by giving her companionship and social life, extolling her virtues as a homemaker, tendering her the affection her feminine heart craves and lauding her ambitions and successes in motherhood.

USEFUL ADJUSTMENT TECHNIQUES

Adjustment is an art which some enjoy by natural ability but others must acquire by strenuous effort. Many studies are available to point out factors which are likely to lead to success in marriage. The author of one of these studies has recognized that the *ability to adjust* is one factor that seems to have been neglected.

But, so far, it has been rather difficult to say whether these problems which the interviewer is able to predict will be disruptive or whether the couples will be able to solve them. This seems to *depend in large part upon the adaptability* [italics ours] of one or both members of the couple. The factor which we have not adequately identified, either in statistical or clinical prediction, is the characteristic of adaptability, or a capacity for problem solving.[17]

---

[16] Paul James, "The Expressed Results of a Certain Premarital Lecture Course" (Master's thesis, Catholic University of America, June 1953), p. 85.

[17] E. W. Burgess, "The Value and Limitations of Marriage Prediction Tests," *Marriage and Family Living*, Vol. XII (1950), p. 55.

Natural flexibility and a knowledge of adjustment techniques are two of the most valuable assets a partner can bring to his marriage. With these qualities all problems which are at all reconcilable can be solved. There are many methods of adjustment—both positive and negative—of which the following are, perhaps, the most important positive ones.

Compromise implies the willingness of both parties to sacrifice a part of their position. It is clearly a two way adjustment in which both must cooperate. Some think it to be the most frequent method employed in marriage to resolve differences. The ability to compromise might be compared to the willow tree and contrasted to the sturdy oak. In a violent storm the willow will adjust to accommodate the wind without being torn from its root position. The oak, since it will not yield, is torn up roots and all. Like the willow, couples should be ready at all times to modify their opinions, attitudes and behavior *without ever surrendering the basically important life principles*. Religious principles, for instance, can never be compromised. At the same time the sturdy oak temperament will make a difficult partner. He may mistake inflexibility for strength; actually, it is sheer obstinacy and willfulness.

Acceptance is another useful adjustment. There are occasions when the wisest attitude is simply to take one's partner as he is despite his shortcomings. While remembering the duty to correct one's spouse, there are many instances where this is not feasible and can only worsen an already poor relationship. In such an eventuality the attitude expressed in prayer is imperative:

> O God, grant me the serenity to accept
> the things I cannot change;
> Give me the courage to change the things
> that must be changed,
> And the wisdom to distinguish the one
> from the other.[18]

Conversion implies a complete and total surrender to the position of a partner in marriage. This is likely to be achieved only if one retains an open mind on differences, an unemotional approach and the humility to admit the error of his own position. This requires genuine maturity of character.

---

[18] Reinhold Niebuhr.

Sublimation is often the only adjustment possible. If all others fail or are not feasible, this technique remains available. By it a partner accepts the inevitable in his or her spouse for entirely noble and lofty reasons. The wife of an unfaithful husband who accepts her cross in a religious spirit, conscious that through her acceptance and suffering, the grace for his conversion will be won—this wife has learned the meaning of sublimation.

Counseling is a useful method of removing differences when one or both parties through emotionality or wrong attitudes have lost their true perspective on marital relationships. In such instances, a person selected because of his ability to counsel and to remain objective may prove the only effective aid.

Abandonment to Divine Providence is an adjustment which leads one to see the designs of a loving Father and to sense His paternal protection in the midst of the most trying situations. On the natural level, it is a strong defense against physical or mental breakdown; on the supernatural level, it will propel a partner to great heights of holiness in marriage.

RESOLVING DIFFERENCES

In the best of marriages some differences or misunderstandings occur. Even the just St. Joseph misunderstood Our Lady's pregnancy! However, differences are not as important as the way in which partners react to them. *Less real harm is done by misunderstandings than by the way in which they are handled.* Successful partnership is not due to the absence of differences but to the ability of the couple to resolve them.

Some advice on this matter is given by the experiences of 476 husbands and wives married ten years or more, who indicated the best ways of letting one's spouse know one differs from him are as follows:

Be frank

Be tactful

Discuss your differences

State reasons for your opinion

Select the proper moment for discussion

Listen to the other partner's side

Try to reach an agreement

Don't delay in doing so

Discuss matters in private

Ignore small things

Agree on getting outside advice

Don't rehash old faults

Don't nag

Write it out

Mention between decades of the rosary said together [19]

---

[19] Dunn, *op. cit.,* Table 63, p. 168.

It is most important to establish, preferably in the first year of marriage, machinery for solving problems and disputes. Those who have done so rarely run into serious difficulties in their marriages. The experience of marriage counselors has shown that most who must resort to counseling have never mastered the art of resolving tense situations. Those entering marriage or those whose marriage is beset with frictions, might consider the following practices:

1. Try to recognize your partner as a person having the right to opinions, tastes and preferences which differ from yours.

2. If your partner shows hostility or resentment try to realize that few people are malicious and that your partner must be suffering internally very much.

3. Remember it is better "to lose the battle and win the war"; it is better sometimes to submit or agree than win a point and ruin a marriage.

4. Learn to understand your partner's way of looking at a situation; with such understanding, malice and growing ill-will usually will disappear.

5. Never attribute ulterior motives; more resentment broods over suspected motives than over differences themselves. Doing so without solid reasons for it, is also a sin of false suspicion or rash judgment.

6. When moody it is best to keep quiet; in all probability the wrong thing will be said and the situation will only deteriorate. At such times, speaking to God will help much more.

7. Don't make decisions when emotionally upset; they will almost always be wrong and cause regret later.

8. A sense of humor can be a saving factor. Some can learn to laugh at the childishness into which they have drifted during an argument.

9. If your partner will not take offense or if there has been a prior understanding about it, leaving in the middle of an argument may save the situation.

10. Although such steps will eliminate quarrels, they will not resolve them. It is important, therefore, that as soon as feasible two partners in marriage try to talk out *calmly and rationally* the point of dispute. Such mature discussion kept on the intellectual level, is the supreme technique for solving problems.

11. Remember that a discussion is intellectual; when it degenerates to the emotional level, it becomes a quarrel.

12. To insure against quarreling try to select the strategic moment for reopening discussion. Such would usually be moments when both are relaxed and in a good humor; perhaps the tactful time is at a party or after an enjoyable day's outing. Moments of fatigue or worry will not lend themselves to calm discussion. On the other hand, such discussion should take place as soon as possible. Shakespeare has well written:

Resist beginnings: all too late the cure,
When ills have gathered strength through long delay.

13. Write it out. A letter to your partner will probably not be charged with emotionalism. He will read it calmly in your absence. In the process of your writing and quiet thinking you may often discover where the mistake really lies or that the whole matter is quite childish. Or perhaps, you may find that you are unable to write your complaints because they existed in your emotions and not in your partner.

14. Admitting one is wrong, though it is difficult and requires real maturity, will usually dissipate an argument and its attendant ill-feelings almost immediately.

15. While partners must learn how to apologize, the art of accepting an apology gracefully is equally important.

16. Ideally speaking, small things should be ignored. In reality, most marriage breakdowns occur because of the accumulation of small things which were not resolved, which festered like sores and eventually grew into a cancer. Partners must recognize that nothing is too trivial to cause serious damage to a marriage if left unsolved. This is why one marriage expert has labeled small differences "tremendous trifles." [20]

17. Patience is a cardinal need especially in new marriages. Completely satisfactory adjustment is a process that comes only with the passage of time. A study of 818 spouses showed that among those married an average of 20 years, adjustment in some areas was a slow process. In sex relations only 52.7 per cent agreed from the start; in spending family income, 56.2 per cent; in social activities 67.1 per cent; in in-law relationships 68.6 per cent; in religious activities 74 per cent and mutual friends 76.4 per cent. [21]

18. Once a matter has been settled, the door should *promptly and permanently* be slammed on it. A serious mistake commonly

---

[20] J. T. Landis and M. G. Landis, *The Marriage Handbook* (Englewood Cliffs, N. J.: Prentice-Hall, Inc., 1948), p. 256.

[21] Landis and Landis, *op. cit.*, p. 243.

made is to rehash old mistakes, continue grudges and "drag old skeletons out of the closet." This shows genuine immaturity.

19. Efforts should be made to repair wrongs done and assuage hurt feelings. Expressions of affection, complimentary remarks, praise, gifts and the like will help here.

20. The Old Testament advised us never to let the sun set on our wrath. This might be paraphrased for marriage by urging that partners "never let the sun set on an argument." Were this done, were all differences resolved, were small sores not left to fester deeper on the morrow—no couple would ever look for the divorce court. This practical technique has been more aptly and beautifully expressed in a "Goodnight for Husbands and Wives":

This day is almost done. When the night and morning meet it will be only an unalterable memory. So let no unkind word; no careless doubting thought; no guilty secret; no neglected duty; no wisp of jealous fog becloud its passing. For we belong to each other— to have and to hold—and we are determined not to lose the keen sense of mutual appreciation which God has given us. To have is passive, and was consummated on our wedding day, but to hold is active and can never be quite finished so long as we both shall live.

Now, as we put our arms around each other, in sincere and affectionate token of our deep and abiding love, we would lay aside all disturbing thoughts, all misunderstandings, all unworthiness. If things have gone awry let neither of us lift an accusing finger nor become entangled in the rationalization of self-defense. *Who is to blame is not important; only how shall we set the situation right.* And so, serving and being served, loving and being loved, blessing and being blessed, we shall make a happy, peaceful home, where hearts shall never drop their leaves, but where we and our children shall learn to face life joyfully, fearlessly, triumphantly, so near as God shall give us grace [italics ours].[22]

ADJUSTMENT IN THE DIVINE PLAN

Success in marriage can mean only the attainment of the goals and purposes designed by God. For this achievement, couples must change their attitudes, emotions and conduct. They must adjust vertically to the nature of marriage and horizontally to each other. Only by making both types of adjustment can they

---

[22] F. A. Magoun, *Love and Marriage* (New York: Harper & Brothers, 1936), p. x.

find happiness in marriage. While some are blessed by nature with adaptable personalities, all must work at becoming more adjustable by growing toward maturity, selflessness and self-control. Adjustment is an art which only the willing learn over a period of time. It is only through adjustment that the "soul union," which Pius XI stated was more important than bodily union, can be effected.

10

Ties That Bind

WHEN ADJUSTMENTS have been made, marriage will have the unity of cooperation toward all marital goals. To achieve these goals a wise Providence has included in the nature of marriage a pattern for social living. Basic to it are certain processes and forces which can forge deeper and deeper the bonds of attachment and unity. Sociologists have identified many of these internal processes—proximity, interaction, domination, competition, cooperation, assimilation, imitation, communication, suggestion, social control.

Though all are important forces, in our urban family life special attention needs to be given to two—proximity and communication. Our industrial and urban culture has so shattered these two in both industrial and domestic areas that many people pass their entire lives without sensing their real importance. The same lack of proximity and communication which industrial relations experts detect in our huge business enterprises, marriage experts detect in the home. It is by proximity that husbands and wives, parents and children remain close to one another, sharing and cooperating in all of life's activities. It is through communication—whether by word, look, gesture, attitude, posture or otherwise—that the various members of a family share and cooperate with each other's thoughts and feelings. In an analysis of two studies which dealt with communication, it was

164

found that it was much greater among happily married couples than among those who were later divorced or separated.[1] Through both proximity and communication families grow in unity and enjoy the sense of accomplishments jointly achieved.

These processes operate in *all* the areas which compose social living. A certain psychiatrist once pointed out that from the cradle to the grave, human beings do only four things. They work, they play, they worship, they love.[2] It is, accordingly, in the economic, recreational, religious and affectional areas that families must be close to each other, to share, to cooperate and to communicate. If they do so the bonds of unity will automatically be forged deeper; if they do not, the growing together of marriage and family life can scarcely be effected.

FORGING FAMILY BONDS

Marriage and family life is a serious responsibility involving much work and many sacrifices. Nor have laborsaving devices lessened the burden significantly. The rearing of children and the maintenance of a home are a joint enterprise of wife, husband and children. Unfortunately our urban civilization separates the husband from the work-life of the home during the day. Yet the growing participation by many husbands in home chores is evidenced by their care of children and the growth of the do-it-yourself industry. Any effort made to avoid solitary occupation and to effect a cooperative work pattern in the home, will help produce the desired result of forging family bonds.[3]

One reason for the superiority of the farm home is its greater sharing of work. However, even city homes can, if they will, develop cooperative work patterns. Husbands and children can participate in homemaking; this becomes increasingly possible as the hours of employment shorten and more time is available in the home.

Home-centered recreation and family outings are equally

---

[1] H. J. Locke, G. Sabagh, and M. M. Thomas, "Primary Communication, Empathy and Family Unity," *Abstracts of Papers Delivered at the Fiftieth Annual Meeting of the American Sociological Society* (August 31–September 2, 1955), p. 59.

[2] W. S. Sadlier, *Worry and Nervousness* (Chicago: A. C. McClurg & Company, 1923), p. 327.

[3] For further discussion see Chapter 17.

useful in this respect. In fact, since opportunities for proximity and communication in the work area are, in urban families, very limited, there is greater reason for more rather than less joint recreation. The paradox of our culture is that although most farm couples who have worked close to their children all day will often spend the evenings playing together as well, many city couples who are separated for large portions of the day from each other and the children will rarely do so. There seems to be a special significance in "playing together" in view of the "association of ideas." Play situations are happy ones; it is natural that the agreeable feeling of a play situation will transfer itself from the game to the participants. Wives and husbands will find their attachment to each other and their children grow as they share mutually enjoyed recreations.

The custom of family recreation after dinner—games, arts and crafts, instrumental or vocal renditions—can be perpetuated. Holidays and week ends are excellent opportunities for picnics, trips, outings of various sorts or simple visiting of friends and relatives together. Typical of a father who understands this is the President of Lehigh Structural Steel Company. In his own words:

My children and I have been close friends ever since their childhood a quarter of a century ago. Our intimate relationship stems, I believe, from a family custom that originated then and is still being maintained—a walk in the evening after dinner. So today is a motorized era, and things are done somewhat differently. But my son is still with his children in the evening, out in the open, under the stars. That, I feel, is what is really important.[4]

Religious life is basically social and corporate. An understanding of religious doctrines, such as the Mystical Body of Christ, will indicate that joint religious living is preferable to the solitude of personal religious life. The individualism of our age had shattered this concept and its practices until relatively recent years. Now there is an encouraging revival of proximity in religion through practices such as family shrines, family pilgrimages, family rosaries and family communions. The motto

---

[4] T. R. Mullen, "A Walk in the Evening," *Parade* (June 12, 1955), p. 2; also see Chapter 16.

has now become almost a household maxim: "The family that prays together, stays together." But much more than this, the family that enjoys proximity and the sharing of inner religious living by communication, will be well on the road to sanctity.[5]

If proximity and communication are found in the work, recreational and religious lives of the family members, growth in love is normally automatic and inevitable. The error of our culture is to believe that since fewer children mean more time for the couple to spend with each other, greater love will result. Love, like happiness, is a by-product; it results from sharing in all other life activities. Annually at commencement day in our colleges and universities, new proof is afforded this fact. Those women graduates who four years previously were complete strangers and now are in tears at the prospect of parting, have learned to love each other. Their love did not grow by direct cultivation but was an affectional tie of steady but sure growth. For four years they did nothing more than work and play and pray *together*. Love automatically grew and waxed strong. The experiences of the last two World Wars also gave countless instances of boys who remained lifelong "buddies," simply because they shared all life's activities in great proximity and with much communication.

RURAL LIFE AND FAMILY UNITY

Despite the prejudice against rural living, few will deny that the proximity found in members of rural families effects a greater solidarity, stability and unity. The smaller rate of divorce, broken homes, suicide, neuroses or delinquency in rural areas seems to attest this fact. Rural society in contrast to "industrial society which works against the family and in favor of divorce, desertion, temporary unions, companionate marriages . . . is characterized by the strength, permanence and unity of the marriage bond and the comparative rarity of its dissolution." [6]

Ever since Pius XI spoke of the family's need for "light, space and air," many have been confused, conscious that this implies the need to live in the rural milieu. Through the centuries

---

[5] For further discussion see Chapters 11 and 14.
[6] National Catholic Rural Life Conference, *Manifesto on Rural Life* (Milwaukee: The Bruce Publishing Company, 1939), p. 3.

Catholic tradition has held steadfastly to the position that "God made the country and man made the town"—with effects proportionate to the makers. St. Thomas, at a time when the largest city had a population of about 30,000, noted that cities are centers of avarice and materialism while solid virtue fared much better in the rural scene. Pius XII, addressing farm families said: "You are called upon . . . to perform an indispensable function as *source and defense* [italics ours] of a stainless moral and religious life. For the land is a kind of nursery which supplies men, sound in soul and body, for all occupations, for the Church and for the state." [7] On a similar occasion he stated: "Of all the goods that can be the object of private property, *none is more comfortable to nature . . . than the land . . .* only that stability which is rooted in one's own holding, *makes the family the vital and most perfect and fecund cell of society* [italics ours]".[8]

The higher birthrate of the rural culture indicates a continuing superiority in attaining the family's first goal. The equal purpose of "education" of the children is also enhanced by the conditions and circumstances of rural life. On the natural level nothing is more important than character and personality formation. Conscientious urban parents deplore the outside influence on their children by the neighbors and neighborhood, the corner drugstore cliques and the like. Such parents are the first to realize why the incidence of delinquency recedes as one moves from the heart of a large city to the rural scene. According to a survey of 1,229 children, good personality adjustment was higher among rural children, who were also found to be more self-reliant, to have a greater sense of personal worth and belonging, to be free from nervousness, to have greater social skills and superiority in school and community relations. The teachers rated rural children superior as "normal, healthy, wholesome persons." [9] In a more recent study of 403 adolescent girls it was

---

[7] Pius XII, "Al Particolare Compiacimento," *Acta Apostolicae Sedis,* Vol. XXXVIII (1946), p. 433.

[8] Pius XII, "La Solemnita della Penticoste," *Acta Apostolicae Sedis,* Vol. XXXIII (1941), p. 224.

[9] A. R. Mangus, "Personality Adjustment of Rural and Urban Children," *American Sociological Review,* Vol. XIII, No. 5 (October 1948), p. 566–575.

found that discipline was stricter and more consistent in rural homes, unhappiness was more frequent in urban families, and more urban girls smoke and drank.[10] Some of the prediction studies for happiness in marriage indicate the better bet is a boy or girl from the country or small town.[11]

During the past two decades many American families have, through bitter experience, come to realize the superiority of the rural environment for family living. Forced by circumstances to dissociate themselves from their city jobs, they have started an outward movement first to the suburbs, then to the fringe areas, and then to the open country—a nationwide movement of major proportions. This is confirmed by a study based on 100 interviews in two suburbs of Chicago in which familism was found to be the most important reason for the trend away from the city.[12] In 1953 there were 91.5 million people in our metropolitan areas; 37.5 million in the cities proper; 30 million in the suburbs; 12 million in fringe areas and 12 million beyond the fringe. This trek is evident because the suburbs have grown faster than the cities. Though the population of the nation between 1947 and 1953 had risen 11 per cent, that of the suburbs had risen 43 per cent.[13]

The fringe areas around large cities have also had a mushroom growth. Between 1940–1950 cities grew 13 per cent but fringe areas grew 34.7 per cent.[14] Studies of these families confirm the superiority of even the semi-rural environment. Family size is increased and family functions remain intact.[15] However, an increasing number of families are only content with a totally rural culture. Some studies show that all classes and occupa-

---

10 E. M. Duvall and A. B. Motz, "Are Country Girls So Different," *Rural Sociology*, Vol. X, No. 3 (September 1945).

11 From Schroeder, and Burgess and Cottrell.

12 Wendell Bell, "Familism and Suburbanization: A Case For the Hypothesis of Social Choice," *Abstract of Papers Delivered at the Fiftieth Annual Meeting of the American Sociological Society* (New York: American Sociological Society, 1955), p. 29.

13 "The Changing American Market IV," *Fortune* (November 1953), p. 130.

14 P. K. Hatt and A. J. Reiss, *Reader in Urban Sociology* (Glencoe, Ill.: Free Press, 1951), p. 68.

15 E. G. Jaco and I. Belknap, "Is a New Family Emerging in the Urban Fringe?" *American Sociological Review*, Vol. XVIII, No. 5 (October 1953), p. 556.

tions, all educational levels (especially the higher ones) are moving onto small farmettes varying, in one study, from 7.9 to 26.8 acres in size.[16]

Obviously not all urban families find it possible to move to a small town or farm. But it is equally obvious that many have learned how inferior the city milieu is for family living and are moving outwards to more rural areas—often at great personal inconvenience.

THE KINSHIP FAMILY

Another internal force of great importance to the "conjugal family" (husband-wife-children) is the "kinship family" (near blood relatives). In-laws bound together by deep ties of reciprocal aid and enjoying a strong sense of group solidarity constitute a family type recognized by both sociology and morality. The conjugal family is not self-sufficient, though in our age of independence we like to think it so. It's needs, in part, must be met by others outside the conjugal family itself. Nature and morality indicate that the in-laws should be the first outside persons to serve the conjugal family. Charity obliges here, for one of the determinants of a duty in charity is *proximity* and none are normally closer than the kinsfolk.

Though serious study of this problem is yet to be made by science, sociologists widely hold that the kinship family system, especially in the city, has suffered serious deterioration. Instead, we are being confronted with a growing in-law problem. As a result of the failure of kinship relations, conjugal families are relying more and more upon other outside aids—commercial sitters, nurses, community centers, homes for the aged, day nurseries, orphan homes and the like. There are those who argue convincingly that behind the cry of our age for "social security," is the insecurity of the family deserted by its kinsfolk in time of need.

The naturalness of the kinship family is suggested in the words of a noted Catholic anthropologist:

It has operated at high efficiency in practically all cultures known to us and as far back as our evidence reaches. It has suffered its

---

[16] N. P. Gist, "Developing Pattern of Urban Decentralization," *Social Forces,* Vol. XXX, No. 3 (March 1952), pp. 257–267.

severest setback in only recent centuries as a result of industrialization. . . . At any rate more of the familial burdens, hitherto shared largely by the composite family group, will have to be carried by the conjugal family alone and by the state and other non-familial institutions.[17]

When properly functioning the kinship family can act as a cushion to soften the impact of the blows which a non-familial culture deals to the conjugal family. More positively it can, and in charity is obliged to, assist in all ways including economic and personal service. Were this done many of the hardships now experienced by families would be minimized; and probably parents would in many instances be willing to have larger families.

In-law problems

Unfortunately the breakdown of the kinship family is so dominant that many marriage authors do not even mention the in-laws except as problems. This attitude may lead readers to the conviction that in-laws are always liabilities. Certainly it fails to impart the concept of the kinship family as an invaluable asset. This emphasis upon in-law problems can be misleading.

However, in a study of couples married happily for 20 years or more, the wives listed in-law interference as their *second* while husbands listed it as their *third* most serious problem. Another study of 544 young couples, found this problem placed *first*.[18] In a study of Catholic couples less than 10 per cent were separated as a result of in-law troubles; this problem rarely led to complete breakdown, and it occurred most often in the early years of marriage.[19]

It would seem that mothers-in-law are more likely to cause trouble than any other relative, while the possibilities of trouble are generally greater from the wife's family.

However, the happy fact is that most couples seem to get along with their relatives. In a study of 1,444 couples married 18 or

[17] J. M. Cooper, "Family Origins" (Unpublished workshop paper, Catholic University of America, June, 1949).
[18] J. T. Landis and M. G. Landis, *The Marriage Handbook* (Englewood Cliffs, N. J.: Prentice-Hall, Inc., 1942), pp. 287–289.
[19] J. L. Thomas, "In-Laws or Out-Laws," *Social Order*, Vol. III, No. 10, (December 1953), pp. 435–441.

more years it was disclosed that 63.4 per cent of the husbands and wives disagreed "very little" with the in-laws, and 17.8 per cent just "a little"; this means a total of 81.2 per cent of these couples had no serious problems with the in-laws.[20]   A study of 210 husbands and 213 wives indicated that over 90 per cent of them were happy though living with their in-laws.[21]

In such cases both the couples and their relatives realize that marriage places a husband and wife before parents; that couples are entitled to privacy to work out a pattern of life according to their own and not their parents' preferences; that charity implies overlooking shortcomings and differences; that the common bond of family relationship is more basic and important than superficial differences of culture, status, education or economic position; that to wreck a good relationship between a husband and a wife, or a child and its parents is a conscienceless wrong of great magnitude; that acting out the charitable obligations of mutual assistance, does much to remove the tensions which might otherwise be present.   Furthermore, whereas wise relatives realize the need of a "hands-off policy," wise married partners realize that the parents of their spouses regardless of shortcomings remain their parents and persons greatly loved by them.   To expect a spouse to develop resentment, antagonism, or even a lack of contact with his own blood-relations, is to expect both the unnatural and the unethical.

When in-laws are aged

Like the general in-law problem, that of the care of the aged relative is one which must be seen in its full context.   Whenever feasible, providing for the aged within rather than outside the family structure is a rightful function of the kinship family. With the weakening of kinship ties and the accompanying charity, the aged become a "problem."   In a strongly functioning kinship family, providing for the aged is accepted as normal and

---

[20] R. B. Reed, "Social and Psychological Factors Affecting Fertility," *Milbank Memorial Fund Quarterly,* Vol. XXV, No. 4 (October 1947), p. 388.

[21] Georg Karlson, *Adaptability and Communication in Marriage: A Swedish Prediction Study of Marital Satisfaction* (Uppsala: Almquist and Wiksells Boktryckeri, 1951), Table 16, p. 183.

natural. Doubtless urbanization, inadequate housing and other social factors are operative here. More basic, however, are the waning of charity, the independence of both the couples and the aged, the idolization of youth and the lack of reverence for old age. A group of distinguished psychiatrists has noted that:

Whereas the Spanish-American or Chinese parent would expect not only to live with his children but to receive their continued respect and devotion, older people in our society can expect to be told that they are old-fashioned, their opinions out of date, and their capacity to give helpful advice based on long experience with life strictly limited. . . . The Council of Elders is notable for its absence, and the role of elder statesman finds hardly an applicant.[22]

The problem of the aged is being intensified by their growing numbers in our culture. In 1955 the age expectancy at birth rose to a new high of 70 years, more than twice that in 1894. The aged are now one in twelve in our total population; their number in 1955 was 14,128,000.[23]

In 1951 there were nine million aged living in their own households, two and three-quarter million in the homes of relatives, a half million rooming or boarding with strangers and 700,000 in institutions.[24] The vast majority of aged are clearly not living in the bosom of the kinship family. This is due, in part, to those aged who permit pride, independence or their own inability to relate well to their children stand in the road; it is due, in part, to the married children who, because of either circumstances or selfishness, refuse to accept their aged relatives into their homes. One study, at least, has shown that Catholic families and rural families stand ready to aid the aged relative more than those of some other religions or of the cities.[25]

---

[22] Committee on the Family of the Group for the Advancement of Psychiatry, *Integration and Conflict in Family Behavior,* Report No. 27 (Topeka, Kansas: August 1954), p. 16.

[23] "Longevity Reaches Three Score and Ten"; also "Our Aging Population," *Statistical Bulletin,* Vol. XXXVII (Metropolitan Life Insurance Company, September 1956), pp. 1–6.

[24] Federal Security Agency, *Fact Book on Aging* (Washington, D. C.: United States Government Printing Office, 1952), p. 1.

[25] R. M. Dinkel, "Attitude of Children Toward Supporting Aged Parents," *American Sociological Review,* Vol. IX (August 1944), pp. 370–379.

Just as there is a growing national opinion that in-laws are usually liabilities, so there is an increasing belief that aged parents usually disrupt the peace of a family. Both of these opinions are incorrect according to the best surveys available. In most other cultures this negative attitude toward accepting aged parents into one's family does not prevail. Our civilization given to a hedonistic philosophy of life, loving ease, comfort and convenience will understandably pose excuses for the difficulties and hardships which are implied in caring for the aged.

On the other hand, if the presence of aged relatives proves a serious danger to the marriage or the members of the family, such aged persons should be maintained somewhere besides the family household. Studies show that having the aged live in their own household is quite satisfying to many.[26] However, those living in institutions are found to have fewest family contacts, and their adjustment and zest for living is low.[27]

The hastening pace of institutionalizing the aged indicates a misunderstanding of their needs. Many seem to act on the assumption that economic support is all an aged parent requires, and that aged persons are no longer fully human. Actually, aged and young alike need acceptance, a sense of being wanted and needed, a sense of belonging, group life, freedom of judgment and choice, a share of responsibilities, attention, freedom from lonesomeness, a feeling of continued usefulness and the warmth of human love and affection. Most of these needs cannot be filled in institutions for the aged and are best satisfied in the homes of the families themselves.

Something must be done to turn downward the present upward trend of institutionalizing everyone who becomes burdensome at home because of age. . . . Unless indicated for sound medical or social reasons, the placing of older people in institutions is contrary to the American heritage that makes family life the foundation of our nation. It denies to chronically ill patients the powerful tonic of care at home amid familiar surroundings. It substitutes for this essential type of care the devitalizing and impersonal care that stresses almost

---

[26] J. I. Landis, "Social-Psychological Factors of Aging," *Social Forces,* Vol. XX (May 1942), p. 469; also E. W. Burgess and P. Wallin, *Engagement and Marriage* (Chicago: J. B. Lippincott Company, 1953), p. 111.

[27] R. Cavan, "Family Life and Family Substitutes in Old Age," *American Sociological Review,* Vol. XIV (February 1949), p. 72.

entirely bodily needs and does little to minister to the needs of the mind and the spirit which, in the end, are the patient.[28]

Despite the clear need of the aged for a normal family atmosphere and environment, "Two-thirds of the old persons in the United States feel unwanted and many of them are right. . . . The attitude toward old age in our country is contradictory and lukewarm at best, often negative and scornful." [29]   Even from a subjective point of view aged parents are often real assets.   In a study of this aspect of the aged, it was pointed out that they serve in various cultures the following functions:

1. Auxiliary services—act as sitters, maids in the home.
2. Specialized skills—contribute the products of their talents such as child care and rearing, home nursing.
3. Rights and privileges—enjoy the role of "elder statesman."
4. Experience—affords the knowledge of a lifetime in many domestic and familial matters.
5. Administer rituals—a special role of usefulness in times of crisis such as births or deaths.[30]

The aged also have a role to play in making themselves an asset in the homes of their children.   They need to accept the fact of old age, rejoicing in the rewards of greater leisure.   They must adjust to the benefits of true progress, or at least refrain from meddling when their married children accept such benefits. They should devote themselves to others, maintain an open-mindedness, learn to live in the present world and not in the past, refrain from complaining and nagging, avoid overdependence, but gracefully accept assistance when needed.   They must realize that another generation is running the home with new methods and concepts.[31]

[28] C. H. Lerrigo, *The Better Half of Your Life* (New York: The John Day Company, Inc., 1951), p. 228.

[29] Dr. E. Ackerknecht, "Problems of Our Aging Population," (Address given at Northwestern University Centennial Conference, June 7, 1951).

[30] L. W. Simmons, "Social Participation of the Aged in Different Cultures," *Annals of American Academy of Political and Social Sciences,* Vol. CCLXXIX (January 1952), p. 46.

[31] Robert Tyson, "Adjusting to Old Age," *Current Mental Hygiene Practice, Journal of Clinical Psychology,* Monograph Supplement, No. 8 (January 1951), chap. xi, pp. 79–87.

RITUAL IN THE FAMILY

Another integrating factor in marital and familial living is the use of rituals, those practices which by regular and repeated use have become more or less fixed patterns of interaction. Only in recent years have studies revealed the importance of rituals. The best known rituals in our family culture are probably those fixed ways of celebrating special occasions such as Christmas and birthdays. They tend to develop chiefly around holidays, anniversaries, meals, vacations, leisure time and religion.[32] They have been found to intensify family integration, foster likemindedness, increase family consciousness, inculcate self-discipline in favor of the group, serve as an educational instrument and promote religious living.

If we would but stop and reflect a moment all of us would realize perhaps how far we have wandered away from the *little* things—the little practices and customs that united the members of our families so closely . . . we do not always see how God, working through them, enriched our own lives and at the same time imposed upon us a responsibility to carry on the customs and ideals and traditions for our children.[33]

After a study of 530 Catholic homes representing four ethnic groups—Polish, German, Italian and Irish—the investigator was impressed that "the rituals although not practiced as extensively or as rigidly as in the native country, are nevertheless being observed to some extent in the average Catholic home today." [34]

Religious rituals seem to be on the increase in this country due doubtless to the various family, liturgical and similar movements. The rosary crusade has enlisted millions of families, while the Enthronement of the Sacred Heart in the Home [35] has spread

---

[32] For extended discussion see J. H. Bossard and E. S. Boll, *Ritual in Family Living* (Philadelphia: University of Pennsylvania Press, 1950).

[33] G. B. Bennett, *The Family Apostolate* (Washington, D. C.: National Catholic Welfare Conference, Summer 1952), p. 7.

[34] Sr. M. Sheila Burns, "A Study of Catholic Rituals in a Selected Sample of Catholic Families" (Master's thesis, Catholic University of America, 1953), p. 5.

[35] See Mateo Crawley-Boevey SS. CC., *Jesus King of Love* (Washington, D. C.: National Center of Enthronement of the Sacred Heart, 1945).

with great rapidity. Long discarded liturgical rituals, associated with the celebration of baptisms, weddings, Christmas, Lent, Easter are enjoying a hearty and encouraging revival.

INTEGRATING FACTORS IN THE DIVINE PLAN

Divine Wisdom not only placed goals in marriage but gave it sacramental aids to achieve these goals. In addition, certain *natural* forces and factors were given which would, if utilized, enhance family unity. Among these were the internal processes of proximity, sharing and communication in the work, play, religious and love areas of life. The external milieu of the rural environment was meant to be the natural habitat of the family. Family needs were to require for their fulfillment the close cooperation and assistance of in-laws. The charity that binds would have kinsfolk help the young conjugal family and in later years have the conjugal family provide for the aged relatives in turn. Fixed patterns based upon rightful practices were to be used to further the solidarity, education and religious living of the family.

11

Religion and Marital Success

THE RELATIONSHIP between the practice of religion and marital success is confused in the minds of many. There are those who believe that religion alone can insure marital success. They forget that grace presupposes nature and that natural factors also play a role in success. However, this type of thinking is on the wane. Far more common is the failure to recognize that religion, while not the *only* factor, is by far *the most important one* for marital success. Perhaps in part, this is due to those people who are "devout" without being truly "religious"; to those who frequent devotions and engage in Catholic activities while making life a continuous martyrdom for their families. True religious living implies the worship of God not only in public and private prayer but in public and private conduct. *It means the will of God translated into practical application to the smallest details of everyday life.* In fact it is precisely because religion relates to these minutiae of daily living also, that the Divine Plan for Marriage goes beyond the purely supernatural aspects and into the mundane aspects of marriage.

Doubtless the disregard for religion as a factor in marital success is one reason why in 1952, 35 million in our nation never attended church, 38 million did so sometimes and 35 million did so weekly; and why 18 per cent of the Catholics, 32 per cent of the Protestants and 50 per cent of the Jews never attended church.[1]   This attitude has affected our intellectuals also.   In a survey of several hundred college students only 4 per cent said they most wanted religious values in their marriage.[2]   Perhaps this is why the Bishops of the United States thought it important to call the attention of the nation back to this fundamental relationship.

Religion, necessary to individual man, is necessary also to human society.   From the very beginning the family, the primary unit of society, has been intimately dependent on religion, and from it has drawn its unity, its stability and its holiness.

Apart from its divine origin and sanction, parental authority, upon which the family is founded, becomes but an arbitrary application of force to be superseded by any stronger power.   Where religion has grown weak the family has shown a corresponding tendency to disintegrate.   When religion remains strong, it stands as a protective armor, safeguarding both individual and family.[3]

THE CHURCH AND MARRIAGE

The reason religion is the most potent factor for success is that it teaches and makes possible the Divine Plan for Marriage, outside of which there can be only failure.   Through its dogma and its laws the Church educates us to the proper principles, attitudes and facts of marriage; through the Mass and the sacraments, the sacramentals, prayer and sacrifice, it offers those supernatural helps so indispensable for marriage.   In addition, the Church aids families in a material way.   The far-flung charitable activities and institutions of the Church's apostolate make her one of the greatest boons to the family in a material way.   Her orphan homes, day nurseries, hospitals, schools, homes for the aged; her thousands of clergy, nuns, brothers, social workers—all stand ready to assist the family, especially in times of emergency.

---

[1] *Catholic Digest Poll,* (Huntington, Ind.: Sunday Visitor Press, November 1952).

[2] C. Adams, "Making Marriage Work," *Ladies' Home Journal,* Vol. LXXII, No. 2 (February 1955), p. 30.

[3] Bishops' Statement at Annual Meeting, *Religion, Our Most Vital National Asset* (Washington, D. C.: National Catholic Welfare Conference, 1952).

Religion and holiness

However, it is chiefly because they have the true way to holiness that religion and the Church serve marital success. Not only does the Church assure us that the married state is conducive to holiness, but also that it can lead families to the very pinnacle of sanctity. This is true basically because holiness means doing the Will of God. It is doing what we ought to do, when we ought to do it, in the manner in which it should be done and for the right reasons.[4] It is easy to forget that "A bricklayer, laying bricks all his life and doing little else, may thus attain the . . . glory of a Saint Therese! All God asks from us in requiring us to 'pray always' is that we *perform the actions that our station in life requires of us, with the intention of pleasing Him* [italics ours]."[5] Were this understood, we would have less grumbling about the monotony of homemaking, less neglect of children and greater harmony in the home. Husbands and wives would give more of themselves to marriage, family, home, and less to their own interests, their careers, their pleasures. There would be larger families and more well-trained children. In general, there would be more faithfulness to the duties which marriage imposes.

However, devotion and behavior must be predicated upon certain beliefs or dogmas. It is from religion that we learn the Divine Plan for Marriage; that in it marriage is a sacred thing and even a sacrament. Through religion we come to know the nature, the purposes, the goals of marriage. Religion teaches us the nature of true love, the complemental natures of the sexes, the roles of husbands and wives, the supernatural dignity of sex, the place of the family in the Mystical Body of Christ. Furthermore, the *morals* of religion give us sure rules of conduct leading to success. It points out clearly through ethical concepts the road to good adjustment, to the achievement of all of the goals of marriage, and to order and peace in married life.

Through its *liturgy*, religion provides indispensable supernatural aids to success. Without the Mass, there would be no grace;

---

[4] F. LeBuffe, *Hard-Headed Holiness* (St. Louis: Queen's Work, 1950).

[5] J. Haffert, *Mary in Her Scapular Promise* (New York: Scapular Press, 1942), p. 193.

without the Sacrament of Matrimony there would be no continuing reservoir of grace available at every moment throughout the duration of a marriage; without the Sacrament of Penance, many could not avail themselves of the peace and strength, the wise counsel and the wisdom which that sacrament affords; without the sacramentals—the crucifixes, statues, blessed pictures, holy water, rosaries—the multiplication of needed graces would not be so facile.

Again, religion points out in its *ascetics,* the value of poverty, chastity and obedience in marriage even as in the state of religion. Millions of families struggling on a limited income can know from religion that theirs is the road to holiness if they will sublimate their poverty. Living within the family income and generosity to Church and charity are further exercises of the virtue of *poverty.* The right use of sex, the avoidance of unnatural means to family limitation, and the necessary periods of enforced abstinence allow married couples to grow toward sanctity through the practice of *chastity.* Wives who humbly adhere to their husbands' reasonable decisions and husbands who support their families by subordination to an ill-tempered boss, are practicing a type of *obedience* which will also expedite greatly their growth in spirituality. Finally, religion emphasizes those two great virtues—humility and charity—without which no marriage can succeed or home can be peaceful, and which make adjustment, harmony, happiness and true success inevitable.

Religion and adjustment

Various studies on factors associated with happiness in marriage tend to agree on the importance of religion in adjustment. People who attend church services several times a month, who were married by a minister of religion and in a church or rectory, who had considerable religious home training, who had formal education in religion beyond their eighteenth year, who went through courtship free from unchastity are the best risks in marriage.[6]

Whereas religious partners have the highest happiness rat-

---

[6] Studies by Bernard, Burgess and Cottrell, Davis, Hamilton, Hart, Kirkpatrick, Landis and Landis, Popenoe, Schroeder, Terman.

ing, irreligious spouses seem to have the highest divorce rate. Among 13,528 Maryland families it was found that the divorce rate of Catholics was 6.4 per cent, of Jews 4.6 per cent, of Protestants 6.8 per cent, of mixed marriages 15.2 per cent and *of irreligious partners 16.7 per cent.*[7] The reasons for this were pointed out long ago by Leo XIII when he advised that:

. . . there would be a calm and quiet constancy in marriage if married people would gather strength and life from the virtue of religion alone, which imparts to us resolution and fortitude. For religion would enable them to bear tranquilly and even gladly the trials of their state: such as, for instance, the faults that they discover in one another, the difference of temper and character, the weight of a mother's cares, the wearing anxiety about the education of children, reverses of fortune, and the sorrows of life.[8]

An important part of religious living is the practice of certain virtues which are by their nature conducive to good adjustment. Conversely, the opposite vices are factors making for poor adjustment or for marital breakdown. Although it is difficult to understand how any two religious partners could fail to be happy with each other, it is even more difficult to understand how a marriage can be successful in the presence of evident vices. Certainly in most cases of breakdown in marriage at least one of the two partners has been departing from the ethical code of virtues proper to marriage (see Table 8).

Perhaps it is safe to state that, excepting those instances where mental ill-health has deprived an individual of responsibility, every marriage failure is the result of an accumulation of sinful practices of one kind or another.

Abandonment, conformity and adjustment

Among the positive factors in religious living that make for adjustment in marriage, is simple conformity to God's Will and abandonment to His all-wise Providence. Those partners who

---

[7] H. M. Bell, *Youth Tell Their Story* (Washington, D. C.: American Council on Education, 1938), p. 21.

[8] Leo XIII, "Christian Marriage," *Social Wellsprings*, Vol. I, annotated and arranged by Joseph Husslein, S.J., Ph.D. (Milwaukee: The Bruce Publishing Company, 1943), p. 45.

TABLE 8

THE RELATIONSHIP BETWEEN THE SEVEN CAPITAL SINS AND GRIEVANCES
AND FACTORS OF MARITAL BREAKDOWN
(as shown by scientific studies)

Capital Sin	Grievances and Breakdown Factors *
PRIDE: excessive love of self	Domination, inconsideration, conceit, excessive ambition, preoccupation with career, opinionatedness, quarrelsomeness, insistence on own way, irreligion, snobbishness toward in-laws.
AVARICE: excessive love of worldly goods	Gambling, extravagance, penny-pinching, refusal to give wife adequate money, preoccupation with work, excessive ambition, discontent with lot, "keeping up with Joneses," birth control.
LUST: inordinate love of pleasures of the flesh	Excessive sex demands, sex for pleasure only, lack of consideration in sex relations, adultery, birth control.
SLOTH: laziness and shirking of duties	Disorderliness, slovenliness, neglect of home and children, laxity in religion, irresponsibility, sex refusal, lack of affection, non-support, husband's refusal to help overburdened wife.
ANGER: inordinate displeasure at wrongs done to us	Cruelty, irritability, faultfinding, tendency to complain and nag, quarrelsomeness, physical and mental abuse, revengefulness, hatred, resentment, hostility.
ENVY: tendency to be sad at the good fortune of others	Cruelty, deprivation of rightful respect, suspicion, detraction, gossip, "keeping up with Joneses."
GLUTTONY: excessive pleasure in eating and drinking	Drunkenness, cruelty, excessive sex demands, greediness, strife, coarse language, immaturity, irresponsibility.

* From studies by Thomas, Brinkman, Terman and others. Also see Chapter 18.

have trained themselves to see the will of a loving Father behind every circumstance of life, will enjoy peace and tranquility at all times. No event, large or small, is viewed without their seeing "the finger of God" in it. In addition, they remain secure in an abiding sense of constant love, assistance and protection of a God who is ever a loving Father. The wife of an inconsiderate husband will see in the hardships resulting from his selfishness (but not in the sin itself) the hand of a provident Father who permits this for her highest good. She remains mindful of the fact that "to those who love God, all things work together unto good." Similarly, the victim of a nagging wife will accept as a providential opportunity to practice patience and humility, the difficulties of his married life. He will remain tranquil, conscious of the sustaining and protecting hand of a kind Father who can change the situation at His Will or turn it into spiritual coin of greater worth.

Unfortunately many richly endowed souls neither understand nor heed the solicitations of a God of Love, and few respond to His call. . . . They had but to take the one decisive step to reach the threshold of the forge where heroes are fashioned, and there, without changing their vocation or dress, by merely *sanctifying the heroism imposed on them by their state of life*—that is to say by super-naturalizing the martyrdom of their daily life—many of these excellent Christians could be truly saints [italics ours].[9]

BENEFITS OF MARRIAGE

Amid the secular confusion of our day, religion more than anything else preserves and teaches the unchanging and unchangeable benefits of married life. By retaining the correct attitudes toward these benefits, when most others have adopted false attitudes, religion proves a bulwark against failure and a potent factor for success.

The Old and New Testament alike affirm and reaffirm that the first great benefit is children. Fertility, in the eyes of religion, is a blessing; sterility a misfortune. In this day of family limitation and child spacing this benefit needs realization anew. Despite propaganda for contraception, children still spell happiness to normal men and women, act as a tie and a security against divorce, develop the character and personality of the sacrificing parents, act as a security and solace in old age, and become the source of countless graces now and after death. Socially children maintain the nation's virility, populate the Mystical Body of Christ and can afford an eternal glory to God in the world to come.

The companionship of married life is another of its benefits. Our age recognizes the advantages of a partner in marriage who

---

[9] Mateo Crawley-Boevey SS. CC., Jesus King of Love (Washington, D. C.: National Center of the Enthronement, 1945), p. 164.

dispels one's lonesomeness, tenders love and affection, affords security and complements one's needs. However, with easy awarding of divorce, it fails to realize the need for companionship in old age.

The sacramental graces and bond remain the chief benefits of marriage. Not only are special graces assured the married couple throughout their married lives, but the bond of unity is forged deeper by the Sacrament of Matrimony. With these special graces the Mystical Body of Christ is extended quantitatively through childbirth and qualitatively through child training.

Even the physical and mental well-being of partners is enhanced by marriage. Statistics indicate that married people outlive both the divorced and the unmarried. In 1940 the death rate of single men was one and a half that of married men, the rate of divorced men twice that of married men. The death rate of divorced women was one and a half that of married women; in fact, even during the chief childbearing ages (20–29 years) married women had a lower death rate than the divorced.[10] "The chances of survival are greater for the married than for the single, much more so among men than among women. . . . Obviously, marriage is a stabilizing influence in the life and health of the individual." [11] In the half-century between 1900–1950, "married men have enjoyed a considerably lower mortality than the unmarried at *every* age period; and in recent years women have been in the same situation." [12]

UNITY, STABILITY AND RELIGION

The advantages of married life, cannot be enjoyed unless both unity and permanency are present. Because of the decline in unity today, families are giving us a large number of neurotic

---

10 L. I. Dublin, *The Facts of Life: From Birth to Death* (New York: The Macmillan Company, 1951), p. 10.

11 "The Married Live Longer," *Statistical Bulletin*, Vol. XXIV, No. 7 (New York: Metropolitan Life Insurance Company, 1943), pp. 5–6; also C. Jones, "A Genealogical Study of Population," *Quarterly Publication of the American Statistical Association*, Vol. XVI (1918).

12 "Married Women Show Striking Decline in Mortality," *Statistical Bulletin*, Vol. XXXI, No. 4 (New York: Metropolitan Life Insurance Co., April 1950), p. 2.

children and a high divorce rate. This is doubtless due in great measure to the failure to realize the profundity of the union in marriage. Religion speaks of "two in one flesh" and "he who hates his wife hates himself." It is a unity so profound that it almost borders on identity. There is also the union of both partners with Christ—the silent third partner to every marriage. Even if there were a legitimate reason for divorce from one's partner, what reason could prevail for breaking the partnership with God which marriage is? Those tempted to sever their marital union might well consider the fact that marriage between Christians is a symbol of Christ's union with the Church. More than once have members of His Church broken anew the heart of the Divine Bridegroom; but never has He resorted to rejection or divorce. Instead He has wooed them back again by the ineffable virtues of His Sacred Heart.

RELIGION AND THE DIVINE PLAN FOR MARRIAGE

Marriage was not intended to be successful without the aid of religion. On the contrary, nothing was to be more important for marital adjustment and success. Religion was to teach the truths by which marriage should live and prosper; it was to afford both the supernatural aids of the Mass, the sacraments, the sacramentals, prayer and sacrifice, and the natural aids which are the practical effects of charity. Religion was to afford that supernatural point of view (through conformity and abandonment) which would insure adjustment, peace and harmony despite difficulties. It was to hold firm to the sacredness of marriage and its benefits, to its unity and stability when secularism would deny them all.

12

Marital Love

LOVE BETWEEN partners in marriage is unique in that its rightful expression is consummated in the *total* embrace of soul and bodily union. Outside of marriage, love may find a limited expression only—a hug, a kiss, a handshake, or a pat on the back. But marital love is total and complete; it is the self-surrender of one's total personality to another. Marital love is unique in still another aspect. While love between any two human beings of the same sex may have its complementary aspects, it does not comprise completion in the physical area. Married love, on the other hand, is based in part upon physical differences and physical completion.

THE SUPER-NATURE OF SEX

A basic, widespread, error obscures the true nature of marital love. It is the mistake of tearing physical sex out of its general context and, in so doing, making it ugly. We are told that the human eye, properly located in the context of the human face, is the most beautiful part of the human anatomy. In a similar sense, sex, when rightly understood and kept in its spiritual and psychological context, is one of the noblest acts a human being can perform. On the other hand, the human eye dislodged from the socket is one of the most disgusting sights observable. So, sex devoid of its spiritual and psychological components is perhaps one of the most degrading and animalistic acts of which human beings are capable.

Sex, like marriage itself, can be a merger of two Christians, reflecting the union of Christ with His bride, the Church. As such it is an act of great spiritual beauty and deep spiritual significance, for marital love between Christians in the state of grace is a merger of two bodies which are temples of the Trinity and a merger of two souls sharing the same Divine Life. Love of God is thereby intensified and magnified since both partners share to an increased extent their participation in the life of grace. The Church is rendered fertile to the bearing of spiritual offspring through the embrace of Christ's love in the waters of baptism. Even so are wives rendered fertile to the bearing of human offspring who can become children of God and co-heirs with Christ. "The truth is: nowhere is God more intimately present than in the act of married love, for nowhere is His activity so immediate." [1]   Furthermore, the marital act can include the virtues of justice, charity, chastity and even of religion. It can be the virtue of justice since it renders the debt contracted at the time of marriage; the virtue of charity since it is an expression of love and reduces the temptations to infidelity of one's partner; the virtue of chastity since this virtue consists in the right use of sex; the virtue of religion since through its effects (children) God its Author is glorified while the partners grow in Godlikeness.[2]

PSYCHOLOGICAL NATURE OF SEX

Sex is something which relates to the entire personality of a human being. Individuals are singled out as being "manly" or "womanly." There is an aversion to the masculine woman and a greater aversion to the feminine man. The clear implications of all this are not only that sex is something associated with the whole human person but also that it differs in its traits as between men and women.[3]

It is precisely because of these differences that the two sexes match and complement each other. Further, it is because of

---

[1] E. Mersch, *Love, Marriage, and Chastity* (New York: Sheed & Ward, Inc., 1939), p. 5.
[2] St. Thomas Aquinas, *Supplement to the Summa Theologica*, Q. 41, art. 4.
[3] For detailed treatment of this point see Chapter 9.

varying traits that both are capable of discharging their roles—
the man as husband and father, the woman as wife and mother.
A close study of sex in both its psychological and physical aspects clearly indicates that it is oriented toward the goals of
generation and education of children.

The psychological differences between a man and a woman
through which each complements and matches the qualities of
the other, lie at the basis of the mysterious component of love.
This is the reason, for instance, that a feminine man will be attracted to a masculine woman, the dominating male will be
attracted to a submissive woman and vice versa. In the deep
union of souls in marriage which true love implies, there will be
an inevitable overflow into the physical which will induce a desire
for bodily union also. From the standpoint of the *individual*
the embrace of physical sex is the culmination, the terminal point
of human love. From the *social* viewpoint, however, physical
sex is the indispensable means and has its rightful termination in
the generation of another human being. Sex not prompted by
true love is a nonhuman experience similar to animal mating.
For this reason we speak of *mates* among animals but of *partners* or *spouses* among human beings. On the other hand, physical sex union artificially diverted from its natural goal of generation is something less than animalistic. For this reason deliberate
birth frustration is an act of perversion unknown to the animal
kingdom, akin to a sacrilege.

IMPORTANCE OF SEX

Though sex is a minor portion of the totality of married life,
it is an extremely important one. Economists assure us that
though the exports of a nation are often a small percentage of the
total production, any significant decrease in them will lead to
disaster in the whole economy. Similarly, the importance of sex
cannot be estimated from its proportionate part of total marital
living but from its impact upon all other aspects of married life.
Without it a marriage is not considered consummated, nor can
all of the purposes of marriage be served. When properly used
it becomes a source of union, harmony, peace and adjustment.
It intensifies the love between husband and wife and acts as a
shield against infidelity and incontinence. The entire human

personality, even in its supernatural aspects, is prospered by sex since the act of marital love also merits grace. The deeper love generated by it overflows into charity toward neighbors; the very incompleteness of it causes the soul to yearn for the perfect union with God. Furthermore, the physical and mental health of men is benefited by it; and women are transformed physically and morally. "It has been recognized for a long time that . . . sexual relations have profound physiological effects, especially on the female," [4] because the spermatic fluid is absorbed by women and plays a dynamogenic role, promoting equilibrium.[5] In general, the act of marital love promotes relaxation, vigor, self-confidence, exhilaration, general sense of well-being, sense of security, and a forgetfulness of minor frictions and tensions in marriage.

On the other hand, the importance of sex in marriage can be and often is seriously overestimated. In a study of 476 Catholic husbands and wives (married 10 years or more) sex was listed 13th among the chief causes of happiness, 22nd among the things most desired by wives; 12th among things most desired by husbands; 21st among factors making for success in marriage.[6] Another study of 108 Catholic husbands and wives indicated that 40 thought sex necessary for happiness while 68 thought it "desirable but not overly important." [7] In a secular study of 665 engaged men and 645 engaged women only 5.1 per cent considered sex adjustment the first factor in success, 15.1 per cent the second, and 8.8 per cent the third factor.[8] Less than one-third listed sex as one of the three most important factors in success.

The importance of sex as a factor in marital breakdown is also grossly overrated by many. In one of the earliest studies sex

---

[4] Raoul de Gutchenere, *Judgment on Birth Control* (New York: The Macmillan Company, 1931), p. 156.

[5] *Ibid.*, p. 206.

[6] Hugh Dunn, S.J., *A Study of Some Catholic Marital Attitudes, Practices and Problems with Special Reference to the Implication for Premarital Instructions* (Washington, D. C.: The Catholic University of America Press, 1956), Tables 30, 34, 38.

[7] P. M. James, "The Expressed Results of a Certain Premarital Lecture Course" (Master's thesis, Catholic University of America, 1953), p. 82.

[8] E. Burgess and P. Wallin, *Engagement and Marriage* (Chicago: J. B. Lippincott Company, 1953), Table 59, p. 403.

was *not found* among the first five causes of breakdown;[9] in a study of 7,000 broken Catholic marriages sex was sixth as a causative factor.[10] In opinions of 26 experts on marriage, sex was not even named as one of the nine major causes of divorce.[11] Less than one-third of all the cases counseled in a Catholic family clinic included sex problems,[12] and in another marriage counseling agency among 2,566 cases only about 15 per cent involved sex.[13] After reviewing the marriages of 600 husbands and 629 wives, it was concluded that though the "odds are strongly in favor of the person with good sex adjustment having a high success score," nevertheless, "A substantial proportion of men and women with *low* sex scores have *high* marital success scores [italics ours]."[14] This clearly indicates that factors other than sex are more important for happiness in marriage.

MORALITY OF SEX RELATIONS

Despite its great dignity and high purpose, sex is a dangerous area of human living. Certainly it is one of the many things which God made and which on the seventh day he called *good*. However, one of the effects of original sin was to take away the full autocratic control over sex. As a result, few instincts are more easily stimulated, few temptations more easily aroused. Furthermore, no other instinct has the same easy tendency to become intensified to proportions which becloud reason and overwhelm the will. This is why, contrary to modern ideas, a certain sense of shame is rightful here. "If the sexual instinct were completely obedient to reason, there would be no indecency or shame attached to it."[15] In a study by a psychologist of 162

---

9 E. R. Mowrer and H. R. Mowrer, *Domestic Discord, Its Analysis and Treatment* (Chicago: The University of Chicago Press, 1928).

10 J. L. Thomas, "The Urban Impact on the American Cathoilc Family," *American Sociological Review,* Vol. X, No. 4 (December 1949), pp. 256–268.

11 C. S. Mihanovich, *Current Social Problems* (Milwaukee: The Bruce Publishing Company, 1951), pp. 231–232.

12 Wilma Dunn, "The Social Worker Helps Mend Broken Homes," *Hospital Progress,* (August 1949), p. 247.

13 E. H. Mudd and M. G. Preston, "The Contemporary Status of Marriage Counseling," *Annals,* Vol. CCLXXII (November 1950), p. 104.

14 Burgess and Wallin, *op. cit.,* p. 692.

15 E. C. Messenger, *Two in One Flesh* (Westminster, Md.: The Newman Press, 1948), Vol. II, p. 118.

American and 69 British men and women, nearly two-thirds reported a sense of shame when exposed to their own sex; and 84 per cent felt shame when exposed to the opposite sex.[16] This is also the reason why filling the minds of our children and adolescents, under the guise of sex education, with sex facts is hazardous and most unrealistic.

The great dignity, nobility and high purposes of sex should make it evident at once that any misuse of it is immoral. Clearly sex, like marriage, is by its nature *social,* implying cooperative and reciprocal action with another of the opposite sex. Like marriage, also, its clearly discernible purposes in nature are first, the procreation and education of the human race, and second, the personal advantages to the partners. Whenever sex is used in such a way as to frustrate its purposes, it is immoral. The solitary use of sex offends against its social nature and purposes, as does the use of contraceptives; directing sex toward the same sex militates against its intersexual nature and its purposes.

It is apparent from a number of surveys made at the Catholic University of America of Catholic married couples that many are still uninformed, despite even higher education, of many moral aspects of the marital act. Since thoughts and desires are rightful preliminaries to marital love, they are entirely lawful provided they concern one's spouse and there is no serious danger of orgasm (complete satisfaction) outside of the marital act itself. The same is true of actions such as kissing or embracing, regardless of how intimate they may be. Intercourse is likewise lawful at any time in married life provided there is no frustration of the natural act and no grave danger to the health of husband, wife, or of an unborn child.

Many couples fail to recognize or accept the fact that accommodating the serious desire of their spouse for the marital act is a matter of contractual *justice.* A partner in marriage may not reject his or her spouse sexually except for *very compelling reasons;* this may mean, at times, a duty of compliance despite considerable inconveniences. Many fail to see not only the injustice implied in refusal of sex but also the danger of exposing

---

[16] John J. Evoy, "A Study of the Psychology of Sex Shame and Modesty," (Doctoral dissertation, Loyola University, Chicago, 1955).

their spouses to infidelity and their marriages to deterioration. There are few forms of rejection more likely to breed bitterness, resentment and antagonism. When 593 husbands and 592 wives were asked whether they refuse their spouses, 10 per cent of the women said "very frequently" or "frequently" and 28 per cent said "sometimes"; well over a third apparently rejected their husbands sexually at least sometimes.[17] In another inquiry 122 Catholic husbands and wives were questioned as to the gravity of refusing the marital act; 37 out of the 122 thought granting the act either a light obligation or no obligation at all.[18]

In the same context, many seem to ignore the dangers inherent in temporary separations from each other. Since a principle of justice and rights is involved again, a spouse may not leave his partner without his consent; and such separation may not prove an occasion for incontinence for either party. The readiness with which some husbands and wives part from each other to spend separate vacations, against the wishes of their spouses, indicates considerable misunderstanding or laxity in this matter.

The morality of sex does not, however, rest so much upon its negative as upon its positive aspects. Sex actions are good and virtuous when properly employed. In fact, contrary to what some think, the virtue of chastity consists not only in the renunciation of sex but also in *its proper use*. Married people as well as the religious can and do exercise the virtue of chastity.

SEXUAL ADJUSTMENT

One of the reasons for sex rejection of spouses is the failure to attain a satisfactory adjustment. Studies show that of all areas requiring adjustment, none takes longer than the sex area. This seems due to the natural differences between men and women in their conception of sex. The observation of Chesterton that men and women are naturally incompatible is clearly noticeable here. The meaning and concepts are so different that unless love and reason dominate, no satisfactory adjustment is possible. Because of this, a significant amount of sex education and a large amount of patience and understanding are imperative. Both

---

[17] Burgess and Wallin, *op. cit.*, Chart 49, p. 664.
[18] James, *op. cit.*, Q. 18, p. 53.

sexes need to realize that men are more easily aroused, more active and reach the peak of satisfaction more quickly than women; and that sex is more specific and localized in men, more general and diffused in women. With this realization both spouses can find themselves as one in understanding and patterning of sex. Like love, with the passage of time sex will take for both a new meaning; it will serve as a vehicle of greater unity and deepened love together with an increased appreciation of the spiritual implications.

Physical facts and sex adjustment

Despite the widespread opinion to the contrary, an extensive knowledge of physical facts is not necessary for good sex adjustment. If one reviews the literature, he is forced to conclude that scientific studies in no way indicate a need for detailed data on sex matters.[19] Two investigators in this field found in all their researches that the physical factor was basic in the cases of only one out of every hundred frigid women.[20] Another student of the question reported that in regard to frigidity "nine-tenths of this type of cases that come to the clinic were known to have had original capacity and desire for the husband at some time. Their coldness then was initiated some place along the line, not in the beginning." [21] Clearly not ignorance of physical facts but other factors are operative in the great majority of sex maladjustments. There is, at present, a growing number of experts who believe that an extensive factual and detailed knowledge of the physical, defeats rather than promotes sex adjustment. They believe that a certain amount of revelation and discovery is a favorable factor and that a physician's knowledge of sex details can render a naturally spontaneous act excessively scientific.

Those experienced in marriage counseling affirm that many couples have made very good sex adjustments with a bare minimum of knowledge of physical facts. This minimum of "'facts

---

[19] A. H. Clemens, "Unscientific Aspects of Sex Education," *Marriage and Family Living,* Vol. XV, No. 1 (February 1953), pp. 11–13.

[20] Terman *et al., Psychological Factors in Marital Happiness* (New York: McGraw-Hill Book Company, Inc., 1938), pp. 373–377; also G. Hamilton, *A Research in Marriage* (New York: A. and C. Boni, Inc., 1929), pp. 333–391.

[21] R. L. Dickinson and L. Bean, *A Thousand Marriages* (Baltimore: The Williams & Wilkins Company, 1934), p. 129.

of life" is imperative because without a knowledge of them bungling and maladjustment can easily result. Yet these minimal facts are few and could be told in less than ten minutes. They have been simply stated by a very careful student of the question in the following terms:

1. There is a substance (life-giving fluid, material, etc.) in a man (seed) and a substance in a woman (egg) which, when united by a marriage embrace, may become a child. Menstruation and seminal emission are an indication of such power in each sex.

2. The marital embrace consists in a union of bodies for which the sex organs are designed. In this union the seed of the man is placed deep within the body of the woman. The pleasure connected with this act is very intense which God uses as a reward and inducement for the propagation of the human race.

3. The new baby develops for about nine months within the mother's body and is delivered through the vagina, the passage through which the seed originally traveled.

4. After birth, the baby is normally fed (nursed) at the mother's breasts.[22]

In addition to these facts, couples should be well advised to learn the technique of physical love-making. However, this knowledge is of no use until marriage and prior to that time can serve only to stimulate the imagination and provoke temptation. Here again marriage counseling experience indicates that instinctive and experimental methods have effected extremely good sex adjustment by many uninstructed in the detailed art of physical love-making.

A knowledge of extensive physical facts and technique are also useful in abnormal cases which need competent counseling. They have little use in *normal* marriages except, in the words of Pius XII, to intensify the pleasure of the act, which he labels an un-Christian motive.

Too often anti-Christian hedonism does not blush to raise this theory to a doctrine by inculcating the desire to intensify continually enjoyment in the preparation and carrying out of the conjugal union. . . . To calm the timid consciences of couples, common sense, natural in-

---

[22] Henry Sattler, *Parents, Children, and the Facts of Life* (Paterson, N. J.: St. Anthony's Guild Press, 1952), p. 182.

stinct and a brief instruction on the clear and simple maxims of Christian morality are usually sufficient.[23]

Art of good adjustment

No amount of physical facts can substitute for the real components of good sex adjustment. Nature has dictated only one method for attaining success in this area—a method in which women enjoy a deeper insight than men. The basis of good adjustment is an acceptance of the natural fact that the sex act is a psychophysical unity, and that the psychological element is far more important than the physical. The latter must at all times be kept in its rightful psychological context; to tear sex away from the psychological, like ripping an eye out of its socket, reduces it to the ugly and abhorrent.

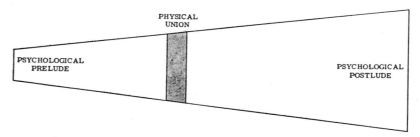

Sexual intercourse must always be regarded as a spiritual relationship wherein two persons are fused together into a glorious unity of love; a profound emotional experience which is intense and satisfying in proportion as the actors cease to be two individuals and become figuratively "one flesh and one personality." This is just another way of saying that sexual experience is never perfect unless it involves the mind and soul as well as the body. Otherwise, all the spiritual possibilities of the act are blasted.[24]

Women understand this better than men. Their romantic, affectionate dispositions enable them to understand physical sex as an interlude between a previous prelude of affectional love and

---

[23] Pius XII, *Moral Questions Affecting Married Life* (Washington, D. C.: National Catholic Welfare Conference), pp. 22–23; also *Acta Apostolicae Sedis,* Vol. XLIII (December 20, 1951), pp. 855–860.

[24] Paul Popenoe, *Preparing for Marriage* (Los Angeles: The American Institute of Family Relations, 1938), pp. 7–8.

a postlude of an even deeper emotional, intellectual, volitional love. The more passionate and impulsive natures of men, on the other hand, will incline them into considering the physical aspect more important and an end in itself rather than a transition stage. Men tend easily to forget that

Love in a monogamous marriage includes sex; but sex, in the contempoary use of the term, does not imply either marriage or monogamy. Every woman instinctively realizes the difference between the two. . . . Man is driven by pleasure; woman by the meaning of pleasure. She sees pleasure more as a means to an end, namely, the prolongation of love in herself and in her child.[25]

It is this varying approach to the act of marital love which occasions most maladjustment and most frigidity.

Women should understand men's more impetuous and impulsive sexual nature. But even more important, because it is more correct, men must understand and accommodate their approach to women's and nature's pattern for sex adjustment. They must see that without a preparatory stage of affection and psychological love-making, the sex act is more nearly animal than human. They should also realize that as important as is an emotional, romantic and affectional approach to the marital act, equally important is a constant day by day affectional relationship. If this is not sensed and acted upon, women will interpret the marital act for what it has really degenerated to—an animalistic experience in which they are being used as a tool for their husbands' pleasure. Men must also forestall their passionate natures by remaining aware that physical union is not a culmination of the marital act but a transition to a deeper and more intense love of the entire person. Husbands who fail to understand the even greater desire by wives for affectional love after the physical embrace, can expect their wives to find their feminine natures frustrated and their former ardor turned into frigidity.

Other factors also operate to induce sex maladjustment and frigidity. Some of these factors were listed by 154 women in the order of the importance as follows:

Physical factors: fatigue, ill-health, sleeplessness.

---

25 F. J. Sheen, *Three to Get Married* (New York: Appleton-Century-Crofts, Inc., 1951), pp. 4–5.

Psychological factors: fear of pregnancy, preoccupation with other cares, childhood inhibitions, emotional upset, lack of interest, demanding husband, drinking husband, unkind husband.[26]

Clearly the proper factors for good adjustment here are, among others, relaxation, freedom from worry and fear, absence of tensions, mutual attention, emotional poise, and realistic expectations.

Some erroneous notions

The emphasis in our marriage literature of the importance of experiencing an orgasm (complete satisfaction) is inducing a great deal of needless misery. The Kinsey Report, for instance, indicated that a great deal of maladjustment in marriage is due to the lack of complete satisfaction by women.[27] Those reading such literature are led to believe that without an orgasm there is something seriously wrong with their love life and that they cannot enjoy happiness in marital relations. Almost 20 year ago one of the first scientific studies disclosed the fallacy of that attitude. Out of 792 couples, 63 wives never experienced an orgasm, 191 sometimes did, 338 usually did and 168 always did. Yet in the group of those who *never* experienced it, every shade of adjustment and happiness was found.[28] Subsequent researches have confirmed the position that although such experience is highly desirable, spouses need not fear that failure of orgasmic experience is necessarily fatal to their happiness or their marriage. Usually proper timing and adequate love cultivation will do much to achieve the desired result.

Another error permeating current thinking is that we must educate couples to drain the cup of sexual pleasure. The great emphasis upon sex technique is today, in part at least, an effort to intensify to the utmost its pleasurable aspects. It is also an effort to compensate on the physical sex level for the couple's

[26] C. T. La Follette, *A Study of the Problems of 652 Gainfully Employed Married Women Homemakers,* Contribution to Education No. 619 (New York: Bureau of Publications, Teachers College, Columbia University, 1934), Table 61, p. 145.

[27] A. C. Kinsey, *et al., Sexual Behaviour in the Human Female* (Philadelphia: W. B. Saunders Company, 1953), p. 172.

[28] Terman *et al., op. cit.,* pp. 373–408.

failure to adjust on the level of emotions and attitudes. Pius XII has noted that this is the result of de-emphasizing the procreative purpose of sex and exalting its personal advantages. He warned that:

This modern cult of pleasure is empty of all spiritual value and unworthy of Christian couples. . . . Banish from your minds the cult of pleasure and do your best to stop the diffusion of literature that thinks it a duty to describe in full detail the intimacy of conjugal life under the pretext of instructing, directing and reassuring.[29]

MARITAL LOVE IN THE DIVINE PLAN

Of all the possible ways Divine Wisdom might have employed to keep the human race alive, He designed the act of marital love for that purpose. It was further intended to deepen the love between husband and wife so that they, in turn, could employ that enhanced love in the formation and education of the children. Not only did God invent sex but He gave it high natural and supernatural dignity. In addition, He surrounded it with certain natural norms and laws, the violation of which spell sin, maladjustment and discord. The adherence of this Divine Plan for sex leads to not only the perpetuity of the race but the development of the spouses' personalities; it rewards them by legitimate pleasure and affords them an increased physical and mental health.

---

[29] Pius XII, *op. cit.*

13

Physical Parenthood

Even in a planned parenthood era, the role of reproduction is inescapably an integral part of marriage. In nineteen leading textbooks used in our colleges and universities, some other roles and functions were omitted, but none failed to mention that of physical parenthood.[1] Anyone studying closely the biological and psychological constitutions, aptitudes and capacities of men and women, cannot fail to recognize that they are oriented by nature toward physical parenthood. This has been recognized, and procreation has been accepted by Catholicism as the first and chief goal of marriage.

DIGNITY OF PARENTHOOD

This primacy of purpose dignifies parenthood from either the supernatural or natural standpoint. No other natural act associates man's creativity so closely with that of God. It is often said that man "joins hands" with the Creator in fashioning another human being. Actually man does more; in a sense he *forces* the hand of the Creator, for God never denies a soul to a

---

[1] J. A. Curtin, "Analysis of Family Theory Found in Some Standard Textbooks Commonly Used in the Basic Courses in Sociology in Colleges and Universities" (Washington, D. C.: Master's thesis, Catholic University of America, July 1951).

body which is generated. We seem to have forgotten that in reproducing a human being, man reaches his creative role by reproducing the masterpiece of all creation. It is easy to write off as poetic imagery the statement that the greatest piece of literature struck from the pen of man, the greatest invention sprung from his mind, the greatest work of music or architecture formed by the genius of man are insignificant as compared with the generation of another human being. Yet this is not poetic fancy or literary exaggeration; on the contrary, it is a *literal fact*. Our current sense of values needs sharpening in this respect. If we add the further truth that other products of man's genius will eventually decay, while the human being lives on endlessly, the dignity of reproduction is heightened still further. In the eyes of faith the newly generated human being will continue for an eternity as an additional worshipper of the Godhead.

Were this properly recognized and accepted in action, parents would dedicate themselves more to their families and less to their careers; they would find their sense of accomplishment and achievement more satisfied by the number of their children than the number of their dollars, honors or awards. Despite worldly and economic mediocrity they would abide in a sense of natural and supernatural worth. The art of homemaking, so often deplored as menial and monotonous, would be raised to new heights of gratification and satisfaction. This was probably part of the reason General MacArthur answered a reporter's question about his son's pride in his military success by commenting that he would prefer that his son remember him as a father rather than as a soldier. Similarly, in a narrative of Cardinal Mindzenty's life is an incident which occurred in the slums of Budapest. Apparently while he was driving through this area, Communist agitators started to pelt his limousine with stones. The Cardinal asked his chauffeur to stop the car, left it and addressed the agitators. In his remarks, we are told, he asked them to spare above all his chauffeur, the father of a number of children, adding: "He cannot be replaced as their father but the Pope can create another Cardinal in 24 hours." This sense of the transcendent dignity of parenthood must be restored before the full dignity of marriage is recognized and before the contraception crusade can be arrested.

DIGNITY OBSCURED TODAY

The preoccupation of parents in their personal ambitions, comforts, honors and pleasures is obscuring the vision of parenthood's nobility. Perhaps if we accepted the fact that "It probably takes more endurance, more patience, more intelligence, more healthy emotion, to raise a decent happy human being than to be an atomic physicist, a politician or a psychiatrist," [2] we would witness an inversion of our sense of values.

Childless marriages are not the rarity in our culture that they have been in most other cultures. Children are frequently accepted with no sense of dignity but as objects to satisfy parental emotional needs. In this there is the competitive tendency to keep up with (but not exceed) the Joneses. The expectations and pressures, as well as the values, of our culture do not encourage having childen in any numbers. In a study of 996 men and 993 women, 27.5 per cent of the men and 26.6 per cent of the women wanted children only *mildly,* while 6.1 per cent of the men and 5.6 per cent of the women objected to having any children; [3] this indicates about one-third who had no strong desire for children.

The small family system now characterizing our society markedly contrasts to the penchant for "bigness" in the same society. The couple who doesn't want a big family, more often than not wants a big car, a big wardrobe, a big income, a big house. They will usually prefer to live in a big city, enjoy big parties, attend big theatres, send their children to big colleges and universities, pride themselves on being employed by a big corporation, want a large circle of friends, are ambitious for great honors, and live in the hope that they might have a big funeral. This has been noted by a distinguished sociologist who labeled it "the culture of quantitative colossalism." Having studied all previous civilizations he recognized it as " a fairly uniform symptom of disintegration," consisting in "the substitution of quantita-

---

[2] M. R. Saperstein, *Emotional Security* (New York: Crown Press, 1948).

[3] E. W. Burgess and P. Wallin, *Engagement and Marriage* (Chicago: J. B. Lippincott Company, 1953), Table 65, p. 409.

tive colossalism for a sublime quality; of glittering externality for inner value; of a show for a substance." He points out that Pliny's comment is as applicable today as in his day: "Not being able to make our values beautiful, we make them huge." [4] We seem proud of bigness in most things today, but are often humiliated at the arrival of an additional member of the family. So badly have our natural and Christian sense of values been distorted by the materialism and neopaganism of the age, that bigness in families is often enough the subject of ridicule and abuse. Parenthood is being sold short and lesser values are taking its place.

ADVANTAGES OF EXPECTANT PARENTHOOD

This penchant for small families and big cars shows a failure to recognize the genuine advantages that accrue from parenthood. This may be due in part to the fact that obstetrical research in this country has been almost sterile in discovering the beneficial effects of pregnancy and childbirth. To learn these advantages recourse must be had to research done in French medical science and that of other nations. These benefits are so many that they are evident immediately. From the onset of pregnancy to old age, the rewards of parenthood continue. Pregnancy is viewed by most couples with some dismay. The nausea, the physical inconvenience and sometimes an irritability and a lessened sex drive on the part of the wife induce dread. Actually it should be a time when these very factors draw a couple closer together through an understanding, patience and mutual anticipation of the child to come. Whatever the discomforts of the normal pregnancy, the advantages more than offset them. The living fetus acts upon the expectant mother as a therapeutic element constantly renewing its chemical messengers. It exerts a marvelous curative influence on the mother's entire organism.[5] Perhaps this is why a study of 112 wives indicated that 56 per cent experienced the same good health in pregnancy as before, 33

[4] P. Sorokin, *The Crisis of Our Age* (New York: E. P. Dutton & Co., Inc., 1942), pp. 252–255.
[5] For medical opinions see Jacques Leclercq, *Marriage and the Family* (New York: Frederick Pustet Co., Inc., 1947), pp. 298–305.

per cent found their health improved and only 11 per cent were poorer in health.[6]

The child in process of formation is no mere parasite fastened to the mother and living with her. He does not merely receive from her the materials needed for his growth, which she has the duty of drawing from the outside and of adapting. He further brings her special stimulation which will arouse dormant activities in her; these will bring about her physical completion and call forth hitherto unsuspected sentiments to complete her morally. This is the source of that wholly charming bloom whose starting point in the young woman is pregnancy.

Important as this phenomenon is, it is not the only one to take place during the silent labor of gestation. The fertilized germ, which from the first day has life of its own, is not just any being whatsoever; it is the father who becomes incarnate in the mother. It will live, and grow in her and when it quits her to become an altogether distinct individual, it will leave in her something of itself and of its father with which she will never be able to part.[7]

"If it is true, biologically speaking that the child receives a deep impress of the mother's temperament and health it is likewise true that the mother is permeated to the marrow by her child." [8] Besides general well-being, pregnancy often has a marked curative effect upon physical and emotional ailments, sometimes of long standing. The stimulation of the endocrine glands in pregnancy often restores to health women who are suffering from dyspepsia, anemia and the like. An authority speaks of "the normal pregnancy, which enriches the somatic and psychic energies of the woman to a degree that she becomes able to master emotional conflicts which were disturbing her at other times." [9] Explaining this statement, she adds: "We have ob-

[6] J. T. Landis, T. Poffenberger, and S. Poffenberger, "Effects of First Pregnancy on Sex Adjustment," *American Sociological Review*, Vol. XV (1950), pp. 767–772.

[7] Dr. Desplate, "Bulletin de la Societe de Saint-Luc" (August 1938), quoted by Leclercq, *op. cit.,* p. 300.

[8] Rene Biot, "Ce que la biologie nous apprend de la nature de la femme," *Semaines Sociales de France* (Nancy, 1927; Paris, 1928), quoted by Leclercq, *op. cit.,* p. 143.

[9] Therese Benedeke, "The Psychosomatic Implications of the Primary Unit: Mother—Child," *American Journal of Orthopsychiatry*, Vol. XIX, No. 4 (October 1949), p. 64.

served that many neurotic women, who suffered severe anxiety states before, have become free from anxiety during pregnancy. Others become free from depression and from desperate mood changes." [10]

One of the best things a husband can do during this period is to make his wife feel that the baby is wanted. His role is scarcely less important than hers, though of quite a different nature.

The father who understands won't have his feelings hurt if his pregnant wife is sometimes cross, weary, nervous, excited, irritable. That is the time for him to be his very sweetest. He might suggest doing something she likes to do. Sometimes just a word of cheer, a look, a bit of loving will make up for a whole day's weariness.

She needs understanding and help through a long and tiresome piece of work. At no time in her life does a woman need her husband's understanding and love more than when she is pregnant. No one else can do for her and for their baby what he can do by making allowances for her ups and downs and by sharing the work and the fun of getting ready for the baby and of caring for him by caring for his mother.[11]

ADVANTAGES OF PARENTHOOD

The relationship between children and happiness is being subjected to considerable scrutiny. We have studies seemingly giving contradictory answers to this question. However, it is quite apparent that what these studies are showing us is simply that normal couples find children a source of happiness while those abnormal couples (who resist nature's deepest instinct of parenthood) find children a source of misery. In reply to the question of how important children are to their happiness, out of 118 Catholic husbands and wives 59 replied that they were "very important," 21 "most important," 13 "desirable." [12] A study of 8,370 couples throughout the nation indicated a higher degree of happiness among parents of three or more children than among childless couples.[13] Another family specialist found that among

---

[10] *Ibid.*

[11] Anne Stevens, *Maternity Handbook: For Pregnant Mothers and Expectant Fathers* (New York: Maternity Center Association, 1932), p. 16.

[12] P. M. James, "The Expressed Effects of a Certain Premarital Lecture Course" (Master's thesis, Catholic University of America, 1953), p. 95.

[13] Paul Popenoe, *Modern Marriage* (New York: The Macmillan Company, 1940), p. 268.

450 old people, over half said the happiest period of their lives was when they had their children at home with them.[14]   Among 653 couples who had at least one child (20 per cent had two or more) there was compelling evidence that children were a source of happiness; 81.3 per cent found children "added very much" to their happiness and 13.7 per cent that they "added considerably" to happiness.[15]

A noted marriage counselor and scholar assures us that children are a unique educational experience for parents, bind parents together, rejuvenate them, give aid and love in old age and confer immortality upon the parents.[16]   He furthermore found that the more intelligent college men have more children;[17] whereas the mothers of the largest families live the longest.[18]   Longevity benefits of paternity are confirmed by recent data officially released.   The lowest death rate of four groups, the single, widowed, divorced, and married, during the childbearing ages (25–34) was that of the married.   Out of 100,000 population the death rate for the single was 308.6, widowed 495.2, divorced 386.7, but for the married only 144.9.   The same low death rate for married people is evident between the ages of 35 and 44; for the single it was 629.9, widowed 728.3, divorced 748.5, for the married it was only 307.0.[19]   One of the deepest students of the family has summarized the data regarding the advantages of children as follows:

It is definitely established that familism is related to a series of biosocial differences.   The differences are found between the celibates and the married, between the divorcd and undivorced, the widowed and the unwidowed, those with children and those without, and those

---

[14] J. T. Landis, "What is the Happiest Period in Life," *School and Society,* Vol. LV, No. 1432 (June 6, 1942), p. 643.

[15] Burgess and Wallin, *op. cit.,* Table 98, p. 707.

[16] Popenoe, *op. cit.,* pp. 244–247.

[17] Paul Popenoe, "Fertility and Intelligence of College Men," *Science,* Vol. LXXXVII (1938), pp. 86–87.

[18] Paul Popenoe, "Long Life Means Many Children," *Journal of Heredity,* Vol. VII, No. 3 (March 1916), pp. 99–100; also C. Jones, "A Genealogical Study of Population," *Quarterly Publication, American Statistical Association,* Vol. XVI (1918).

[19] National Office of Vital Statistics, United States Department of Health, Education, and Welfare, *Mortality from Selected Causes by Marital Status, United States, 1949–1951,* Vol. XXXIX, No. 7 (Washington, D. C.: United States Government Printing Office, May 8, 1956), Table 2, p. 376.

with more than two children compared with those with only one or two children. These differences are reflected in the greater ability of the more familistic persons to resist the conditions leading to suicide, to live longer, to have better physical and mental health and to have more rounded personalities.[20]

Spouses cannot experience the sacrifices and joys of becoming the parents of a number of children without finding their lives, characters and personalities profoundly changed. Nor can they do so without having their spiritual life grow significantly. Important advantages are the countless graces accruing from the responsible discharge of parenthood and obtained for parents by their children's prayers and sacrifices. In old age dutiful children also afford an economical and emotional security not enjoyed by childless couples. Even after death, the conscientious parent can be assured of the continued prayers of his children, often after others have forgotten him.

SOME DIFFICULTIES OF CHILD REARING

Even the most ardent advocate of children is not unmindful of their costs in time, energy and money. For this reason, many young couples are tempted to defer the start of their families. Such delay, without compelling and justifiable reasons, is unethical and hazardous. Among other advantages nature intends the first child to refill the cup of marriage somewhat reduced by the disillusionments, waning romance and adjustment difficulties of the first year. When much of the poetry has worn thin, a child once again renews the love and community of life together. Furthermore, the temptation to defer continuously the first child is great when the wife is working and the couple is enjoying the double income and the pleasure of a relatively carefree pattern of marriage.

When children come, a new set of adjustments must be effected. More than before, both partners must then adapt themselves to the fuller meaning of marriage. This is a difficult adjustment because it demands the sacrifice of self to the interests of children. Time schedules, vacation plans, religious activities and many

---

[20] Carle Zimmerman, *Family and Civilization* (New York: Harper & Brothers, 1947), p. 680.

other elements will have to be modified or changed in favor of the best interests of the children. However, all of these accommodations are made easier and lighter by the pervading happiness of being a parent.

In our time the financial cost of rearing children is of great concern to most. Studies show this to be one of the chief reasons for family limitation. We are told, by some, that it will cost a parent $20,000 to raise each child to the 18th year. This would be, if true, enough to frighten most parents into a reconsideration of their family planning. A detailed analysis of the various items, however, shows them to be incomplete. Parents would be well advised not to take such figures at face value but to inquire into what such totals include. Studies of this type usually do not consider the possibilities of home production, of hand-me-down clothes, and the like; on the other hand, they prorate the use of family conveniences, such as an automobile, charging a significant percentage of the cost to an infant, though he may rarely be taken for a ride. They also fail to include the ability of children to produce in the home or to earn money by part-time jobs. Normally, every additional child is less costly than the previous one— a fact not taken into account in these studies. Furthermore, these amounts for child rearing are not an estimate of *absolutely necessary costs* but of what many parents *prefer to spend,* including many luxury items.

PARENTS AND CHILDBIRTH

Another factor inducing couples to either remain childless or limit the number of their children, is an exaggerated fear of childbirth. There are many such fears; death, weakness, subsequent invalidism, defective children, inheritable defects.[21]

Actually most of these fears are grossly exaggerated. The poet may induce phobias by speaking of a mother's "going down into the valley of death," but only about one out of a thousand mothers die in childbirth; many of them because of primitive con-

[21] Sprague Gardiner, "The Study of Personality and Situational Factors in Obstetrics," quoted by P. V. Lemkau, *Mental Hygiene in Public Health* (New York: McGraw-Hill Book Company, Inc., 1949), p. 268; also R. K. Stix, "The Place of Fertility Control in Public Health," *American Journal of Public Health,* Vol. XXXVI (March 1946), pp. 209–318.

ditions of delivery. In some places the maternal death rate is much less than the national figures, as is evident from the statement of a Catholic obstetrician:

Now let's analyze the risks. The number of women who are avoiding pregnancy because of real or implied medical reasons is legion. Surely, we should have bigger and better cemeteries to receive all these frail bodies whose lives are going to be terminated by pregnancy. Yet in 1950, in the city of Philadelphia, only three women died per 10,000 live births, and in the words of the Chairman of the Maternal Mortality Committee, two-thirds of those deaths were preventable. A remarkably low risk when one considers that in every 10,000 live births will be young and old mothers, twins, large babies, anemias, cardiacs, diabetes, tuberculosis, toxemia and kidney cases, caesarians, etc. and also when one considers that 35 per cent of all the cases delivered at Philadelphia General Hospital are unregistered cases.[22]

The fear of the pain associated with delivery is also greatly exaggerated in the minds of many. In a study of childbirths with a minimum of discomfort, fear was found the factor causing psychoses after birth.[23]

The normal woman takes her pregnancy in stride. Under proper medical attention she is guided through her prenatal course with a minimum of discomfort and is thus spared the unnecessary ill health of the neglected patient. When labor ensues she is in excellent physical condition. This sense of well-being undoubtedly allays the fears of labor so frightening to the expectant mother of past generations. The doors of our modern well equipped and excellently staffed hospitals swing open to welcome the woman in labor. She is made comfortable by the newer developments in obstetrical analgesia and anesthesia. The screaming, pain-wracked patient of former times is now a rarity. Instead we witness the labor of a quiet patient so relieved of her pains that she barely recalls the event. Again the obstetrician is aided by scientific instruments and drugs in the proper treatment of any complication which may arise. The expectant mother is practically assured of a safe delivery of a healthy child.[24]

---

[22] Dr. James Quindlen, "Marriage: the Obstetrician's Point of View," *Villanova Alumnus,* Vol. XVII, No. 1 (October 1953), p. 16.

[23] M. Strater, "Psychological Factors During Pregnancy and Childbirth," *Canadian Medical Association Journal,* Vol. LXX, No. 5 (May 1954), p. 510.

[24] E. F. Daley, "Medical Aspects of Marriage and Child-Bearing," *The Family Today: A Catholic Appraisal* (Washington, D. C.: National Catholic Welfare Conference, 1944), pp. 89–90.

The "childbirth without fear" movement in recent years has done much to allay such phobias. By stressing the importance of a relaxed, fearless, poised attitude, the discomforts of delivery have been reduced measurably. The practice is growing of returning the husband to his *natural* role beside his wife during her moments of fearful anticipation and delivery. Experience has shown that this is a great moral support to both wives and husbands at such times, and also that poor relationships between spouses are often improved and the two are brought closer together than ever before.

The experience of childbirth has its consolations and rewards. The initiator of the movement to dispel exaggerated fears surrounding delivery has words of assurance for such mothers.

Many women have described their experiences of childbirth as being associated with a spiritual uplifting, the power of which they have never previously been aware. I have witnessed this so often, and become so profoundly conscious of the implacable transfiguration of women at the time of their babies' arrival that I have been led, as usual, to ask: Why this? It's not sentimentality; it is not relief from suffering; it is not simply the satisfaction of accomplishment. It is bigger than all those things. Can it be that the Creator intended to draw mothers nearest to Himself at the moment of love's fulfillment? Can it be that it is the natural reward of those who perfect their ultimate purpose in life? [25]

BREAST FEEDING

Obstetrical science is rediscovering the superiority of nature's method of feeding infants over man's attempts at substitution. More and more obstetricians are discouraging the use of artificial bottle feeding in favor of breast feeding, when it is feasible. Moralists have traditionally urged the same thing, pointing out that breast feeding is a moral obligation, though only a light one, when it is possible and feasible. The advantages of breast feeding are so many and weighty that one would think only the most compelling of reasons would induce anyone to favor artificial feeding.

---

[25] Dr. Grantly Dick Read, *Childbirth Without Fear* (New York: Harper & Brothers, 1944) pp. 6–7. Reprinted by permission of Harper & Brothers and *The Reader's Digest*.

An internationally famous authority has given us the following account of the benefits of natural lactation. Though bottle feeding of babies is a well-developed technique with frequently excellent results, public health officials, obstetricians and competent general practitioners still prescribe breast feeding as the ideal. Breast feeding, because of its importance for the child's development as a healthy and happy member of society, is one of the first duties of the mother to her child, and the mother also benefits from the exercise of this normal, natural function.

The physical relationship between mother and child during pregnancy is so close that the child is "one with the mother and all the organs of her body after birth. This close relationship is intended to last, though less intimately, for several months. Mother and child still remain interdependent, . . . united by chemical, physiological and mental bonds." [26] These bonds cannot be broken abruptly through substitution of bottle to breast feeding without depriving both mother and child of valuable benefits.

Let us outline as briefly as possible the benefits the child receives. Suckling, the first effort required of man:

brings about the optimum development of the jaws, nose and roof of the mouth. It enhances the beauty of the face and the quality of the voice. The process of aspirating milk through a rubber nipple in no way adequately replaces suckling. The milk runs down too fast into the stomach, whereas the breast is a faultless distributor of milk. The absence of muscular effort and the poor shape of nipples are partly responsible for "the protruding upper jaw, recessed chin, ill-formed nose, flattened mouth-arch which many children display today. These malformations cause defective dentition, and predispose to infections of the tonsils, pharynx, ears and sinuses.[27]

Breast feeding provides automatic regulation of the diet.

It is a striking fact that the amount of milk secreted by the breast increases with the needs of the child. It varies from a few ounces during the first days to 1.5 and even 2 quarts a day after 8 months. Its composition is also adapted to the requirements of growing human tissues. Woman's milk contains proteins of the same nature as those

---

[26] Alexis Carrel, "Breast-Feeding for Babies," *The Reader's Digest*, Vol. XXXIV, No. 206 (June 1939), pp. 1–7.
[27] *Ibid.*

constituting the body of the child. These proteins never bring about the changes in reactivity, called allergy, which cow's milk may produce on account of its foreign nature. The amount of protein, phosphorus and calcium contained in the mother's milk is more precisely adjusted to the child's requirements than any artificial formula can possibly be. As the child grows, its rate of growth decreases. Simultaneously, the mother's milk undergoes a corresponding reduction in proteins and salts.[28]

As a result of this marvelous adaptation of the composition of the mother's milk to the needs of the child, breast feeding reduces mortality.

In a survey of 2,000 babies made in Chicago by Dr. Clifford G. Grulee, the mortality of the artificially fed children was ten times greater than that of those breast-fed. . . . Secondly, occurrence of disease is also decreased. . . . In statistics compiled by Dr. Grulee, 64 per cent of artificially fed babies were affected with diseases of lungs, throat, stomach and intestines during the first year. But only 37 per cent of the breast-fed children became ill during that period.

[Moreover] many physicians believe that breast feeding gives to children not only better health, but also greater bodily endurance and nervous equilibrium. There are people, as is well known, who are never ill, resist infectious disease and completely ignore physicians, surgeons and hospitals. Generally, these people when infants were fed on human milk. Such a high degree of health depends on the peculiar quality of tissues and blood.[29]

So much for the benefits derived by the baby. Now how does nursing affect mothers? Breast feeding done with the appropriate care can contribute to the physical and mental development of women. It is not a menace to beauty. "If trained by wise physicians, women keep their beauty even after having suckled several babies. . . . Suckling has never been shown to predispose the gland to cancer." [30] The breasts are affected by the ovaries and the pituitary gland, and in turn influence the ovaries and the uterus. Suckling brings about rhythmic contractions of the uterus which prevent the occurrence of hemorrhage. Also,

---

[28] *Ibid.*
[29] *Ibid.*
[30] *Ibid.*

these contractions help the organ return to its normal condition. As menstruation ceases during lactation, breast activity gives a period of rest to the ovaries.

Feeding the baby is an occasion for mothers to learn how to live. They see "the ill-effects of tobacco, alcohol and coffee, which enter the blood and directly affect the child. They have to lose many bad habits. They cannot afford to be nervous and temperamental." [31]

Breast feeding also carries moral benefits for the mother. She needs strict self-discipline, for suckling is a hard and monotonous task. She learns selflessness and love. "She has the joy of giving more health and strength and beauty to her child," thereby preparing her own happiness for future years.

More recently a paper read at a medical convention indicated that the incidence of breast cancer is much less among mothers who breast-fed their babies.[32] Surveying this whole problem very carefully, several research scholars stated that despite conflicting testimony two conclusions are tenable in the light of evidence now available:

1. That breast feeding increases the child's resistance to infections during the first year of life.

2. That breast feeding lays the foundation for healthy emotional development and mental health.

They further wrote:

That so many different people working independently should reach the same conclusions leaves little doubt of the validity of such conclusions, namely that lack of maternal care causes grave personality defects later in life. Stunting of the child's physical, mental and emotional development, a failure to conceptualize and think in abstract terms, and a failure to give or receive affections, all contribute toward the development of an inadequate personality.[33]

Another group of research workers found that anemia developed in the first six months among bottle-fed babies when

31 *Ibid.*
32 Dr. Percy Stocks, paper noted, "Pathologists Hear Three Utah Scientists" (Washington, D. C.: *Post and Times-Herald* September 10, 1954).
33 Ann Burgess, John Burton and Priscilla Milton, *Health Educational Journal* (London, July 1952), quoted in *Family Life,* Vol. XII, No. 10 (October 1952), p. 4.

emotionally disturbed but not among breast-fed babies.[34]   In an investigation made at the request of the United Nations Children's Fund it was found that the high mortality rate of children in the localities studied was due chiefly to malnutrition and this malnutrition began *after the babies were weaned.*[35]

It seems an alarming fact that in our urban culture only about half of our mothers are able to breast-feed their children.   There are many reasons for this, among which is the little suspected role of the emotions.   A relatively recent set of findings indicate that emotions can cause poor secretion of milk.   They also point out that in most instances when mothers were anxious to breast-feed, they had much milk.   They further show that mothers who did not care to breast-feed their children found their babies refusing their efforts to do so three times more frequently than the mothers really eager to breast-feed.[36]

CHILD SPACING

Another departure from nature's pattern which is widely practiced without regard to consequences, is that of spacing children according to personal preference.   Scientific findings indicate the need for serious consideration of this problem.   A study made a few years ago is still unrefuted; the examination of 5,158 patients indicated these conclusions:

1. The mortality rate of infants born 12 to 24 months apart is no greater than that of others; nor are there any greater complications.
2. The longer the interval between births the greater the danger of the mother suffering from toxemia of pregnancy.
3. Youth is a better guarantee of maternal and child welfare than spacing.[37]

Scientific studies indicate that *natural* child spacing leads to children having a superior body composition, fewer infant deaths,

---

[34] G. H. Pollock and J. B. Richmond, "Nutritional Anemia in Children: Importance of Emotional, Social and Economic Factors," *Psychosomatic Medicine,* Vol. XV, No. 5 (September–October 1953), pp. 477–485.

[35] G. D. Schultz, "Breast Feeding Miracle," *Ladies' Home Journal,* Vol. LXXII, No. 9 (September 1955), p. 93.

[36] Niles Newton, *Maternal Emotions* (New York: P. B. Hoeber, Inc., Medical Books Department of Harper & Brothers, 1955) p. 44.

[37] N. J. Eastman, "The Effect of the Interval Between Births on Maternal and Fetal Outlook," *American Journal of Obstetrics and Gynecology* (April 1944).

less gastro-intestinal trouble, lower respiratory infections and even a greater immunity to measles.[38]

A specific danger of artificial child spacing is a tumorous condition of the female organs, called by medical experts "endometriosis." The most noted authority on this subject traces its causes to late marriages and the avoidance of pregnancy. "It is usually," Dr. Meigs tells us, "among patients who can afford private practice surgery that endometriosis is found. They are . . . the patients who marry late and avoid pregnancies. They have fewer children and six to seven times as much endometriosis." [39] He further notes that due to greater child spacing the incidence of this affliction is higher among the educated than the poorly educated.

Breast feeding has long been recognized as a *natural* method of child spacing. Ordinarily ovulation does not occur during lactation, and conception is then unlikely. In one study, only 9.2 per cent became pregnant, whereas 90.8 per cent did not.[40]

Rh FACTOR

This factor, named Rh because it was first found in Rhesus monkeys, was discovered in 1940. It is an element in the blood stream which about 85 per cent of white people have; these are called Rh-positive. The 15 per cent without it are "Rh-negative." The marriage of an Rh positive and negative couple in some cases affects their children. There is damage, at times, to liver, brain, and many other tissues. These changes may result in the death of the infant, or if it is born alive, a severe neonatal jaundice, anemia or brain injury, but in recent years by transfusions and other means, many of these infants are being spared the results of this factor. The first child born is rarely affected; but with additional childbearing a mother may become "sensitized." Usually the mother's own health is not affected.

However severe the effects, fortunately this need not be a

38 Newton, *op. cit.*, pp. 52–54.
39 J. V. Meigs, "Endometriosis," *Journal of Obstetrics and Gynecology,* Vol. II, No. 1 (July 1953), pp. 47–52.
40 Rose Goiosa, "Incidence of Pregnancy During Lactation in 500 Cases," *American Journal of Obstetrics and Gynecology,* Vol. 70, No. 1 (July 1955), pp. 162–174. See also I. C. Udesky, "Ovulation in Lactating Women," *Journal of Obstetrics and Gynecology,* Vol. 59 (April 1950), p. 843 and F. W. Rice, "The Function of Lactation," *The Family Today* (Washington, D. C.: National Catholic Welfare Conference, 1944), pp. 96–100.

source of undue concern to married persons. Among whites the wife is Rh-negative and the husband Rh-positive in only one in 10 marriages, *only one in 25 is likely to have trouble,*[41] *and only one in about 300 pregnancies will be accompanied by complications* from this source. Also, proper care before and after childbirth can often do much to prevent the worst effects. Obviously having the blood of both men and women typed is advisable to determine the presence or absence of this factor.

INFERTILITY AND ADOPTION

Apparently in our civilization sterility is increasing. Some studies indicate that half of our city families are childless. The smaller number of children in completed families also confirms the growing incidence of infertility. It is difficult to determine how much of this is voluntary, due to contraceptives and other forms of family limitation, and how much is involuntary. Venereal and other diseases often rob persons of their reproductive ability. Some studies also indicate a relationship between nervousness, tension, fatigue and infertility; while others suggest the probability that artificial living in our city environment is taking its toll here.

Since any normal woman entering marriage greatly hopes to have children, the failure to do so often leads to an extreme sense of frustration and discontent. It is important in such instances that the cause be determined, as often it can be remedied with little difficulty. Marriage counseling experience indicates that most husbands are quite uncooperative in this matter, refusing to have the necessary tests made to determine whether they or their wives are the source of infertility. No doubt this is often because the male ego dislikes facing the possibility of being something less than what is falsely thought to be masculine. If such reluctant husbands realized the number of outstanding athletes who are sterile, they might feel their pride less injured. However, in having tests made

one must never obtain a specimen of semen in a manner which is clearly and plainly contrary to moral law. We regret to state that

_____

[41] *Briefs,* Vol. XVIII, No. 1 (New York: Maternity Center Association, February, 1954), p. 11.

many times the specimen is obtained as a result of wilful masturbation or by the equally immoral use of a condom (male contraceptive) at the time of coitus. We cannot use words too strong in our condemnation of these two methods.[42]

Those permanently unable to have children should seriously consider the question of adoption. Many are deterred from so doing by phobias which seem to have become deeply ingrained in our culture. The greatest fear in this respect, and the most groundless, is that of hereditary defects in adopted children. This attitude shows failure to realize that education and environment are more important than heredity. It is based upon the false assumption that most children available for adoption have come from "bad stock." Actually, many such children are born of parents from superior families—religiously, culturally, socially and economically. Furthermore, the risks of adoption are really less than those of having one's own child. Due to the standards of many agencies, most children are tested and screened with great care before being placed for adoption. But even geniuses can have a "Mongolian idiot" born to them as their own!

Others fear an inability really to love a child not their own. Such couples fail to understand the nature of the love process; proximity and daily attention will cause love and affection to sprout and flourish. One of the reasons few adopted children become delinquents is that they were loved and wanted, which is not always true of children of the parents' own blood. In considering this matter, couples might also remember that few types of charity exceed that of adopting the homeless child whose personality cannot develop normally except through the personal care, love and attention of a normal, wholesome home.

Some childless couples in their desire for a child are resorting to artificial insemination. Speaking of this practice before the Fourth International Convention of Catholic Physicians, Pius XII warned that "the simple fact that the desired result is obtained by this means does not justify the employment of that method itself; not yet does the desire of marriage partners—most legitimate in itself—to have a child, suffice to prove the lawfulness of

---

[42] F. L. Good and O. F. Kelly, *Marriage, Morals, and Medical Ethics* (New York: P. J. Kenedy & Son, 1951), p. 133.

a recourse to artificial insemination for the fulfillment of that desire." [43]

CESSATION OF CHILD BEARING

The end of the long road of active parenthood is commonly called the "menopause," instead of the "climacteric," which is more accurate. It implies that the wife has now entered that period in which, due to a gradual slowing down of the reproductive glands, her capacity for motherhood is coming to an end. It is a period of both bodily and psychological change. The lessened functioning of the ovaries causes other glands to compensate by speeding up. This in turn induces physical and nervous symptoms. It is clear (Table 9) that the symptoms

TABLE 9

FREQUENCY OF VARIOUS SYMPTOMS ASSOCIATED WITH THE
MENOPAUSE OF 96 WOMEN *

Nervous Symptoms	Per cent	Circulatory Symptoms	Per cent	General Symptoms	Per cent
Nervousness ...	92.7	Hot Flashes	91.6	Lassitude, fatigue	78.1
Excitability	72.9	Palpitation:		Constipation ...	72.9
Irritability	61.4	dyspepsia	72.9	Gaining weight .	51.1
Headache	50.0	Vertigo	71.8	Menstrual	
Decreased		Cold hands and		disorder	97.7
memory and		feet	23.9	Cessation of	
concentration .	54.1	Numbness	29.1	menstruation .	41.5
Depression	60.4	Pulse average			
Psychosis	35.4	per min.	78.3		
Sleeplessness ...	59.3	Pulse pressure average	50		

* August Werner, "The Climacteric or Menopause in Women," *Acta Endocrinologica*, Vol. XIII (1953), pp. 92–93.

vary considerably between one woman and another. A vast majority experience nervousness, excitability, hot flashes, heart palpitation, dyspepsia, lassitude, fatigue and constipation. The more aggravated emotional symptoms are experienced by slightly

---

[43] Pius XII, "To Catholic Doctors," *Catholic Mind*, Vol. XLVIII (April, 1950); also *L' Osservatore Romano*, Vol. LXXXIX (October 1, 1949).

more than half. Perhaps this number would be even smaller if some women did not *misinterpret* the menopause as meaning the end of their attractiveness, womanliness or sex life. Also, the onset of this period implies, in the minds of many, advancing old age—an unpleasant prospect to those who worship youthfulness.

Few experiences in the "life together" which marriage means, demand greater understanding, insight and patience on the part of both husbands and wives. Without these and the assistance of the graces of the Sacrament a good marital relation of long standing can be seriously jeopardized. However, this marital storm can be weatherd by employing certain attitudes and practices, such as the following:

1. Both must face the fact that the difficulty is due to the menopause and not to other causes.

2. Accordingly, they should resort to every expedient—medical care and, in more aggravated cases, psychiatric counsel. Many women benefit greatly—both physically and emotionally—by the administration of estrogenic hormones, though medical science is divided on their use, and some doctors believe such hormones induce tumorous conditions.

3. Both should realize that this experience is a normal one in marriage and accept the consolation that it lasts usually for a quite limited time only. In some cases the glandular imbalance may not exceed three to six months, though in rare instances it may be prolonged for six or even more years.

4. The wife will benefit by realizing the nature and symptoms of her ailment. She should readjust her time schedule so as to reduce fatigue. On the other hand, she should engage in more pleasant diversions which are restful, relaxing and quieting.

Indeed, the one who can help her best is she, herself. Her intelligent control is essential. . . . A sensible woman can help herself in many important ways. . . . She can guard against overwork. . . . She can see that she gets the rest she needs. . . . And she can cut down on coffee and cigarette consumption. . . . But most important of all, she must captain the good ship *Self* and keep a steady hand on the helm.[44]

5. Husbands mindful of the implications of the situation should devise methods of reducing the strain of work and worry for their wives. They should try to understand that this is the time that strains women's souls and bodies. They should understand the irri-

---

[44] F. S. Edsall, *Change of Life* (New York: Whiteside, Inc., 1949), pp. 67–68.

tability, vacillation and fatigue of their wives and make allowances for them. Instead of lessening their attention or affection, they should increase and intensify them, treating their wives with an even greater kindness and consideration than previously.

6. If their wives' condition is of a more aggravated nature, they must understand why the wife who never was jealous before now shows marked signs of suspicion; why the placid wife now becomes worrisome and fretful; why the cheerful and optimistic wife now exudes gloom and depression; why the amiable, tolerant, charitable wife now engages in chronic nagging. Not only should they understand all this, but they should not allow these *temporary* swings from the truly admirable qualities of their wives to become sources of friction or tension.

7. Both should remain as poised as possible throughout this experience, mindful of the fact that if properly and wisely handled, the wife will emerge healthier and happier and their marriage will have new life and prosperity.

8. Both should be aware of the urgent need for spiritual aid and employ every means—Mass, sacraments and prayer—with greater vigor than at other times.

9. Both might view these trials, coming at the close of their career as parents, as a providential design to make reparation for the mistakes and shortcomings of that career. They will see "the finger of God" in it all, and retain a spiritual composure through conformity to God's Will and abandonment to His fatherly Providence.

DECLINING PARENTHOOD

The eugenic tragedy

One of the greatest comic-tragedies of our age is the program of that group of eugenists who revel in having an all too simple formula for the world's ills. They would improve society by *keeping* misfits out of it through abortion, sterilization, and contraceptives; and of *weeding* misfits out by euthanasia (incorrectly called mercy killing). Their simple formula, however, rests upon an extremely complex assumption, that we know a great deal about the laws of heredity. This is the comic aspect of this school of thought because our knowledge of heredity is actually too limited to tell, in most instances, who would prove fit or unfit parents. Not only do we know extremely little about *what* is inheritable but we know even less about *when* it is inherited. Some hereditary qualities skip generations before re-appearing. After reviewing the whole field of findings about heredity of mental traits a scholar assured us that "no results of scientific value have yet been reached in this field." [45] In 1953 Pius XII repeated the same thought to a group of experts in genetics: "We Ourselves," the Pope told them, "urged the further-ance of research in the hope that *some day* perhaps results might be achieved *which one could be sure of, for up to the present nothing definitive has been obtained.*" [46] The same conclusion was voiced by a world famous scientist at a meeting of experts under the auspices of the United Nations:

While the effects of the evolutionary factors mutation and selection have been thoroughly analyzed in animal experiments and rich knowl-edge could be gathered in this field, *we yet are very insufficiently in-formed* about the processes in domestication and evolution in man-kind. Investigations on the mutation rates of deleterious human genes *are still in the preliminary phase* and the estimates of the rates include *many possibilities of error* which more than heretofore must be taken into consideration.[47]

At the same convention another world expert pointed out that "not more than 2–3 per cent of the total population suffer from severe hereditary affections, *i.e.,* disease which eventually depend on pathogenetic genes." [48] One known fact is that everybody has some undesirable genes. On the other hand, there is a *possibility* of transmission by heredity of syphilis, epilepsy, schizophrenia (split personality), deaf-mutism, and bleeding (hemophilia). In these, as in similar medical matters, couples should consult a specialist who is as Catholic in his practices and viewpoint as he is learned in his science.

---

45 G. Dahlberg, *Race, Reason, and Rubbish* (New York: Columbia Uni-versity Press, 1942), p. 131.

46 Pius XII, "Iis qui Interfuerunt Primo Symposio Intenationale Geneticae Medicae," *Acta Apostolicae Sedis,* Series II, Vol. XX, No. 12 (October 3, 1953), pp. 596–607.

47 Hans Nachtssheim, "Mutation Rate and Mutagenic Factors," *United Na-tions Economic and Social Council,* Dist. Gen. E/Conf. 13/247, Meeting No. 23 (June 8, 1954).

48 Tage Kemp, "Prevalence of Genetically Based Physical and Mental Defi-ciencies and the Frequency of Related Genes," *United Nations Economic and Social Council,* Dist. Gen. E/Conf., 13/193, Meeting No. 23 (May 17, 1954).

Prospective mates and parents should be much more concerned about passing on to children *predispositions* to virtue or vice, than about the many hereditary factors unknown to us. Pius XII, in one of his many discourses to married couples, told one group: "You inherit good natural *dispositions* from your ancestors and transform them into virtue by repetition of acts"; he also spoke of "individual *inclinations* to the natural virtues, that you the parents have communicated to them the children through generation [italics ours]." [49]   The Holy Father advised couples before marriage to select partners in the light of these facts. Parents, on the other hand, conscious of such hereditary leanings in their children can make special efforts through grace, education and environment to curb the weak tendencies and to supplant them by the opposite virtues.   Spiritual writers inform us that every person has some central weakness from which all of his lesser failings flow.   Doubtless this "chief sin" follows an innate tendency.   If parents remained conscious of this and the need to especially teach children the control of these chief faults, character training would surely be facilitated.

Decimating heaven

For over a century our culture has been committed to a policy of declining parenthood.   Between 1800 and 1930, the birth rate declined 75 per cent.   The reproductive activities of the family had dwindled from a population growth rate per decade of 36.4 per cent for 1790–1800 to a mere seven per cent for 1930–1940.[50]   From the 19.4 per cent rate of 1940, a rise occurred to the 26.6 per cent rate of 1947—the highest since 1922— then birth rates fell to 24.9 per cent in 1951, and rose again to 25.1 per cent in 1952.[51]   In 1954, only 67.5 per cent of wives had any children, 21 per cent had only one child, 18.1 per cent had two children, 9.5 per cent had three and 7.1 per cent had four or more.   In other words, 84.4 per cent had less than

---

[49] Pius XII, *Atti e Discoursi di Pio XII,* Vol. V, (Rome: Instituto Missionares Pia Societa San Paolo, 1943), p. 39.
[50] United States Census Report (1940).
[51] National Office of Vital Statistics, United States Department of Health, Education, and Welfare, *Summary of Natality Statistics, United States, 1952,* Vol. XL, No. 8 (Washington, D. C.: United States Government Printing Office, 1952), Table 1, p. 186.

three children.[52]   Those prematurely heartened by the increased birth rate need to remember that the current rates are still about 50 per cent below those in 1920.   Also it should be noticed that the rate of second births, which continually increased from 1933 to 1952, has again begun to decline.[53]   It is expected by many that the current high rates will not hold up once prosperity is lessened and child-rearing begins to interfere with the economic and material comforts of the family.   The fact remains that the average family does not exceed three children (though it has 3.64 cats and dogs.)   On the other hand, only about 15 per cent of completed families among white women are completely childless.

Many and complex factors influence the birth rate and family size, some of which are not yet known.   Among the well known factors for small families are involuntary sterility, employment of women, desire for a high material standard of living, late marriages, the impact of urban living, the pleasure craze and the decline of religious values in family life.   Perhaps the most widespread and obvious techniques are abortion, contraceptives, and rhythm.

Murder of the innocents

Despite the enormous hazards we have in the nation from one-half to two million abortions each year.   The former Surgeon General of the United States warned the nation that: "For every 100 women who die in pregnancy or childbirth, 24 perish from abortion.   Three-fourths of these deaths are due to blood poisoning.   Hemorrhage accounts for many more.   These appalling figures represent only the *known* causes and constitute only a small fraction of the total number." [54]   One study of 1,712 abortions in Japan showed that 47.3 per cent suffered abnormal conditions afterwards; [55] another Japanese study of 1,382 dis-

---

52 "The American Wife," *Statistical Bulletin,* Vol. XXXVI, No. 10 (New York: Metropolitan Life Insurance Company, October 1955), p. 2.

53 "The Birth-Rate: Recent Trends and Outlook," *Statistical Bulletin,* Vol. XXXVII (Metropolitan Life Insurance Company, October 1956), pp. 2–3.

54 J. Ward, "What Everyone Should Know About Abortion," *The American Mercury,* Vol. LIII (August 1941), pp. 194–200.

55 Yoshio Koya, "A Study of Induced Abortion in Japan and Its Significance," *Milbank Memorial Fund Quarterly,* Vol. XXXII, No. 3 (July 1954), p. 11.

closed that almost half of the women complained of some ailment after abortion.[56]

Danger to the mother is often alleged as a reason for abortion. Reference has already been made to the fact that out of 10,000 live births in one of our large cities only one maternal death was unavoidable. Therefore, therapeutic abortion does not seem to be indicated by necessity. In fact, those who favor abortion are less and less indicating the need for it. In a 20-year study made in a Los Angeles hospital, it was found that while 20 years ago there was one abortion in 106 births, during the last five years there was only 1 abortion in 2,864 and in the last year only 1 out of 8,383 births. This study also noted that despite fewer abortions the maternal mortality rate declined during these years.[57]

The incidence of maternal death in childbirth is extremely low according to the latest official data. Between 1949 and 1951 at all ages and for all races there was one maternal death in about 1,235 births; during the childbearing ages the incidence was one in about 870. For white mothers at all ages only one in 1,655 died in childbirth.[58] It must be remembered that this includes mothers suffering from all types of diseases; the rate for non-diseased mothers would be significantly less than the above.

Of the many leading medical experts who are opposed to therapeutic abortion, one has stated: "If abortion is to have any scientific justification, evidence must be sought showing that in general the harmful effects are avoided if the pregnancy is being interrupted. A study of the literature will soon convince any impartial person that *no such evidence exists* [italics ours]." [59]

---

[56] M. Muramatsu, "Summary of Preliminary Report of a Survey of Health and Demographic Aspects of Induced Abortion in Japan," *United Nations Economic and Social Committee,* Dist. Gen. E/Conf. 13/77, Meeting No. 8 (April 26, 1954).

[57] K. P. Russell, "Changing Indications for Therapuetic Abortion," *Journal of American Medical Association* (January 10, 1953), p. 108.

[58] National Office of Vital Statistics, United States Department of Health, Education, and Welfare, *Births by Age of Mother, Race, and Live-Birth Order, United States, 1954,* Vol. XLIV, No. 8, Table 6, p. 167, and *Mortality from Selected Causes by Marital Status, United States, 1949–1951,* Vol. XXXIX, No. 7, Table 1, pp. 362–364 (Washington, D. C.: United States Government Printing Office; July 24, 1956, and May 8, 1956).

[59] Dr. Jacobs, quoted by Dr. John Cavanagh, *Fundamental Marriage Counseling* (Milwaukee: The Bruce Publishing Company, 1956).

Among other reasons for the prevalence of abortion is the popularity of contraceptives. It is easy logic to assume that those who reject children through use of contraceptives will, when such means fail, often resort to the more extreme measure of abortion. The hospital records of 25,000 white women showed an abortion rate much higher among the users of contraceptives than the nonusers.[60] In another study "illegal abortion was *ten times* as frequent in the cases of women who had been using contraceptives." [61] Even the United Nations conferences have taken cognizance of this link between the two practices:

Furthermore, abortion has increased markedly in recent years along with contraception. It is noticeable that abortion is far more frequent among married couples with contraceptive experience than among those without this experience.[62]

Unborn children

Another practice which many have urged under the guise of science, is birth control through use of contraceptives. The moral attitude toward this practice has been clear since God called Onan's unnatural practice of family limitation a "detestable thing" in the sight of the Lord and struck him dead on the spot. By reason, too, it is clear that such a direct blocking of nature's clear intentions is unnatural and sinful. It remained for modern pseudo-science to tell us that far from being wrong, the use of contraceptives is to be encouraged.

Science has not conclusively proved contraceptives to be harmful, neither has it proved them to be harmless. The fast-accumulating scientific evidence is tending to confirm the injurious nature of this practice rather than disprove it. Our national attitude toward contraceptives is as unscientific as that in regard to the use of sulfa drugs, penicillin, and polio vaccines. In each of these three instances we dashed impulsively, but not scientifically, ahead into their widespread use before waiting to deter-

---

[60] R. Pearl, "Fertility and Contraception in New York and Chicago," *Journal of the American Medical Association,* Vol. CVIII (1937), p. 122.

[61] F. Rice, "A Catholic Physician's Views on Family Limitation," *American Ecclesiastical Review,* Vol. CIII (July 1940), pp. 60–67.

[62] Honda Tatsu, *U. N. Economic and Social Council,* Dist. General E/Conf. 13/128, Meeting No. 8 (April 30, 1954).

mine the results. And in each instance, we found some serious "secondary reactions." In like manner as a nation we are employing contraceptives *without being sure of their harmlessness and despite increasing evidence of their injurious nature.*

Even some ardent advocates of contraceptive use admit the unnaturalness of this practice. An internationally famous Dutch gynecologist and advocate of birth control wrote:

The great majority of contraceptive measures are, up to a point, incompatible with ideal marriage. These methods prevent perfect union, for they interfere with the stimulus, disturb the normal reactions, offend the aesthetic sense, and destroy the spontaneity of complete abandon.[63]

Reference was made earlier to the physiological fact that the spermatic fluid when absorbed by the female, prospers her physical and mental health. Wives employing contraceptives cheat themselves of this natural and intended benefit of physical union. Worse even than this is the link between contraceptives and the growth of tumorous conditions in women (endometriosis). The most noted specialist on this disease tells us that it is caused by the failure to interrupt the span of menstrual activity; that this link is so clear that "the best medical treatment for endometriosis is *pregnancy* [italics ours]."[64] Another specialist and clinical professor of obstetrics and gynecology told his medical colleagues: "It is noteworthy that the frequency with which the diagnosis of endometriosis is made parallels the increased use of contraception. . . ."[65]

Psychiatrists are now stressing the emotional impact of this practice. One of the Freudian school assures us that "If a woman rejects motherhood emotionally and hates the whole business of creating a comfortable home atmosphere, *that is neurotic* [italics ours]."[66] A woman psychiatrist whose clientele was largely female tells us that her experience indicates that contra-

---

[63] Dr. Van de Velde, quoted by Raoul de Gutchneere, *Judgment on Birth Control* (Baltimore: The Carroll Press, 1950), p. 140.

[64] Meigs, *op. cit.,* pp. 47, 50.

[65] Dr. C. T. Bucham, speaking on a panel of the meeting of the American Medical Association and quoted by G. D. Schultz, "Women Without Children," *Ladies' Home Journal,* Vol. LXVIII, No. 9 (September 1951), p. 198.

[66] Edward Bergler, *Divorce Won't Help,* (New York: Harper & Brothers), p. 206.

ceptives are destructive of emotional and mental health and that mothers of large families seldom seek her services.[67] Even a layman can understand that couples violating their consciences by prolonged use of contraceptives will have a rightful sense of guilt not conducive to emotional peace. Others not so sensitive to ethical considerations, but conscious of the risks involved in contraceptives not yet made completely reliable and effective, continue to fear that prevention may fail.

Great spiritual evils also accompany this deleterious practice. The case records of the Marriage Counseling Center of the Catholic University of America make it abundantly clear that this practice causes many couples to grow lax in religion and many others to renounce it completely. Furthermore, from the supernatural point of view the external glory of God is being robbed by this practice to an enormous extent. Couples rejecting only *one* child see no harm greater than the lack of one human being in heaven, if indeed they see even that. However, the long range effects through many generations are not the deprivation of one but the deprivation of many thousands of souls who some day might worship eternally at God's throne. The accompanying table is an attempt to indicate in somewhat crude fashion the potential loss in this respect.

TABLE 10

COMPARISON OF THE CUMULATIVE EFFECT OF NO BIRTH FRUSTRATION
AND THAT OF ONE FRUSTRATED CHILDBIRTH IN FIRST GENERATION

Generations	Number of children No family limitation	Number of children reduced by one in first generation only
1	4	3
2	12	9
3	36	27
4	108	81
5	324	243
6	972	729
7	2,916	2,187
8	8,748	6,561
9	26,244	19,683
10	78,732	59,049
11	236,196	177,147
12	708,548	531,441

[67] F. Lundberg and M. F. Farnam, *Modern Woman: The Lost Sex,* (New York: Harper & Brothers, 1947), chap. xii.

It assumes that of four possible children in the first generation, one is not conceived because of contraceptives and one will either not marry or be unable to bear children; it further assumes no birth frustration for the next eleven generations, but that one out of four children will not become a parent. Under these conditions, the generations not practicing family limitation would have in time reproduced some 708,548 human beings; the progeny resulting from one child frustration in the first generation would be only 531,441 children. The net result of the frustration of *only one childbirth* in the first generation would be the *loss of 177,107 souls* through 12 generations who would have contributed to the eternal glory of God. Here we begin to sense the deeply irreligious nature of birth control. Perhaps this is what the poet, John Davidson, had in mind when he penned the lines:

> Your cruelest pain is when you think of all
> The hoarded treasures of your body spent,
> And no new life to show. Oh, then you feel
> How people lift their hands against themselves
> And taste the bitterest punishment
> Of those whom pleasure isolates.
> Sometimes
> When darkness, silence and the sleeping world
> Give vision scope, you lie awake and see
> The pale, sad faces of the little ones
> Who should have been your children, as they press
> Their cheeks against your windows, looking in
> With piteous wonder, homeless famished babies,
> Denied your wombs and bosoms.

The practice of birth frustration indicates not only a loss of religious insight but also a loss of social consciousness and of a sense of professionalism. Motherhood is not the only profession which at times requires self-sacrifice in the line of duty. The doctor, nurse, fireman, policeman, soldier, seaman and many others accept the risks inherent in their work even when they jeopardize their lives. In fact, by a strange contradiction in our culture, society expects the members of these professions and occupations to face death if duty requires it and castigates them as "cowards," "traitors," "deserters," if they fail to do so. However, when it comes to the more important task of parenthood, society easily excuses those rejecting their clear duty on the pretext of sympathy, pity, or mercy. No wonder Chesterton once mentioned the characteristic weakness of our age as being that of driving virtue to an extreme and so making a vice of it.

Natural family limitation

Nature and its Author have not been as exacting of parents as many think. At least two methods are found quite in accord with biological nature for limiting family size. One has previously been discussed, breast feeding of infants. The other is that periodic abstinence from the act of marital love, commonly called "rhythm." It is a theory based upon the alternating periods in women of fertility and sterility. The most recent studies indicate that women are perhaps able to conceive a child on only two days in a month. The rhythm method of family limitation implies refraining from the marital act at this time of greatest sensitivity to conception. Its effectiveness as determined by a number of studies is as great as is that of contraception.[68]

Even though the rhythm method is not a direct blocking of a natural process, as is contraception, and is, therefore, in accord with nature's biological laws, it is nevertheless not ethically right in itself. Pius XII made it clear that the very nature of marriage imposes on married people the obligation in social justice to contribute to the preservation of the race. At the same time he indicated that there are reasons of a medical, eugenic, economic or social nature which will justify the use of the rhythm method of family limitation; in fact, such reasons could be so compelling as to excuse a couple from having any children.[69] In fact, contrary to what many think, the Church does not teach that women are mere "breeders"; on the contrary, much as she prizes children, she also acknowledges certain justifiable and prudential reasons for not having an unlimited number. Pius XII pointed out that

---

[68] For a summary of such studies see Mihanovich, Schnepp and Thomas, *Marriage, and the Family* (Milwaukee: The Bruce Publishing Company, 1952), Appendix.

[69] Pius XII, "The Apostolate of the Midwife," *Moral Questions Affecting Married Life* (New York: Paulist Press), pp. 14–15. This address was given October 29, 1951.

". . . the Church knows how to consider with sympathy and understanding the real difficulties of the married state in our day. Therefore . . . we affirmed the legitimacy of a regulation of offspring, which, unlike so-called 'birth control,' is compatible with the law of God." [70]   However, it is often forgotten that even in the presence of compelling reasons rhythm cannot usually be employed except with mutual consent and the absence of any serious danger to incontinency or the stability and peace of the marriage.   A noted moral theologian has pointed out that three questions must be answered in the affirmative to justify rhythm: 1. Are both parties *willing;* 2. Are both *able* to practice it; 3. Do they have a sufficient reason? [71]   Every couple contemplating its use should consult their confessor or a priest to determine whether their alleged reason is a justifiable one and whether all the conditions which free it from guilt are present.   This is important since so frequently couples have an inadequate knowledge of the moral complexities of rhythm.   In addition, they are so close to the problem which they allege as a reason, that in all probability their perspective is distorted, making them rather poor judges of its justification.   Some of the reasons listed for us in a careful theological study of rhythm are as follows: [72]

For permanent use of rhythm

1. Because conception will very probably result in death or a permanent state of bad health for the mother.
2. Because it is almost certain that the mother cannot bring forth living children.
3. Because the mother can bring forth only abortive children (i.e., miscarriages).
4. Because it is practically certain that the children will be born with serious and incurable hereditary defects, especially insanity.
5. Because it is morally impossible for the husband to support another child.
6. Because the mother has proved to be utterly incapable of fulfilling the usual maternal duties relative to the care and training of children either physically or morally.

---

[70] Pius XII, "Morality in Marriage," *Catholic Mind* (1952) Vol. L, p. 311.
[71] G. Kelly, "A Moral Theologian Looks at Rhythm," *Grail* (March 1955), p. 15.
[72] Orville Griese, *The Morality of Periodic Continence* (Washington, D. C.: The Catholic University of America Press, 1942), chap. vii, pp. 75–79.

7. Because one of the spouses is absolutely opposed to having children or another child (lesser of two evils).

8. Because it is the only way of stopping or preventing the use of onanistic methods in marital relations.

9. Because it is morally certain that one of the parties will otherwise fall into sins of incontinence.

Ordinarily sufficient only for the temporary practice of periodic continence

1. Because of a temporary physical sickness or weakness or period of convalescence on the part of the mother, e.g., gaining strength after childbirth or after an illness.

2. Because of the extraordinary inconvenience and expenses associated with childbirth in an individual case, e.g., Caesarean deliveries.

3. Because of the exceptional fecundity of the mother—necessity of "spacing" children.

4. Because of the difficult financial conditions at the present time, unemployment, misfortune, etc.

5. Because the young wife is not yet physically fit to assume the cares of motherhood.

6. Because of the temporary nervous strain on the part of the wife; simply cannot bear the thought of another child.

7. Because the birth of another child will actually render the mother incapable of properly rearing the children already born, at least for the time being.

8. Because the wife has to work and help support the family when the husband's salary is insufficient or employment irregular.

The concept of "temporary" implies the use of rhythm for a *limited* period of time *only*. This time interval depends upon the reason for it. Since reasons differ, the length of time will also differ. For instance, the exceptional fertility of a couple would justify rhythm for perhaps six months but not for two years. In general, once the cause for child spacing has disappeared the justifiable use of rhythm also vanishes.

Insufficient motives

1. Because the wife has an unfounded fear of the ordinary pains and inconveniences of pregnancy and childbirth.

2. Because the man and wife wish to "enjoy life" while they are young—or any other motive which indicates an excessive love of ease and comfort.

3. Because of any malicious motives such as hatred of children, contempt for the Divine Plan or for the authority of the Church.[73]

Even as it usually is unwise for couples to decide the presence or absence of a justifiable reason, it is unwise for them to try to determine unaided the exact time of fertility. Marriage counseling practice makes it clear that many couples conclude that "rhythm doesn't work with us" when, as a matter of fact, it has never been correctly tried. Often it is evident that rhythm hasn't failed, but that the couple have failed in their own calculations. In other instances, couples will, on occasion, fail to conform to the rhythm schedule and then blame the schedule instead of themselves.

Although less is known about the effects of rhythm than of contraception, many of the same results seem to be present. Both are abetting the small family system unmindful of the advantages of more children; both are often accompanied by an abiding sense of fear lest their best efforts at prevention fail; both deny the spontaneity of marital love; both may lead to unwanted and neglected children; both may be conducive to rendering the wife infertile; and rhythm, unsuccessfully employed, often leads to the use of contraceptives. For these as well as other reasons of a more social nature, rhythm, even in the presence of a justifiable reason, should be used with great circumspection.

Large families

The Judaic-Christian tradition has ever exalted the large family. The Old and New Testaments abound in references to children being a blessing. In many instances they are regarded as a reward for faithful service to the Lord. Our materialistic and lazy age looks upon a large family as a virtual curse and to devious means of sparing us its labors.

A realistic study of a typical American community, notes that a family of 6 to 12 children was commonplace 50 years ago; now such a family is rare even among the more prolific lower class people. The author of this investigation commented:

Such large families are both ridiculed and condemned, and are attributed to selfishness, laziness or carelessness on the part of the

---

[73] *Ibid.*

husband, or, in some very religious lower class families, to an "old-fashioned" idea that children are the gift of God, whose will should not be interfered with.[74]

This may be one reason why our culture, so bent upon social research, has practically ignored the study of the large family system. In one of the few serious attempts to study large families, the investigator detected certain definite advantages. His study abounds in expressions such as a "distinct way of life . . . produces entirely different personality type . . . distinctly different kind of child with different behavior patterns and problems . . . tends to develop certain patterns of an active acceptance of fate . . . take minor crises in stride . . . makes for adjustment to the changing vicissitudes of a realistic world . . . emphasizes the group rather than the individual." [75]

A study of the children of 173 one-child families, 679 two-to-six-child families, and 148 seven-or-more-child families revealed that the children of the large families enjoyed the best mental health. They were found to be "significantly less emotionally disturbed, less likely to do poor school work, more prone to have unintelligent fathers and mothers and more likely to come from poor homes." [76] It was also found that the incidence of broken homes was much higher in small families. As we noted earlier, available studies on happiness in marriage indicate that children of large families are the best risks in marriage; this is thought to be due to their greater adjustability and the greater maturity of their personalities.

In another study of 100 large families of from 6 to 16 children, it was found that their undoubted advantage lay in personality development. The relatively greater number of mature individuals led the authors to conclude that "to grow up in a large family is to come to terms with life." [77]

In large families, for reasons of survival if no other, children

---

74 James West, *Plainville, U.S.A.* (New York: Columbia University Press, 1947), pp. 57, 165.
75 J. H. S. Bossard, *Parent and Child* (Philadelphia: University of Pennsylvania Press, 1953), pp. 105–108.
76 A. Ellis and R. M. Beechley, *Journal of Genetic Psychology*, Vol. LXXIX (1951), pp. 131–144.
77 James H. S. Bossard and E. S. Boll, *The Large Family System* (Philadelphia: University of Pennsylvania Press, 1956), p. 319.

must and do perform part time duties as maids, cooks and nurses and learn the arts of homemaking; children *cannot help* but learn child psychology and care (especially the older children); they *must* learn to adjust, adapt, sacrifice and subordinate personal wants to family needs. Furthermore, children *will* discipline one another frequently with greater firmness and vigor than is done by parents. These and other qualities *must* prevail in large families if there is to be any semblance of order and organization. On the other hand, in small families the pressure for these same characteristics is not as great, and unless parents make special efforts, will not exist. In a study of 136 young married and 75 unmarried persons, it was disclosed that "almost unanimously, the children from the one-child family expressed regret that they had no brothers or sisters. . . ." [78]

Nor are the parents without benefits from their many children. Some studies indicate that the mothers of the largest families live the longest,[79] and the observations of an experienced Chairman of the Department of Medicine of a sizeable clinic caused him to comment upon the large amount of emotional health among them: "The group in my part of the country having emotionally induced illness *least* often are the farmers' wives with families of 9 or 10 who, in addition to their housework, also help out on the farm . . . they are too busy taking care of other people to think of themselves." [80]

PHYSICAL PARENTHOOD AND THE DIVINE PLAN

Few marvels of nature are more striking than the physiological and psychological mechanisms which Providence has devised so that His Plan for the perpetuation of the human race would succeed. Not only has He created a complex but orderly network of factors for this purpose, but He has made them so profound that medical science is only now beginning to understand a few of their inner secrets.

---

[78] A. Bates, "Parental Roles in Courtship," *Social Forces,* Vol. XX (May, 1942), pp. 483–486.

[79] Paul Popenoe, "Long Life Means Many Children," *op. cit.,* pp. 99–100; also Jones, C., *op. cit.*

[80] Dr. J. A. Schindler, *How to Live 365 Days a Year* (Englewood Cliffs, N. J.: Prentice-Hall, Inc., 1954), p. 9.

In placing the reproduction of children as the first purpose of marriage, the Divine Plan not only insured the future of the race, but included benefits of incalculable value to the partners themselves. These advantages, however, are being obscured today by the selfishness which is rejecting parenthood. Pseudo-science lends support to this parental failure, whereas genuine science is constantly confirming anew the timeless laws of this Divine Plan for parenthood.

14

Educational Parenthood

THE GREATEST role that married couples play is that of educators of their children and each other. "It is by his communication of truth, by teaching his fellows, that man plays his chief part in divine government." [1] If man joins hands with the Creator in procreating human beings, he does the same in educating them. "Nature intends not merely the generation of the offspring, but also its development and advance to the perfection of man. . . ." [2] Unfortunately, both of these roles are on the decline, and the full scope and meaning of the educational function seems little realized in family life today.

Education implies the full development of all of man's innate capacities—natural and supernatural, personal and social; it is the responsibility chiefly of the home. The supernatural life of grace and virtue needs cultivation; the natural and personal capacities of will, intellect, emotions and body need development; the social inclinations of man toward his fellow need expansion. "In fact it must never be forgotten that the subject of Christian

---

[1] W. Farrell and M. J. Healy, *My Way of Life—The Summa Simplified for Everyone* (Brooklyn: Confraternity of Christian Doctrine, 1952), p. 146.

[2] St. Thomas Aquinas, *The Summa Theologica of St. Thomas Aquinas*, tr. by the Fathers of the English Dominican Province (New York: Benziger Bros., 1948), Vol. III, Q. 41, art. 1, p. 2712.

education is man whole and entire, soul united to body in unity of nature, with all his faculties natural and supernatural. . . ." [3]

METHODS OF EDUCATION

Today it must recognized anew that *formation* of personality is much more important than *information*. There is a continuing tendency in our age of quiz contests to place the premium upon encyclopedic knowledge rather than traits of personality. Were this interpretation correct, the home would be a very minor agency of education compared with the school. For it is in the school that the *formal* education of lectures, assignments, and application to study dominate.

The educational process of the home, though resorting to formal teaching at times, remains chiefly an *indirect* and *informal* process. It is not only what a person is "taught" but also what is "caught" that comprises total education. This has been well expressed by a prominent educator:

But a great deal of teaching is done outside schools. Some things— and some of the most important things—are taught by mothers and fathers to their children. This kind of teaching begins as soon as the baby reaches for a knife and his mother takes it away. No, it begins earlier than that. It really begins when the baby gives its first cry and is first answered. In those days, before he can see or hear properly, he is finding out something about the world and himself, he is communicating and being answered, he is exerting his will and being victorious or controlled or frustrated, he is being taught to suffer, to fear, to love, to be happy, or to be violent.[4]

This is the sort of indirect but highly effective education that, for the most part, characterizes the efforts of the home. It is learning by the example set by the objects of children's hero worship. It is the influence of the home atmosphere—cultured, refined, poised and serene or primitive, crude, and tense. It is the training of the home environment—order, system, art, music, books, symbols of religion—or the absence of these. It is the product of "learning by doing," that participation in all phases

---

3 Pius XI, *Christian Education of Youth* (New York: The America Press, 1936), p. 19.

4 Gilbert Highet, *The Art of Teaching* (New York: Alfred A. Knopf, Inc., 1954).

of home life—work chores, recreation, religious practices, love and affection. The educational process in the home is, in short, the immersion in a certain social-cultural-religious milieu which finds a minimum of resistance from the student chiefly because it is so largely an unconscious process. Day by day, little by little, children and adults absorb from their home environment the tiny sinews of character, intelligence, emotional maturity, physical strength and religion—moral fibre. This type of learning does not superimpose a veneer of culture from without which, if slightly scratched, reveals the savage beneath; rather it is supreme, since it integrates into the warp and woof, the very sinews of a healthy, wholesome personality.

TEACHERS PAR EXCELLENCE

Doubtless this is why a noted educator spoke of the home as "the school of schools" and parents as the "teachers par excellence." But there are further reasons to confirm the truth of this statement. The parents have the child in its most formative and plastic years; their relationship and influence is the most intimate and marked. The home provides every life situation in which a child needs training; it is the home which first socializes the child, teaching him to relate well or poorly with others. Early habits are planted in the home, a fact which has caused an educator to state that "we send our children to school when they are too old to be educated." Even after a child starts school it is under the supervision of parents more than 7,000 hours during the course of a year as compared with about 1,000 hours at school.

Our culture seems to be forgetting the importance of parents as teachers. Education is being identified more and more with formal schooling. Home training is being weakened rather than strengthened. Many parents are too slothful, indifferent or preoccupied with other interests to educate their children effectively. Many homes lack the facilities—books, periodicals, musical instruments, creative toys—while others have few chores left for children to participate in and to learn. The small family system is depriving children of the great educational values of brothers and sisters. Increasing home tensions are stunting and warping the personality formation of children. And all the while, outside agencies, all too willing to take the child into their care, are quickly multiplying. This is noted by sociologists, one of whom has well expressed this tendency:

With almost a menacing eagerness agencies organized to supplement family activities have grasped at the chance to take up responsibilities which parents seem desirous of escaping. . . . Parents who find it more comfortable to shift their responsibility to an organization accept the dictum that "parents are ignorant and do not properly understand child psychology and the needs of children." They further are inclined to assume that parents are not only ignorant, but cannot learn. Hence we find an ever increasing number and an ever increasing demand for boys' clubs, girls' clubs, preschool nurseries, ad infinitum —a frantic effort to save babies from their parents." [5]

With this trend has also come a decreasing interest by parents in the schools their children attend. A nationally famous Catholic educator, the assistant director of education for the National Catholic Welfare Conference, has pointed out that this will result in a "professional dictatorship" over the nation's school "no less dangerous than those of a government dictatorship." He suggested that this trend be counteracted by substituting parent-teacher interviews for report cards and by attracting more fathers into existing Parent-Teacher Associations.[6]

At this time parents should relearn the Church's teaching on their obligations as educators. According to the Code of Canon Law, the official position of the Church is found in the following:

Canon 1113: Parents are bound by a most grave obligation to provide to the best of their ability for the religious and moral as well as for the physical and civil education of their children, and for their temporal well-being.

Canon 1372: From childhood all the faithful must be so educated that not only are they taught nothing contrary to faith and morals, but that religious and moral training takes the chief place.

Canon 1374: Catholic children must not attend non-Catholic, neutral, or mixed schools, that is, such as are also open to non-Catholics. It

---

[5] M. C. Elmer, *Sociology of the Family* (Boston: Ginn and Company, 1945), chap. xxvi, p. 496.

[6] Rev. William McManus, quoted in *The Catholic Herald,* St. Louis, Missouri (September 19, 1947).

is for the Bishop of the place alone to decide, according to the instructions of the Apostolic See, in what circumstances, and with what precautions attendance at such schools may be tolerated, without danger of perversion to the pupils.

Canon 1375: The Church has the right to establish schools of every grade, not only elementary schools, but also high schools and colleges.

The obligation to send children to Catholic schools actually increases as the child goes to high school and college. A noted theologian points out that the prohibition against attending non-Catholic schools "extends to all schools, secondary as well as primary and more so to universities." [7]

SCHOOL OF THE SERVICE OF THE LORD

The home is the basic school for religious education of children. It is not the pastors or school sisters who have the primary duty here, but the parents. One can sense this because from the child's baptismal day till its sixth year, the Church leaves its religious formation in the hands of the parents exclusively. Also, the right to judge whether a child is sufficiently disposed for his First Communion belongs, after the confessor, to parents (Canon 860). The Spanish have a proverb reading: "An ounce of the parent is worth a pound of the clergy." Pius XII noted the basic role of the home when he wrote: "When churches are closed, when the image of the Cruicified is taken from the schools, the family remains the providential, and in a certain sense, *impregnable* refuge of Christian life." [8]

Evidence is constantly accumulating to indicate that parents do not realize their full roles as religious educators. One of the top Air Force chaplains observed that "40 per cent of the families of America give no effective spiritual training to young men." [9] When a poll was taken of the nation's Catholics asking where they would want their children taught religion, 27 per cent said Sunday school, 74 per cent said religious or parochial school and

---

[7] Henry Davis, *Moral and Pastoral Theology,* Vol. II (New York: Sheed & Ward, Inc., 1935), p. 73.

[8] Pius XII, *Acta Apostolicae Sedis,* Vol. XXXI (1939), p. 444.

[9] *New World,* Vol. XXIII, No. 2 (January 14, 1955).

only 20 per cent said the home.[10]   In a survey of 20,691 Catholic children in 33 states the percentages of preschool children receiving religious instruction in the home were indicated (see Table 11).

TABLE 11

PERCENTAGE OF ITEMS IN RELIGIOUS EDUCATION OF 20,691 CATHOLIC
PRESCHOOL CHILDREN *

Item	Percentage
KNOWLEDGE OF PRAYERS	
Can make the Sign of the Cross	52.9
Can recite the "Our Father"	23.2
Can recite the "Hail Mary"	33.0
Knows prayers at meals	14.1
Knows prayer to Guardian Angel	15.5
UNDERSTANDING OF DOGMA	
Has some knowledge of story of Creation	24.9
Has some knowledge of Adam and Eve	13.1
Has some idea of the Christmas story	34.2
Knows that Jesus is in the Church	33.0
Knows the story of the Crucifix	30.6

* J. L. Thomas, "Religion and the Child," *Social Order*, Vol. I (May, 1951), Table 1, p. 205.

Parents are charged with training children in dogmatic beliefs, in the liturgy and the use of the Mass, sacraments, in the moral conduct and even in the way of the counsels to some extent. However, they should remain on guard against a widespread misinterpretation today—that religious growth is equated with pious practices.   If asked how to become holy, many would indicate more frequent attendance at Mass, or an increased practice of devotions; few would point out the simple fact of doing God's will better in their duties in school or at home; still fewer would mention purifying their intentions.   From earliest days parents could inculcate with relative ease habits of duty consciousness, seeing the Will of God in all thangs and abandonment to it.   By the time they have reached adult life, these habits could be second nature to them.

Parents attempting to educate their children in our culture to a

[10] "Do Americans Want Their Children to Receive Religious Instructions," *Catholic Digest*, Vol. XVII, (September 1953), p. 12.

full and rich Christian life, can expect to meet with many difficulties.

One of the most frustrating things that a married couple find in raising a family is that the parents cannot completely educate or supervise the education of their children. . . . No longer can married people think they can raise a family the way they would like to. *The cards are too heavily stacked against them* [italics ours].[11]

Secular influences of movies, television or companions, etc. will be felt unless the greatest vigilance is exercised. Yet one of the worst enemies Catholic parents have in this respect is their fellow Catholic parents who are more secular than Catholic. The parent who recognizes no restrictions on the children's movies (such as the Legion of Decency listings), who is unconcerned about late hours for teen-agers, who fails to chaperone teen-age parties in his home, who tolerates or condones indecent clothing is one of the major difficulties confronting the conscientious Catholic family. If a majority of parents were Catholic in their child rearing, a circle of Catholic culture would be created for children. Not only would the children themselves obtain much moral support from one another but the parents would find the fight against secularism relatively facile.

The task of teaching religion to children is a "most grave obligation" and a "most serious duty" (Canon 1113). In a close scrutiny of this question a theologian pointed out a Church Council's warning "that without doubt parents guilty of neglect on this score would, on the day of judgment, find themselves held responsible for all those sins of their children which would not have been committed if the parents had faithfully discharged their duty." [12]

CHARACTER TRAINING

After religious formation, character training is by far the most important educational goal. Success and failure, happiness and

---

[11] D. J. Geaney, *You Are Not Your Own* (Chicago: Fides Publishers, 1954), pp. 108–109.

[12] D. M. Enderbrock, *The Parental Obligation to Care for the Religious Education of Children within the Home with Special Attention to the Training of the Pre-School Child* (Washington, D. C.: Catholic University of America Press, 1955), chap. ii, p. 31.

unhappiness, good or poor adjustment are much more a matter of character than of intelligence. Since character is the strength of will that impels a person to act on principles and not on expediency, it makes for stability, security, maturity and dependability. The person of character can be trusted and relied upon; he can, as Kipling indicated, keep his head when most are losing theirs. The business world puts a premium on character, and history exalts a Washington or Lincoln for his sturdy adherence to principle. The world today is beset with endless problems and is looking for the leadership which can come only from men of will, force of personality and strength of conviction.

If we are left devoid of adequate leadership, it is largely the fault of the home; for the formation of character is more the task of the home than any other agency. Yet if the home is to achieve this task it will need to forsake its present efforts to surround its children with soft luxuries, ease and creature comforts. It must, instead, expect sacrifices, hardships and difficulties of children. A wise sociologist has observed that when our large universities turn their luxurious fraternity houses into something like monastic cells or army barracks, they will once again furnish the nation and the world the leadership both need. *Character is rarely forged in the lap of luxury.*

There is no greater gift to the young than the formation of character entailed in hardship and self-denial; and the parents who remove all the vitamins of suffering from the spiritual nourishment of their children must not be surprised to find them develop mental and moral scurvy. . . . For this reason the poorer classes are the regenerators of society.[13]

EDUCATING THE MIND

Though intellectual training may seem the peculiar realm of the school, the home even here plays a prominent role. Common sense judgments are most likely to be observed in children whose parents show common sense—a species of parents quickly vanishing from the scene these days. The ability to think objectively by overcoming biases and prejudices (such as race discrimination) is a habit taught early in life or acquired later only with

---

[13] F. J. McGarrigle, *My Father's Will* (Milwaukee: The Bruce Publishing Company, 1944), p. 227.

great difficulty. The proper use of the native tongue, a genuine appreciation for things intellectual—books, music, art—are "caught" from parents rather than "taught" in school. Assisting children with their homework also helps to expedite their intellectual growth.

EMOTIONAL AND PHYSICAL CULTURE

Few personality traits are more often discussed today than emotional maturity. Though its definitions are almost as varied as its proponents, an implication in all definitions is *self-control,* or dominance of mind and will over emotions. When we are told that we must not be sensitive, irritable, subjective or vengeful, we are really being told to exercise self-control. St. Paul told his listeners that when they became adults, they laid aside the things of childhood. Psychologists today repeat the same advice about childish emotional splurges and tantrums. The supremacy of will over emotions is a habit to be developed from earliest childhood. Experts quite generally believe its lack is one of the basic causes of marital breakdown.

Poise and serenity are associated with emotional control. These are best developed by the parents' example and by a home atmosphere devoid of tensions. Apparently many homes are failing in these respects. A government spokesman assured us that 3 million out of the 30 million school children in 1949 suffered *serious* emotional problems and that 3 out of every 30 children were destined for mental hospitals sometime in their lives.[14]

The physical care of children is, in general, better provided by the home today than any other type of care. Yet there are two dangerous trends that need watching. Television is becoming a serious threat to children's sleeping habits. Among 3,691 children surveyed 26 per cent watched television till 10 P. M. or later; 60 per cent of the 5–7 year olds till after 8 P. M.; and 42 per cent of the 10–11 year olds till after 9 P. M.[15]

The other tendency (discovered by government research workers) is malnutrition of children. In 1947 one-third were poorly

---

[14] J. L. Thurston to the Senate Subcommittee of the Economic Report, *Washington Post* (December 13, 1949).

[15] C. F. Housen, *Washington Post* (May 11, 1950).

fed and another third had a "fair" diet; only the remaining one-third had a fully adequate diet.[16]   It was noted that many of the undernourished children were from homes of wealth and affluence.   Obviously, the "coke and candy" diet so prevalent today is making inroads on the health of children.   Another study made on a large scale by famous nutrition experts indicated that three-fourths of our teen-agers were not eating enough energy foods, about half were not obtaining enough protein foods, and all their diets were short on minerals, fats and vitamins.[17]

Some are unduly enthusiastic about the improved diet of the nation in the past 20 years.   They are impressed with the fact that more money is being spent on food than previously, without inquiring into whether the foods consumed have higher nourishment content.   The most recent study available indicates that "Today the average person is eating more pounds of food but about the same number of calories as prewar. . . . Thus, consumers are getting more of the foods they want the most. . . . The 12 percent increase in the index reflects mainly a shift from less expensive to more expensive foods."   The nutritive index has by no means gone up proportionately.[18]

SOCIAL CULTURE

In our individualistic age a serious lack of altruism is not surprising.   The early cries of the infant must eventually be turned outward in sympathy for others.   The infant hand outstretched for personal gain must be ready to aid those less fortunate.   The innate propensities for social relations must be cultivated into a deep social-consciousness.   Parents with social vision who practice the virtues of social justice and charity toward other races, classes and peoples, will find their example a most forceful preachment.   Children brought up in a large family find that the circumstances and needs of the other members of the family re-

---

16 F. Baily, "We Feed Our Hogs Better Than Our Children," *American Magazine* (October 1947); also H. K. Stiebeling, *Are We Well Fed?* (Washington, D. C.: United States Government Printing Office, 1941), p. 7.

17 Gaylord Hauser, "Teeners Don't 'Eat Right,'" *American Weekly* (December 18, 1955), pp. 4–5.

18 F. V. Waugh, "Food Supply and Prospects," *Proceedings of the National Food and Nutrition Institute,* Handbook No. 56 (Washington, D. C.: United States Department of Agriculture, 1953), p. 19.

quire the curbing of their own desires and preferences for the welfare of all. At relatively early ages children can be enlisted in causes and movements that will make them aware of others' needs and willing to sacrifice for them.

EDUCATION FOR MARRIAGE

It is generally agreed by marriage counselors that lack of education for marriage is at the basis of the high divorce rate. What is not equally accepted by parents is that the fault lies chiefly in the home. Many parents today place the blame on the school and the Church. Yet the traits of character and personality formed early in life are more important for success than is knowledge. From their vantage point in the midst of a family, children learn daily the good or bad patterns of marriage. Observation, experience, participation, example are all theirs in the home. Nowhere can they learn the art of loving and being loved, of extending and receiving affection, of adjusting and sacrificing better than in their own family. There they first learn the art of human relations and, if the family is sizable, the different psychologies of the sexes and how to adjust to them. In the home nursery children learn the principles of child growth, care and psychology. By direct participation boys develop the skills of masculine home chores and girls the arts and crafts of homemaking. For these types of home education for marriage, courses, lectures and books are useful but inadequate substitutes. It should be noted that parents have a moral responsibility to so prepare their children for married life.[19]

CHILDREN ARE TEACHERS TOO

Children imitate, correct and teach one another. In fact, children often censure and discipline one another more strictly than parents do. Furthermore, for children with varying dispositions and temperaments to learn to live harmoniously together is a major educational process. Here again the advantages of large families become evident.

But more than this, children educate their parents more than

---

[19] John J. O'Sullivan, *The Moral Obligation of Parents to Educate Their Children for Marriage* (Washington, D. C.: The Catholic University of America Press, 1955).

is usually suspected. Conscientious parents will improve their conduct when they see how imitative their children are. They will also benefit by their children's example, or introduce educational features not before enjoyed, for the sake of the children. The sacrifices exacted in childbirth and child rearing strengthen the character and moral fibre of parents, and through the prayers and works of children parents will also grow in spiritual stature and holiness.

HUSBAND-WIFE INTERACTION

The personality perfection of husbands and wives is an important goal of marriage. It was intended "that man and wife help each other day by day in forming and perfecting themselves in the interior life; so that through their partnership in life they may advance ever more and more in virtue and above all that they may grow in true love towards God and their neighbor." [20] The "mutual aid" important to marriage, refers chiefly to assistance in the growth and expansion of all levels of the personality. Everybody has a duty of "fraternal charity" to help improve his friends and associates, and this duty is certainly even greater toward those closest to them by ties of marriage.

This, of course, does not suggest "nagging" but rather the quiet force of example, gentle persuasion, stimulation to better things, subtle change of attitudes and cheerful encouragement to personal progress. It means also, the constant gaining of grace for one's spouse, for nothing is more important. The biographer of St. Thomas More excellently illustrates his quiet influence for good upon his wife. Though quite advanced in years and averse to learning music, she nevertheless took up the study of several instruments because (we are assured) *of the subtle flattery of her saintly* and wise husband. A little recognized method of mutual improvement is found in the doctrine of "vicarious suffering." The graces won by a spouse through resignation in trial and affliction, may often be the source of the conversion of one's partner or the overcoming of a special weakness or vice.

So many and so effective are the interactions between husbands

---

[20] Pius XI, "On Christian Marriage," *The Catholic Mind,* Vol. XXIX, No. 2 (January 22, 1931), p. 28.

and wives that one of the rightful norms for success of a marriage, is the degree of progress made in the perfecting of their personalities.

SEX EDUCATION

Because of its importance and its frequent neglect by parents, sex education requires special attention today. Parents have a strict moral obligation to impart it to their children. Without it youth cannot be expected to understand or practice chastity. On the contrary, they may easily become the victims of a culture which gives them either a distorted puritanical notion or a secularistic outlook of license and excessive preoccupation with sex.

Sources of sex information

The home's serious neglect in this respect has led youth to obtain its sex information elsewhere, often from unwholesome sources. When 1400 Catholic high school students were questioned, one-half stated they were "still in the dark" about sex matters in their senior year; 58 per cent got sex knowledge outside the home; and only 56.5 per cent thought they were adequately informed.[21] The investigator of another group of 740 university students commented as follows: "It is to be noted that of the students who expressed an opinion as to how much sex education they should have had, more than twenty-three times as many students said they should have had more than said they should have had less sex education. About four times as many thought their sex education should have come earlier rather than later.[22] In a survey of Catholic parochial school teachers it was found that two-thirds had noticed a need for sex education of the pupils not being met by the home; in fact, out of 118 teachers only 10 per cent thought the parents were giving adequate sex education.[23]

---

[21] Sr. M. Jessine, "Our Children Need Sex Education," *America*, Vol. LXXXV, No. 15 (July 14, 1951), pp. 376–378.

[22] R. A. Skidmore and A. S. Cannon, *Building Your Marriage* (New York: Harper & Brothers, 1951), p. 553.

[23] Sister Mary John Murray, "A Study of the Attitudes and Practices of Catholic Elementary School Teachers in Washington, D. C. on Education for Marriage and Family Life in the Elementary School" (Master's thesis, The Catholic University of America, 1950), p. 42.

A summary of 29 different studies is given us by two marriage scholars:

1. The majority of young people have received little or no sex education from their parents, and only a small minority feel that they can discuss sex problems with their parents.
2. One-half to three-fourths of young men and women have obtained most of their sex information from contemporaries and from books. Most of them considered their sex education inadequate.[24]

One of the reasons, no doubt, so many parents neglect this responsibility is their feeling of inadequacy for the task. They are not sure when to give sex education, what to tell or how to impart it.

When to give sex education

Sex education, like the learning of one's native language, should be a gradual, informal process starting in the earliest years. Children witnessing their baby brothers and sisters being breast-fed, bathed or dressed, are being introduced to sex differences in the best possible manner. As they grow older (perhaps by the age of four) they will be taught habits of privacy and chastity in dressing, bathing, and the toilet. Ideally no significant amount of formal sex education should be required until about the thirteenth year. However, due to the precocity of our age, many children need it long before that time. In general, the proper time for such formal sex education is just *before* the need arises rather than afterward; this calls, of course, for alertness on the part of the parents. Just prior to the onset of adolescence parents must explain the nature of the natural processes involved and the moral hazards that lie ahead. If this is not done, a traumatic surprise may shock the adolescent and permanently affect his attitudes. Certainly complete sex education must be given prior to marriage. The literature advisors and counselors customarily give prospective married couples to read, would be entirely unnecessary and the couple's education could be very much superior were it given by their parents.

---

[24] L. D. Rockwood and M. E. Ford, *Youth, Marriage, and Parenthood* (New York: John Wiley & Sons, Inc., 1945), p. 4.

What to impart

Three things are required for effective sex education—guiding principles, correct attitudes and facts. The principles are found largely in the area of religion; the attitudes in psychology; and the facts in physiology.

Religion points out the sacredness and dignity of sex; it also teaches the principles for the right use of sex.[25] Sex must be equated with love and, according to Pius XII, *always* ought to be linked with the concept of parenthood. In addition, youth should be trained to apply these principles so that they can make their own decisions. Knowledge is not enough; correct habits must also be inculcated. This calls for training in mortification and self-control. It implies the frequent use of Mass, the sacraments, prayer and the avoidance of companions and places (movies, parties) which prove an occasion to sin.

Correct attitudes follow logically from correct principles. A right appreciation of sex will foster attitudes of nobility, dignity and respect towards it. Youth will come to know that nature's deepest secret demands protection and not revelation; that attire, posture, and speech should always show respect for the sacredness of sex. They will avoid both the "hush-hush" attitude of puritanism and the current attitude of neopaganism which makes sex the butt of every cheap joke. It is attitudes such as these that will largely determine a chaste or unchaste preparation for marriage and a good or poor adjustment to sex in marriage.

Physical facts, as was earlier indicated, are the *least important* part of sex education. While a knowledge of a *few* such basic facts is, of course, *essential,* it is questionable whether more than these few serve any purpose; perhaps they will even defeat the purposes of sex education. In imparting such facts, it is probably best immediately to acquaint the children with the proper medical terms, so that they will have a common sex language and one understood by those (such as doctors) with whom they need to discuss sex matters later in life.[26]

---

[25] See Chapter 12.
[26] See Chapter 12 for physical facts.

How to give sex education

Sex education is best given informally by easy, gradual stages as circumstances and needs indicate.

The mother produces healthy attitudes more by her general reaction when the subject comes up casually; less and usually very little by studied and planned verbal instruction. . . . She does not paint a precisely detailed picture, knowing that one's sexual life cannot be modelled upon that of another and that the removal of spontaneity is destructive. Sex is not nakedly exposed. Enough of its inner veilings are left intact so that later in life the child will have the satisfaction and the maturing value of making his own discoveries.[27]

Parents and educators should answer *all* questions children ask about sex. Refusal to do so may discourage future questions or give the impression that the subject must never be discussed. In all probability, they will find the answers to their questions elsewhere and from less wholesome sources.

For similar reasons their questions must be answered *truthfully*. It is best to tell them the truth always, but not usually all of the truth. Nothing is more important than retaining the children's complete confidence so that they will bring their problems without fear or hesitation to their parents. This becomes even more important as children grow to adolescents and later to adults. Parents who keep the confidence of their children will find it a great personal satisfaction; and it will be an invaluable asset to the youth during their dating and courting periods.

Some of the things that destroy such confidence in children and youth are parental attitudes of shock, surprise, fear or excessive shame when approached about sex matters. Sex education, as all education, is "caught" as well as "taught." Children are sensitive enough to detect any such attitudes. Instead, parents should discuss sex matters with ease and poise, to engender similar attitudes in their children.

Much sex education in the past has been almost entirely negative. Sex was mentioned only when parents and educators

---

[27] E. A. Strecker, *Their Mother's Sons* (Philadelphia: J. B. Lippincott Company, 1946), pp. 42–43.

treated sins against chastity. Little wonder that many grew to adult life associating something sinful with sex even in marriage! It seems imperative that the *positive* aspects of sex be included in any proper education. The beauty, dignity, goodness, sacredness and virtuousness of sex should also be emphasized.

Who should give it

The very nature of sex education clearly indicates that the parents are the rightful educators. If such education begins very early, if it is a gradual process, if it slightly anticipates the needs of each child, if it is repeated time and again and if children differ vastly in their needs and the age of those needs—obviously no other persons are in a better position to meet all these than the parents. Furthermore, they should have more of their children's confidence than any other. However, if, because of their own shortcomings, parents must select another to educate their children in sex matters, they should select one who will keep sex in its spiritual and psychological context and who has the child's confidence. They must remember that really effective sex education cannot be given to children in groups. The needs of each child vary, and such group instruction will be precocious for one and not sufficiently advanced for another's needs.

The schools should supplement the education given at home. "Even in the lower grades the instruction on the sixth and ninth commandments . . . should be sufficiently clear and explicit to meet the needs of the child placed in the surroundings that modern life in America has produced." [28] In addition, the Church has a role to play in sexual preparation for marriage.

Sufficient prenuptial instruction should be given to every couple preparing for marriage. The undeniable fact is that sometimes the entire course of instruction is crowded into an hour or a half-hour. Sometimes the fault is on the part of the couple, who do not approach the priest sufficiently soon or sufficiently often for a proper series of instructions. . . . In the instruction immediately preceding the marriage the priest must explain the Catholic moral principles regarding

[28] F. J. Connell, "The Obligation of the Home, School and Church To Educate for Family Living," *Marriage and Family Relationships,* ed. A. H. Clemens (Washington, D. C.: The Catholic University of America Press, 1950), p. 17.

the fundamental duties of married life, and although this does not mean that he is expected to dwell on the physiological aspects of conjugal intercourse, he must emphasize the evil of contraception, and the duty of each to render to the other his or her rights when they are reasonably sought.[29]

EDUCATIONAL PARENTHOOD IN THE DIVINE PLAN

One of the chief purposes of marriage as indicated in the Divine Plan, is the perfection of the personalities. The circumstances, rights and obligations of family life are such that both the supernatural and natural aspects of the human personalities will prosper. Through the process of family living, husbands, wives, parents and children are intended to grow in grace and godliness, in character, in intelligence, in emotional control and maturity, in physical strength and in social aptitude. In so doing, they will all enjoy a progressive victory over the effects of original sin and grow into a closer likeness to God, until they reach the full fruition of their family education in the joys of the Beatific Vision.

---

[29] *Ibid.*, pp. 17–18.

15

Personality Building

It CANNOT be repeated often enough that, in the education of a child, what the child *is* becomes more important than what the child *knows*. A good personality (including a well-formed character) is the most valuable natural asset parents can give their children. When a child is born, it comes into the world in possession of certain hereditary tendencies toward good and evil, and also with a capacity to absorb and be molded. Through the repetition of attitudes and actions, habits take root which, in time, become "second nature" to the individual. Psychologists realize that people are to a great extent a "bundle of habits," acting in the vast majority of their daily actions upon them rather than upon extensive deliberation and careful thinking. One of the goals of education should be to make the individual less a creature of habit and more a person of thought.

It has long been recognized that parents are most responsible for the formation of these habits of personality. The "way the twig is bent, the tree inclines" has been accepted for centuries, though perhaps no age has given it the study and attention which ours has. Much controversy and considerable theorizing has come to bog down and confuse our current child psychology. Theories of child development, lacking scientific support, and frequently in complete contradiction, jostle one another for acceptance. We are told, for instance, that the plastic, formative period of childhood is so important that all adult behavior should be analyzed in terms of unconscious drives stemming from childhood. On the other hand, an emerging school of thought would have us believe that the early years of life have been overemphasized, and that most formation takes place later in life. Actually, current research indicates that neither overindulgence nor lack of affection are desirable. Rather does it point to a combination of affection and discipline.[1] The amazing fact is, that despite countless theories of child training, not a *single one* has any compelling scientific data to support it. After reviewing the literature in the field of child psychology, a scientist concluded that this field is prolific with theories but devoid of a substantial scientific basis.[2] Here, as elsewhere, if we want security in the quest for answers to our problems, we need to resort to religion, reason, common sense, experience and ordinary observation.

IMPORTANCE OF PERSONALITY FORMATION

Perhaps the importance of the role of parents can best be seen in the factors contributing to personality. Heredity, environment, training, free will and the grace of God are the causal factors in personality development. Although parents cannot control heredity, they can, through alertness, detect innate desirable and undesirable dispositions and work to teach the child how to handle them. The training of children is obviously more under the control of the parents than any others. With attention to these two factors, and through the inculcation of proper principles, ideals and motivations, parents can hope that the free choices of their children will prove, on the whole, proper ones. By obtaining grace, and training the children to intensify their own supernatural life, parents afford the most important of all the factors in personality development.

This training in proper habits of will, mind, emotions and body is reflected in quite a number of studies on adjustment in marriage. It is generally agreed that maturity of personality is the

---

[1] R. P. Knight, "Parents and Children in a Time of World Crisis," *Child Study*, Vol. XXVIII, No. 3 (Summer, 1951), p. 5.
[2] Harold Orlansky, "Infant Care and Personality," *Psychological Bulletin*, Vol. XLV, No. 1, pp. 1–48.

basis of such adjustment and that personality development is the distinctive role of the home.

The importance of personality formation can be detected negatively from its prominence as a cause of disagreement and friction between parents. One investigator found that the most common cause of tension among 409 young married couples was disagreement about infant training.[3] This is one of the few times that this cause has appeared in current studies. Most of the studies on factors of breakdown in marriage do not reflect this factor, and their accuracy may well be held suspect for this reason. Marriage counseling experience indicates that friction over child training is not only a very frequent factor, but one of increasing frequency as children grow older.

DIFFICULTIES TODAY

The task of the parent in child training was never an easy one, but it is enormously more difficult in the urban environment of today. The physical conditions of city homes, the strain of maintaining a higher standard of living, the increased expectations on the part of the children, the quick tempo of change creating a gap between youth and age, the education of children beyond the cultural level of the parents, the religio-moral breakdown and the disappearance of sanctions flowing from a common ethical heritage—these and other factors are complicating the problem of child rearing for parents.

An important obstacle to effective personality development by the parents is the constant pressure of the urban environment. Investigators found this factor operative in a careful study of American family life in a typical Midwestern city, named fictitiously "Middletown." They noticed that:

Child rearing is traditionally concerned by Middletown chiefly in terms of making children conform to the approved ways of the group. A "good" home secures the maximum of conformity, a "bad" home fails to achieve it. Today the swiftly moving environment and multiplied occasions for contact outside the home are *making it more*

---

[3] J. T. Landis and M. G. Landis, *Building a Successful Marriage* (Englewood Cliffs, N. J.: Prentice-Hall, Inc., 1948), p. 443.

difficult to secure adherence to established group sanctions [italics ours].[4]

To the arduous task of teaching a child of Adam to curb his innate tendency toward certain faults and weaknesses, is now added the burden of persuading the child "to be different" in the face of a secular and hostile environment. The failure of so many parents to train their children properly imposes an added difficulty upon those who would do so. In a nationwide poll, 49 per cent thought the main fault of parents today to be weakness in disciplining children, being too lenient and letting children have their own way; 28 per cent thought it to be neglect and lack of supervision.[5] The homes of conscientious parents appear to be surrounded by those where a lack of discipline prevails. Such a situation exerts a detrimental influence over the proper personality development of both parent and child.

WHAT IS A GOOD HOME?

Homes in which parents realize and act upon the principle that the home is the training school for adult personality development are the need of our times. Both formal and informal methods are used to inculcate right habits of living in such homes. Parents find their chief occupation a study of their children's wholesome and unwholesome traits and tendencies. These are the homes that radiate the warmth of affection, the orderliness of discipline, the reverence of religion and the security of love. They are places where the example of good parents remains one of life's most cherished memories. They are the homes to which tired, discouraged, worried children and youth can return with a sure expectation of being understood, encouraged, inspired and solaced. They are, in short, the one place in all the world that children hold most precious and to which they will ever want to return after their absences. But these attitudes, preferences and sentiments are not the result of mere accident; rather are they

---

[4] R. S. Lynd and H. M. Lynd, *Middletown: A Study in American Culture* (New York: Harcourt, Brace & Company, 1929), p. 132.
[5] *Public Opinion Quarterly*, Vol. XIII (1949–1950), p. 349.

the product of certain very definite qualities indigenous to such homes.

The absence of these home qualities is generally agreed to be basic in juvenile delinquency. In a study of 165 reformatories in 25 different nations, it was found that out of 18,376 families of delinquent youth 15,045 were abnormal. The author concluded on this note: "The primary cause of juvenile delinquency is the deficient family." [6] After hearing the testimony of the nation's experts, a Senate committee on juvenile delinquency concluded:

No child is born delinquent, but he is subject to a wide variety of influences and conditions which tend to either lessen or increase his chances of becoming delinquent. He is subjected, first of all, to the profound influence exerted by his parents and immediate family. The child of parents who provide affectionate and consistent care, correct instruction and example, who can offer support and protection and yet give sufficient freedom for growth and development, has little need or inclination to become seriously delinquent. He has found the world a friendly place. He has not built up abnormal hostilities. He has learned to trust others. He feels worthy of love and respect. He faces new situations with at least some security and confidence. A solid foundation has been laid down for the development of normal self-discipline and self-control.[7]

In the same vein, studies show that most happy couples have come from homes where children developed a deep attachment to both parents, had little or no conflict with either parent, were firmly disciplined, were happy in childhood and adolescence, had parents who were happy in their marriages, attended church regularly and were given religious home training.[8] In the Milwaukee public school system, teachers were asked to select 158 happy, adjusted children. The homes and parents of these students were investigated. Among the most important factors found in these homes were the role of religion, joint work and recreational activities, mutual love of the fathers and mothers, and the love and

---

[6] Odette Philippon, *La jeunesse coupable vous accuse* (Paris: Recueil Sirey, 1950), p. 68.

[7] *Juvenile Delinquency,* Senate Report No. 1064 (Washington, D. C.: United States Government Printing Office, 1954), p. 9.

[8] Bernard, Burgess and Cottrell, Davis, Hamilton, Hart, Kirkpatrick, Popenoe, Schroeder, Terman.

respect of the parents for the children.[9] A nationwide poll of parents was taken in which parents were asked how to reduce delinquency; they agreed on three steps, two of which were *more* home supervision and stricter home discipline.[10]

A national conference on juvenile delinquency has pointed out that a good home embodies 14 elements.[11] These points are incorporated in the following:

1. It is a home that affords a sense of being *loved,* which springs from the basic human drive for emotional security; this includes a sense of being *wanted* which likewise induces a feeling of security. The lack of love relationship in the home had its effect on the draftees of World War II. One investigation of 2,228 patients with neuroses in military hospitals showed that 48 per cent were timid, immature, dependent and frustrated. "On the whole," the research workers found, "this group revealed marked evidence of love-deprivation in childhood." [12]

2. It is a home in which children are weaned from total dependence upon parents or others; it affords progressive growth in self-reliance and self-confidence, obviating "momism."

3. In it children develop a feeling of *belonging;* the social instinct of humans is so deeply rooted in nature that we must feel as though we are a member of a group, accepted by them and contributing to them.

4. It furnishes *time and space* for the children; time in which they are free to develop their own potentialities according to the innate inclinations peculiar to each (this presumes such inclinations are good ones). Oversupervision of child growth is as bad as too little supervision. To some extent, children grow through neglect, correctly understood. They need *space* of their own, where they can keep their clothes, toys, and the like. This will not only help to develop a sense of ownership, but also of responsibility for the proper care of such space.

5. In a good home there is always *discipline*—firm but not harsh;

---

9 J. W. Stout and G. Langdon, "A Study of the Home Life of Well-Adjusted Children," *Journal of Educational Sociology,* Vol. XXIII, No. 8 (April 1950), pp. 442–460.

10 *Family Life,* Vol. XV, No. 1 (January 1955), p. 4.

11 *National Conference on Prevention and Control of Juvenile Delinquency: Report on Home Responsibility* (Washington, D. C.: United States Government Printing Office, 1947), p. 8.

12 H. G. McGregor, *Journal of Neurology, Neurosurgery, and Psychiatry,* Vol. VII, No. 21 (1947).

not a single top authority on child care any longer subscribes to the "permissive" theory of child training. This concept has given way to the need for firm discipline. Harsh discipline, however, breeds resentment and obviates the sense of being loved, wanted and belonging mentioned above.

6. Here children are *understood* as children; adults learn to view childish actions and attitudes from the viewpoint of the child and not from their more mature point of view. Children have a different sense of values from adults; once this is recognized, many actions of children that on the surface appear delinquent become upon proper understanding a childish prank, mischievousness and the like.

7. In such a home, children are made to feel *needed;* feeling wanted will not alone develop their rightful sense of importance or sense of responsibility; once children sense that they are actually *needed* in the home—useful and contributory—they develop importance, participation and responsibility.

8. In it their abilities are *appreciated.* Constant faultfinding not counteracted by proportionate praise and commendation may breed resentment, discouragement, introversion and so forth. On the other hand, nothing succeeds like success, provided that the children are commended for it.

9. In it there is a regulated *freedom of speech* without hesitancy or shame; through this rightful self-expression parents come to understand their children and their problems. This is especially true in matters of sex education. All this means that parents first instill and then remain worthy of the confidence of their children. This confidence, so imperative, will be shattered if the children come to feel inhibited in their freedom of speech.

10. In a good home, there is no *jealousy* among the children. Positively viewed, this means that parents do not give children an occasion to become jealous. To avoid the growth of this untoward trait, therefore, parents need to treat all children, not equally, but equitably, to love them all sincerely and without discrimination, to give them all the same essential things, though not necessarily the same incidental things.

11. A good home develops a sense of *responsibility.* Most people do not develop this trait even late in life. It can only be brought about by responsibility; it cannot be learned by reading or lecturing alone, but requires active and frequent participation in responsible work. Work around the home is an excellent technique here. Responsibility is one trait *learned by doing.*

12. Above all, a good home gives children *ideals* which, in the last analysis, spring from *religion.* Children are born idealists, with

a keen sense of justice and high purpose. Parents must not destroy these traits, but embellish them. This can best be done by and through the graces, motivation and principles of religion; for an ideal is simply a set of principles.

13. Finally, a truly good home imparts to children a sense of *being loved by God*. This pervading relationship gives children a realization of a fatherly Providence, a sense of security and of acceptance which no crisis can destroy.

CURRENT APPROACHES

There are, perhaps, only three types of parental approach to personality development. In the last analysis, these stem from three basic theologies of life and the family.[13] One of them is the literal application of the principle that "children should be seen but not heard." It is a form of domestic tyranny that, far from expanding a child's personality, actually stunts and distorts it. Children of such families usually lack self-confidence, suffer from inferiority complexes, fail to confide in their parents and are the victims of many fears. Careless "family experts" have, in many instances, confused this type of approach with that of a reasonable discipline by parents and have labeled it "authoritarian."

Another approach is what was originally called "self-expression," then "progressive education," then "permissive" and more recently "developmental." It is based upon the unbelievably fantastic theory that children should be left uninhibited by parental direction. The assumptions, of course, are that *nature* will properly direct the growth and development of the child's personality, and that, if the child is restricted by parental rules, it will develop a neurosis. The widespread lack of parental discipline and supervision today indicates that this theory is still quite widespread. Fortunately, the field of child psychology, once obsessed with the permissive approach, has at this time *not a single nationally famous expert who any longer subscribes to this theory*.

Still another approach is that which prompts parents to employ reasonable direction and guidance of their children's personality formation. It assumes that at very early ages parental intel-

---

13 See Chapter 2.

ligence and experience must substitute for the lack of both by the small child. As the personality develops (and with it rationality) parental discipline relaxes and changes in technique by degrees until the child reaches maturity. Not only will children, under this approach, be given progressively more freedom to make their own decisions, but the methods of discipline will change gradually from the more forceful (such as physical punishment or deprivation) to the more persuasive (reasoning, appeal to honor, sentiment, loyalty, religion and the like). Parents seem to make two mistakes in this approach today: either they fail to wean their children from them gradually by means of a progressive education in self-direction and decision making; or they tend to allow too complete freedom to make important decisions (even ones having profound ethical implications) to adolescents not yet matured in reason or experience.

TYPES OF PARENTAL FAILURE

Among the many varieties of parent-educators are found the *inhibited* parents. They are the persons who, in all probability, have been raised in overly strict homes. Replete with self-strictures on their own conduct, they impose them upon the behavior of their children also. These parents usually find it difficult to express their affections, engage in recreation with their children or impart that sense of relaxation and confidence which will induce the children to look upon them as confidants and friends.

The *overprotective* parents are those who will not permit children to hazard the ordinary risks of life. The youngsters may not have bicycles for fear of an accident; boys may not play football lest they receive an injury; daughters may not attend properly chaperoned dances because they might meet an unwholesome boy. Children brought up under a sheltered existence will likely either never learn to face the normal risks of adult life, or, in a spirit of revolt, will turn out to be "daredevils."

The *rejecting* parents are, perhaps, more numerous than any other distorted type. There are, of course, those who openly reject their children by displaying overt dislike, resentment or even hatred against them. But much more frequently found are parents whose rejection is so subtle that often they themselves do not realize it. The parent who *neglects* a child *rejects* it; the working mother who prefers office work to child care is a rejecting parent. The countless parents who deprive their children of time, attention, affection, esteem, love, companionship, supervision, discipline, religion are rejecting their children even though they may little suspect the fact. This is one of the worst natural results of the practice of family limitation. The "contraceptive baby" or "rhythm baby" is likely to prove as rejected later as it was unwanted originally. Studies of rejected children indicate that rejection results in plays for attention, showing-off, hostility to parents, brothers, sisters and society, feelings of inadequacy, anxieties, frustrations or extreme independence.[14]

Perfectionists are a very subtle species of repecting parents. They revel in unrealistic fantasies of living in a world, a neighborhood, a home without blemish or imperfection. They would force their children into this dream world by making them conform to the strictest type of rule and regulation. The housewife poring over magazines for long hours, studying with great care the "model home," is likely to end in having very unideal children. The spotless, scratchless, perfectly regimented model house is not a nursery, school or recreation center for children. We cannot have model homes and model children at the same time; one or the other must become frayed. The parent who insists upon ideals that are too high of attainment, or who demands all the embellishments of adult conduct from young children, is a perfectionist. It is out of such homes that flow the many unrelaxed, prudish, extremely formal and overly rigid, regimented children. An insistence upon top grades in the long record of school achievement may develop a "brain," but, in many instances, it is likely to develop a distorted personality. Not only does the perfectionist parent err in trying to impose an inhuman routine upon the home, but also in a lack of human sympathy, understanding and warmth.

The *indulgent* parents are at quite the opposite pole. Instead of rigid adherence to a militaristic orderliness, they are driven to

---

14 O. S. English and G. H. Pearson, *Emotional Problems of Living* (New York: W. W. Norton & Co., Inc., 1945), pp. 15, 133; also P. M. Symonds, *The Dynamics of Parent Child Relationships* (New York: Bureau of Publications, Teachers College, Columbia University, 1949), pp. 11–50.

giving excessive privileges to their children, often from a sense of misguided love. These are the parents who have forgotten (if they ever knew) that the sinews of character are built on denial and suffering. Their children are frequently seen draped over corner drugstore counters sipping Cokes by the hour, roaming the streets late or night, or driving dad's car into a prominent eating place at two in the morning. They are never expected to assist with home chores, and the parents do most of the homework assigned by the school. Many of them were found among the 1,825,000 men rejected for military service; a situation which provoked a book by the chief psychiatrist of the armed services.[15] In it he deplored the fact that "momism" had ruined so many boys by overindulging them. He believed this growing phenomenon in our culture to be due to the fact that boys are so much of the time under women's supervision (in both home and school) and so little under that of men. These children are the forerunners of the immature adult, who runs away from the realities of a life not equally as indulgent as his parents, and finds an escape in drink, drugs, or sheer irresponsibility.

The *domineering* parents are still in our midst also, though their number is diminishing. Inflexible by temperament or training and often nagged by an inferiority complex, they tend to carry into the adolescent and adult ages of their children the same rigidity of their early childhood training. They, too, like the indulgent and perfectionist parents, never permit their children to grcw to maturity. All decisions, major or minor, are made by them and their growing children may never use the expanding powers of reason and self-direction which nature gives them. Not only will such children become indecisive adults, but they will probably go through life with a fear of, and a possible and proportionate disrespect for, all authority.

PARENTAL TRAITS AND SUCCESS

To achieve success as the parent-educator of personalities is a task that requires certain traits in the parents themselves. Here, as in all education, what is "caught" by the children from the parents is often more important than what is "taught" to them.

---

[15] E. H. Strecker, *Their Mother's Sons* (Philadelphia: J. B. Lippincott Company, 1946).

Children have a keen natural ability to sense parental attitudes and feelings despite occasional attempts by parents to conceal them. They will know clearly whether they are really wanted or merely tolerated or, perhaps, accepted as a dutiful responsibility. Children will know if their parents have a genuine and deep interest in them or a feigned one; they will know with certainty if they are truly loved for their own sakes or for selfish reasons.

Parents, on the other hand, will ever try to meet the varying needs of children at different ages and stages of growth. Conscious of the fact that child rearing is a great responsibility, they will consider no sacrifice too great which serves such a rightful purpose. Parents need to look upon themselves as expendable for the formation of their children. They will, if they enjoy the full vision of the vocation of parenthood, work at it and continuously try to improve themselves in all ways as educators. Aware of their limitations, they will continue to learn and grow in their professional knowledge even as do the doctor, the lawyer, the teacher. Above all, they will ever remain mindful of the importance of grace both for themselves and their children; and being mindful, will exploit the channels of grace at their disposal.

NEEDS OF CHILDREN

Nature has ingrained in the personalities of children certain *inescapable needs* that must be attended if wholesome development is to be expected. One of these is simply *personal care and attention.* Our extensive current experience with children in institutions, such as orphan homes, where personal care is impossible, confirms this need beyond any doubt. It is a well-known fact that many such children, when adopted or placed in foster homes, experience a transformation in their personalities which is very marked and striking. In a study of infants reared in institutions, the following characteristics were found: diminished interest, excessive preoccupation with strange persons, general retardation, blandness of facial expression, impoverished initiative, ineptness in new social situations and language retardation.[16]

---

[16] A. Gesell and C. Amatruda, *Developmental Diagnosis: Normal and Abnormal Child Development; Clinical Methods and Pediatric Applications* (New York: Harper & Brothers, 1949).

Equal if not more important is the need for *love and affection*. It is at least as necessary for the nourishment of the soul as food is for the body. The significance of parental love was emphasized in a World War II report on our youth. Despite the stresses and strains of separations, crowded housing, economic worries, and the like, adolescents did not show serious evidence of such strains when *parental love and affection were strong*.[17]

In the first place, there is abundant evidence that deprivation can have adverse effects on the development of children. . . .The evidence suggests that three somewhat different experiences can each produce the affectionless and psychopathic character: (a) lack of opportunity for forming an attachment to a mother-figure during the first 3 years; (b) deprivation for a limited period . . . during the first 3 or 4 years; (c) changes from one mother-figure to another during the same period.[18]

A very striking observation was made in two institutions in which all factors were the same except one—personal affection. The children not given affection "never learned to speak, to walk, to feed themselves. With one or two exceptions in a total of 91 children, those who survived were human wrecks who behaved either in the manner of agitated or of apathetic idiots." [19] During a two-year period, furthermore, out of 239 children observed, none of those receiving personal love died, but 37 per cent of those unable to be given such affection did.[20]

The need of children for *security* will usually be satisfied if they are given personal attention, love and affection. Young children require a sense of complete assurance that they are wanted and that all their needs will be met by the parents. Without this they can only develop those vague feelings of insecurity that are basic in so many emotional disturbances in adult life.

---

[17] E. R. Groves and G. H. Groves, "The Social Background of Wartime Adolescents," *Annals of the American Academy of Political and Social Sciences,* Vol. CCXXXVI (November 1944), pp. 26–32.

[18] J. Bowlby, *Maternal Care and Mental Health* (Geneva; Palais des Nations, World Health Organization, 1951: and New York: Columbia University Press, 1951), p. 47.

[19] Rene Spitz, "Motherless Infants," *Selected Studies in Marriage and the Family,* eds. R. F. Winch and R. McGinnis (New York: Henry Holt & Co., Inc., 1953), p. 187.

[20] *Ibid.*

World War II afforded a striking example of the meaning of parental security to a child. During the severest bombings of London, children remaining with their parents showed no serious disturbances, whereas those evacuated to rural camps and separated from their parents showed marked psychological regressions.[21]

It is easy to overlook the need of children to have their dignity *respected*. (This is especially true when their parents have tendencies to dominate, or be perfectionists.) Children not only have all the innate dignity of human beings, but also the rights inherent in that dignity. More than this, they have a keen sense of justice and fair play concerning these rights. Too often parents will have this vision fail them in moments of anger and will resort to discipinary measures that violate both the dignity and rights of the child.

In our age of neuroses and psychoses, few things are more necessary than a *serene home atmosphere*. The nervous systems of children are sensitive and impressionable and will suffer severely from the emotional debauches of parents mentally ill or lacking in self-control. In our age, when children are subjected to the same neurotic pressures that adults experience in urban living, they need all the more a home that is a haven of peace, serenity and harmony. For the same reason, nagging and excessive criticism (often never offset by praise) can be damaging. In a study of 2,957 children in public schools who were given various psychological tests, it was found that only 5 per cent of them made a poor adjustment if their homes were free of nagging, while 25 per cent of the children subject to severe criticism were poorly adjusted.[22] Another study of 126 children showed that mental disorders were rife if their fathers were excessively demanding or were antagonistic.[23]

Though nagging, antagonism and excessive expectations de-

---

[21] A. Freud and D. T. Burlingham, *War and Children* (New York: Medical War Books, 1943), pp. 156–157.

[22] E. W. Burgess, *The Adolescent in the Family* (New York: Appleton-Century-Crofts, Inc., 1934), p. 274.

[23] J. E. McKeown and C. Chyatte, "The Behavior of Children as Shown by Normals, Neurotics and Schizophrenics," *American Catholic Sociological Review*, Vol. XV, No. 4 (December 1954).

stroy personality growth, praise is constructive. Normally, children need the approval of their parents to sustain their morale. This is also true of adults since any human being who loves and is loved and wanted in return desires to have this good relationship confirmed by words of commendation. On the other hand, few things are more damaging to a child than ridicule, which offends his innate sense of dignity.

Children also need clear-cut *principles* constituting an ideal. By nature they are idealists but they should have their zeal in these respects, guided and directed. The absence of such ideals in parents can be disappointing and disillusioning; and conflicting principles between parents cause doubts, perplexities and neuroses.

Children also require the aids and motivations which *religion* alone can bring. They have a natural tendency toward religion and reverence that demands cultivation, not discouragement. Late childhood and adolescence in particular, need sorely the principles, graces and motivations and self-discipline of religion. This is especially true in our age where we are soon subjected to pagan influences and must form our own moral decisions earlier than formerly.

The need for discipline

Discipline is indispensable in child development. It is practicing the habit of doing the right thing at the right time regardless of the difficulties or sacrifices involved. It means adherence in practice to one's principles despite the costs entailed. Children need discipline, not only for character training but also for their own sense of security. A child without respect for authority is a child lacking in feelings of assurance. Students polled in colleges throughout the nation indicated this fact. The director of this research concluded:

If we believe the critics of modern youth, our adolescents want nothing better than to be left alone and untrammeled. But our survey shows precisely the contrary. What the adolescents want is guidance, the security of firm ground under their feet, the knowledge of right and wrong. They want a home that is more than a provider of food, shelter and clothing—a place that has absolute standards and definite authority. This present generation is perhaps the first generation of young people in modern history which does not clamor for more freedom but wants less freedom and more security. . . . Even more surprising for the critics of modern youth will be the age limits which the adolescent himself sets for parental control. Only in the case of radio was the average opinion inclined to the view that parental control should stop before high school age; and while some felt that parents should not interfere with the child's listening after the age of 10, others held that control should be exercised up to the age of 16. The majority believed that radio listening should be under supervision up to the age of 12, and movies and reading up to the age of 15. As to smoking, drinking, making friends, and staying out late, most students wanted parental authority right up to college age. Many felt that even this was too early an age to be left without parental guidance. And although some of the students questioned must have been below 21, a considerable percentage held that parental authority on these activities should continue up to 21, that is, up to the time when the average college student goes out into the world to earn his own living.[24]

Many parents do not seem to realize how much children and youth want and expect to be disciplined. Whether it be laziness and indifference or only an erroneous belief that youth can be trusted to discipline itself, the fact remains that quite generally youth is being allowed excessive freedom by parents. This seems especially true in regard to the leisure time pursuits of youth.

Perhaps one of the reasons for this lenient attitude toward children and youth is the large number of fathers who fail to take an active part in discipline. According to the study just cited, interviews disclosed that in 14.8 per cent of the cases parental authority was about equally divided, in 57.9 per cent it was more in the mothers' hands, and in only 27.3 per cent of the instances did the father have the dominant role in discipline.[25]

How to discipline

Two common errors about discipline are that it is exclusively prohibitive and, accordingly, only negative; and that it exclusively imposes hard things—punishments, denials, refusals and sacrifices. Doubtless these somewhat militaristic attitudes ex-

---

[24] Doris Drucker, "Authority for Our Children," *Harper's Magazine*, No. 1089 (February 1941), pp. 279–280.
[25] *Ibid.*, p. 280.

plain why many American parents rebel against disciplining their children. Correctly understood, however, a child's personality is formed as much by the positive action of doing right things as it is by the negative action of prohibiting wrong things.

In the words of a distinguished neurologist and psychiatrist "the first two essentials of successful training and discipline are to have something to teach, and to build such a loving and friendly relationship with our children that they will gladly accept it from us. The third is example. . . . The fourth great factor . . . is reward or punishment." [26] To these should be added a fifth, the power of religious living.

Parents need clearly conceived and imparted principles for their children before any progress in discipline can be made.

Discipline rests on love and a rapport with the children (setting them an example, and affording them the motives which religion supplies), not upon punishment. As a matter of fact, punishment should be considered a means of last resort, much as the fear of hell when love of God is not present. If this is understood, the reason some parents "have a hard time with the kids" and must so frequently resort to force, is the absence or breakdown of religious motivation, love or example. Parents who find themselves often using punishment and threats should examine their general relationship with their children. Children do crave the approval of parents, as a rule, and their worst dislike is parental disapproval and disfavor if there is a deep mutual love between parents and children.

If children are to be trained in right conduct they must, of course, be given directions. However, many seem to make serious mistakes in doing so. When parents must give directions, they should follow these rules:

1. Directives must be firm, not subject to change; children knowing a parent's weakness to vacillate will play upon it; they need to feel the parent "really means business."
2. They must be consistent. To permit an action today and deny it tomorrow will not command respect; nor will a certain command from one parent and the opposite command from the other parent.

---

[26] R. P. Mackay, "Children Without Neuroses," *Ladies' Home Journal,* Vol. LXV, No. 11 (November 1948), pp. 278–279.

A united parental front is imperative or children become confused and perplexed.

3. They should not be vague and indefinite but very clear and specific so that the child knows precisely what is expected.

4. They should be reasonable.

5. Directives once given should usually be executed to their final completion or children will soon learn that future threats are only "half-meant."

6. They should not be too frequent. Constant "don'ts" can prove an excessive pressure and lead to unwholesome inhibitions.

7. Directives should be given for both the natural and supernatural welfare of the children.

8. They should never be given as a mere convenience for parental sloth or laziness.

9. Though as a rule, directives should be accompanied by reasonable explanations, it is perhaps well at all ages to expect an occasional "blind obedience"; this habit is necessary not only for adult experience in the world but also as an aid to developing trust in a Providence Whose ways are often mysterious.

10. They should frequently be accompanied with religious motivation; to insist upon a child's performing a distasteful chore because "God wills it," "for the sake of the poor souls" or "for sinners" is to sublimate personality formation to its ultimate heights.

Just as some parents do not know the methods of giving commands, so too many do not know how to administer required punishments. In fact, they are less likely to punish properly since the subjective element is often very strong. Some generally accepted rules of punishment are as follows:

1. Punishment should usually be given promptly. Thus given, it is associated directly with the misdeed and the emotion will soon subside. When punishment is delayed, emotions often remain ruffled and grudges develop; the too frequent habit of delaying punishments till father returns means that his arrival is much the same as that of a policeman or executioner. It is usually (except for special offenses) an admission of the mother's inability to control the children.

2. All punishments should be proportioned to the offense committed and not to the degree of parental anger. This is clearly a matter of simple justice as well as good policy; when in a rage, postpone punishment.

3. Some punishments, at early ages especially, must be physical; it is quite idealistic to expect children to be sweet and rational at all

times, furthermore, an advantage of physical punishment is its promptness and its association of disagreeable sensations with wrong acts— an association which can be a lifelong asset; child psychologists are, at this time, rapidly returning to the Biblical injunction not "to spare the rod, and spoil the child."

4. One of the most effective punishments is to deprive a child of objects or experiences it cherishes the most.

5. Once a threat of punishment is attached to an act or omission, it should be carried through. Not to do so will make successive threats meaningless.

6. Repeated threats before eventually administering punishment, will have much the same effect; threats should be given only once.

7. Punishments should never be given unless the child is aware of the seriousness of the act; this calls for a large measure of understanding of the child.

Parents need, in addition, to verbally rebuke, correct or scold children. Here, too, mistakes can occur. It is well to glean from experience again some elementary rules:

1. Rebukes and corrections should usually be given in private, or children may "lose face" with others or feel disgraced or excessively humiliated.

2. They should be given as calmly as possible. Angry words usually make the listener equally angry and often defeat the correction.

3. Parents should try not to show impatience in their corrections or to forget the child's innate dignity by offensive language or attitude.

4. Rebukes that show hostility on the part of the parent, are very damaging.

5. It is wise policy to point out some good trait or deed of the child before confronting him with his offenses. This is recognized as clever in adult human relations but is not stressed enough in parent-child relations.

6. Parents should employ both natural and supernatural motives in correcting a child. They will single out a misdeed as an offense against other children or society, but all too seldom will they point out the same act as an offense against God.

7. Since rebukes and corrections have only one purpose, the improvement of the child, they should be accompanied with suggestions relative to the need of grace to help correct an undesirable trait or habit.

However, it is not only through punishments but equally through rewards that personalities are trained. This is so widely recognized as a spur to achievement in the professional, academic, business, political and even religious groups that it needs little comment. Yet there are those parents who misuse rewards because they misunderstand their purposes. Experience seems to have pointed out certain wise rules in this respect also:

1. Rewards when deserved should be fully given.
2. They should never deteriorate into bribes. To promise a certain favor if a certain act is performed is "buying off" a child and is quite useless as a disciplinary technique. In fact, if often indulged, it will teach the child that one never makes sacrifices unless he will be paid—a very widespread principle in our times. Rewards for a deed performed are not as promises but as tokens of appreciation.
3. Rewards should not become a matter of regular daily occurrence; they will soon be interpreted as bribes or they will lose their novelty and appeal.
4. They should always be proportionate to the good deed done or misdeed avoided; excessively small rewards will lose their stimulus to effort, while extravagant awards will tend to spoil children.

PERSONALITY FORMATION OF PARTNERS

It would be a serious mistake, and one all too commonly made, to fail to recognize that marriage is intended also for the development of the personalities of the parents. Although nagging is widespread and indicates a general desire to improve one's spouse by *wrong* methods, the fact cannot be ignored that partners have a clear duty to assist each other toward the perfecting of their personalities. The basic methods are not unlike those employed by parents toward children. Partners in marriage need to employ all the resources of religion in this task of helping each other. They need to exert a mutual influence toward progress in personality growth through a deep, genuine love and an abiding and good relationship. One partner should not ignore attempts at fraternal correction on the part of the other, and rewards and an appreciation and recognition of merit have an important part to play.

PERSONALITY FORMATION AND THE DIVINE PLAN

It was clearly intended that the home be the instrument for forging human personality. This is the tremendous responsibility of parents in the Divine Plan, that they can in such large measure shape the destiny of their children and of themselves.

Not only has this goal been fixed, but also many of the means for attaining this goal have been fixed in the Divine Plan. It has posited for us the inescapable qualities of a good home, the correct approach to personality development, the traits of parental success, the natural needs of children, the rules for human discipline. In addition, the Divine Plan has supplied the many supernatural aids of religion for the use of parents and children. Few aspects of marriage and parenthood have evoked more emphasis from the Author of the Divine Plan than the weighty responsibility of personality development. If on the one hand, He has asserted "Woe to those who scandalize the little ones," He has, on the other assured parents that "Blessed are they who *do* and *teach* for their place shall be high in heaven."

16

The Role of Recreation

Though always important, the role of recreation in the family is of growing concern today. Not only does increasing leisure magnify its importance, but some current trends in recreation are dangerous. The nature and purposes of recreation are widely misunderstood. Many view it as an end in itself rather than as a means to other goals. Such persons work in order to play, rather than play so as to recreate themselves for their life work. Others equate recreation with dissipation; late hours, overeating and excessive drinking are mistaken for play and recreation. Many interpret it in terms of dollars and cents; the more costly the recreation, the better. Others have decided that recreation outside the home is superior to that in the home.

WHAT TRUE RECREATION MEANS

Each of these attitudes indicates a lack of insight into the meaning and purposes of recreation. There are many complicated theories these days about the nature of recreation but none is as practical as the simple, concise definition given us by St. Thomas: "anything which delights or gives joy." One might wonder that a theologian should interest himself in matters seeming so mundane. However, this is understood when he further observes that "Joy is the necessary companion of virtue, and to be virtuous one must be joyful . . . for it happens that when virtue is sad it will not be long endured." This emphasizes one of the important reasons for recreation.

Chesterton also noted the close connection between religious living and recreation. "The countries," he observed, "in Europe which are still influenced by priests, are exactly the countries where there is still singing and dancing and colored dresses and art in the open air. Catholic doctrine and discipline may be walls," he added, "but they are the walls of a playground." [1]

PURPOSES OF RECREATION

Not only is religion recreative but also religious living depends upon joyful living. This is why so many moderns who seem cheerful when dissipating at parties, lack that constant, pervading and ever present cheerfulness and joyousness of a truly religious person.

On the natural level recreation restores energies lost through work so that the individual is again capable of effective industry. However, there are less evident but equally compelling reasons for play. Perhaps we do not realize sufficiently its great educational effectiveness. This is especially true when so much of our recreation comes from the mass media—movies, television, radio, books, periodicals and newspapers. Collectively these constitute a university of greater influence than all the formal colleges and universities together. The significance of educational recreation can be seen most easily by its important role in the lives of small children, who spend most of their time and receive most of their basic training through play situations.

Professional educators have long realized the character building potential of recreation. For this reason, the athletic director is often more influential in personality formation than are the teachers. The boy, for instance, who would never stop smoking at the advice of a teacher, will usually do so at the insistence of the coach. In a similar sense, parents can often train their children more effectively in a play situation than in any other; but this presupposes that parents will interest themselves in, supervise and share their children's recreation. If it takes the form of manual

---

[1] G. K. Chesterton, *Orthodoxy* (New York: John Lane Co., 1908), pp. 268–269.

hobbies or sports, recreation will also teach skills which can prove lifelong assets.

While our culture has given us many who work to play, it has also given us many who rarely or never relax. The hypertension and heart conditions so prominent today are probably due in many instances either to dissipating forms of play or to failure to play at all. The Mayo Clinic tells us that the cause of many ailments they treat in men, is failure to rest, relax and recreate. The price of success in our highly competitive economic life is too often physical or mental ill-health. Apparently we have forgotten that play is an absolute necessity which gives spice to life and balances the diet of living between work, love and religion. Children should be taught wholesome, lasting recreational habits which will keep the next generation from suffering what some psychiatrists have labeled "Americanitis."

Another important purpose of recreation is its social one. Few group experiences will more deeply cement the attachments between husband and wife, parents and children than will play. A family that has spent an enjoyable, relaxing outing together, or an evening of games together, will have strengthened the bonds by which families live and upon which marriage thrives. Separate, individualistic types of recreation common today ignore this significant purpose of family recreation.

RECREATION OUTSIDE THE HOME

The tremendous growth of recreation outside the home, usually the individualistic type, is further evidence of the failure to realize the social and unitive aspects of play. Commercialized amusement has prospered to the advantage of the business world and the disadvantage of the family. Parents, especially, must clearly realize just what is happening in this respect. Much of our outside recreation is highly individualistic; it often lacks adequate supervision of children and youth; it tends to equate dissipation with recreation (and teaches this false lesson to children); it is dominantly secular and frequently immoral; too much of it is stimulating and exciting rather than peaceful and relaxing; often it has little or no educational value; it is generally artificial rather than natural; it encourages the breaking of family budgets for pleasure purposes; and it is highly passive, giving us the phenomena known as "spectatoritis." It seems very revealing of our failure in this respect, that when 476 Catholic husbands and wives (married 10 years or more) were asked what they found was the best recreation between husbands and wives, they placed at the top of the list "outside activities"; the same reply was given for the best recreation for parents and children.[2]   Another study of 50 tenth grade students and their parents, confirmed earlier investigations, which indicated that the most enjoyable recreation of families today is found outside the home.[3]

Though recreation outside the home ought never take priority over home centered types, parents yet should promote and encourage limited amounts of outside recreation in our crowded cities.   This is particularly true in areas so congested that children have little yard and play space; in such instances, parents might well realize it a rightful and required social action on their part to have parks, playgrounds and the like provided. It is equally imperative that parents of teen-agers encourage and assist personally in supervising parish centered activities for the youth.   They should recognize that traditionally parishes were not only places of worship but also social centers for persons of all ages.   Experience has shown that where this is the case, parish spirit flourishes; there is a deeper rapport between clergy and laity, and between families; Catholic life prospers and mixed marriages are significantly reduced.   Since a part of every Catholic family's leisure time should be given to charitable aid to others, parents and youth also ought help return to the parish level many of the charitable aids extended by central agencies such as Catholic Charities offices.   Were this done effectively, a parish would once again become what it is intended to be, a family of families, in which no single family would remain in either material or spiritual need.

----

[2] Hugh Dunn, S.J., *A Study of Some Catholic Marital Attitudes, Practices and Problems with Special Reference to the Implication for Premarital Instructions* (Washington, D. C.: The Catholic University of America Press, 1956), Tables 67, 69.

[3] R. Connor and T. B. Johannis, "Family Recreation in Relation to Role Conceptions of Family Members," *Marriage and Family Living,* Vol. XVII, No. 4 (November 1955), p. 308.

FAMILY CENTERED RECREATION

While such extradomestic recreation resources are useful, it would be a serious mistake to permit them to supplant home recreation. The century old trend away from home play has been reversed somewhat by the exodus from the city proper to the suburban and fringe areas. Television also, has helped to keep members of the family home more; but the strictures of complete silence so often associated with viewing it, can scarcely be deemed an ideal family or group type of play. Despite these changes toward home recreation, the lure of the outside agencies of pleasure is still dominant and seemingly irresistible to millions of families.

It is still generally true that group play shared between husbands and wives, parents and children in the home is not too common. The individual preferences and hobbies, the constant busyness of parents, the frequent evenings out of members of the family, the lack of facilities, the laziness of parents, the "passing the buck" to outside organizations and their leaders—are all factors keeping recreation from becoming fully family centered again. Added to these are the false sense of dignity some parents have, which they feel suffers if they stoop to play with the children; and the failure of so many parents to really *enjoy their children*—a factor that in later years is often a source of very bitter regret.

Doubtless, the chief reason for the decline of home centered recreation has been the simple failure to appreciate its superior merits. Bonds of attachment are deepened and education and character forming are being done by the parents instead of by a less effective substitute. If desired, family recreation can also be active rather than passive and include all the superior effects which active recreation implies. Human beings are meant to be active organisms, not passive spectators. It is generally agreed that participation in play activities brings more relaxation, more education, more development of useful skills and crafts, more wholesome and healthful results than sitting and listening to a radio or watching television or a movie.

Another important aspect of family recreation is its moral effects.   Parents can use play situations very effectively to develop in their children self-control, meekness, honesty, fair play, justice, charity and other virtues.   If family parties were encouraged rather than discouraged (by parents who place model homes before their children), the proper supervision of such mixed gatherings of the sexes could be assured.   Unfortunately, there is a growing number of all too trustful and puerile parents who, when they do permit home parties, leave the youth completely unsupervised.   In one locality recently observed, Catholic parents of fifth grade children arranged mixed parties in their homes and then went out for the evening, leaving the pre-teen-agers of both sexes on their own.   A psychiatrist after a seven-year study of influences affecting child behavior wrote:

It is becoming more and more apparent that what all delinquent children have in common is unprotectedness.   I have found in every delinquent child that one time or another he had insufficient protection.   That implies not only material things, but social and psychological influences.   Of course children get hurt at home and by their parents.   But the time when children in the mass are most defenseless, when they are most susceptible to influences from society at large, is in their leisure hours.[4]

Still another advantage of family recreation is a religious one. It is quite evident that purveyors of pleasure outside the home rarely use their facilities to promote religious values.   The "Song of Bernadette," for instance, represents a type of movie so infrequent as to be an insignificant per cent of the total output of the movie industry.   Families, however, can employ play situations more frequently for religious purposes.   They might recall that most dramas produced in the "Ages of Faith" were enacted either around miracles or mysteries of religion; and that the greatest occasions for merriment were Holy Days.   England received its title of "Merry England" when it was Catholic!   Today, too, parents can use hobbies to erect shrines, home altars and other religious articles; instead of the usual picnic at a beach, they could occasionally make a pilgrimage to a neighboring shrine; into their home musical renditions they could sometimes introduce hymns

---

[4] Fredric Wertham, *Seduction of the Innocent* (New York: Rinehart & Company, Inc., 1954), pp. 155–156.

and the beauties of the Gregorian Chants. These and many other things which Catholic ingenuity can devise, could be made part of the recreational heritage of children.

We can see the recreation pattern of the 476 Catholic husbands and wives who were asked what play plans were found most feasible for husbands and wives. The first twelve named (in order of their frequency) were—outside activities together, visiting or entertaining friends, movies, cards, occasional night out alone, sporting events, dances, dining out, mutual home interests, reading, picnics and motor trips.[5] The same group, asked about their parent-child play pattern, listed (in the order of frequency) picnics and outings, motor trips, family group activities, home games, movies, visiting and entertaining, sports, reading, vacations, children's play and swimming.[6]

Those who do not appreciate family centered recreation, should be reminded that even some of those who devote their professional lives to recreational projects outside the home (and might be expected to have a bias in that direction), recognize the superiority of home recreation. One of these specialists gave the following reasons for his preference of home centered play:

1. It develops deeper understandings between parents and children.
2. It provides opportunities for individuals to learn to live together.
3. It contributes to the total development of the individual.
4. It strengthens the spiritual life of the family.
5. It indicates the strengths and weaknesses in individuals and the treatment needed.
6. It provides opportunities for guidance and counsel.
7. It gives a golden opportunity to parents to live up to the ideal of them held by their children.
8. It develops a pride in achievement.[7]

SUPERVISING RECREATION

The highly secular and immoral nature of many leisure time activities today, and the frequency with which children and youth are exposed to them, demands alert and constant supervision by

---

[5] Dunn, *op. cit.*, Table 67.
[6] *Ibid.*, Table 69.
[7] Daniel Culhane, "Family Recreation," *Marriage and Family Relationships*, ed. A. H. Clemens (Washington, D. C.: The Catholic University of America Press, 1950), p. 128.

parents.   Companions, parties, movies, television and radio programs, comics, periodicals and similar items in children's recreational diets need watching.   After warning parents and teachers of the need to supervise children's leisure interests, Pius XI continued:

It is no less necessary to direct and watch the education of the adolescent, "soft as wax to be moulded into vice," in whatever other environment he may happen to be, removing occasions of evil and providing occasions for good in his recreation and social intercourse; for "evil communications corrupt good manners."

More than ever nowadays an extended and careful vigilance is necessary, inasmuch as the dangers of moral and religious shipwreck are greater for inexperienced youth.   Especially is this true of impious and immoral books, often diabolically circulated at low prices; of the cinema, which multiplies every kind of exhibition; and now also of the radio, which facilitates every kind of reading.   These most powerful means of publicity, which can be of great utility for instruction and education when directed by sound principles, are only too often used as an incentive to evil passions and greed for gain.   St. Augustine deplored the passion for the shows of the circus which possessed even some Christians of his time, and he dramatically narrates the infatuation for them, fortunately only temporary, of his disciple and friend Alipius.   How often today must parents and educators bewail the corruption of youth brought about by the modern theater and the vile book! [8]

This warning of the Holy Father has since been verified by experience.   In addition to the moral effects of many radio programs, 90 per cent of the 344 experts questioned by the Los Angeles Tenth District PTA agreed that many radio programs have a detrimental psychological effect on children.[9]

Comic books

Perhaps a greater threat to our children are the tons of comic books which fill their minds with murder, theft, obscenity and similarly depressing scenes.   In 1949 there were 50 million comics sold every month, with some 70 million people annually

[8] Pius XI, *Christian Education of Youth* (New York: The America Press, 1936), p. 31.

[9] *Family Life,* Vol. VIII, No. 2 (February 1948), p. 3.

buying them, 40 per cent of whom were children between 8–18 years of age. Surveys suggest that perhaps 98 per cent of all children between 8–12 years read comics.[10] The situation has become so serious that in 1954 the U. S. Senate held extensive hearings about comic books. One bit of testimony was submitted by a Cincinnati interfaith committee to evaluate comics. They found that of 555 comic magazines only 57.47 per cent were suitable for children and youth.[11] A similar study was made by a joint committee of the New York State legislature which concluded about comic books: [12]

That these publications continue to adversely affect the physical, social and religious welfare of children and of emotionally unstable adults, and contribute to juvenile delinquency.

That the reading of these publications contributes to juvenile delinquency, stimulates sexual desire, lowers standards of morality and interferes with the normal development of sexual tendencies in both adolescents and adults. That the continued and unrestrained dissemination of material of this type will do lasting harm to the spiritual, mental and physical health of the people of this State, undermining our standards of morality.

Until public opinion brings this detrimental industry under control, parents themselves must be responsible for keeping harmful comics away from children and helping to form neighborhood and parish groups to combat the sale of such literature in their neighborhood stores and newsstands.

Television homes

The radio's influence is quickly being superseded by that of television. Unlike radio, television has produced a major revolution within the home itself. Many people have completely readjusted their work, recreation, food and sleeping habits to conform to television programs. Many families with sets dis-

---

10 J. Frank, *Comics, Radio, Movies and Children,* Public Affairs Pamphlet No. 148 (New York: Public Affairs Committee, Inc., 1949), p. 3.

11 *Juvenile Delinquency,* Hearings before Subcommittee of U. S. Senate Judiciary Committee (Washington, D. C.: United States Government Printing Office, 1954), p. 46.

12 *Report of the New York State Joint Legislative Committee to Study the Publication of Comics* (Albany: Williams Press, Inc., 1955), pp. 136–137.

turbed their budgets to buy them. The graceful arts of visiting and conversation have received mortal blows. Often visitors are expected to wait until a favorite family program is finished before they receive any significant attention, and none present may speak above the briefest of whispers. Instead of becoming a servant, television (more than any other recent invention) has made the family its victim. One survey showed that television families did less visiting of friends, less driving, saw fewer movies, listened to the radio less, engaged in much less reading and much less conversation.[13] In a nationwide poll two effects, one on adults and the other on children, were indicated by those interviewed. The findings (which included the fact that 58 per cent said there is little or no talking during TV programs) led the survey directors to conclude:

It appears that the increased family contact brought about by television is not social except in the most limited sense and that of being in the same room with other people. . . . The nature of the family social life during a program could be described as "parallel" rather than interaction and the set does seem quite clearly to *dominate family life* when it is on [italics ours].[14]

Television was found to cut down on children's outdoor and indoor play time; there was less active play, fewer household tasks and less creative play. About one-third of the families had problems regarding bedtime for children.[15] A survey of elementary school children in Evanston, Illinois, made in 1950–1951 disclosed that:

About half of the teachers cited minor or serious behavior problems associated with TV; for example, increased nervousness on the part of some children, and drowsiness, disinterest and irritability on the part of others. About a third of the parents cited similar difficulties and stressed particularly the undesirable influence of TV on reading and study habits.[16]

---

[13] McDonagh *et al.*, "Television and the Family," *Sociology and Social Research*, Vol. XXXV, No. 2 (November 12, 1950), pp. 113–123.
[14] *Public Opinion Quarterly*, Vol. XV, No. 3 (Fall 1951), pp. 427–429.
[15] *Ibid.*, pp. 421–445.
[16] Paul Willy, "Children's reaction to TV—A Third Report," *Elementary English* (December 1952).

Another survey made in 1952 showed that 88 per cent of the homes of elementary school children had television and that an average of 23 hours weekly was devoted to watching it. One study revealed that many children view TV as an escape and that this accounts for the long hours spent before the television set.[17]

It is quite clear from a survey of 850 grade school and 350 high school students, that those who believe television is of great educational value do not know all the facts. The selections of these groups are obviously based mainly on entertainment and not cultural values. In contrast, the teachers surveyed showed a marked preference for programs with educational content. Four research agencies investigated the preferences of television viewers during various weeks in November 1955. It was striking that among the first ten ratings only one program had any significant educational value; the remaining nine were dominantly entertainment programs.[18]

Not only is television apparently not being used for educational purposes to any great extent, but it is serving extremely harmful purposes instead. The Federal Committee that investigated television programs between 4–10 P. M. on all stations in Washington, D. C., reported that 20 per cent of that time was given to crime and violence. Nine other cities studied showed the same pattern. In 1953 in New York seven television stations in a six-day period showed an average of 15.2 cases of violence each hour on children's programs and 6.2 on adult programs. In 1951 a survey given the Federal Judiciary Committee showed that crime and violence dominated about 40 per cent of the programs shown.[19]

These facts led the State legislators of New York to conclude:

1. That radio and television programs continue to feature programs dealing with terror, brutality and violence and that such programs are exerting an undesirable influence upon children.

2. That there *is great need of increased parental supervision* [italics

---

[17] E. E. Maccoby, "Why Do Children Watch TV?" *Public Opinion Quarterly,* Vol. XVIII, No. 3 (Fall 1954).

[18] Lawrence Laurent, "But Who Cares About Ratings?" (Washington, D. C.: *Post and Times Herald,* December 18, 1955), p. J3.

[19] Report of New York State Joint Legislative Committee to Study the Publication of Comics (Albany: Williams Press, Inc., 1955), p. 119.

ours] of the reading material of children and of the listening and viewing habits of juveniles having access to radio and television.[20]

Pius XII has also noted the dangers inherent in television. In a letter to the Bishops of Italy he referred to the "poisoned atmosphere of materialism, of frivolity, of hedonism . . . brought into the very sanctuary of the home . . . one cannot imagine anything more fatal to the spiritual health of a country." [21] He further urged that both the clergy and laity prevail on public authorities to curb these abuses.

Television *can* be a real advantage to the family if made the servant and not the master of the home. It can help restore family recreation, prove a cultural and educational asset and even serve the purposes of religion. To effect these purposes, however, programs must be selected discriminatingly.

Movies

The effects of movies are similar to those of television so far as their influence for good or evil is concerned. The pernicious nature of so many movies has called for a Legion of Decency. However, authorities of the Legion readily admit the failure to stop the production of indecent movies; in recent years this type has been on the increase. Again the fault seems to lie largely with parents.

D'Youville College decided to investigate this problem. The students interviewed theatre managers and heads of police departments; they also obtained information from 1,800 students in private Catholic high schools in Buffalo. Among their findings were the following:

1. *B* and *C* ratings by the Legion had "little, if any effect on attendance," unanimously agreed the theatre managers, most of whom were Catholic.

2. Almost 75 per cent of the girls and 60 per cent of the boys went to movies one or more times weekly.

3. When asked what the Legion of Decency was, almost 50 per cent of the boys and 34 per cent of the girls did not know the answer. Less than 12 per cent of the boys and only 16 per cent of the girls knew the essential facts about the Legion.

---

[20] *Ibid.*, p. 137.
[21] Pius XII, "Television: Its Public and Private Effects," *The Pope Speaks*, Vol. I, No. 1 (January 1954), pp. 7–8.

4. Only a little more than 44 per cent of the girls and 21 per cent of the boys knew what the different ratings meant.

5. Only half of the girls and 60 per cent of the boys stated their parents ever forbid them to attend certain motion pictures.

6. The survey disclosed that "the typical Catholic high school youth attends . . . pictures indiscriminately, as his personal fancy dictates."

7. "If the Legion could get its rating lists into the parish bulletins, and if the parish priests could awaken the local parents to the need for a close check on the pictures seen by movie loving Johnny and Betty, then the Legion would not have to look for some way to stop objectionable pictures before they are produced."

8. "The parents must be made more conscious of their obligations toward their children in the matter of the pictures they let their children see." [22]

Rules for good recreation

In working out a pattern of recreation for a family, the nineteen principles of the National Recreational Association should prove useful. Some principles of special relevance to the family follow:

1. Every child needs to be exposed to the growth-giving activities that have brought satisfaction through the ages—to climbing, chasing, tumbling; to singing, playing musical instruments, dramatizing; to making things with his hands, to working with sticks and stones and sand and water; to building and modeling; to caring for pets; to gardening, to nature; to trying simple scientific experiments; to learning team play, group activity, and adventure, comradeship in doing things with others.

2. Every child needs to discover which activities give him personal satisfaction. In these activities he should be helped to develop essential skills. Several of these activities should be of such a nature that he can keep them up in adult life.

3. Every man needs to know well a certain limited number of indoor and outdoor games which he himself likes, so that there will never be an occasion when he cannot think of anything to do.

4. Every man should be helped to form the habit of finding pleasure in reading.

5. Every man should be helped to learn how to make something

---

[22] "The Movies Your Children See," *The Oblate World*, Vol. X, No. 1 (February 1948), p. 9.

of beauty in line, form, color, sound or graceful use of his own body. At least he should find pleasure in what others do in painting, woodworking, sculpture, photography, if he cannot himself use these forms of expression.

6. Every man should be encouraged to find one or more hobbies.

7. Rest, repose, reflection are in themselves a form of recreation and ought never to be crowded out by more active play.

8. Those recreation activities are most important which most completely command the individual so that he loses himself in them and gives all that he has and is to them.

9. Ultimate satisfaction in recreation comes only through one's own achievement of some kind.

10. A man is successful in his recreation life in so far as the forms of activity he chooses create a play spirit, a humor, which to some extent pervades all his working hours, helping him to find enjoyment constantly in the little events of life.[23]

RECREATION AND ADJUSTMENT

One of the four major adjustments in marriage is in the recreational-social area. If done well it can deepen bonds of unity, love and attachment; if not, it can and does lead to friction and breakdown. A study of 818 spouses indicated that 5.3 per cent took from 1–20 years to adjust their social life while 13.8 per cent never did. A mutually satisfactory adjustment to social activities was enjoyed by 72 per cent of another 409 couples investigated.[24]

To assist in making this adjustment partners should remember the nature and purposes of recreation. If they act on the principle that the best recreation for their spouses is whatever their spouses enjoy the most, many difficulties would be removed. At least an attitude of tolerance, if not the more mature one of genuine encouragement, would result. This is an area in which a great deal of broad-mindedness is required. The favorite recreation of one spouse may appear to the other to be childish, silly, boring or empty. However, if effective recreation comes from doing what one *enjoys,* whether it is puerile or not really makes no difference; and partners should see this fact. Some

---

[23] National Recreation Association, *Introduction to Community Recreation* (New York: McGraw-Hill Book Company, Inc., 1949), pp. 218–219.

[24] J. T. Landis and M. G. Landis, *Building a Successful Marriage* (Englewood Cliffs, N. J.: Prentice-Hall, Inc., 1953), pp. 243–245.

people, for instance, think card playing a complete waste of time since it is in no way a creative type of relaxation. If, however, card games are the chief leisure time delight of such persons' mates, they would be wise, indeed, to encourage it. If they discouraged it, they would be robbing their spouses of their most relaxing form of recreation.

Often couples wonder whether separate nights out occasionally are desirable. It would seem that in so doing spouses have an opportunity, on occasion, to pursue their own interests unqualified by the interests of their spouses; they can meet with friends who sometimes would be boring to their spouses but interesting to them; the freedom from being responsible in part for the evening's enjoyment of one's spouse, is in itself a relaxing factor; and such brief separations can help to stave off the possibility of monotony creeping into the husband-wife relationship. After all, while marriage is a merger of two persons, it does not demand the complete submerging of one's autonomous personality into the other's.

RECREATION IN THE DIVINE PLAN

Recreation was made an imperative not only for individual survival, but also for marriage and family success. In the Divine Plan it was intended to bring joy to the family circle and to provide relaxation needed to offset tensions. But more than this, recreation was to help deepen affectional ties, form personality and promote moral and religious living in the family.

The departure of so much recreation from the home is not in accord with the Divine Plan for Marriage. It not only serves less well all the purposes of recreation, but also involves many moral hazards. Parents are intended to develop home centered play situations such as home parties, games, and the like. They are also charged with the weighty responsibility of supervising the leisure time pursuits of their children and of setting them an example in preferring wholesome types of recreation only. Husbands and wives should have a charitably tolerant attitude toward the recreational interests of their spouses. They should encourage (even when they do not prefer) their spouse's enjoyment of his particular play interests; and charity would prevent them from imposing a form of recreation on their partner which he finds entirely joyless.

17

Family Economics

$\mathbf{N}$O MARRIAGE or family can attain its rightful goals without a wise handling of its economic affairs. This must be true because economy means making limited resources meet all needs. That families' financial resources are quite limited in view of the great responsibilities to be met, seems obvious. In 1954 before taxes were deducted, 23 per cent of our consumers had incomes under $2,000 a year, 37 per cent under $3,000 and 53 per cent under $4,000 a year.[1] In 1955 one-fifth had incomes under $2,000 while two-fifths had incomes ranging between $2,000 and $5,000. This meant that only two-fifths had incomes over $5,000 a year.[2] With incomes so low, most families can meet their needs only by wise management. This is hard to detect by observing the careless way so many use their limited incomes. The secular spirit of materialism has so exalted a luxury standard of living that the common pattern is to spend in haste and repent at leisure. The same families who today revel in all the gadgets that our economy has produced for comfort and ease, tomorrow experience the sad awakening of an empty

[1] *Federal Reserve Bulletin* (Washington, D. C.: United States Government Printing Office, March 1955), p. 3.

[2] United States Department of Commerce, *Current Population Reports*, Series P-60, No. 22 (Washington, D. C.: United States Government Printing Office, September 1956).

chest when real needs are pressing. This secular spirit of the age has permeated Catholic families too, and prevented them from understanding the right use of money.

THE CATHOLIC APPROACH

Nothing seems more necessary here than that families return to fundamentals once again. · One of the facts we must remember is that the first claim on family funds is the family and its proper goals and needs. Since the rearing and education of children is the primary purpose of marriage, family finances must be employed for this purpose before any other. This implies not only provision for today but an inheritance for tomorrow. Providing security for children in case of the death of the breadwinner, or for their adult life is a strict moral obligation.[3] In practice, this means for many the sacrifice of a car, a television set, a fur coat or a clothes dryer so that money will be available tomorrow for the educational and other needs of the children. It may mean less expensive clothes, less expenditure for pleasure and a greater outlay for the security of life insurance. The important things must be put first, even though the Joneses may not think so.

A second fundamental we must relearn is that things economic have an effect on things religious, especially the salvation of souls. We were advised centuries ago by St. Thomas that "Two things are necessary for man to live a good life: first, to act in a virtuous manner; and second, to have a sufficiency of those bodily goods whose *use is necessary for an act of virtue* [italics ours]."[4] Parents who fail to handle family economics *wisely* are toying with the possibility of future distress in this world and also in the next. For instance, repeated studies show that the use of contraceptives is induced by economic factors as often as any other. Doubtless there are millions of families who misuse their funds for luxury living to the point where they will reject having another child because of the costs entailed. Had they embarked upon a simpler standard of living, the temptation to unnatural family limitation would not be present.

---

[3] C. A. Dames Aertnys, *Theologia Moralis,* Tomun I, Editio Decimaquarta (Torina: Casa Editrice Marietti, 1944), p. 436.

[4] *De Regimine Principum,* I, c. 14.

There are those, on the other hand, who believe the Catholic approach to things economic biased with puritanism. They should recall that the poverty of a Trappist monk would be sinful for a family. "Comtemplatives may with praise abstain from certain pleasures, but those engaged in active work and generation of species *may not* with equal praise refuse these pleasures." [5] In fact, contempt for worldly goods on the part of parents would be a sin of insensibility.[6] On the contrary, parents have a genuine obligation to work industriously, manage carefully and conserve wisely so that family purposes will all be fully served.

The Catholic approach actually encourages a progressively higher standard of living in all respects—spiritual and material. However, this laudable ambition is not as unrestricted as our current attitude would have it be. In the Catholic sense, a standard of living ought to be proportioned to the family's position in life. It should also be free of vulgar and ostentatious display which betrays sheer pride. If the Catholic approach favors a higher standard, it is of a pattern of living designed to promote the development of personality—supernatural, intellectual, and otherwise. Vanity and rivalry with others is not a part of the Catholic concept. For these reasons, even wealthy Catholics will, if this is understood, show a simplicity in keeping with their correct position in life.

Catholic families will resist the lure of riches mindful that they are serious stumbling blocks to virtuous living and, more likely than not, will spoil the children. They will prefer to sacrifice even innocent pleasures, at times, to assist the Church and those less fortunate. Nor will they, in determining their own standard of living, forget the need to rescue Christ from the dinginess (and stinginess) of dark basement parish chapels.

In general, the Catholic approach is based upon the principle that the family is not the owner but the *trustee* of family finances. As such, it is required to employ the funds (as any trustee would)

---

[5] St. Thomas Aquinas, *The Summa Theologica of St. Thomas Aquinas*, tr. by the Fathers of the Dominican Province (New York: Benziger Bros., 1948), Vol. II, Q. 142, art. 2, p. 1772, 153, art. 3, ad. 3.

[6] Veermersch, *Theologiae Moralis*, Vol. II (Rome: Universita Gregoriana, 1926), p. 611; also H. Davis, *Moral and Pastoral Theology*, Vol. II (London: Sheed & Ward, Ltd., 1938), p. 271; and Lehmkuhl, *Theologia Moralis*, Vol. I (Friburgi Brisgoviae: Sumtibus Herder, 1898), p. 483.

according to the intentions of their real Owner. His intentions are that the purposes of family life, primarily the rearing of children, should be served.

The right and wise management of family funds is more than an economic matter; it is also the application of the virtues of prudence, thrift, industry, poverty, humility and detachment. A family is not prudent that does not enjoy correct Christian attitudes or an adequate knowledge of the complexities of family economics. "Dollars can be spent only once; *the right disposition of funds becomes a duty of the Christian* [italics ours]." [7]

CURRENT STANDARDS OF LIVING

One of the reasons families are unwise about these matters is that they believe erroneously that most others are enjoying a high standard of living. This boast issued largely by big business, repeated in political oratory and endorsed by economists, is of course, quite widespread. It is based upon *incomplete* facts such as those in the 1950 census—that 94 per cent of our nation's homes have electricity, 95.6 per cent have radios, 80 per cent have mechanical refrigeration and 14.6 per cent have electric stoves. What is not so widely publicized is that (in 1946) 37.6 per cent of the people had 8 years or less of school; 24.4 per cent went only to grade school; and only 31.9 per cent attended high school.[8] It is not generally known that (in 1953) only 17 per cent of our people were reading books as contrasted to 55 per cent in England, 34 per cent in Australia and 31 per cent in Canada. In the United States there were 1,450 fairly complete bookstores, in Denmark (with half the population of New York City) there were 650; if the same proportion existed here, we would have had over 23,000 such stores. Our standard of living afforded us 7,500 public libraries while in Sweden (population 7 million) there were 3,500; proportionately we should have had 77,000 public libraries.[9] Only one-third of our families in 1941

---

[7] John J. O'Sullivan, *The Moral Obligation of Parents to Educate their Children for Marriage* (Washington, D. C.: The Catholic University of America Press, 1955), p. 33.

[8] Subcommittee of the Economic Report, U. S. Senate, *Low Income Families and Economic Stability* (Washington, D. C.: United States Government Printing Office, 1949), p. 15.

[9] George Gallup, Institute of Public Opinion Poll, *Washington (D. C.) Post* (November 15, 1953), p. 7b.

were well-fed; and a million and a half of our boys in the prime of life were rejected for defects as draftees. We have inadequate health facilities, overcrowded schools and underpaid teachers, deficiency in housing and a serious shortage of churches. In addition, only about half the nation places religion in its standard of living in any visible manner. The cultural level of our movies, radio and television programs, comics, popular periodicals and books is low. In many nations opera is a preference of the masses; only "soap operas" are sufficiently popular here to entice radio and television sponsors.

In general, couples harried by the vaunted high standard of living of others, should realize that it is a highly materialistic standard premised upon secularism and not a Christian standard replete with cultural and other spiritual values. The family that places its money in a collection of operatic high fidelity records has a higher standard of living (in a Christian sense) than if they had purchased an automatic garbage disposal.

HOME PRODUCTION

The real forgotten men and women of our economy are those who produce at home. Economists practically ignore them, the government fails to include them in its annual studies of national production, and they are not counted a part of the labor force. This is to be expected of an age given to commercial gain and a growing penchant for labor saving. From this neglect of the home producer, incalculable harm has come.

Despite the inventions of industry—new canning processes, frozen foods, and the like—home production of many items is still a very important advantage to families. Controversy may rage over individual items, comparing the cost of canned or frozen foods, of factory baked goods to home processed foods. Usually, two mistakes creep into the picture here: first, there is made only a price comparison and not quality comparison; secondly, satisfactions such as taste and palatibility are ignored. In some instances factory processed foods are devitalized as compared with home processed foods; while none dare deny the superior taste of home baked over factory produced bread or pie. These considerations also apply to many other items. Furthermore, frozen and canned foods are usually higher in price than home processed foods bought in quantity when in season. "The meals using ready-to-serve foods cost over a third more . . . as did meals for which more preparation was done in the home. Meals emphasizing use of partially prepared foods were a sixth higher in cost. . . ." [10] Another study made by the department of home economics of the University of California revealed that the quality of packaged spinach and tomatoes was definitely inferior; that packaged spinach cost 113 per cent more and packaged tomatoes 44 per cent more than in bulk form.[11]

Home production can significantly elevate the family standard of living. Some economists have estimated that the improvement can be as large as 15–20 per cent. One of the most noted interpreters of the economic Encyclicals reminds, further, that "It is by no means a natural condition, or one demanded by nature, that the family shall have no other means of support than the wage income of its father and head. Neither is it the will of nature or its Creator that the other members of the family permit themselves to be supported by the working head of the family without contributing their share for the common support." [12]

A national example of the significance of home production can be seen in our wartime home gardens. In 1939 we had 4,800,-000 home gardens which produced $200 million in vegetables.[13] Another example is the amount of sewing being done in homes. In 1953 30 million were sewing their own clothes, having bought $51 million worth of notions and novelties, a half billion dollars in yard goods and 200 million dress patterns.[14] Two women gave the home producing wife special study. One concluded that the average woman could earn more as a housewife than an office or factory worker; the other studied the value of the farm

---

10 G. S. Weiss, "Time and Money Costs of Meals Using Home—and Pre-kitchen—Prepared Foods," *Journal of Home Economics*, Vol. XLVI, No. 2 (February 1954), p. 98.

11 J. V. Coles, "Packaged and Bulk Spinach and Tomatoes: Quality, Price, Availability, and Consumers' Reactions," *Journal of Home Economics*, Vol. XLVI, No. 5 (May 1954), p. 320.

12 O. Nell-Breuning, *Reorganization of the Social Economy* (Milwaukee: The Bruce Publishing Company, 1939), p. 174.

13 United States Department of Agriculture, *Bulletin No. 483* (Washington, D. C.: United States Government Printing Office, February 1942).

14 Dorothy Thompson, *Ladies' Home Journal*, Vol. LXX, No. 5 (May 1953), p. 14.

woman's labor over a period of 30 years and estimated it worth at least $3,500 to her family.[15] This was when the price level was half that of the present; the housewife's economic value at today's price level is proportionately higher.

Apart from such economic advantages are the health and educational benefits of home production. Busy wives are usually not among those lounging on the couches of psychiatrists or annoying doctors with imaginary ailments. One woman psychiatrist traces feminism and its attendant neuroses to the discontent of women who fail to find a sense of worth in the home since they are no longer producers; instead of regaining the lost sense of importance in the home, they try to gain it where men do, in offices, stores and factories.[16]

The benefits to children of home production would vindicate its worth were there no other advantages. The participation of children and youth in home chores develops character, teaches skills, develops a sense of contribution to the group; traits such as industry, cooperation and application to duty wax strong, and the cult of pleasure has no chance to grow. Choreless homes are usually homes with added disciplinary problems and frequently with children who are bored with life.

These advantages of work for children are realized by many productionless parents who induce them to work outside the home. Often such parents do not realize the dangers of some such types of employment.

In a study of child employment in theatres, the Bureau of Standards concluded with the reminder:

This review of experience in the employment of minors under 18 in these industries, brief and incomplete as it is, indicates excessive cost to many young persons in loss of time for sleep, rest, study, and the type of play with youngsters of their own age that develops qualities of teamwork. It also shows over-long hours of after-school work, night work, and physical strain, that are likely to affect health,

---

[15] F. G. Orr, "How Much Is A Wife Worth," *The Cincinnati Enquirer* (December 4, 1938).

[16] F. Lundberg and M. F. Farnham, *Modern Woman: The Lost Sex* (New York: Harper & Brothers, 1947), chap. vii.

and shows in some cases surroundings undesirable for the impressionable young person.[17]

Surely in view of such findings it is better if children have chores at home.   Working together around and in the home also welds the group solidarity of the family.   It protects children from the notion that without money one cannot get the good things of life.   The aptitudes and skills making home chores easy probably will also foster a liking for such work—something sorely needed today.   Furthermore, working with parents can teach children that one does not work for money alone, nor for one's self alone but for a natural form of self-expression and a thing which, in charity, one does for others.

Of all socially "cementing" elements that of joint production is indeed particularly missing.   The fact that the rural population has a smaller percentage of divorces, broken homes, etc., than the urban, may be due to some extent to the comparatively greater degree of living and working together on the farm.[18]

TABLE 12

WORK CONTRIBUTIONS TO THE HOME MADE BY HUSBANDS *

Type of work	Number	Percentage
Food preparation	48	27
Food preservation	37	21
Dishwashing	70	39
Care of house	39	22
Care of clothing	13	7
Care of family members	90	50
Marketing and records	101	56
Driving	154	86
Chores or gardening	142	79
Repair of house	40	22
Total	179	

* M. M. Knoll, "Economic Contributions to and from Individual Members of Families and Households," *Journal of Home Economics*, Vol. XLVII, No. 5 (May 1955), p. 324.

---

[17] United States Department of Labor, *They Work While You Play*, Bulletin No. 124, (Washington, D. C.: United States Government Printing Office, 1950), p. 25.

[18] F. H. Mueller, *American Institute of Socio-Political Thought*, Vol. II, No. 4 (January 1946).

One of the strange upsets in our culture is that while wives are producing less, men are working around the house more. This is evident from the growth of the do-it-yourself industry, by the fact that 65 per cent of houses are painted by husbands, and also by men's increasing help in wifely chores A nationwide poll indicated that 62 per cent of husbands help with general housework, 40 per cent with cooking and 42 per cent with the dishes.[19] On the other hand, the importance of the wife's knowing home skills is revealed by some studies. In one of them 67.2 per cent of the husbands and 76.3 per cent of the wives stated the wife's knowledge (and presumably use) of home production "very important" for a successful marriage.[20] Perhaps this is the reason Pius XI stated:

We bless your schools of domestic economy and in general all that tends to help the formation and the instruction of the woman in housekeeping and for the care of her home and the care and education of her children.[21]

SUBSISTENCE HOMESTEADING

An increasing number of families are finding a small, part time farm the answer to many of their problems. Not only is their standard of living increased, but family life as a whole prospers and child training is facilitated. The benefits to health and family solidarity are difficult to exaggerate.

Even a small plot of ground can aid family income significantly. Enough fruits and vegetables, for instance, can be raised on a half acre of ground to supply the needs of a family of five for an entire year. However, despite the obvious advantages, families must be willing to sacrifice much to obtain them. Vacations may be shorter, and wives and children will have to take over if the husband is away on trips. It will mean more than an 8-hour day or a 40-hour week; gardens and animals are not subject to hours established by law. It may mean longer distances and more time in commuting and the increased

---

[19] *Public Opinion Quarterly,* Vol. XIII (1949–1950), p. 543.

[20] P. M. James, "The Expressed Effects of a Certain Premarital Lecture Course (Master's thesis, Catholic University of America, 1953), p. 121.

[21] "Holy Father Encourages Women in Interest of Family and Youth," *Catholic Action,* Vol. XXXI, No. 9 (September 1949), p. 9.

cost of the same. When the children are ready for high school new problems may be posed if none is in the vicinity. Despite these difficulties an increasing number of families are moving onto such small farms and finding the advantages superior to the trouble involved. In fact, rarely do such families care to return to the more crowded suburban areas (much less the city proper) once they have discovered the freedom and naturalness of a family in its proper environment, where children prove an asset and not an economic liability.

THE FAMILY GOES SHOPPING

In our urban culture the American family does not seem to be too wise as a consuming unit. Predatory advertising, salesmanship and merchandising have triumphed over common sense in this respect. The attempt to "keep up with the Joneses" and the luxury mindedness of the age have also helped circumvent the basic wisdom of good consuming habits.

Many families must learn the basic elements of wise buying, wise spending and wise saving. Experts estimate that the average family could increase its standard of living 15–20 per cent by more careful buying habits, such as knowing *where, when* and *how* to make purchases. In our competitive system every sizable locality has a great variety of places where a given article can be bought. Through shopping and exchanging experiences with friends, families can learn the places where any given article can be bought most economically. Women are more skilled in this than men, a fact that occasions not a few arguments between careful wives and careless husbands.

Knowing the best time of year to obtain particular articles is also indispensable to good buying. Most people, for instance, will look for a home in the spring when prices are highest; the same house in the middle of winter would probably have sold for considerably less. Others buy at the start of a season clothes that could have been purchased at the close of the previous year's season for much less. Fruits and vegetables bought in *quantities* and at the *right season,* are more economical than those available in all other ways.

Knowing how to buy is probably the most difficult and time consuming ability. It requires information about many articles and an ability to judge quality. With this knowledge one can avoid being "taken in" at false sales; with it one can select at genuine sales the one item of fifty that is an unusually good purchase. Families should take special pains with large and costly purchases such as homes, cars or large appliances. They should learn just what qualities and characteristics to investigate in such purchases before buying. Instead of being attracted to a house by superficial qualities such as lighting fixtures, formica top sinks, and other gadgets that have "eye-appeal," they will check the plumbing, the roof, the foundation and other substantial qualities.

Wise buyers also know that to the original cost of many items must be added the upkeep. Many families seem unable to calculate for themselves the real cost of a home including the hidden items such as taxes, insurance, depreciation and upkeep. Many do not realize that they are often paying more to finance the home than the original cost of the house. Others seem not to realize the very high costs of operating a new car as compared to a used car in average good condition. By first acquainting themselves with *all the costs* involved in certain large purchases, many families would make better decisions than are currently observable. Learning how to buy takes time, patience and work; but it is an art which will richly repay the family.

FAMILY BUDGETING

Wise management requires some plan for family expenditures. This sort of planned spending is usually called a budget. It is necessary because present income must not only carry present expenses but also anticipate future expenses and help provide for them. Sociologists have outlined seven steps in a normal family cycle, each having distinct economic responsibilities:

1. Starting a family—costs are minimal and savings should be effected.
2. Children preschool—costs increase because of maternity and child care; some savings are indicated.
3. Elementary school—costs continue to rise; some savings continue.
4. High School—significant increase in expenses; further savings.
5. College—even more significant outlays demanded; still some savings if possible.

6. Recovery—children are raised and making their own way; costs decline and savings mount.

7. Retirement—expenses once again minimal.

Obviously any young couple who can see the large expenses awaiting them, will try to build as large a saving in early marriage as possible. This calls for the willingness to work long and hard, and also frugality, thrift and careful planning. When 61 husbands and 59 wives were asked the import of a planned family economy, 51.6 per cent thought it "very important" and 32.5 per cent "desirable." [22] When 190 husbands and wives were asked if success in marriage depended more upon income or management, 83.5 per cent replied that it depended more on proper management.[23]

Expenditure patterns

Anybody who studies the expenditure pattern of our families as a whole, is forced to conclude that it is not a wise one. This pattern is reflected in the data available on consumer expenditures, which reveals a materialistic luxury pattern devoid of adequate spiritual values. The secularism of the age again becomes evident for "Those who are totally disinterested in God clothe themselves with jewels and finery to compensate, whether they know it or not, for their inner spiritual poverty." [24]

It is immediately evident from the data (Table 13) that, as a nation, our families spend too heavily for material things and luxuries and much too little for spiritual items and necessities. The low amounts spent, for instance, for religion, welfare and education as contrasted to the amounts spent for recreation and personal care are very disproportionate. This suggests why commercialized amusements and beauty salons thrive while churches and schools must *beg* for support. Clearly a better sense of values and more careful planning are needed by a large number of families.

---

22 James, *op. cit.*, p. 124.

23 Hugh Dunn, S.J., *A Study of Some Catholic Marital Attitudes, Practices and Problems with Special Reference to the Implication for Premarital Instructions* (Washington, D. C.: The Catholic University of America Press, 1956), Table 57.

24 Fulton J. Sheen, "Preface," *Mary in Her Scapular Promise,* by John Haffert (New York: Scapular Press, 1942), p. viii.

TABLE 13

How We Budget Our Expenditures
(billions of dollars)

	1929 to 1941 *	1935 to 1936 †	1943 ‡	1952 §	1954 ¶
Food and tobacco	19.1	17.0	36.6	F 70.1 T 5.0	F 76.3 T 5.2
Clothing and jewelry	8.1	5.3	14.8	C 23.3 J 1.5	C 22.9 J 1.6
Personal care	0.9		1.8	2.5	2.7
Housing	8.9	9.5	10.4	25.6	29.7
Household operation	9.1	16.2	13.3	28.8	30.7
Medical	3.1	2.2	4.7	10.5	11.7
Personal business	2.5		2.9	9.3	11.3
Transportation and automobiles	6.0	4.6	5.7	T 23.2 A 19.8	T 26.9 A 23.6
Recreation	3.2	1.6	5.0	11.3	12.2
Education and research	.5	.5	.8	2.3	2.6
Religion and welfare	.9	.6	1.5	2.8	3.2
Travel	.5		.1	1.6	2.0

* *Survey of Current Business,* Vol. XXIV, No. 6 (June 1944).
† National Resources Committee, *Consumer Incomes in the United States: Their Distribution in 1935–1936* (Washington, D. C.: United States Government Printing Office, 1938).
‡ *Survey of Current Business, op. cit.*
§ *Survey of Current Business,* Vol. XXXV, No. 7 (July 1955), p. 19.
¶ *Ibid.*

This lack is also evident in the expenditures for specific luxuries. The Family Economics Bureau, for example, estimated that the average alcoholic beverage bill per family was $60 for each member; this meant about 20 gallons per capita.[25] A nationwide poll also showed that 46 per cent of the families with

[25] *Family Life,* Vol. XIII, No. 2 (February 1953), p. 6.

incomes under $2,000 a year, and 53 per cent of those under $3,000 a year had television sets; [26] while over a third of the families with incomes under $2,000 and about half with incomes under $3,000 had automobiles. [27] Perhaps this is why 32 million spending units saved money in 1948 but 15.5 million *spent in excess of their incomes;* [28] and why we had slightly less than $3,000 in life insurance per person in 1952. [29]

The model budget

There can be little doubt that our families need to learn and apply the art of budgeting. The recognition of this fact is, perhaps, the reason that we find so many articles and books on this subject. Unfortunately the scientific trend of our age has led to a supposedly scientific budget generally called a "model budget." Unthinking millions including writers and lecturers have erroneously adopted this as the answer to the problem.

The model budget allocates *fixed* percentages or amounts to various uses—food, clothing, shelter, personal care and the like. It attempts to quantitize what simply *cannot* be *fixed* for *all* families. It appeals greatly to the impractical pragmatist but cannot be sustained in the light of harsh realities. It is as unrealistic to try to tailor the same budget for all families as it would be to tailor the same suit for all members of the family.

Personal and family needs differ between individuals, social and professional position, climate and other factors. A budget for clothing in the South would be inadequate in the North; a fixed food budget for a family with naturally small appetites would not satisfy the hearty eaters of other families; a fixed clothing budget for a plumber would not meet the needs of a bank cashier. Then, too, families who produce their own foods and other items would not need the same budget as an unproductive family. But apart from all these variations are the realistic changes that cause prices in our economy to fluctuate between different items, localities and times. Food may become more

---

[26] E. E. Macoby, "Television: Its Impact on School Children," *Public Opinion Quarterly,* Vol. XV, No. 3 (Fall 1951), p. 422.

[27] *Federal Reserve Bulletin,* Vol. XLI, No. 5 (May 1955), Table 9, p. 478.

[28] *Federal Reserve Bulletin,* Vol. XXXVI, No. 1 (January 1950), p. 14.

[29] *Statistical Bulletin,* Vol. XXXIII, No. 5 (May 1952), p. 1.

costly just when clothing drops in price—and the model budget no longer applies. A young couple given a fixed budget in Chicago may find it impractical, and even harmful, as a guide in Atlanta. In 1950, for instance, average expenses for housing in Chicago were $110 while in Atlanta they were only $65.[30] Again, a model budget for a period of low prices may be quite useless in a period of high prices. This is why the model budget is not model but highly theoretical, having been devised for a mythical average family living in a static, and not a dynamic, economy.

Recent years have brought an increasing awareness of the defects of the fixed budget.

The trouble with most family budgets is that they aren't elastic. Consequently, lack of flexibility can, and no doubt often has, disarranged the best efforts of many an amateur budgeter.

Still another difficulty commonly encountered is that the budget does not fit. A tailor-made one is essential in order to avoid fruitless attempts to make the individual conform to some standardized distribution of income.[31]

A practical budget

Since any practical budget is flexible, it must be based, not on *rigid rules* but on *principles*. Centuries ago St. Thomas noted that economic goods fell into three classes—absolute necessities, conventional necessities, luxuries.

A thing is necessary in two ways: first, because without it something is impossible . . . secondly, a thing is said to be necessary if a man cannot live without it in keeping his *social station* [italics ours], as regards either himself or those of whom he has charge.[32]

Anything which is not one of these two types of necessity he called a "superfluity" or a luxury. This basic sense of values is almost completely lost in our culture, and yet it is absolutely imperative for wise management of family economics. Any ob-

---

[30] M. Smith, "Monthly Cost of Owning and Renting New Housing, 1949–1950," *Monthly Labor Review*, Vol. CCLXXVII, No. 8 (August 1954), p. 854.

[31] E. C. Harwood and H. Fowle, *How to Make Your Budget Balance* (Great Barrington, Mass.: American Institute of Economic Research, 1947), pp. 5–6.

[32] St. Thomas Aquinas, *op. cit.,* Vol. II, Pt. 2, Q. 32, art. 6.

jective person must realize that there are many families who clutter their budgets with luxury items before they provide for the two types of necessities.

This may be due, in part, to their failure to realize *all* the items falling under these necessities. Usually, for instance, the only absolute necessities are thought to be food, clothing and shelter; actually religion; education; health; security against contingencies, unemployment and old age; and recreation are also absolute necessities. This is not known or practiced by those who have swanky cars but little life insurance; fur coats and expensive recreation but no home of their own; money for gadgets and creature comforts but none for the Catholic education of their children. The simple principles beneath all wise budgeting are, as they have ever been, to allocate funds *first* to absolutely necessary items, *secondly* to the needs of the professional or rightful social status of the family, and only *thirdly* to other items. Any family consistently following these principles will never be mistaken regardless of price changes, moving from one locality to another, or individual differences in family needs. However, to do so requires maturity, self-control and strong character. It means standing out against the Joneses who have a "model budget" which neither fits their needs nor is followed. It means being different because the family will be Christian.

The problem becomes a moral one when we come to the attribution of the family income in accordance with the relative demands of real and conventional necessities. A choice must be made and the various monetary units apportioned. *In a particular civilization the conventional necessities may have so expanded that they encroach on what is necessary for decent sustenance.* At a given moment there may be a serious disequilibrium, and a society may have created for itself a multitude of artificial needs which really reduces the standard of life when this is viewed from the moral and cultural and not from the purely material viewpoint. It may be costing us too much to keep up a standard of respectability at the cost of the solid family virtues which are necessary for social stability. *In this case the family wage is being misapportioned, its allocation is out of line with the moral purpose it was meant to subserve* [italics ours].[33]

---

[33] P. McDevitt, "The Spending of the Living Wage," *Irish Ecclesiastical Record,* Vol. LV (February 1940), p. 148.

Principles and practice

Only by translating these principles into practice can a family come to a truly practical and realistic budget. In the first place, they can sense the luxury aspect of things often deemed necessities and, will, if necessary, budget accordingly. For instance, studies have shown that only 41 per cent of the clothing dollar is spent for protection against weather and only 56 per cent of the food dollar for satisfying hunger.[34] Obviously, if and when necessary, families can cut large slices of the luxury aspects of common items such as food and clothing without injury and, in many cases to their physical advantage.

With a little effort any family can, on the basis of these principles, devise a budget to fit its own peculiar needs. Three things must be done. First determine fixed items such as taxes, regular church contributions, savings and insurance. Second, determine variable expenses such as food, clothing and home furnishings. Third, provide a contingency fund for unexpected, emergency or unusual expenses not included among the fixed or variable because it is so infrequent. Having determined these three, the total cost for a year can be divided by twelve, by fifty-two, or any other number, depending upon the preference or feasibility of budgeting by the month, the week or otherwise.

Some families find an envelope system convenient; the allocated amounts are placed into separate envelopes regularly. Others dislike the inconvenience of this method and prefer to keep records, which they regularly check against their planned budget allowances. Still others will also devise a system of separate allowances for husbands, wives and children. There is much to be said in favor of this system provided such allowances are adequate and husbands and wives do not cross-examine each other about the way they are spent. Women generally prefer this system to the awkward and humiliating experience of having to beg repeatedly from not-too-generous husbands. Many arguments could be avoided by an allowance system between husbands and wives.

---

[34] K. Kernan, "Americans Spend Only One-Third of Their Income for Necessities," *St. Louis Post Dispatch* (February 9, 1936), quoting studies made by Professor E. L. Thorndike of Columbia University.

Ideally, partners should share family funds jointly even as they share all other aspects of life together. A joint bank account, for instance, is to be recommended unless one of the two is overly extravagant or prodigal. If children are given an allowance, it should be given with understanding and supervision regarding wise handling. Indiscriminate handouts to children can prove detrimental, but a supervised allowance can become a valuable education in wise management. Children can and should be taught to buy wisely, to save if even a tiny amount, and give at least something to Church and charity. Even when children earn money, they should understand that it is not exclusively their own but that the family has a right to call upon it if necessary; nor should they then be allowed to feel that, having earned it, they can do as they please with it.

It often happens that quarrels arise over who should handle family funds. This, like other matters, is ideally the right of the head of the family. However, with this right goes a heavy duty to see that such funds are managed with prudence, care and wisdom. This right would be best exercised in most families by thorough consultation with wives. Unfortunately there are many husbands who keep their wives so uninformed of family financial affairs that, if they died, their wives would have little knowledge of what they left or where it was. When husbands have little ability or prodigal spending habits, it is much wiser to delegate the family funds to the more capable and thrifty wife.

FINANCES AND ADJUSTMENT

The amount of income does not cause frequent friction in marriage. On the contrary, studies made during the depression indicated that lessened or curtailed income often welded families closer together.[35] But tension over money *management* is exceedingly frequent. In a study of 476 Catholic husbands and wives, 83.5 per cent said success in adjustment depends on management rather than income.[36]

The material is the basis of division; it is that which divides men in society; that which gives rise to quarrels and wars. And it is the

---

[35] R. S. Cavan and K. H. Ranck, *The Family and the Depression* (Chicago: The University of Chicago Press, 1938).

[36] Dunn, *op. cit.*, p. 156.

basis of division because in dividing material things, there is question of how to divide justly, for one may or should get less or more.[37]

In a nationwide poll money arguments were listed by couples as the first of 10 causes of disagreement.[38] Another study (210 couples in Los Angeles) showed that excessive spending, debt and lack of savings are associated with poor adjustment.[39] In studies money varies from first to tenth place as a cause of serious breakdown. In the experience of the Marriage Center of Catholic University of America it is clear that while money is rarely the chief cause of trouble, it is often a contributing factor and is present in a high percentage of the cases. Most clients are in debt, many heavily so.

On the whole, husbands contract more debts and worry less about them than their more conservative wives. This seems to be the most frequent reason for disagreement and quarrels. Apparently many families fail to realize that borrowing should not be risked except for dire emergencies, for purposes which will be self-liquidating (a sewing machine to make one's own clothes) or a *genuine need* (a home) that can be obtained no other way. The current pattern of loans is quite uneconomic. Borrowing for luxuries and gadgets (jewelry, hi-fi recordings, electric dishwashers) is scarcely wise management and quite a costly proposition since interest rates on installments are higher than usually suspected.

ATTAINING FAMILY SECURITY

Families seem more security conscious than before, yet are less willing to work to attain it. Our historic experience and heritage has made us an adventurous, risk-taking people.[40] The pioneer who hazarded his whole family's future on one big gamble, has a counterpart today. It is the family which spends its present income as though there were no tomorrow; or which lives in the

---

[37] F. J. Sheen, *The Cross and the Crisis* (Milwaukee: The Bruce Publishing Company, 1939), pp. 89–91.

[38] G. Gallup, The Gallup Poll, *Washington (D. C.) Post* (January 18, 1948), pp. 79–80.

[39] R. C. Williamson, "Economic Factors in Marital Adjustment," *Marriage and Family Living*, Vol. XIV, No. 4 (November 1952), pp. 298–300.

[40] J. T. Adams, *The Epic of America* (New York: Triangle Books, 1941).

hope that its "ship will come in" some day and no provision need be made for the future. As a nation we are inclined to play the horses, and speculate on the stock market to obtain security, rather than to follow the long, arduous road to security by constant hard work, much frugality and thrift, and very careful investing.

This becomes evident when most families' security planning is contrasted with norms given us by experts, such as Babson. His plan is simple but difficult, calling for character and self-sacrifice. It has five steps *to be followed in the order in which they are named:*

1. Provide a liquid emergency fund—money placed so that it is easily available when an unusual need arises; a bank account serves this purpose.

2. Buy adequate insurance—few can purchase the full amount of insurance necessary (life, property, auto, etc.) for all purposes but they should have a reasonable amount. For most insurance is the *only* method of affording security for contingencies; and parents have a moral obligation to protect their families against insecurity in the event of the death of the breadwinner.

3. Purchase a home—this usually means savings, stability, and a greater incentive to home production.

4. After the above three are provided, any surplus funds should be invested in only the *most secure* type of investment; at this point families do not yet have full security, and their funds cannot be risked in speculative ventures.

5. After complete security for a family is attained by the first four steps, any surplus can now be used for more risky speculations.

Clearly many families are not following this slow, difficult but sure road to security. The heavy debts already noted, the little life insurance previously mentioned and the fact that only about half the families are buying homes of their own indicate our lack of wisdom. If one also notices the money spent on flashy cars, luxurious recreation, gadgets and costly clothes, very uneconomic patterns emerge.

FAMILY ECONOMICS IN THE DIVINE PLAN

God intended that the family attain its goals through the proper use of material goods and services. These have been placed in the hands of families, who act merely as *trustees* of His wealth. In this Divine Economy, such funds must be employed primarily for family purposes (children and self-development) and only secondarily for personal comfort or convenience.

This calls for many virtues, particularly that of *prudence*. To exercise this virtue families need not only the Christian sense of values but also a considerable amount of knowledge about mundane economic facts and methods. With this sense of values, current materialism, luxury-mindedness and rivalry with the Joneses will give way to an ambition for a more spiritual standard of living, contentment with an unostentatious pattern of material living. Christian self-control and mortification will aid adherence to the principles of wise budgeting; charity will remove stinginess toward spouses and others; detachment will eliminate extravagance. Children will be trained in industry by chores, in wise money management by example and supervision of their allowances. They will be protected against the dangers of ambition for riches by the simplicity of life and the attitudes of their parents.

The spirit of poverty will keep families from useless borrowing and will find them willing to attain security by the sure and safe road of sacrifice rather than by foolish speculation.

18

Marriage Failure and Family Rehabilitation

Some SECULAR and professional optimists try to comfort us with the assurance that the family is suffering from nothing more serious than a temporary change to urban living. They offer us the additional solace that once this transition is effected, we may have families superior to any before. However, all recent Popes have thought otherwise. They have detected something more profound than environmental changes in the process of the de-Christianization of family life. Pius XI and Pius XII have stressed that this de-Christianization is the goal of many today and that there is actually an *attempt* to break down the Divine Plan for marriage.[1] "The life of the family is, beyond doubt," Pius XII asserted, "the thing which *suffers most* from the great poverty of our times, whether in material or in spiritual things, and from the countless errors which are its miserable consequence [italics ours]." [2]

---

[1] Pius XI, "Christian Marriage in Our Day," *Social Wellsprings,* Vol. II Annotated and arranged by Joseph Husslein (Milwaukee: The Bruce Publishing Company, 1943), pp. 140–142.
[2] Pius XII, "Summi Pontificatus," *Acta Apostolicae Sedis,* Vol. XXXI (October 28, 1939), pp. 413–453.

DESTROYING GOALS

One of these errors is that the chief goal of marriage is personal gain, so that this becomes the norm for judging success or failure. However, viewed from the natural and Christian point of view, the chief goal is children and the norm for failure is the frustration of family purposes.

Even a superficial review of the family situation today discloses a widespread failure to attain these proper goals. The small family system and the high incidence of childless couples, indicate the frustration of the primary purposes of marriage. The growing trend of juvenile delinquency, of immaturity, of lack of preparation for marriage, of irreligious living bespeak the failure of the educational role of the family. The divorces granted, divorces refused, annulments, separations and desertions imply that even the companionship and happiness goals of marriage no longer are being well served. Nor can personalities find their development in this type of family milieu.

HISTORIC BREAKDOWN

It is not surprising that the bond of love is severed by growing numbers of divorces. All other family bonds have previously been severed or weakened and love cannot thrive on this type of diet. The Reformation dealt the first blow by weakening the religious bond of the family. Luther held that though marriage was still sacred, it was no sacrament. Accordingly, he took it out of the hands of the Church and gave it to the State which, as it became more secular, also helped to secularize marriage.

The Industrial Revolution cut through the work unity of the home by sending men, women and children into factories and offices. Families once working side by side all day, now were separated for the major portion of their working hours. Then outside amusement agencies took the members of the family away from home for separate recreational activities.

A historian a century ago, witnessing the severance of the bonds of religion, work and play, might well have predicted the present divorce rate. The bond of love must grow weak, if the others have deteriorated. For love grows and thrives on proximity, sharing and cooperation in religion, work and recreation. Without them it can scarcely be expected to prosper. Others have traced the current breakdown to the historic change from a compulsive, trustee family pattern in which families were held together by the pressure of kinship, to the familial-domestic type cemented by bonds of genuine love, to the current contractual-atomic type held together by nothing more than a legal contract which can be broken as easily as it is enacted.[3]

The most thorough study yet made of the history of the family, points out that the same practices were found in the decadent Greek and Roman families as exist today. Some of these are:

1. Increased and easier "causeless" divorce.
2. Decreased number of children, population decay, and increased public disrespect for parents and parenthood.
3. Rise of theories that companionate marriage or a permissibly looser family form would solve the problem.
4. Breaking down of most inhibitions against adultery.
5. Revolt of youth against parents so that parenthood became more and more difficult for those who did try to raise children.
6. Rapid rise and spread of juvenile delinquency.[4]

FACTORS THAT CAUSE MARRIAGE BREAKDOWN

The various recent Popes have stressed the fact that the basic cause of breakdown is the de-emphasis of the supernatural aspects of the family. The Divine Plan for marriage requires the assistance of grace and a knowledge of the truths by which alone marriage can live. Neither of these is sufficiently present in our families today. Repeated surveys taken at the Catholic University of America of Catholic married couples indicate a deplorable lack of knowledge of the religious and moral laws of marriage. In one study the average score of husbands was 65.2 per cent, of wives 64.7 per cent and of both 65.1 per cent; in another study the average score for husbands and wives was 68.6 per cent.[5] They show, in general, that the best educated have

---

3 P. Sorokin, *The Crisis of Our Age* (New York: E. P. Dutton & Co., Inc., 1942), pp. 187–192; also Carle Zimmerman, *The Family and Civilization* (New York: Harper & Brothers, 1947), chap. xxix; also see Chapter 2 in this book.

4 Zimmerman, *op. cit.,* pp. 776–777.

5 J. R. Feiten, "An Investigation of the Knowledge and Attitudes of Catholic Married People on Moral Relations in Marriage and the Family" (Master's thesis, Catholic University of America, 1948); also P. M. James, "The Expressed Results of a Certain Premarital Lecture Course" (Master's thesis, Catholic University of America, 1953).

about 70 per cent and the average couple has about 55 per cent of the desired knowledge about the religious and moral aspects of marriage.

On the other hand, the casual manner in which families approach and celebrate the great sacraments—especially Baptism, Confirmation, Holy Communion, Marriage—suggests the probability of a minimum rather than a maximum of grace being obtained. The secular approach to marriage by Catholics, cannot wrest from that sacrament all the graces possible. The decline in family prayer, use of sacramentals, and family religious ritual indicate a further avoidance of the graces so useful to success. Add to this the failure to live up to the morals of marriage in husband-wife relationship, in child rearing and supervision and it becomes readily understandable why the family today is spiritually anemic.

Basic attitudes

Second as a basic cause of breakdown is the presence of *incorrect attitudes*. St. Thomas assured us that attitudes condition conduct and that all social change is preceded by a change in attitudes.[6] Institutions like the family change basically because men's ideas change. "Since men unite for a common purpose, it is *ideas* that serve as the nuclei for institutions. Therefore, changes in institutions are dependent on changing ideas and purposes [italics ours]." [7] These attitudes have been called "isms" —individualism, materialism and the like (Table 14). None is more basic or vicious than the parent of all other "isms"— liberalism.[8] This spirit of independence, of chafing at the wise rules of the Divine Plan for Marriage, is rampant even in Catholic circles.

Unfortunately American Catholics fight shy of calling the blackest of spades, Liberalism, a spade. They may attack the errors flowing from it, and institutions, such as divorce and birth control that have

---

[6] St. Thomas Aquinas, *The Summa Theologica*, Vol. I, Pt. 2, Q. 8, art. 1; Vol. I, Q. 80, art. 1; Vol. I, Pt. 2, Q. 1, art. 1.

[7] Sr. M. E. Healy, *Society and Social Change in the Writings of St. Thomas, Ward, Sumner and Cooley* (Washington, D. C.: The Catholic University of America Press, 1948), p. 32.

[8] Liberalism is understood here in its historico-theological sense, not in its current manifold meanings.

TABLE 14

FAMILY ATTITUDES AND CORRESPONDING PRACTICES

Attitudes	Practices
LIBERALISM Spirit of unrestrained freedom; chafing at restraints.	Undue freedom of sexes in dating, sinful necking and petting, lack of consultation with parents on mate selection, secular marriages, birth control, divorce, freedom between sexes after marriage.
SECULARISM Divorce of religion from marriage.	Marriage not a sacrament; lack of religious preparation; absence of religious approach to marriage; mixed marriages; marriage in rectory or brief Low Mass; no family prayer, ritual, sacramentals; infrequent use of sacraments; breaking moral laws of marriage.
INDIVIDUALISM Lack of social consciousness; seeking personal advantages at expense of others.	Failure to work out group patterns of religion, work, recreation; no family consciousness; neglect of wives by husbands, of children by parents; divorce.
RATIONALISM Rejection of teachings of authority in favor of one's own reasoning.	Rationalizations for departing from the Divine Plan for marriage including Church's teachings on mixed marriages, birth control; anti-clericalism; disobedience by children.
EMOTIONALISM Rejection of both authority and reason in favor of one's heart and feelings.	Romantic concept of love; selecting mates for love only; quarreling after marriage; nagging; carrying grudges; acceptance of birth control and divorce out of misguided sense of pity and sympathy.
FEMINISM Concept of identity of sexes.	Women and men equal in *all* respects; women aping men in clothes, smoking, careers; preferring jobs to homemaking; selecting jobs devoid of motherhood implications.
MATERIALISM De-emphasizes spiritual in favor of material values.	Living beyond one's means; useless borrowing; ostentatious display; keeping up with the Joneses; neglecting family for career; making sex solely physical and all-important; luxury at expense of necessities.
FALSE NATURALISM Cult of obeying instincts and urges but not reason	Failing to admit will and reason as parts of human nature; emphasizing lower natural urges, giving impulses free rein; deeming divorce, birth control "natural."

their origin in Liberalism, but to condemn the entire system in all its ramifications, they seem to lack courage. In consequence, we find Catholics participating in and propagating causes they should condemn and combat.[9]

These attitudes make it clear that the dominant pattern of marriage today is based, not upon Christian, but upon secular attitudes. These are absorbed from our culture which uses every indoctrinating technique available. These outpourings of radio, television and press are part of the conscious conspiracy against Christian values spoken of by the popes.

Immaturity and lack of preparation

It is generally agreed by marriage specialists that immaturity and inadequate preparation are basic causes of marital breakdown. An immature person is arrested in growth of character, intellect and emotions. Though physically adult, he remains adolescent psychologically. Such partners are characterized by weakness of will, vacillating opinions and convictions, infantile attitudes and viewpoints, and lack of emotional control. They will find escape by neglecting responsibilities, drinking and dissipation, gambling, temper tantrums, suspicion, jealousy and similar childish traits. Often they will lean on mother, father, spouses or any other person willing to "mother" them.

In addition, most immature people lack proper attitudes and knowledge of the many aspects and relationships in marriage. They can be compared to a doctor who has had only one year of medical school or a college teacher without a degree or normal school training. Such persons bring to marriage romantic and unrealistic expectations, know little about the homemaking arts and less about child rearing. Their concepts of management of family funds are undeveloped and their insights into methods of adjusting and of solidifying a marriage are few and meagre.

Perhaps they are to be pitied more than blamed, though today most people desiring such preparation can receive it fairly easily. Basically the homes of these couples are at fault. Small families, neglect by parents, absence of training in homemaking and child

---

[9] F. P. Kenkel, *Central Blatt and Social Justice*, Vol. XXIII, No. 6 (September 1930), p. 195.

care, poor parental examples and failure of the home to develop mature, responsible personalities are the factors most responsible. Our schools also have done less than their full educational role in preparing for marriage. Many teachers lack family insight and consciousness and many curricular and extra-curricular activities are devoid of marriage and family content. A pioneer Catholic family specialist has asked the question:

Is the school helping the family? There is no question it is doing something. Equally certain is it, that it is doing more and more. Nonetheless, there is no room for complacence about either the past or present accomplishments. *There is vast room for further advance and improvement* [italics ours].[10]

The proceedings of the National Catholic Education Association for the past 20 years show that marriage and family have not once been a topic for discussion.[11] "In spite of the fundamental role our culture assigns to marriage and the family, in spite of their encompassing importance for a happy personal life, higher education has in the past concerned itself little with preparing students for their role of mates and as parents." [12] Couples are not effectively receiving the religious and moral truths of marriage in our current religious milieu. Many of them even fail to receive adequate instructions immediately prior to marriage, according to surveys made at the Catholic University of America. In one study only 93 out of 167 married people received pre-nuptial instructions from a priest; [13] in another study of 476 married people 54 per cent of the husbands and 51 per cent of the wives received none at all; and 26.5 per cent of them received

---

[10] Edgar Schmiedeler, "Education and the Family," *Marriage Education and Counseling,* ed. A. H. Clemens (Washington, D. C.: The Catholic University of America Press, 1951), p. 22.

[11] Sr. M. Evodine McGrath, *The Role of the Catholic College in Preparing for Marriage and Family Life* (Washington, D. C.: The Catholic University of America Press, 1952), chap. i.

[12] Report of President's Committee of Higher Education, *Higher Education for Democracy,* Vol. I (Washington, D. C.: United States Government Printing Office, 1947), p. 56.

[13] Richard Feiten, "An Investigation of the Knowledge and Attitudes of Catholic Married People on Moral Relations in Marriage and the Family" (Master's thesis, Catholic University of America, 1948), pp. 26–32.

only one.[14]   Local needs of families in distress are not being adequately met by fellow families in the same parish.   The civil and state role is also offending against the family, both by omission and commission.

Though the home, school, parish, and government are not effective enough in correct preparation, our culture and its mass media are imparting most successfully secular notions about marriage.   Until this process is reversed, little hope can be held for a victory over neopaganism in the familial society.

Expectations and failure

The role of expectations in marriage is often neglected.   To counselors with any experience at all, such expectations also appear to be a basic cause of failure.   Most of the disagreements which end in divorce, seem to result from differing expectations as to the roles each was to play after marriage.   This is why some conclude that most divorces had their seeds planted even before the wedding took place.

This implies poor selection of life-partners.   Such mistakes are easy to make in a culture such as ours, with many sub-cultural groups each of which has a different set of concepts about marital roles.   Mixed marriages, whether they be religious, ethnic or otherwise are likely to result in partners with vastly differing expectations.   For instance, the boy brought up in one of the ethnic groups in which the role of the husband is very strong, is not likely to prove a good partner to the girl raised in an equalitarian type of family.

Studies of factors of discord

Quite a number of studies give us factors that do not *cause* but *occasion* failure in marriage.   These studies differ and even contradict one another; yet all help to illuminate marital adjustment.   At least they might be warning signals of the rocks and shoals ahead.

Some secular studies present marriage factors that are associated with discord and breakdown (Table 15).   Though the

---

[14] Hugh Dunn, *A Study of Some Catholic Marital Attitudes, Practices, and Problems with Special Reference to the Implication for Premarital Instructions* (Washington, D. C.: The Catholic University of America Press, 1956), p. 204.

studies often agree on factors, the frequency of their appearance varies considerably. It might also be noted that the most frequent factors were cruelty, finances and incompatibility. The second in frequency were nonsupport, in-laws, drink and sex.

TABLE 15

FACTORS OF DISCORD BY FREQUENCY

Factors	Davis * (2,200 women)	Mowrer † (1,573 cases)	Laird ‡ (Couples in Who's Who)	Schroeder § (410 persons)
Abuse or cruelty		1		1
Bad housekeeping		5	6	
Children of former marriage		12		
Deceit				9
Drink	5	2	10	3
Economics	3	10	1	7
Evil companions		13		
Incompatibility	1			8
Infidelity	4			4
In-laws		7	2	6
Irregular habits		3		
Jealousy		9	4	
Mental deficiency		4		
Nagging		6		
Nonsupport				2
Personal irritation				5
Sex	2	11	7	10
Temper		8		
Children			3	
Different education			5	
Difference in social status			8	

* K. Davis, *Sex Factors in the Lives of Twenty-two Hundred Women* (New York: Harper & Brothers, 1929).
† E. R. Mowrer, *Domestic Discord: Its Analysis and Treatment* (Chicago: University of Chicago Press, 1928).
‡ D. A. Laird, *Why We Don't Like People* (New York: A. L. Glaser & Co., 1935), pp. 73–75.
§ C. W. Schroeder, *Divorce in a City of 100,000 Population* (Chicago: University of Chicago Press, 1939).

The studies of factors of failure in Catholic marriages also show some agreement on factors but little on their frequency of appearance. The first, on the whole, are misunderstanding, finances, drink and cruelty; the second are incompatibility, adultery and drink.

Another interesting observation arising from a comparison of the four studies (Table 16) is the close agreement of the two studies based on clinical evidence (St. Michael's Clinic and Clemens) as to both the inclusion and the frequency of some factors; and the variations in these same factors compared to non-clinical studies. Drink, for instance, is found as first and second in rank by the Chancery Office records, but eighth and ninth in the clinical studies. This is true despite the fact that St. Michael's Family Clinic has an affiliated Alcoholic Clinic which would seem to increase rather than decrease the frequency of cases entailing drink as a factor. It is clearly much too early to label drinking *enemy number one* of the Catholic family, though doubtless it is an important factor in marriage breakdown. Again, sex factors were found second and third in rank in the clinical studies though listed sixth and eighth in studies based on Chancery records.

The variations between these four available empirical studies on the failure of Catholic marriages, make it imperative to withhold conclusions about the frequency or importance of any one or all factors. Further research will be required before we can scientifically demonstrate all of the major factors operative, or their importance and frequency. Even more profound research will be necessary before we can scientifically determine the more basic factors (or causes) of Catholic marriage breakdown. In the meantime we have a list of some known factors which those selecting life-partners would be well advised to study. Those engaged in premarital and postmarital education might also find these known factors worth noting in their writing and lecturing.

Both secular and Catholic studies, seem to have found a dominance of certain factors, among them being incompatibility, drink, cruelty and in-laws. These, in turn, confirm the position that immaturity is a basic cause since each of these dominant factors can be traced to an adolescent type of personality. Sex is obviously not the primary factor of failure which some would believe it to be since it ranks second, eleventh, seventh, tenth, third, sixth and eighth respectively.

The omissions of these studies are as revealing as their conclu-

TABLE 16

FAILURE OF CATHOLIC MARRIAGES BY FREQUENCY OF FACTORS STATED

Factors	St. Michael Clinic * (152 couples)	Thomas † (7,000 couples)	Brinkman ‡ (518 couples)	Clemens (116 husbands and wives)
Adultery		2	4	
Child rearing	8		12	3
Crime			14	
Cruelty			1	
Desertion			5	
Drink	9	1	2	8
Economics	7	9		1
Housing				12
Incompatibility	2	4	7	
Infidelity			6	13
In-laws		5	9	5
Irreligion	6			
Irresponsibility		3		
Jealousy				4
Mental abuse				10
Misunderstanding	1			
Mixed marriage	4			
Nagging			13	7
No interest in the home				11
Non-support			3	
Psychiatric illness	10	7	11	
Conflicting religious views	5	8	10	9
Sex	3	6	8	2

* Wilma Dunn, "The Social Worker Helps Mend Broken Homes," *Hospital Progress* (August 1949), p. 247.

† John Thomas, "Marriage Breakdown," *Social Order*, Vol. II, No. 10 (December 1952), pp. 445–451.

‡ Gabriel Brinkman, "Some Factors Involved in the Breakdown of Catholic Marriages in Several Eastern Archdioceses" (Master's dissertation, Catholic University of America, July 1953).

sions. Marriage counseling experience shows that absorption with careers and a corresponding inattention to wives and children is a frequent factor; and arguments about child rearing appear very often especially in marriages of 10 years duration or more. Perhaps we do not yet know the most important factors of breakdown and the techniques of research employed so far have been not too effective or reliable.

MARRIAGE REHABILITATION

Our society faces the herculean task of restoring marriage and the family to the pattern laid down by its Author.

To this end, it behooves us, above all else, to call to mind that firmly established principle, esteemed alike in sound philosophy and sacred theology: namely, that whatever things have deviated from their right order, cannot be brought back to that original state which is in harmony with their nature *except by a return to the Divine Plan* which, as the Angelic Doctor teaches, is the exemplar of all right order.[15]

The Divine Plan also prevents misguided zeal for reform and points out the road to genuine and complete reconstruction of the family. Today we tend to forget that the entire social universe should center around the family; that every other institution exists to help the family whether it be the Church, state, school, or any other. The family has the right to self-government and the direction of its own internal affairs. Whatever assistance other societies offer should be tendered only when the families cannot or will not help themselves; it should be for no longer period of time than is required; and it should be done so as to restore the autonomy of the family and not destroy it. These principles are frequently forgotten by individuals and groups characterized by more zeal than wisdom. Providing sex education in our schools, for instance, without also persuading parents to resume this basic home obligation, may permanently substitute the school for the home and help weaken and destroy the family's autonomy.

The family helps itself

Unless the family does what it can to restore itself, all the efforts of outside societies and agencies can only be partially effective. This is inescapable since by its very nature, the family receives its vital activity and its source of rehabilitation from *within* and not from the outside. This is true of *all* living organisms; it is also true of the family. Obviously the emphasis in family reconstruction *must be* placed upon the reactivation of

---

[15] Pius XI, *op. cit.,* p. 159.

the internal life of the family rather than on its external environment. For as Cardinal Suhard has reminded us after stating the need for external reform also:

Doing this [external reform], we have not resolved the problem. *The essential factor remains in the family itself.* For if certain economic and social conditions are necessary for the development of the family, they are *not the cause* of it [italics ours].[16]

The first and most important internal factors the family needs are grace and knowledge of the Divine Plan for marriage. In this the family must obviously help itself. The channels of grace are ever at its disposal, as are the religious and moral aspects of marriage. The second important internal self-help is to change current secular attitudes for religious ones. This change will follow automatically from growth in grace and wisdom. The third is the invigoration of character. Families must realize that they must be different, if they would be right and Christian. Families can, if they will, turn their homes from show places to little churches, nurseries, schools, workshops and recreation centers once again. They can effectively train children and prepare them to set up Christian homes of their own some day. The fourth self-help is further education in the worldly aspects of marriage and the family. If couples have been poorly prepared in this respect by the home and school, they can in this day of literature and lectures recoup this loss with little difficulty. These internal forces, this self-determination *must* be employed and every resource strained or external aids will prove of limited value only.

Families can also intensify their liturgical and sacramental living in church and home; they can foster and attend premarital and postmarital lectures and conferences; form and participate in family discussion clubs; make family retreats; read marriage and family books, pamphlets and periodicals; restore some productive chores to the home; handle their money more wisely and so forth. In addition, ties of kinship can be deepened and

---

16 Cardinal Emmanuel Suhard, "Blueprint for A Christian Family," *Grail*, Vol. XXXV, No. 10, (October 1953), p. 43, as taken from *The Church Today* (Chicago: Fides Publishers, 1953).

strengthened to afford an ever ready resource when families need assistance.

Perhaps one of the most useful steps a family can take is to become active in a Catholic family movement. With such help the battle against secularism will be facilitated and their morale boosted. The conviction that a family must fight the battle against secularism *alone* is devastating. Once the Catholic family finds other Catholic families equally conscientious, equally determined to create a Christian oasis in the desert of paganism, the task becomes easier. Unfortunately, the worst enemies of the conscientious Catholic family are the partly secular families who are more worldly and "modern" than Catholic. A hard core of hundred percenters, could build a truly Christian environment despite the rampant secularism of our culture and society.

On the other hand, complete family rehabilitation cannot succeed through internal processes alone. *External aids are imperative* since families are not entirely self-sufficient and since their environment can be an obstacle or an asset to internal reform. For instance, we previously discussed the need for all parents to agree about the supervision of children in their leisure time pursuits. This calls for social action on the part of families themselves to influence their married colleagues to agree in thought and action.

With characteristically keen insight Cardinal Suhard noted the need for two types of what he called "cooperation of families in the apostolate of the hierarchy." One type of Catholic Action is chiefly devoted to the *internal* family life through group study and prayer; the other to the *external* milieu through family social action.[17]

The Church and family rehabilitation

Since grace and religio-moral knowledge of marriage and the family are so basic, the role of the Church in family reconstruction is equally basic. The Bishops currently are employing specialized family movements and organizations to assist them in this pastoral role. Three have been initiated in our country, each with considerable effectiveness. The National Catholic

---

[17] *Ibid.,* p. 13.

Conference on Family Life is a nationwide organization operating chiefly through family life committees of the National Councils of Catholic Men and Women.   Though data is not available to indicate the extent of its activities, their scope seems impressive.   It furnishes literature; operates an information Center; promotes religious family practices; aids family security; employs the radio, discussion groups, the little theatre for family purposes; and annually conducts a convention sponsoring a national family week.[18]   Its initiative and clearing house is the Family Life Bureau of the National Catholic Welfare Conference.

Another channel for family reactivation is the Cana Conference Movement.   In 1950 it operated in 87 dioceses, or 71 per cent of the 122 dioceses in the nation.   It is not a nationally organized movement (though the leaders annually conduct a Study Week on a national basis) but is autonomous on either a diocesan or parish basis.   It holds conferences for married couples; 47 dioceses in 1950 having held 619 such or an average of over 13 for each diocese.   Some 56,000 married persons attended them.   In addition, its Pre-Cana Conferences (existing in 36 dioceses in 1950) are intended to prepare engaged couples for marriage.   The most recent addition has been Cana Clubs or Caucuses, small discussion groups of about 6 couples and a chaplain.   In 1950 there were 112 of these groups in 23 different dioceses.[19]

A third group interested in family reform is the Christian Family Movement.   This movement is based on small groups who engage in study, prayer and action.   A large emphasis is placed on social action in behalf of families, in which the Jocist technique of observing, judging and acting is followed.   At the moment it is active in 105 dioceses, has over 300 priest chaplains and 250 regional leaders.   Like the Cana Conference Movement it has spread to many foreign countries and to other continents.[20]

These three movements are all dedicated to family rehabilita-

---

[18] *The Family Life Bureau of the National Catholic Welfare Conference* (Washington, D. C.: The Family Life Bureau).

[19] A. H. Clemens, *The Cana Movement in the United States* (Washington, D. C.: The Catholic University of America Press, 1953).

[20] George Powers, "The Christian Family Movement in Theory and in Action" (Doctoral dissertation, Catholic University of America, 1957).

tion in every way feasible, but the emphasis in the first two named is largely on internal family reactivation while the third is devoted to social action outside the homes. Both types of movement participate in the work of the hierarchy and are therefore forms of Catholic Action; in fact, various Bishops have employed each of these as they were needed. Cardinal Suhard showed his acquaintance with them both, when he wrote about the family apostolate:

It assumes two forms. On the plane of spirituality one sees more and more Catholic homes reuniting periodically in groups for a triple purpose: prayer in common, mutual spiritual and material aid, and the study of family problems. This formation is also sought in days of recollection, at family retreats, through specialized literature.

On the plane of action, they aid in instilling Christian Family ideals in their daily lives and works. They want to Christianize the whole life of the home. To do this they bring the aid of the large Christian Family Movement to bear on the problem; they bring in addition the testimony of their own family, and in each locale they assume the responsibility for bringing families together in a common ideal of mutual aid and restoration.[21]

He also addressed this reminder to his families: "We ask you to enter immediately one of the already existing family movements. We do not hesitate to urge you to do this as a *grave duty in conscience.*[22]

In providing these various movements the Church is not unmindful of the differences in temperament of various couples. The Holy Father has warned against members of any one of these movements narrowly insisting that theirs is the only form of the apostolate.

Moderation and prudence are necessary. Particular and intimate qualities of mind, as well as certain conditions of life not possessed by all, are necessary to practice the apostolate. Not everyone is a good catechist, orator, or propagator of Catholic doctrine. Not everyone is capable of making his own cause seem attractive to the people with whom he lives. For a lot of people, the task of taking care of the family they are called upon to create, and to which they

---

[21] Suhard, *op. cit.,* p. 40.
[22] *Ibid.,* p. 41.

should always give their first attention, is so absorbing that they cannot devote time to the particular activities of the apostolate.[23]

The parish and the family

The family touches the Church most closely on the parish level. Here families can best be restored to their full Christian splendor and can more immediately make their contribution to the Mystical Body of Christ. Pius XII so clearly realized this that he penned words of greatest emphasis to urge the reactivition of parish life in behalf of the family.

For the love of our Savior Jesus Christ, therefore, we implore pastors of souls, by *every means* in their power, by instruction and catechism, by word of mouth and written articles widely distributed, to warn Christian parents of their grave obligations. And this should be done not in a merely theoretical and general way, but with *practical* and *specific application* to the various responsibilities of parents touching the religious, moral, and civil training of their children, and with indication of the methods best adapted to make their training effective, supposing always the influence of their own exemplary lives [italics ours].[24]

Many parishes are reactivating themselves and their families by adhering more intensely to the liturgy; by action and study groups, premarital lectures, conferences for the married, libraries and pamphlets on family topics, maternity guilds, and by revitalizing the already existing societies.

Government aids

Pius XII has placed the role of the government second to that of the Church in family reconstruction. In a speech to the Roman Rota, he pointed out that the Church's efforts will not meet with hoped for success unless the state plays its role in cleansing the immoral climate in society.

One of the chief concerns of the Church today, beyond doubt, must be to put a stop, by all means possible, to the decadence of marriage and the family. She is fully aware of this duty but knows well at the same time that her efforts will be successful only to the degree that

---

[23] Pius XII, quoted in *The Catholic Standard,* Vol. VI, No. 41 (October 5, 1956), p. 1.

[24] Pius XII, quoted by Edgar Schmiedeler, *op. cit.,* p. 18.

conditions generally in the economic, social and above all the moral sphere, make it less difficult in practice to lead a married life pleasing to our Lord. *In this regard public authority must shoulder a very serious responsibility* [italics ours].[25]

In practice this means a positive and a negative role. The state should recognize the family as a juridical unit and establish a national program for family welfare. This would include such factors as family allowances, better housing, and widows' pensions. The ever present danger that government aid may make the state a permanent substitute for the family must be avoided. On the other hand, divorce, contraceptives and the immoralities permitted on the mass media need government attention.

In these respects families should impel state assistance. Using the ballot more discriminatingly, writing letters to Congressmen, serving on civic committees and even attaining public office are imperative if the Christian concept of family life is once again to influence state efforts. Perhaps it is not premature but long overdue to urge the formation of family unions similar to those in Europe, which could help protect and promote family interests in civil circles.

Schools and families

As complements to the home in all other educational matters, schools should also assist the home in family education.

As in the home, so in the school, those who have the responsibility of guiding the young must start with the presumption that each of the pupils will one day enter the married state. Naturally, the education for marriage becomes more definite and more detailed with the advance of the child in school grades. However, even in the elementary school this type of education must be regarded as a requirement even though its relation to marriage is only remote and general.[26]

Through Parent-Teacher organizations closer cooperation between school and home can be effected. It is one of the

---

[25] Pius XII, *Acta Apostolicae Sedis,* Vol. XXXVII, No. 391 (October 6, 1946).

[26] F. J. Connell, "The Obligation of the Home, School and Church to Educate for Family Living," *Marriage and Family Relationships,* ed. A. H. Clemens (Washington, D. C.: The Catholic University of America Press, 1950), pp. 13–14.

anomalies of our times that the two educators of our children—parents and teachers—so seldom meet, interchange ideas or discuss the objects of their common aim and concern.

Both high schools and colleges can assist the home in this serious task of marriage preparation.   It is a sad commentary on our schools that explicit training has been given for all other aspects of life but not to the same extent for that which will be for most their *major vocation*.   Doubtless this is why Pius XII said:

We bless also *your schools of domestic economy* and in general all that tends to help the formation and the instruction of the woman in housekeeping and for the care of her own home and the care and education of her children [italics ours].[27]

Some practical steps which high schools and colleges might employ have been suggested after a very thorough study of the situation by the president of one of our Catholic women's colleges:

1. Sequence of studies in marriage and family living could be offered.

2. The number of courses relating directly or indirectly to the family could be increased.

3. Instructors could interpret and evaluate all courses in terms of marriage and family living.

4. Marriage education might reach more students if taken out of the home economics or social science departments and made part of the general curriculum.

5. Such courses should not be limited to juniors and seniors; most need some of this knowledge before that age.

6. Counselors of students might improve their abilities for marital counseling.[28]

Marriage counseling

No marriage preparation course can be completely effective without the added resources of personal counseling.   Human personalities are too varied to fall into standard patterns, averages

---

27 Pius XII, "Holy Father Encourages Women in Interest of Family and Youth," *Catholic Action*, Vol. XXXI, No. 9 (1949), p. 9; also *Acta Apostolicae Sedis*, Vol. XLI (September 6, 1949), pp. 415–421.

28 Sr. Mary Evodine McGrath, *op. cit.*, pp. 123–127.

and generalities with which group instructions must be concerned. Only personal and private interviews can serve this purpose effectively. For this reason, group instructions should not be accepted as an adequate substitute for premarital counseling.

Due to inadequate education increasing numbers of couples require additional guidance after marriage. Facilities must be provided for these couples if we hope to improve marriage relationships and prevent marital breakdown. In addition, are couples whose relationship has been so seriously impaired that they can no longer view their problems with objectivity and a proper perspective. These couples, tensed by resentments, hostilities and antagonisms need more than guidance. Without counseling, to restore their perspective, there will be little hope for the continuance of their marriages.

This type of case is frequently very time consuming. It calls for a genuine ability on the part of the counselor. Many think it demands skills that require specialized training in marriage counseling. This conviction is quickly gaining acceptance throughout the nation and is giving rise to a new profession.

Traditionally Catholics have gone to priests with such problems, usually with good results. However, today large numbers of Catholics are consulting secular marriage counseling agencies, sometimes with untoward effects upon their Catholic beliefs and practices. A nationwide survey indicated that one-third of all the clients of secular agencies are Catholic couples. This national trend to professional marriage counseling is impelling Catholic circles to consider the need for marriage counseling resources of their own. Catholic couples need counselors who can assist them within the framework of Catholic beliefs and practices. Few areas of life have more religious and moral implications, the complexities of which only a person trained in the Catholic way of life is likely to master. Fully alert to this need, the Catholic University of America has opened a Marriage Counseling Center specifically to train such specialists. The recognition of this need is also impelling the opening of marriage counseling agencies under Catholic auspices in various dioceses and charitable institutions.

Perhaps the growth of such facilities will encourage couples to avail themselves *sooner* of their services. It seems tragic that so many couples permit their marriages to deteriorate for years (to the misery and harm of parents and children) before seeking assistance. With the growth of facilities and the greater acceptance of such counseling by couples at large, it may be expected that more families will use these facilities and that they will resort to their use *earlier*.

THE FAMILY AND THE DIVINE PLAN

There is only one plan for success in marriage. The rejection of the Divine Design for marriage means failure; its acceptance cannot mean anything but success. In this design children and youth were to have their personalities matured, educated and informed chiefly by the home, Church and school. The state was to use its facilities to promote family welfare and eliminate an immoral climate. All societies were to help and perfect the society of the family and in so doing, to perfect the individual in the family. The family was so constituted by Divine Design that it alone, in the last analysis, could save and perfect itself. However, to do so it would require the assistance of all other societies. Just as their assistance would prove largely ineffectual without internal family reform, so family self-help would be partially frustrated if other societies did not function fully and completely.

19

Design For Successful Marriage

IN THE VAST silence of eternity, before time began, the Divine Wisdom planned a design for the universe. In that eternal Now, the infinite fullness of love between Father and Son had overflowed, giving issue to the uncreated Holy Spirit. This eternal Love and Divine Triad was to be mirrored in God's creation. Divinity was to wed humanity for "There is a certain spiritual wedlock between the Son of God and human nature. Therefore, in the Annunciation the Virgin's consent was besought in lieu of the entire human nature." [1] In this Divine Romance, God would share His friendship with men through the life of grace. Humanity, in turn, inspired by Divine Love would reach out to its fellows in the embrace of wedded love and so share in the great creative act of the Godhead. Husband, wife, and child were to reflect the Trinity in their family life.

When in the fullness of time the Divine Wisdom was to create angels, He created the entire angelic multitude in one

---

[1] St. Thomas Aquinas, *The Summa Theologica of St. Thomas Aquinas,* tr. by the Fathers of the English Dominican Province (New York: Benziger Bros., 1948), Vol. II, Q. 30, art. 1, p. 2179.

mighty act. With mankind, however, it was to be otherwise. Only two human beings were to be created. Through them, with the passage of time, the entire human race would, by a gradual creation emerge. Unlike the angels, man was to share in the great creative act of God. In this Divine Plan men and women would unite into families to develop the human race. The children of that race were to be nurtured in the bosom of the family to a greater Godlikeness until they finally found their way back to God, from Whom they came. Each family, Dom Columba Marmion assures us, was to represent a "Divine Thought"; and the family's holiness would consist "of carrying into effect this thought which God conceived of before creation." [2] This is the utterly wise and sublimely beautiful Divine Plan for marriage.

It is this Plan—designed by the same Infinite Mind that created marriage—that alone can assure success and happiness in the family. Only within this Plan can the family find peace, harmony, holiness, and security. Only deviation from it can cause marital dissolution and failure. Outside of it is chaos, discord, sin, and insecurity. Pius XI has repeatedly reaffirmed that marriage can once again be restored to its original stature only by "a returning to the Divine Plan" and that nothing is of greater moment than that "all should bear in mind what is the Divine Plan." [3] It can be learned chiefly from the Church's tradition. This, according to Cardinal Newman, consists not only in her dogmas and laws but also in the habitual (and sometimes unconscious) way in which she views things. Though this Design for marriage is supernatural in its origin and in its goals, it also embraces the natural. "The finger of God writes His directions in the very fibres of the things He makes and directs; those Divinely written directions we call nature's directions or nature's laws . . . they are a record of His governing intelligence." [4]

Those understand this Plan amiss who think of it only in terms of religion, prayer, the sacraments, morals, and dogma. God's

---

[2] Dom Columba Marmion, *Christ the Life of the Soul* (St. Louis: Herder Book Co., 1929), chap. iv.

[3] Pius XI, "On Christian Marriage," *The Catholic Mind*, Vol. XXIX, No. 2. (January 22, 1931), p. 52.

[4] W. Farrell and M. J. Healy, *My Way of Life* (Brooklyn: Confraternity of the Precious Blood, 1952), p. 110.

design for marriage can as much be seen in love, sex attraction, or balancing the family budget. The natural differences between male and female are as integral a part of the Divine Plan as the sacramental nature of marriage. Those who would grasp the true meaning of marriage must resort to religion and its teachings; but they should tap the fonts of scientific knowledge as well. On the other hand, they will fail utterly to understand God's design for marriage if they contend that "durable knowledge of the family can only be achieved through the use of the scientific method." [5] We must recognize the relative merits of different sources of knowledge:

> First of all we should know the relations of creatures to God; second in rank is knowledge of their relation to man; and least of all is the knowledge of their material relations to one another in the "scientific laws." Yet the majority of the world's intelligentsia deems that there is naught to be learned more noble than the third class of lore. . . . The result is, naturally, that they are led into repeated gross errors in the fundamental knowing of creatures because they would study strands of God's intricate tapestry of creation outside their setting.[6]

The supernatural presupposes the natural but the natural indicates the need of the supernatural. In our present state of things the two are intimately intertwined. For " the effort to draw a clear line of distinction between religion and life, between the supernatural and the natural . . . as though they had no relation with each other, and as though the rights of God had no validity in the multiform relationships of daily life—human and social—is completely alien to Catholic thought and is openly anti-Christian." [7]

To be Catholic in our concept of marriage we must be "universal" in our outlook. Catholicism is a total and integral thing which does not ignore the natural but employs it to serve the supernatural. It is the latter part of the Divine Plan which posits the ultimate goals for marriage and the supernatural means. It is the natural portion which posits for us natural and equally in-

---

[5] R. F. Winch and R. McGinnis, *Marriage and the Family* (New York: Henry Holt & Co., Inc., 1953), p. v.

[6] F. J. McGarrigle, *My Father's Will* (Milwaukee: The Bruce Publishing Company, 1943), p. 14.

[7] Pius XII, "All' Alba della Storia," *Acta Apostolicae Sedis*, Vol. XXXXIX (1947), pp. 60–61.

dispensable means. In God's Design for success in marriage we need only know these goals and the art of employing both sets of means to attain them. In other words, for success in marriage, we need above all else the great virtue of prudence. It is not accidental to note that when St. Thomas treated the family and the Plan by which it is to be guided, he did so under the virtue of prudence.[8] This is the virtue which orders all means toward their rightful goals. In a certain sense the sole purpose of this book is to explain prudence in every one of the many relationships of marriage; to indicate how grace, love, sex, money, recreation and so forth can be made to serve the goals of marriage. If each human relationship is oriented toward the rightful goals of marriage, success and happiness are insured.

But this order . . . will be quite faulty and imperfect, unless man's activities harmoniously unite to imitate and, as far as humanly possible, attain the marvelous unity of the Divine Plan. This is the perfect order which the Church preaches with intense earnestness, and which right reason demands; which places God as the first and supreme end of all created activity, and regards all created goods as mere instruments under God, to be used only in so far as they help toward the attainment of our supreme end.[9]

SUPERNATURAL AND NATURAL TRUTHS

This Design for success in marriage consists of sets of truths, laws and relationships. Since they were known by God for all eternity, they have been labeled the "Eternal Law." In this eternal plan are truths both supernatural and natural. The supernatural truths have been given us through revelation and theology. Though the deposit of truths constituting the Catholic faith has been with us since the beginning, the fuller understanding of these truths has come with the development of theology. With the passage of time, for instance, the supernatural splendor of the vocation of marriage has been more fully grasped and understood. A noted theologian has called this to our attention:

It is unfortunate that many Catholics are not fully aware of the sanctifying power of matrimony. However, in a sense this is to be expected

---

8 St. Thomas Aquinas, *op. cit.*, Vol. II, Pt. 2, Q. 47, art. 11; Q. 50, art. 3.

9 Pius XI, "Restoring the Christian Social Order," *Social Wellsprings*, Vol. II, annotated and arranged, Joseph Husslein (Milwaukee: The Bruce Publishing Company, 1943), p. 228.

since the Church itself came to the full consciousness of the effectiveness of marriage as a means of holiness only gradually down through the centuries; and it can safely be asserted that in the course of time an even deeper understanding of this sublime subject will enlighten the minds of the faithful.[10]

The natural truths (laws and relationships) are discovered by man through and in the sciences of philosophy, sociology, psychology, physiology, education, recreation, economics and others. With the passage of time more and more light is thrown on God's Plan for marriage. Every new scientific discovery about marriage is a further revelation of the great Design for it. The Rh factor, childbirth without fear, the advantages of breast feeding, the superiority of active over passive recreation, the laws of psychology and child training and numerous other scientific findings are merely the unraveling of the intricate and marvelous skeins that make up the Design for success in marriage. In addition, Church and state devise laws that are merely applications of the natural and supernatural truths already known. Accordingly, there are both Canon and civil laws indicating the road to success in marriage.

THE DIVINE PLAN FOR MARRIAGE

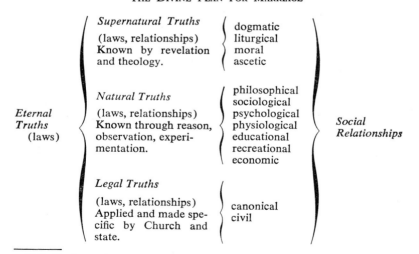

Eternal Truths (laws)	Supernatural Truths (laws, relationships) Known by revelation and theology.	dogmatic liturgical moral ascetic	Social Relationships
	Natural Truths (laws, relationships) Known through reason, observation, experimentation.	philosophical sociological psychological physiological educational recreational economic	
	Legal Truths (laws, relationships) Applied and made specific by Church and state.	canonical civil	

[10] F. J. Connell, "Marriage as a State of Religious Perfection," *Marriage Education and Counseling,* ed. by A. H. Clemens (Washington, D. C.: The Catholic University of America Press, 1951), p. 30.

A SOCIOLOGICAL APPROACH

The same scheme and truths issuing from the Eternal Law are also arrived at by reviewing the family as a social institution. The family, as all other societies, is ". . . a system of dynamic relationships purposely organized. . . . Out of the common action for a common purpose arise *relations* which, when they become relatively stable, may be designated as *institutions*. Human relations resulting from common activity and common purpose that tend to become permanent are institutions [italics ours]." [11]

Any attempt to list the relationships existing in the family, will reveal the same scheme already derived from the Divine Plan. On the supernatural level, are social relationships like those of the Mystical Body of Christ, the doctrine of vicarious suffering, Matrimony as a social sacrament. On the natural level, are social relationships such as the kinship family, family recreation, the complementalness of the sexes, marital love, child bearing and rearing.

AN INTEGRAL PLAN

At first thought, this design of truths, laws and relationships may appear disconnected or departmentalized. It may seem to lack coherence and integration. However, careful scrutiny reveals that, on the contrary, this intricate network of truths and relationships which constitute marriage and the family is extremely well integrated into an over-all pattern.

In the first instance, the supernatural truths alone give us the full scope of the purposes of marriage. In addition, they furnish the supernatural aids or means indispensable to the attainment of these marital goals. The natural relationships and truths, are also indispensable means for the achievement of goals. Here the virtue of prudence becomes an integrating factor; it indicates the manner in which each natural relationship is to be used to serve the supernatural and natural purposes. For instance, to use family economic resources to attain best the natural goal of rearing of children and the supernatural purpose of saving the

---

11 Sr. M. Edward Healy, *Society and Social Change in the Writings of St. Thomas, Ward, Sumner and Cooley* (Washington, D. C.: The Catholic University of America Press, 1948), pp. 6, 16.

souls of family members, calls for prudence of a high order. All relationships must be used wisely if marriage is to succeed and the family is to prosper. There is an intimate connection between the supernatural and natural by which each serves the other. If grace builds on nature, nature needs grace for its maximum achievement and attainment.

The integral nature of these relationships is also visible in the fact that, on the natural level alone, each affects the other and is, in turn, affected by all the others. Sex maladjustment (psychological-physical), might be caused by the poor treatment given by a spouse to the partner's relatives (sociological), by lack of affection (psychological), by disputes over child training (educational), by failure to share social life together (recreational), or by quarrels over money matters (economic).

THE SCOPE OF THE DIVINE PLAN

In fact, so completely integral is this Divine Design that every factor and every problem in marriage must be viewed from the standpoint of each and every relationship. To try to find, for instance, the right age for marriage from just one relationship could prove a serious mistake. The physiological relationship would indicate the desirability of late teen-age marriages; [12] and the sociological would caution against such early marriages.[13] To be sure of the correct position of many elements and factors in marriage, it is imperative to consult *all* the relationships.

For the same reason, any premarital preparation or educational endeavor that fails to impart the proper insights and knowledge of every relationship is incomplete; it cannot educate for the totality of marriage. Success in marriage itself means living out *all* the truths, laws and relationships found in these various areas. By the same logic, those who would educate for marriage or engage in marriage counseling with maximum effectiveness, must be well equipped with the knowledge of all these areas and relationships.

DESIGN FOR MARITAL SUCCESS

In the Divine Plan marriage is an institution enjoying liberty but not license; it is regulated by the wise laws of God and man.

---

12 See Chapter 13.
13 See Chapter 6.

Though the rearing and education of children are its chief goals, many personal advantages including happiness, are also served. By its nature marriage is a natural contract and a social institution, elevated to the supernatural as a sacrament, and regulated by good laws of Church and state. It is one of the four major vocations—a vocation to a higher life of spirituality and to the quantitative and qualitative extension of the human race and the Mystical Body of Christ. Its nature and purposes require certain functions be performed without which the family could not grow strong and attain its goals.

Love is at the heart of marriage and family life. Through self-sacrifice for one another, children are nurtured and all grow in love of God. Husbands, wives, parents and children must discharge certain roles to attain the goals and functions proper to marriage. A diminution of these roles means a proportionate lessening in functions and an equal failure to achieve rightful purposes. The man's role is that of creativity and leadership in all respects; woman's role is motherhood.

Marriage is prepared for by long and careful training starting in infancy in the home and completed with the aid of the Church and school in adolescence. Boys and girls should mingle and meet one another, to learn to adjust to the opposite sex. In time, they should court to select wisely a proper life-partner. In this important selection, the purposes and goals of marriage should be the paramount consideration; mixed marriages of various types—religious, social, cultural, educational—are to be strenuously avoided in spouse selection.

Once married, couples should dedicate themselves to the goals of marriage, sacrificing self in the interest of the group. Partners must adjust to group purposes and living as well as to each other. To accomplish the latter, both must understand the differences between the sexes and the arts of adjustment.

Conscious that good marriages are made only through strenuous effort, partners develop deep ties of affection by sharing in all of life's activities. They realize that the rural milieu is most conducive to this pattern of life together. Aware of the inability of families to work out their destiny unaided, they also develop strong bonds with close relatives with whom there remains a continuing and mutual spirit of assistance and support. From childhood through old age till death, the kinship circle remains the natural place for youth and age alike. Family rituals are fostered for their unitive, educational and religious values.

Religion teaches, governs and sanctifies the family, and the family is basically responsible for the religious formation of children and adults alike. No stronger force for success and happiness in marriage exists than adherence to religious living. Natural factors also have an important role to play. Sex (properly used in marriage) is considered a noble, dignified act that is, at once, an act of the virtues of justice, charity, purity and religion. It not only prospers the race but brings physical and emotional health to the partners and a deepening of mutual love. Sex adjustment is an art which must be learned, and sex education is a duty of parents.

Childbearing, though not devoid of the discomforting effects of original sin, is a physical and spiritual experience of great merit and advantage to both parents. Parenthood has the high dignity of joint-creativity with God and a participation in his extension and governing of the human race. It ultimately implies populating heaven with saints. The ideal of large families remains intact. Any force militating against such large families also militates against the Divine Plan.

Equally important is the total education of children in religion, character, intelligence, emotions, physical care and family living. Sex education is to be given by parents according to definite rules. The home is to give the basic training in each of these respects, assisted, but not substituted for, by outside agencies. Spouses are to assist each other in perfecting their personalities, especially in growth of holiness. Children, in turn, are an asset in developing the supernatural and natural aspects of their parents' personalities. A good home, based upon nature's unchangeable demands, is given children so that their budding personalities develop normally and healthily. Parents, in addition, take pains in instilling proper habits of soul and body into children through correct rules for discipline and the supervision of their environment and associates.

Recreation is family centered and shared by husband, wife, parents and children. As such, it provides the most wholesome and least expensive types of play, active rather than passive participation; it deepens bonds of unity between members of the family, promotes their education and enhances their religious living.

Family economic resources are viewed as a stewardship, to be used chiefly for family goals and purposes. To insure the attainment of these goals, families have all members share in home production; engage in wise buying; use the principles of good budgeting; conserve their resources through frugality and simplicity of living; and attain economic security through gradually building an estate upon proved rules of investment.

The wise laws of Church and state are respected and followed, as specific applications of the Divine Plan for marriage, to concrete situations and problems. The family makes a studied effort to divest itself of secular practices and attitudes which militate against God's design for marital success. Couples are aware of the danger that immaturity, irresponsibility and inadequate preparation will hasten marriages to their doom. Certain vices such as drinking and infidelity are viewed with alarm. Conscious of the importance of religious living to success, the family intensifies its religious life and practices.

In order to restore itself to its full stature as indicated by the Divine Plan, the family tries to reactivate itself by every form of self-help. It works to obtain grace in increased amounts and changes its attitudes to more correct ones; it also labors to change the external environment to a more Christian one. Church, school, state and all other agencies should be centered around the family. They should bring needed assistance without destroying the autonomy of the family.

All these various forces, and relationships constitute a complex and intricate Design for success in marriage. These are truths and laws, unchanging and unchangeable, springing ultimately from the Eternal Law of God Himself. This is, in short, the whole scope and sublimity of the Divine Plan for marriage.

"O the depth of the riches of the wisdom and of the knowledge of God!" [14]

---

[14] Romans: 11:33.

Unscientific Aspects of Marriage Literature

THROUGHOUT the pages of this book studies reputed to be scientific have been used quite generously. An attempt has consistently been made, however, to use them in such fashion that the reader would realize that they are not *conclusive* findings. Their use in this book as well as the prominence of surveys and investigations in much of our popular literature, calls for a word of caution in their interpretation. The Kinsey Reports, for instance, became best sellers before readers had inquired into their scientific worth; had they done so, these reports might never have attracted nationwide attention except to evoke negative criticism. Many authors more facile in writing than learned in scientific research hasten to expound the findings of new pieces of research in exaggerated terms. Often they easily brush aside the warning attached by the research worker to such findings, that they apply only to the persons studied and none other. They often create a minor sensation by applying such findings to all persons or couples throughout the nation.

The disconcerting and somewhat discouraging fact remains that not a single piece of empirical research on marriage and the family (nor all of them combined) has given us knowledge of

TABLE 17

SOME INSTANCES OF SAMPLING IN EMPIRICAL STUDIES ON MARRIAGE

Author	Study	Sample	How obtained	Comment
L. M. TERMIN	*Psychological Factors in Marital Happiness* (1938)	900 persons; all residents of California; majority upper or middle class.	Volunteers obtained through church groups, court records, etc.	Sample in no way representative; confined to one state; lower class not adequately represented; volunteers constitute a biased sample.
E. W. BURGESS AND P. WALLIN	*Engagement and Marriage* (1953)	1,000 couples who were engaged or its equivalent; 795 interviewed; white collar class; urban Protestant chiefly.	Questionnaires distributed by students to anybody they chose; those interviewed not selected but whoever was available.	Samples not representative; interviewees not selected, hence consisted only of those willing to be interviewed—a bias here; confined to one city only.
J. T. LANDIS	*Length of Time Required to Achieve Adjustment in Marriage* (1946)	409 couples; mostly parents of college students; income and education above average.	Students asked to send questionnaires to their parents.	Only those included who were willing to reply—bias here.
E. W. BURGESS AND L. S. COTTRELL	*Predicting Success and Failure in Marriage* (1939)	526 questionnaires; all subjects from Illinois; married one to six years; about half were Protestant; some case studies.	Questionnaires distributed by students, friends, social agencies, lists of divorces, lists of young married couples.	Samples not representative; no distinction in findings between results of questionnaires and of case studies; all located in or near Chicago.

Author	Study	Sample	How obtained	Comment
KINSEY, et al.	Sexual Behavior in the Human Male (1948) and Sexual Behavior in the Human Female (1953)	5,300 men 5,940 women	Interviews picked up wherever possible; little systematic sampling.	Bias exists in interviewing only the willing; unduly high per cent of interviews with abnormals—prostitutes, gamblers, prison inmates, thieves, etc.; uneven geographic distribution; more educated than nation as a whole; Catholics and Jews underrepresented.
JOHN THOMAS	Some of the Factors Involved in the Breakdown of Catholic Marriages	7,000 couples applying for separation.	Records of the Catholic Chancery of the Archdiocese of Chicago	Sample not representative of any couples other than the 7,000 studied; broken marriages not applying for separation not included; unduly weighted with ethnic groups; confined to one city only.

any premarital or marital relationship that is applicable to couples generally throughout the nation. This is true simply because none of them have measured up to all the rules and requirements demanded by true scientific inquiry. While there are many such norms to be followed faithfully, none presents greater difficulties than those relating to sampling.

Unlike the research worker in physics, chemistry, botany, or other natural and physical sciences, the social scientist studies people and groups with hundreds of variable characteristics. Instead of identical traits he is confronted with a bewildering array of varying characteristics. Accordingly, the facts, attitudes, and motives he may discover among persons or groups in one locality or of one culture, may not be true of people in a different locality or culture. The factors, for instance, contributing to marriage failure in the northeastern section of the nation or in cities may not apply to failing marriages in the southwest or in rural areas.

The only way social science can ever arrive at valid generalizations of this sort, is by an adequate sampling technique or by a survey of each and every person or couple in the nation. The latter method is obviously so vast and costly an effort that it has not been done and is not likely to be in the foreseeable future. The social scientist, accordingly, must select out of the total population a limited number of people, couples, or families. All of the available studies in the field of marriage relationships are based on such samples. However, he must select only those for his sample who will be so *representative* of all others that whatever findings he will make are equally true of both those in and those outside the sample. Many are impressed by the *size* of the sample, without considering how truly *representative* it is. Size is no guarantee of representation. The accompanying table gives instances of some of the best empirical studies on marital relationships available together with the reasons for their failure to sample the nation scientifically. It will be noted that not only is the failure to carefully select samples a common weakness but also that those selected are often clearly biased by the fact that they were volunteers. Studies have been made by careful students indicating that when volunteers are used for interviewing the result is seldom a normal sample of the population; [1]

---

[1] *Science*, Vol. CXX, No. 3114 (September 3, 1954).

and marked differences have been found between those who respond and those who fail to respond to questionnaires sent to them.[2]

It seems clear that, apart from other defects, the available empirical studies are too inadequate in their sampling techniques to permit any generalizations or universally applicable conclusions about relationships before and after marriage.   Their findings must be confined in application to the people actually sampled, usually a very small number.   Furthermore, there are marked and contradictory findings in the best studies available. For instance, a Swedish study [3] discovered that the amount of education, the relative intelligence, membership in organizations, size of home community, number of friends of the same or opposite sex, had little relationship to happiness in marriage. These findings directly contradict those of the best American studies.

---

[2] C. F. Reuss, "Differences Between Persons Responding and Not Responding to a Mailed Questionnaire," *American Sociological Review,* Vol. VIII (1943), pp. 433–438.

[3] Georg Karlsson, *Adaptability and Communication in Marriage* (Uppsala: Almquist and Wiksells Boptryckeri, 1951), pp. 105–111.

Index

Success in marriage (*Cont.*):
the "supernaturalist" and the "naturalist," 7
survey, 148–63
traits tending toward failure, 132
true love, 52
vertical and horizontal adjustments, 150–52
working wives; conditions, 100
Suckling, 211
Suhard, Cardinal, 323, 324, 326
Supernatural, the, 334

Teen-agers (*See* Youth)
Television:
children and, 244, 284–85
crime programs, 285
family life and, 283–86
recreation and the family, 279
Termin, L. M., 344
Theology, 335, 336
Thomas, John L., 345
Thomas Aquinas, Saint, 52, 291, 335
Tobias, 40
Trinity, Blessed, 332

United States:
expenditures, 302
mixed culture of, 18
standard of living, 293–94
Urbanization and family change, 15

Values, 37, 123, 203, 310
Vice and heredity, 222
Virtues, 181, 188
Vocation, 33–34, 335
Vocational guidance, 8

Wages, deductions from, 92
Wallin, P., 344

Wealth, 292
Weddings:
Catholic customs, 145
cost of, 144–45
planning, 144–46
Wife and husband (*See* Husband and wife)
Will, love and, 54, 59
Wives (*See also* Home economics, Housewives):
economic value as producer, 94
happy, 132
subordinate position, 87
Women (*See also* Sex differences; Single women):
psychology, 153
role after marriage (survey), 73
role in marriage and family, 81–84
traits of, 155
traits; to be reserved, to conserve, to serve, 82–83
understanding of sex, 196
working outside the home, 89–100
Work:
home-centered, 165
home chores, 296–97
Worldly goods, 292

Youth:
dating (*See* Dating)
early marriage and, 118–20
false "love," 51
parental guidance wanted by, 268–69
preparation for marriage, 4, 5
recreation (*See* Recreation)
sexual ethics and, 108
steady dating, 116

Zimmerman, Carle, 12, 13